THE GLOBAL MANAGER'S GUIDE TO LIVING AND WORKING ABROAD

Eastern Europe and Asia

Mercer

PRAEGER

An Imprint of ABC-CLIO, LLC

A B C ⬤ C L I O

Santa Barbara, California • Denver, Colorado • Oxford, England

Library of Congress Cataloging-in-Publication Data

The global manager's guide to living and working abroad : Eastern Europe and Asia /
    Mercer.
        p. cm.
    Includes bibliographical references and index.
    ISBN 978–0–313–37590–3 (hardcover : alk. paper) — ISBN 978–0–313–37591–0
    (ebook)
1. Employment in foreign countries. 2. International business enterprises—Europe, Eastern
—Employees. 3. International business enterprises—Asia—Employees. I. Mercer
Consulting.
HF5382.55.G559 2009
658.4'09—dc22   2009009589

13 12 11 10 09 1 2 3 4 5

This book is also available on the World Wide Web as an eBook.
Visit www.abc-clio.com for details.

ABC-CLIO, LLC
130 Cremona Drive, P.O. Box 1911
Santa Barbara, California 93116-1911

This book is printed on acid-free paper ∞

Manufactured in the United States of America

Contents

Introduction   vii

Part One: The Logistics and Psychology of Moving Abroad   1

Getting Ready to Move   3

Arriving: What to Expect   8

Managing Culture Shock   10

Staying Connected to Home   12

Coping When Things Go Wrong   14

Part Two: Living and Working in Eastern Europe and Asia   17

Australia   19

• Brisbane   24

• Canberra   29

• Melbourne   34

• Sydney   39

China   44

• Beijing   49

• Shanghai   55

Czech Republic: Prague   59

Egypt: Cairo   66

Hong Kong   78

Hungary: Budapest   88

India   100

• Mumbai   105

• New Delhi   109

Indonesia: Jakarta   114

Israel: Tel Aviv   123

Japan: Tokyo   132

Malaysia: Kuala Lumpur   141

New Zealand: Auckland   149

Philippines: Manila   158

Poland: Warsaw   166

Romania: Bucharest   175

Russia: Moscow   185

South Africa: Johannesburg   194

South Korea: Seoul   201

Taiwan: Taipei   209

Thailand: Bangkok   218

Turkey: Istanbul   230

United Arab Emirates: Dubai   239

Appendix 1: Securing Work Permits and Visas   255

Appendix 2: Salary/Price Differentials for Managers (Compared to New   275
York City, United States), 2007 (Converted to USD)

Appendix 3: Safety Abroad: Corporate Concerns   277

Appendix 4: Healthcare Abroad   289

Appendix 5: Celsius to Fahrenheit Conversion Chart   303

Index   305

Introduction

The decision to accept a job in another country is an important one, fraught with both great possibility and great challenge. Depending on how mobile your own family was when you were growing up—and on how much you have traveled as an adult—the prospect of leaving your current home and country for another country can be both exciting and daunting at the same time.

The amount of social, cultural, psychological, and linguistic change you will face depends, of course, on how different your new locale will be from the one you are in now. A move from the United States to Canada, or from Germany to Austria, could prove to be no more difficult than a move to another part of your current country. But a move from Tokyo to Johannesburg, or from Helsinki to São Paulo, could be much more challenging.

Another major factor is whether you will be making the move alone, with your spouse, or with your spouse and children. Each of these scenarios presents its own level of challenge and change. It may seem that going alone would be the simplest—yet, depending on how collegial your new work environment is and how big the cultural change is you will face, going alone may turn out to be more difficult than going with your spouse. But there is no denying that going with your spouse and one or more children will have the same sorts of day-to-day involvement with your new city that can put even well-adjusted families under stress.

In this book, we have assembled some advice on how to plan for your move to a new city as an expatriate employee. Ideally, you will learn something about your host city that helps you make the transition more smoothly.

We present some concise chapters addressing the major issues expatriates will face: preparing for the move, what to expect on arrival, managing "culture shock," staying connected to your home, and coping when things go wrong.

The bulk of this book, though, is city-specific advice on personal safety and security issues, healthcare, environment issues, a snapshot of economic data, the city's infrastructure (utilities, air travel, ground transport), where to shop, recreation and entertainment, the sociocultural environment, some demographic data, workplace culture (including how to interact with business associates and how to dress for work), the natural environment, the housing market, financial issues (including banking and personal taxation), and education (for children).

Of the cities we cover, most are the only ones in their country, so all the above topics are covered in one chapter. But for the countries for which we present reports on two or more cities, we have consolidated some of these topics in a country-specific chapter, followed by city-specific information. In addition, besides cities in Eastern Europe and Asia, we cover some in Australia, New Zealand, and South Africa.

Appendices collect specific information on securing work permits and visas, salary/price differentials (with New York as the base), safety issues, and healthcare issues.

If you are considering a job in another country—or are already committed to one—we hope you find the following information valuable as you make this exciting transition.

Part One

The Logistics and Psychology of Moving Abroad

Getting Ready to Move

INTRODUCTION

It is time to move out of the country. The excitement of travel is definitely there—but along with it come the problems of moving out, especially if you are planning to move with your family. Dozens of questions cross your mind: How will my family adjust in the new place? How will the kids like the new place? Can I learn the foreign language quickly enough? How do I transport my things? Are pets allowed?

PREPARING THE FAMILY

Moving out of the country where you may have been for a long time can be difficult, especially for children. Sometimes, expatriates have had to return home prematurely due to their families' inability to cope in the new environment. So it is critical for expatriates to prepare the family before moving out of the country.

The move to a new country may present an attractive career opportunity for you, but your spouse and children will have many questions and concerns. It can be very difficult to break the news to your family. It is always good to discuss the pros and cons of the move with your family before committing to the move.

Learning as much as possible about the host country is the best way to prepare your family for the move. They should be aware of the cultural, climatic, and social differences in the new country.

You have a wide range of information sources you can consult for information on your new host country, including this book. Your local library and the

Internet will be other good resources. You may also want to connect with the host-country expatriate community in your home country and your colleagues or friends who live or have lived there. These resources will give you a better idea on the local customs, practices, and culture. It is also advisable to visit the host country embassy in your home country.

BRINGING CHILDREN

Moving to a new country with children adds a lot of responsibilities and anxieties. There are certain things that you need to know before you enter the host country with your children.

- Is the school certificate in my home country valid in the host country?
- Is there a good foreign language school in the neighborhood?
- Can I find a good childcare service for my child?

To ensure that your child gets enrolled in the international school in the host city, it is advisable to file your child's following educational documents:

- child's marks (or report) card;
- letter from the school head or the teachers and the syllabus followed for the most recent year of schooling;
- copies of assignments done by your child;
- copies of certificates showing extracurricular achievements;
- proof of vaccinations.

You must also check with the host country embassy about the documents to carry and the vaccinations needed to take before traveling there. If it is a long journey, it is important to travel with something to engage your children throughout the trip.

In addition, you need to prepare them for the new country. Adults are mostly unaware of their children's feelings during the move. But children, though they adjust quickly to the new environment, are more worried about their new place.

Suppose you are moving into a country where the cultural and social system is totally different from your home country. Without some preparation, your child may not have the maturity to understand and adjust to the system. Of course, very young children need less advance preparation.

For school-aged children, though, the effect of the stay could be both psychological and sociocultural. Its impact will depend to an extent on the length of your stay. But even with shorter-term stays, children will be concerned with their school, acceptance among peers, making friends, the games they play, and learning the new language.

Longer stays may pose more of a challenge in adjusting to the social system in the host country. If your family maintains its "home" culture at home, but your children see a totally different culture around them, they can have some trouble figuring out their true "identity."

To minimize the shock in the children, it is advisable to give them as much information as possible on the new country. If they are old enough, encourage them to read or get information online about their new country.

LEARNING A LANGUAGE

Learning the language of your host country will ease your transition. Even if you know the host country language, pronunciation and usage may vary in different countries. So it is necessary to learn the specific style of usage of the language in the country you are planning to move to, especially the business usage of the language.

In this electronic age, it is can be relatively easy to learn a new language. There are a number of Web sites which will help you learn the language even before you reach the new country. See www.bbc.co.uk/languages, www.early-advantage.com, and www.word2word.com/coursead.html.

Then there are a number of audio tutorials, tutor-led classes, and books that will also help you learn the language. You can further improve your language skills once you reach the host country. In your new country, you can go for an extension course with your family. It is advisable, also, to try to use the language at home so that you get comfortable with it.

TAKING CARE OF PETS

When moving to a new country, what to do with the pets is an important question many people ask. There are several options. You can take the pet along with you, or you can leave it in the care of someone you know if you are moving for a shorter period of time. You can also sell or give away the pet before you go. Whatever you do you have to plan it accordingly.

Suppose you are taking the pet along with you. The first thing you have to do is ask the specific country consulate about the process of moving your pet. Most countries need a certificate from a vet showing prior vaccination up to a certain month. Clarify the following items with the country consulate:

- Is there any breed, type, or age restriction on moving pets?
- What documents should one have in place to move the pet?
- What vaccinations are needed before the move? How much lead time does the host country need?
- Can I carry the pet on the airplane or train or must I leave it in the baggage area?
- How long will it take to clear customs?

- What is the fee structure for moving a pet?
- Who will feed the pet during travel time?
- Should I put the pet in a cage and should I give it a sedative?

Once all your doubts are cleared, take some copies of your pet's photograph and its documents. Then attach each of these with the pet and keep one in your hand. Write down the name of your pet and also your name and your contact details in case the pet is lost on the journey. Chances are, it will come back to you safely.

PLANNING THE MOVE

Once you have decided on the move and the date is fixed, it is time to plan the move. There are a lot of things you have to take care of before you move out of your home country with your family. List all the things to do and check each off your lists as you finish the task. These lists should have some tasks under various headings: documents to take, people to call, information to get, and so on. Following are some guidelines:

- Ensure all passports, visas, and necessary permits are in order.
- Confirm journey dates and travel tickets/documents.
- Remember to change your address with all companies and persons you correspond with and arrange a mail forwarding service with the post office.
- Cancel all utilities and services you will no longer need and settle all accounts with these companies.
- Decide what essentials you need to carry with you when traveling.
- When packing, take into consideration the climate and availability of products within the host country.
- Find out what you can and cannot take through customs.
- Be aware of any particular rules and regulations in the country.
- Make sure you have some local currency for your arrival in the country, and try to get small denominations of bills and coins, which will be needed to pay the taxi/bus fares from the airport to your hotel or apartment.
- Check whether you have copies of all important documents, such as birth certificates, marriage certificates, wills, insurance policies, deeds, medical records, driver's license, bank statements, school records, and vet records. Leave copies with a friend, an attorney, or a family member at home and take the originals with you. (You may want to scan all these documents and send them to yourself on a noncorporate email account such as Yahoo, Gmail, or Hotmail. Then you can find them again and print them anywhere you have Internet access.)
- If possible, get a plan of your new house and then decide what household items you should take and what you can leave behind.
- List all items you are planning to take. If possible, get a picture of these items. Leave a copy of the list with a friend and take the original with you. It will help you in

calculating the moving charge, and after moving you can check to ensure all your items have arrived in the host country. (Again, you may want to send the pictures to yourself on your personal email account.)

- Decide how you are moving things, whether by yourself or through a moving agency. If you use a moving agency, contact more than one (unless your employer uses only one) and get an estimate of the cost and delivery time. See if the company will cover the insurance for the goods moved or whether you should take additional insurance.
- Arrange for storage of the items you are leaving behind.
- Keep all the papers and receipts related to your move.
- Check whether you have the telephone numbers and contact details of all the people you should contact after you reach the new country. Take along contact information for your children's friends as well.
- Complete any home improvements/repairs you have agreed to do before renters or the new owners of your house move in.

TRANSPORTING PERSONAL ITEMS

Unless you are driving to your new country, you can either transport your items by air or by sea. Both options have advantages and disadvantages.

By air, your things will reach you quickly. But it is expensive, so you should take only essential personal belongings. Sea transport is less expensive but slower. Before you decide on the mode of transport, it is advisable to check the costs and other facts for both modes of transportation. Whatever your chosen mode of transportation, it is advisable to seek the help of a professional mover to pack your household items.

Many countries have restrictions on the import of certain products, so you should learn about what you can import to the country and the quantity allowed. That is one reason why it is a good idea to work with a relocation consultant. That person will help you with moving your belongings, housing, schooling, and also take you and your family through a short course on your host country.

Once your items reach the host country, they will go through customs clearance, a process that can vary considerably by country.

If you are moving your household items through a moving agency, you can cut costs by

- taking only those items that are very important for you;
- choosing a less expensive time to move, like off season (June or July or middle of the month), if possible;
- checking with various moving companies and their tariffs and special rates.

SAYING GOODBYE

Before you leave, you may want to visit each of your friends or schedule a bit of time with them to say goodbye. Save some time for your relatives, too, before you leave. Even if everything goes according to plan, departing can still be difficult. There will be times when you are physically and emotionally exhausted but try not to let things overwhelm you. Do not be shy about asking for help or support, because there are plenty of people who have been there before.

Arriving: What to Expect

INTRODUCTION

Expatriation poses opportunities as well as challenges for one. There can be cultural as well as climatic differences between the home and host country. When these differences are large, the expatriate finds it difficult to adjust to the new circumstances. So, it is advisable to gather some basic information about the host country before he or she makes the actual move. This will considerably reduce the time taken to adjust.

FIRST DAY

An expatriate's first day in the host country can set the whole tone for the foreign assignment, for better or worse. Most employers have expatriate assistance programs to help employees. Usually an expert or an agency that specializes in this field takes care of expatriate employees in the host country—in matters such as finding accommodation, searching for schools, finding ways to commute to the office and home and so on. Some agencies may also conduct language and cultural coaching for new employees.

An expatriate without the assistance of such agencies must find and arrange for everything alone; the challenges faced can add to tension and stress—or can be considered part of the adventure of changing work venues.

GETTING SETTLED

Following is a list of items for an expatriate to handle first:

- Register with the host country government.
- Find a home within a suitable budget.
- Look for foreign language schools in the vicinity.
- Apply for a health card and social security number in countries that require them.
- Open a bank account.
- Learn the local laws.
- Figure out basic transportation.
- Find fellow expats and build contacts.

Settling down can be tough when reality falls short of one's high expectations for the host country. But an expatriate can settle down comfortably and quickly when the host country offers more than what he expects.

The climatic condition in the host country is also a factor that slows down an expatriate's adjustment to this new life—an example would be when a person moves from colder regions of the world like Europe to hotter areas like South American countries or vice versa.

The difference in the natural environment in the expatriate's home and host country may also pose problems to him or her. In any circumstance, a good social network will help expatriates to smoothly transition into their new host environment.

INVESTIGATING SCHOOLS AND HEALTHCARE FACILITIES

One of the first questions that crops up in an expatriate's mind on reaching the host country is "Are there any good foreign language schools available in the neighborhood?" Many expats ask the question the other way round: "What decent housing is available that is reasonably close to good foreign language schools for my children?" Fortunately, finding a good school in any country is not a difficult task. Most countries have quite a number of international, American, and British schools.

It is always advisable to get references from within the expatriate communities and from friends and colleagues before settling for a school. Some agencies assist in finding appropriate school facilities, too.

The schooling system in the host country may differ from that in an expatriate's home country. So parents should help in preparing their kids to face the new scene before they actually get enrolled. In some countries, there is an option of home schooling, which prepares kids to adjust to the local school. This option may not be feasible for everyone. But an expatriate needs to keep an open mind and make the best choice from the array of options available.

It is necessary to have information on good quality medical facilities in the host country, especially if the expatriate has a medical condition. In some countries, healthcare facilities are good, but the cost of treatment is high, unless an expatriate is adequately insured. It is recommended that one check with the country consulate or fellow expatriates about these factors even before leaving for the host country. Expats should keep in mind that in some countries healthcare systems are not funded by the government.

ASSESSING SECURITY ISSUES

In the wake of terrorist attacks and political disturbance in many parts of the world, an expat should research how secure the host country is and what personal safety measures he should take. This is extremely important when a person moves to the host location with his family. Local real estate agents and local consulates are good sources of information on what security matters are paramount in the host city and how most expats address them.

USING ROADWAYS AND TRANSIT SYSTEMS

The traffic system in various parts of the world differs significantly; the divergence is huge between Asian and European countries, for example. Road rules also differ among these regions. In some parts of the world, the public transport system dominates, while private transportation prevails in others. The mode of transport used too is different in different countries. Public transport is the effective mode of transport in most of the European countries. In wealthy Asian countries like Japan and Singapore, traveling by car is almost impossible. Owning a car in Singapore is very costly. Rail transport is the frequently used transport system. In China, until recently, bicycles were the most-used vehicles in the country. Now the use of cars has increased, causing a lot of traffic congestion in cities. In African countries, transport systems are not as well laid out as in Europe or any other part of the world; the public transport system is the most frequently used mode of transport.

Managing Culture Shock

Culture shock (which can include surprise, disorientation, confusion, and even disgust) is a typical reaction to fundamental change—an honest reaction to living and working in a completely different culture. Recovering from it is a process of adjusting to a new environment—realizing, completely, that it is difficult to communicate and get things done and, more importantly, understanding that one never gets the same ease and comfort zone of living on one's home turf. The reaction to this situation will differ from individual to individual. Generally, an extrovert can adjust to a new lifestyle faster than an introvert—although even introverts may learn new levels of self-esteem and motivation as they assimilate.

Basically, there are four stages of culture shock: honeymoon, rejection, adjustment, and recovery. During the honeymoon period, a person is excited about almost every aspect of the new place. But as in the case of marriage, reality slowly dawns on the person. This is the time when the person starts comparing her home country lifestyle with that of the host country. The new place seems strange and frustrating, which leads to stress. The periods of rejection, adjustment, and recovery can be long or short, depending on circumstances, temperament, and time spent in the new culture. (Note that "reverse culture shock" upon returning home after an extended stay in the host country is also quite common and should be expected; fortunately, it generally passes more quickly than the initial shock.)

One of the major causes of culture shock for an expatriate is being cut off from familiar cultural patterns. This sense of loneliness in the country adds to one's level of stress. This stage is characterized by a person's inability to work effectively. Therefore, it is important to examine this phase of intercultural adjustment. Sometimes it can be alarmingly scary, but the shock slowly dies down as the person starts understanding the new culture. It is necessary for an expatriate to realize that opinions and reactions of locals and expatriates are not always based on personal evaluation but can be based on cultural values. Once a person becomes skilled in assessing cultural norms and can understand which of her cultural values and behaviors clash with those of others, it is easier to make adjustments that help in overcoming serious issues.

Throughout the period of cultural adaptation, it is necessary to equip oneself with adequate knowledge on local culture and practices. It is good to read a book or watch a movie in the local language, take a short trip, relax, communicate with friends or family, and spend time with friends. Having a positive approach and concentrating more on the available good things about living in the new country definitely helps. The relative availability of cheap phone and Internet access has helped many expats stay in close contact with their home country family and friends.

Culture shock is normal for any person moving into a completely new environment. It does not mean that the person has made a wrong choice in life. This is one phase that an expatriate generally faces and works through; normally, it passes quickly.

UNDERSTANDING VALUES AND BELIEFS

Reducing culture shock, difficult as it can seem, is all about understanding the values, beliefs, and the traditions in the host country. Each part of the world varies considerably from the rest in many aspects, such as climate, food habits, living style, and so on.

The Internet has made life easier in giving us access to information regarding the sociocultural and culinary habits of any country in the world. An expat needs to start learning about the values, beliefs, and living style of the host country as much as she can before arriving. Doing so will minimize the time it takes to adjust to the new circumstances.

The first few months may pose problems for an expatriate in terms of adjusting. Ideally, a co-worker in the host country will be available to mentor each expat and smooth the transition. Absent such a mentor, the expat should consult others to help her understand the culture better and minimize confusion or misunderstanding. When an expatriate's cultural ignorance may have offended a local person, seeking forgiveness and expressing interest in understanding and learning more about the local culture can ease the tension.

Learning the new culture can be difficult and stressful. A person may commit blunders at the initial period of learning. Instead of taking it gravely, laughing it off saves one from an awkward situation. This lightens and hastens the learning experience.

DEALING WITH DIFFERENT CULTURAL NORMS

The first few days for an expatriate can be full of excitement, challenges, and education. It is common for culture shock to set in after the initial euphoria of arriving in a new country fades out. At this point, one starts to feel frustrated, angry, or sad. Language differences between the home and host country worsen matters further.

Anyone who has moved out of his country or city for whatever reason has experienced some degree of cultural shock. After the initial shock, an expat tries to adjust to the new culture, which can take up to six months. This involves everything from getting used to the food and language to learning how to use the telephone. No matter how patient and flexible an expat is, adjusting to a new culture can, at times, be difficult and frustrating. To ease the shock, one should try the following:

- Get out and explore the neighborhood. Try to interact with neighbors. Check whether any locals speak English. Check out the local cuisine and local shops. Try to use the local transport.

- Understand the similarities and differences between host and home country cultures; understanding similarities will help in coping with the foreign culture better, while understanding differences will help in analyzing and addressing the area of discomfort.

- Try to learn the local language—at least some commonly used words and phrases. Generally, locals will enthusiastically appreciate an expatriate's effort to learn the local language.

- Find a club or social group to join. Involve yourself in collective activities. Examples include the Canadian Women's Club in the United Kingdom and the Amsterdam Book Club for Australian expatriates.

WOMEN WORKING IN MUSLIM COUNTRIES

In Muslim countries, women are often considered second-class citizens and may be restricted as to the kind of work they do. Most Muslim cultures are quite conservative and have a dress code—that of modesty, not too revealing and tight fitting—for women for social gatherings and the workplace. Though the situation is changing, it can be difficult for women expatriates, especially those who belong to the Western culture, to adjust to such circumstances.

In most countries, expat women are required to wear a scarf over their heads, while in others many do not wear a veil. Some countries, like Saudi Arabia, do not allow women to drive a car. But it is not surprising to see that Western women sometimes succeed in Muslim countries better than their male counterparts.

Staying Connected to Home

Distance from family can often be overwhelming when moving overseas, especially when children are involved. Establishing and maintaining a solid home base while staying abroad is more important and challenging than it may seem. In this Internet age, it is less challenging than when the fastest written communication was by air mail. But expatriates placed in locations where the Internet is unreliable or not available face special challenges.

CONNECTING WITH THE OFFICE

Staying connected with the office in the home country is also important. "Out of sight, out of mind" can apply to an expatriate's professional life as well. It is important for the expatriate to stay connected with colleagues and the home office, as it will help him to stay in the loop of what is happening in the home country and also to reduce the stress and tension in the host country. There are numerous ways to keep the contact alive. It can be done through email, online chat, telephone, and also—increasingly popular—by blogging.

CONNECTING WITH FAMILY

After moving out of the country, it is necessary for an expatriate to stay connected with family and friends at home. It is helpful when family members and friends get regular updates on the life and adventures of the expatriate. It helps them feel a part of the expatriate's overseas life and not excluded bystanders. If an expatriate remains available and interested in their lives, even from a far-off country, they can stay close rather than growing apart. Options to stay connected include cellular phones and Voice-over-Internet Protocol (VoIP) phone services such as Skype or Gizmo.

FINDING AND SOCIALIZING WITH FELLOW EXPATS

You may find a ready-made community of expats in your host city, which can be a two-edged sword. These communities can provide a welcoming, safe environment in which to learn about the host city. But they can also inhibit one's adaptation to the foreign culture.

Expat communities vary in size and geographic coverage. There are a number of online support groups for expatriates also. It is easy to find these expatriate groups. Just ask colleagues or friends how to find these forums.

When choosing an expatriate group, note that there may be a difference in choice for long-term and short-term expatriates. Long-term expatriates may not be there in the expat groups' arena. They might have blended with the host country culture. Short-term expatriates are therefore more active in the expatriate forums and groups.

MAKING TRIPS HOME

Before accepting an overseas offer, a potential expat should clarify with the company what the policy is for leaves and trips home. Most employment contracts address this topic directly, but the terms may be negotiable.

Most companies pay for the annual home trip with full pay only for the employee, while others might pay out half of the total cost of travel. Some companies pay for a family vacation.

WORKING WITHOUT A "NET"

Not all countries have speedy, reliable Internet connectivity. Some simply lack the infrastructure, while others discourage Internet use in an effort to control personal expression.

Even without the Internet, work will happen, just as it has for centuries. There are always the telephone, fax, air mail, and other offline methods for communicating.

Coping When Things Go Wrong

Life rarely stays on a steady course wherever one lives and works, and expats should anticipate some bumps in the road when they relocate to their host country. Emotional problems, financial struggles, illness, accidents, and more trivial issues can be challenging enough on familiar ground, but they can seem harder and less tractable without the support of family, friends, or colleagues. Anticipating challenges, planning how to handle them, and maintaining an optimistic attitude can go a long way in resolving the personal challenges that may arise once in the host country.

AVOIDING PROBLEMS

The best way to deal with problems in a foreign country is to stay away from them. Learn what parts of town are riskier than others, know your own limits when it comes to personal behavior such as consuming alcohol, and stay alert.

SOLVING PROBLEMS

Expats, especially those with less knowledge of the language, can face a number of petty problems due to misunderstanding. Clear thinking helps rather than panicking over petty issues. Dealing with the problems as they arise is best. Talking to friends or relatives also helps. During the course of a conversation, an expat could gain insight into solving her problem or come across a fellow expat who may be going through the same issue or might have undergone a similar experience in the past.

DEALING WITH CRIME

Be vigilant in buses, bars, and around railway stations, where thefts frequently occur. In case of theft, contact the local police. Reporting a theft helps for insurance purposes.

CONTACTING EMBASSIES AND CONSULATES

It is prudent for you as an expatriate to register with the local office of the embassy upon your arrival so they know who you are if you need legal help. Consuls, although not able to help an expat in all cases, can help citizens living or visiting foreign countries by

- retrieving lost money or tickets;
- contacting relatives or friends back home;
- transfering money and funds;
- assisting in emergencies by referring to local social services;
- locating local lawyers who can assist in legal matters;
- arranging for messages to be sent to friends and relatives when expats are arrested in a foreign country; and
- sometimes make representations on an expat's behalf to local authorities.

RETURNING HOME

On return to their home countries, expats can get restless with the relative sameness of everyday life. They can lose their drive because they miss the stimulation of the new. Expats can face depression and feelings of dislocation. In some cases, the existing culture will have changed, prompting new feelings of alienation. Some return to an environment where the international experiences they have gained will seem unimportant or misunderstood. Life will also have changed for friends and family at home. Talking to them about what has changed could help. Maintaining relations with overseas friends helps to keep the connections built on the trip abroad. Much of the readjustment depends on how long an expat has lived abroad and the experiences faced there.

Part Two

Living and Working in Eastern Europe and Asia

Australia

PERSONAL SAFETY AND SECURITY ISSUES

Australia's relations with neighboring countries are generally good. Demonstrations and strikes are unusual. Cities are generally safe, but some violent crimes occur, and common sense precautions should be taken when venturing out at night. Foreign nationals must hold a valid passport and a visa before entering Australia. Work permits are fairly easy to obtain. Due to the threat of terrorism, entry into the country has been tightened.

While Australian cities are considered to be safe, it is still wise to avoid certain situations. Some Australians have the reputation of being heavy drinkers, so be cautious after drinking hours. Women can walk around freely, but it is advisable to travel in groups at night. The police are generally efficient and courteous. Foreign business visitors should be careful of becoming victims of petty crimes. Purses, laptops, and briefcases require additional security.

Following are some personal safety tips to remember:

- Do not leave valuables on show in cars or on tables in cafés.
- Avoid dark public spaces when alone.
- Always let someone know where you are and whom you are with.
- Take care when using automated teller machines (ATMs).
- Ensure you have road maps while driving.

- Drink alcohol only in moderation.
- Never drink and drive.

MEDICAL ISSUES

Medical treatment is excellent and almost any treatment can be done in the country. However, due to a shortage of nurses and highly qualified doctors, there have been some concerns about hospital services and availability of beds. Medicines are widely available. An outbreak of dengue fever has been noticed in tropical and subtropical regions, and special care should be taken with regard to sun exposure; sensible precautions should be taken against heat and sunstroke.

The Australian Healthcare Service is mixed, with responsibilities for healthcare divided between federal and state governments. Both the public and private sectors play a role. Government programs offer key elements of healthcare. Medicare, which is funded from general tax revenue, covers all Australians and pays for hospital and medical services. Public hospitals are owned by the state. Overall, the quality of healthcare in Australia is high and doctors and medical staff are well trained and highly qualified. For further information, refer to the Department of Health at www.health.gov.au. A comprehensive list of hospitals (public and private) can be found in the local *Yellow Pages* directory (or online at www.yellowpages.com.au).

ENVIRONMENT ISSUES

Food and water are safe to eat and drink. Air pollution is not a major concern in most Austalian cities. Sand flies and other insects are common in Australia, but they are more of an irritation than a health hazard.

ECONOMIC OVERVIEW, 2008

GDP growth	2.4%
Inflation	3.6%
Unemployment	4.3%

SOCIOCULTURAL ENVIRONMENT

In Australia, there are no major limitations on the freedom of speech or movement or the practice of religion. But there are censorship regulations governing the media with regard to publishing or broadcasting items of an offensive nature. International cable television and international newspapers are available.

DEMOGRAPHIC/WORKFORCE OVERVIEW

Population	20,434,000 (2007 estimate)
Population density	2.6 inhabitants per km^2
Age structure	0–14 years, 19.6%
	15–64 years, 67.3%
	65 years and over, 13.1%
Life expectancy at birth	
Total population:	80.5 years
Male	77.6 years
Female	83.5 years

WORKPLACE CULTURE

Australians are friendly, outgoing, informal people who move to a first-name basis rather quickly. In general, let your Australian acquaintance set the level of informality, and do not be offended if they become quite informal immediately.

Except for situations involving large corporations, Australians are generally result-oriented. They prefer where possible to make quick decisions and move fast to put their decision into action, although most organizations tend to be collaborative and may seek feedback and/or approval from various levels in the organization before action is taken. In smaller businesses, one person could be the sole decision-maker for the entire company and might make a decision immediately. Australians are fairly conservative, however, and the decision-making process reflects this. If the proposal contains unusual or innovative terms, they will generally need time to consider it before committing to a deal. Meetings start on time. If you are going to be late, let your associates know in advance. Men still hold the vast majority of management positions, but Australian women are being hired for higher level jobs and are expected to be treated seriously. If you are dealing with a woman, do not treat her any differently than you would treat a man. Australian companies hire people whose personalities fit the company. In general, business hours are Monday to Friday, 9 A.M. to 5 P.M.; however, work hours are lengthening; many businesspeople are now holding 8 A.M. meetings or conducting business over breakfast. For business meetings, men should wear suits and ties and for women smart suits or conservative dresses are best. Skirts should be at least knee-length, and excessive jewelry and loud fashion accessories should be avoided. Business dress, however, may be more informal in very tropical climates or depending on the region and the company.. Some workplaces have a "casual Friday" policy where casual dress may be worn on Fridays.

The standard greeting in business is a firm handshake with good eye contact. For initial meetings, last names preceded by Mr., Mrs., or Ms. should be used; "Sir" is another term of respectful greeting used until your Australian associate has initiated using a first-name basis. Professional titles are not prominent in Australian business culture and are sometimes dismissed as pretentious. Gift giving is not frequently practiced in Australian business culture; however, if you would like to give a present, it is recommended that you offer something from your home country such as an illustrated book of your region or a specialty food (preserved, otherwise you risk having the items confiscated at customs). Australians generally dislike negotiating and aggressive sales techniques. Australians do not find it difficult to say "no" and are usually very direct, and directness is appreciated in return in all situations in Australian life, especially business; presentations of any kind should be straightforward and clearly show both positive and negative outcomes.

Australians view people who seem too wealthy or powerful with great suspicion and cynicism. In the Austalian culture, there is greater respect for the "underdog." You should never discuss your personal life during business negotiations. If you are invited out for a drink, do not bring up the subject of business unless your host does so; there is a clear divide between business and pleasure in Austalian culture.

When speaking to an Australian, keep an arm's length distance from the person, as it is important in Australia to maintain personal space. Men should refrain from being too physically demonstrative with women. Touching, patting, or hugging other men in public is considered socially unacceptable.

FINANCIAL ISSUES INCLUDING BANKING SERVICES AND TAXES

Banks: There are branches or subsidiaries of many major international banks represented in Brisbane. The banking service is very good and most international transactions can be made without delay. Currency may be exchanged at all banks, post offices, and some hotels. Credit cards are widely used. ATMs are widely available.

Currency: The currency of Australia is the Australian Dollar (AUD). 1 AUD = 100 cents. Denominations of notes are AUD 5, 10, 20, 50, and 100. Denominations of coins are 5, 10, 20, and 50 cents, and AUD 1 and 2.

Cash, traveler's checks, and credit cards: Australian currency is the only legal tender in Australia. Traveler's checks and foreign currency can be easily exchanged at banks, foreign exchange bureaus located in major cities and hotels, and foreign exchange kiosks at airports. Banks offer the most variable exchange rates. Traveler's checks receive a better exchange rate than cash. Traveler's checks are easier to use if already in Australian dollars; however, banks will cash traveler's checks in virtually any currency.

Credit cards are widely accepted in Australia, including American Express, Visa, MasterCard, and Diners Club, as well as bankcards from the larger Australian banks. All taxis accept credit cards, and you can get cash advances with your credit card at many of the ATMs. Long-term visitors are advised to set up a checking account in Australia and get an ATM card.

Taxes: Australian residents are taxed on worldwide income, whereas nonresidents are taxed on Australian source income only. In determining whether an expatriate is an Australian resident, there is a legislative definition and public ruling (TR 98/17). The relevant factors to be considered are intention or purpose of presence in Australia; whether the expatriate is accompanied by family; the extent to which any assets or any bank accounts are acquired, maintained, and located in Australia; the existence of a contract of employment in the home country; the expected length of the visit; and social and living arrangements in Australia. The ruling (TR 98/17) regards an expatriate as a resident if the expatriate's intention to visit Australia is greater than six months from the date of arrival.

A resident in Australia is

- subject to Australian tax income from worldwide sources;
- allowed a foreign tax credit where non-Australian income has been subject to tax in a foreign location, being the lower of foreign taxes actually paid or the Australian tax liability on that income;
- taxed at resident rates of tax;
- entitled to a tax-free threshold of AUD 6,000 or part thereof if a resident for only part of the year of income;
- subject to the Medicare levy and, possibly, the Medicare levy surcharge or part thereof if a resident for only part of the year of income unless not entitled to Medicare benefits or the resident is a member of an Australian registered private health fund.

A nonresident is subject to

- Australian tax on Australian source income only (salary paid for days worked outside of Australia are not taxable in Australia);
- tax at nonresident rates of tax; and
- Australian source interest and unfranked dividend income subject to a final withholding tax of 10 percent and 30 percent (generally reduced to 15 percent where a tax treaty exists with a foreign country in which the taxpayer resides), respectively (Australian sourced fully franked dividends are not subject to withholding tax or income tax).

Any gains on the disposal of assets that do not have a close connection with Australia (such as shares in public companies but assets such as Australian real estate or private companies) will not be taxable here if bought and sold while the expatriate is considered a nonresident.

All goods imported into Australia must be cleared by customs, whether imported by air, sea, or post. Goods brought into Australia may require the payment of customs duty and sales tax; however, travelers are allowed to bring into

Australia the following goods duty and sales tax free when the goods accompany the passenger:

- goods to the value of AUD 900 (AUD 450 for travelers under 18 years of age), excluding alcohol or tobacco, for example, cameras, electronic equipment, perfume concentrate, leather goods, jewelry, watches, sporting goods, and so on;
- 2.25 liters of alcoholic liquor (including wine, beer, or spirits) for travelers aged 18 years and over;
- 250 cigarettes or 250 grams of cigars or tobacco products other than cigarettes for travelers aged 18 years and over. Most personal items such as new clothing, footwear, articles for personal hygiene/grooming, personal goods owned and used for at least 12 months can also be brought into Australia without payment of duty and sales tax (proof of date of purchase may be required). Goods bought overseas or bought duty/sales tax free before leaving Australia are included when determining a duty-free allowance.

Further information on taxes can be obtained from the Australian Taxation Office (www.ato.gov.au).

BRISBANE

MEDICAL ISSUES

Hospitals in Brisbane include the Mater Adult Hospital and the Children's Hospital Foundation. Dr. Malcom Duff offers 24-hour emergency dental treatment. There are detailed listings of pharmacies at www.doctors-4u.com/brisbane/chemists_sub.htm and in the yellow pages (www.yellowpages.com.au). For emergency chemists and those available out of hours, you should check in the local newspapers as some shops operate a "rota" (rotating) system to provide nighttime and evening opening. The following pharmacies are open evenings and on weekends: Costless Chemists, Delahunty's Costless Chemists, and MacArthur Central Chemist.

INFRASTRUCTURE

Utilities and traffic: The telephone system in Australia is very good. The mail service is efficient. Public transport is efficient, comprehensive, and well integrated. There are buses and local rail services. Traffic is often congested during the rush hours and is worsening.

Air travel: Brisbane Airport (BNE) (www.bne.com.au) is located 13 km from Brisbane's Central Business District. The journey into the center, by road, takes around 35 minutes. It offers good connections to other cities in Asia and a fair range of flights to Western Europe and North America. There are two terminals: the International Terminal and the Domestic Terminal. There is a shuttle bus service connecting the two terminals every 15 minutes in the morning and every 20 minutes in the afternoon. This service is free for airline ticket holders. Taxi stands are available at both terminals at the arrivals levels. The fare from the airport to the city costs around AUD 25 plus an AUD 2 airport surcharge.

Coach services are available to Brisbane, Gold Coast, and Sunshine Coast. Brisbane city service offers daily service between the Central Business District and Brisbane Airport every 30 minutes from 5 A.M. to 7:30 P.M. The fare costs AUD 11 one way. Gold Coast service offers daily service every hour via the Gateway Bridge. The approximate price is AUD 35 one way. Sunshine Coast service offers daily service approximately every two hours from 5:50 A.M. to 6:50 P.M. Prices begin at AUD 40 for a single ticket. Air train services are available from both terminals. At the International Station, an all-weather bridge links the station to the arrivals and departures levels. At the Domestic Station, an all-weather bridge links the station to the ground level check-in area. The trip to Brisbane City from Brisbane Airport takes 22 minutes and a single one-way ticket costs AUD 10. The service is available between 5 A.M. and 9 P.M. daily. Online bookings can be made at www.airtrain.com.au. Car rental companies represented at the airport are Avis (www.avis.com.au), Budget Rent-a-Car (www.budget.com.au), Hertz (www.hertz.com.au), Europcar (www.europcar.com.au), and Thrifty Car Rental (www.thrifty.com.au).

Public transport in Brisbane is managed by Translink (www.translink.com.au).

Buses run across an extensive network of routes in the greater Brisbane area through to the city center, where a loop service operates. Translink offers a special service whereby all outbound services departing the city after 9:30 P.M. will set down passengers at any point on the route, where it is safe to do so for both driver and passenger. Pick-ups, however, are available at established stops only. There are 23 zones throughout South East Queensland, and bus passengers pay per the zone in which they travel. The zones radiate as a series of concentric circles from Brisbane Central Business District. Fares for one-zone travel begin at AUD 2 for a single trip and AUD 4 for a daily ticket within one zone.

Rail: A map of the city train routes operating to and from Brisbane city center are available at www.translink.com.au/qt/translin.nsf/index/maps. Rail services are operated by Translink and operate on the same tariff and zonal fare system as the buses. You can either purchase a ticket at one of the ticket booths in any staffed station, or if you are buying your ticket from a ticket vending machine (found in train stations), you just have to enter your destination and the machine will calculate the zones and fare for you. Further information is available either on the Translink Web site, or at www.citylink.com.au.

Ferry: A number of ferry services operate across Brisbane. Fares for train and bus services are operated on a zone charging system. Ferry services along the Brisbane River operate from Bretts Wharf to the University of Queensland (Citycat line), Sydney Street to North Quay (inner city ferry), and Holman Street to Thornton Street via Eagle Street Pier (cross-river ferries). Fares for one-zone travel begin at AUD 2. There is a water taxi operating between Cleveland and Dunwich daily from 6 A.M. to 6:45 P.M. (7:45 P.M. on Friday).

Taxis are widely available in Adelaide and operate on a 24-hour basis. With regard to initial meter charges you should pay AUD 2.50 from 7 A.M. to 7 P.M. and AUD 3.70 at all other times. Rates per kilometer are currently AUD 1.32. Yellow Cabs and Black and White Cabs are the two officially recognized services for Brisbane and surrounding areas.

SHOPPING AND AVAILABILITY OF CONSUMER GOODS

In Brisbane, there is a complete and wide supply of food and daily consumption items. There is a good choice of alcoholic beverages. Almost any model of car is available to buy, though there may be delays in obtaining some models. Angus & Robertson—Post Office Square (www.angusrobertson.com.au); Dymocks Brisbane (www.dymocks.com.au); Bent Books (www.bentbooks. com.au); and McGills (www.mcgills.com.au) are a few bookstores in the area.

Shopping malls, such as The Queen Street Mall, Indooroopilly Shopping Center, Broadway on the Mall, Mt. Gravatt Shopping Center, and The Oasis are located here.

Department stores include David Jones and the Kmart Queen Street Mall, one of the biggest shopping malls in the country, with over 1,200 shops represented, including many of Australia's top department stores. Others are Kmart (Brisbane alone has 15 stores), Freedom, Target, Big W, and so on. Supermarkets in Brisbane tend to open from 9 A.M. to 9 P.M., Monday to Friday, and many are open during normal retail hours on the weekend. Coles Supermarket, Rosalie Gourmet Market (delicatessen-style market), Spar Bakers (located within Supermarket), and Fundamental Food Store (organic) are a few supermarkets located here.

RECREATION AND ENTERTAINMENT

Brisbane has a good choice of prestigious restaurants with high-quality food. There is also a good choice of operas, cinemas, and theaters. Brisbane has numerous organized sport and leisure activities that are easily accessible.

Restaurants: Petries Bistro is known for its spectacular seafood buffet. Michael's Restaurant is a multi-award winning restaurant with an eclectic character to the contemporary menu. Daniel's Steak and Seafood is an award winning restaurant with modern local cuisine and decor celebrating Australia's heritage. There is heavy emphasis on local seafood and meat dishes. It offers superb views of the river. Bali Grill covers traditional Indonesian cuisine served with a modern twist.

Culture and entertainment: The free weekly newspaper *Brisbane News* lists performing arts, jazz and classical music performances, art exhibitions, rock concerts, and public events. The state opera company, Opera Queensland, performs a lively repertoire of traditional as well as modern works, musicals, and choral concerts. Free talks on the opera take place in the foyer 45 minutes before every performance. Most performances take place at the Queensland Performing Arts Centre (QPAC) either in its Optus Playhouse or at its Cremorne Theatre, South Bank. The Queensland Orchestra schedules around 30 concerts per year. The orchestra plays at the Concert Hall in the Queensland Performing Arts Centre or City Hall; more intimate works sometimes play at the Conservatorium Theatre, South Bank. Brisbane Powerhouse Centre for the Live Arts is a dynamic art venue for exhibitions, contemporary performances, and live art.

Cinemas include Greater Union Hoyt's Myer Centre, Valley Twin Cinema, Palace Centro Cinemas, Dendy Twin, and Greater Union Hoyt's Regent Centre.

Museums: Abbey Museum of Art and Archaeology is one of the most popular museums in the region. The museum also hosts a Medieval Tournament, which attracts thousands of spectators each year. Queensland Maritime Museum (www.qmma.ecn.net.au), with sailing ships to WWII memorabilia, is situated at the end of the newly opened Goodwill Pedestrian Bridge. Caboolture Historical Village with over 60 restored buildings provides the visitor with an insight into life in a bygone era. This place includes domestic appliances, weapons, and clothing as well as many other items from everyday life. Queensland Museum (www.qm.qld.gov.au) conducts exhibitions that include some of the best dinosaur collections in the country. Redland Museum has an extensive display of elements of early life in Cleveland—one of the first European settlements in Australia.

Entertainment for children: Moreton Island (www.brisbanetourism.com.au) is one of the largest sand islands in the world (38 km long). Most of the islands offer beaches, freshwater lakes, wetlands, and wildflowers. Fishing, snorkeling, swimming, sailing, and surfing are very popular. Lone Pine Koala Sanctuary has the oldest Koala sanctuary in the world with over 100 koalas. Children can cuddle the koalas and feed the kangaroos. AJ Riding School and Training Center (www.ajridingschool.com.au) has scenic rides and day treks and offers the most popular excursions on horseback and is suitable for all ages and abilities. Laserforce has a high-tech laser tag game and is suitable for children over the age of six. Yeronga Park Heated Pools (www.ourbrisbane.com/lifestyle/health-sport-and-fitness/yeronga-pool) has heated pools that allow swimming all year round. The center also has barbeque facilities, a beach volleyball area and kiosk, plus a fully enclosed children's play area. Lollipops Playland has an indoor playground for children up to 11 years old. Separate party rooms are available.

Nightlife: Supermild Lounge Bar is a cozy retro (1970s) haunt that makes it a top place to unwind. Cocktails and imported beer are sold here. Brisbane nightlife can be sought in bars like Rue de Paris—it has a restaurant and coffee boutique on the pavement where you can watch the world bustle by. A good selection of imported beers is available. The Embassy Hotel has a five-star bar and friendly service. Pub food is also available. O'Malley's Irish Pub is a traditional Irish pub and features live music on Wednesday and Sunday nights. Verve Café has a cultural ambience. Adrenalin Sports Bar is Brisbane's premier sports bar, where many of Brisbane's top athletes often arrive later in the evenings for a postgame drink or a game of pool. At City Rowers the idea is not to stop dancing. If dance music is not your taste, then you could head downstairs for some 1980s and 1990s pop or go into the Rhythm and Blues bar. Friday's has two separate rooms playing either the latest dance tunes or live bands playing rock. Someplace Else is preferred by the more upmarket night-club clientele; this is also a club for the more mature. Club Brazil is a wild party atmosphere with Latino music. Finally, the Monastery is the epitome of the bustling nightlife scene in Brisbane which is the home of house music (electronic mid-tempo dance music) in the city.

Casinos like Conrad Treasury Casino are located here as well.

Sports for children: The Yeronga Swimming Complex (www.ourbrisbane.com/lifestyle/health-sport-and-fitness/yeronga-pool) offers classes for children from as young as six months old. Ambiwerra Sports Centre—LifeTime Tennis (www.lifetimetennis.com.au) has a tennis center with professional coaches. MF Bowling—Kedron (www.amfbowling.com.au) has a family-friendly bowling center with "Kid's Zone" and "Family Special" promotions on Sundays. Happy Coconuts (www.happycoconuts.com.au) has a fun sports program for kids aged three to six years.

NATURAL ENVIRONMENT

Brisbane has a temperate climate with mild winters and hot summers. No natural disasters occur, although cyclones may occur very occasionally and with "flash flooding." Summers can be very hot and humid.

HOUSING

There are many attractive rental properties available in Brisbane, including both apartments and houses. The more prestigious residential districts include Hamilton, Toowong, St. Lucia, Ascot, City Fringe, and Sanctuary Cove. Household appliances and furniture are widely available.

Real estate agencies are usually listed in the local telephone directory. The online *Yellow Pages* have listings of all rental agencies available (www.yellowpages.com.au). Some of the real estate agencies incude PRD Realty (www.prd.com.au/brisbane), L. J. Hooker (www.ljh.com.au), Raine & Horne (www.raineandhorne.com.au), and Sissons Estate Agents (www.sissons.brisbane.homeone.com.au). In order to rent a house or apartment, a lease must be signed between the owner of the house and the tenant. The lease sets down the obligations of the owner and the tenant. In the lease, it should state that the owner is to make sure all utilities are properly installed and working and the tenant must keep the house or apartment in good condition. A first lease is usually set at six months and extendable, based on whether you and the owner can agree on rent increases.

In Brisbane, one month's rent as a refundable deposit is required. A garage is usually included in apartment rental costs. Houses in districts in Brisbane: good areas: Hawthorne, Bulimba, Paddington, Red Hill; very good areas: Hamilton, Spring Hill, Clayfield, St. Lucia, Bulimba; best areas: Ascot, New Farm, Brookfield, Chelmer. Apartments in good areas: Aspley, Bardon, Carsetdine, Chermside, The Gap; very good areas: Hamilton, Aluchenflower, Spring Hill, Teneriffe; best areas: Toowong, St. Lucia, Ascot, City Fringe, West End, South Bank.

There is a good choice of unfurnished accommodations available; however, there is a limited choice of furnished apartments. Accommodation costs can vary considerably, depending on the area and type of housing. On average, the cost of a two-bedroom, unfurnished apartment in a very good area would be around AUD 1,800 per month, rising to AUD 2,300 a month in the best areas.

INTERNATIONAL SCHOOLS AND EDUCATION

There are Swedish and international schools available in Brisbane and there is a good choice of private schools, offering both primary and secondary levels of education.

- Kooralbyn International School (www.schools.ash.org.au/kooralbyn) has international and the International Baccalaureate curriculum. Diploma is offered. The school serves children aged between 5 and 18 years. The school applies a uniform policy, and there is a canteen available for children who wish to eat at school. School hours are 8:30 A.M. to 3:15 P.M.

- Brisbane Boys College (www.bbc.qld.edu.au/home.asp) applies a uniform policy. The school serves students in grades 4 to 12. A school bus service is available. Both day and boarding students are accepted. There is a waiting list for entry. School hours are 8:25 A.M. to 2:55 P.M.

- Peter's Lutheran College (www.stpeters.qld.edu.au), as with other Queensland schools, is based on the Radford System which was introduced in 1971 and later modified under ROSBA (Review of School-Based Assessment). The school applies a uniform policy, and a school bus service is available. School opening hours are Monday through Friday, 8 A.M. to 4:30 P.M. The school has an Olympic-sized swimming pool and a fully equipped gymnasium and weights room among many other excellent sporting facilities.

- Japanese Language Supplementary School of Queensland (www.members .westnet.com.au/jsb/hoshuu) is also located here.

CANBERRA

MEDICAL ISSUES

Hospitals in Canberra include the Calvary Public Hospital, Queanbeyan District Hospital and Health Service, and Queen Elizabeth II Family Centre. Canberra does not have a dental emergency referral service. A reputable dentist in the center of town is Lachland B. Lewis (for emergency calls only on weekends,

Tel: +61 2-6295-9495). There are detailed listings of pharmacies in the *Yellow Pages* (www.yellowpages.com.au). For emergency pharmacists and those available after hours, check the local newspapers, as some shops operate a Rota system to provide nighttime and evening openings. Capital Chemists pharmacy is open evenings and weekends.

INFRASTRUCTURE

Utilities and traffic: The telephone system in Australia is modern and efficient. The mail and utility services are reliable. The public transport network is comprehensive and well integrated. Nevertheless traffic is often congested during rush hours.

Air travel: Canberra International Airport (CBR) (www.canberraairport .com.au) is situated 8 km east of the city center (travel time is 15 minutes) and has a good selection of domestic destinations; other destinations need a connecting flight through Sydney. Taxis and shuttle buses are available to the city center.

Taxis operate from outside the main terminal building. All taxis are metered although average fares can vary from AUD 14 to AUD 16 depending on which side of the city center your destination lies. Taxis are normally available 24 hours a day, although if there is none currently waiting there is a courtesy telephone provided for which you can use to call the taxi office.

Airliner shuttle buses operate on an hourly basis Monday through Friday between the airport and the city center. The shuttle bus stop is located just outside the central terminal. Fares are AUD 7 for one way or AUD 12 for a return ticket. Further information is available from www.deanesbuslines.com.au. Car rental desks are located in the central terminal area. The following rental companies are represented at Canberra airport:

- Avis (www.avis.com.au)
- Budget (www.budget.com.au)
- Delta Europcar (www.deltaeuropcar.com.au)
- Hertz (www.hertz.com.au)
- Thrifty (www.thrifty.com.au)

Transport: Public transport in Canberra is run by Action (www.action.act .gov.au). As well as a city network, Action runs several inter-town routes that operate between the Belconnen, City, Woden, and Tuggeranong interchanges. Tickets can either be purchased on board (single, return, or day tickets only) or from most newsstands. If you change buses, you will be required to purchase a supplement, although the first 90 minutes of your journey are exempt from this. There is a new flexibus system that allows you in the evenings to be dropped near to your destination, regardless of whether it is part of the designated route.

Bus: The city of Canberra is divided into three separate bus zones and ticket prices relate to these zones. All-day/all-zone tickets provide excellent value for your money if you plan to travel extensively on Canberra buses. Another popular option for bus travel in central Canberra is the City Sightseeing explorer buses, which travel to 18 major locations in Canberra and feature hop-on/hop-off tickets. Kingston Train Station, on Wentworth Avenue, is Canberra's main train station and CountryLink trains offer good connections throughout Australia and the Australian Capital Territory (ACT). Most trains in Canberra and the ACT are modern, in good condition, clean, fully air conditioned, and feature good general train facilities. Bicycles are allowed on trains during off-peak times and also on Saturdays and Sundays.

Bicycles are an extremely popular way to travel much of Canberra, including many recreational areas and parks. Canberra is fairly flat and there are plenty of cycle trails in Canberra, often close to Lake Burley Griffin, making cycling an enjoyable and scenic way to travel around Canberra.

Taxis are a popular choice for shorter journeys, and Canberra's taxis travel all over Canberra and the outskirts of the city. Most taxis in Canberra can be hailed on the street or at Canberra's numerous central taxi ranks. The main taxi company in the city of Canberra is Canberra Cabs, which are white taxi cabs containing a yellow and black central stripe. Initial meter charges begin at AUD 3.20 and rates per kilometer vary between AUD 1.31 and AUD 1.51.

SHOPPING AND AVAILABILITY OF CONSUMER GOODS

Most consumer goods are available in Canberra and the selection is broad. A good selection of alcoholic beverages as well as cars can be purchased in Canberra. Angus & Robertson—Canberra (www.angusrobertson.com.au), Koorong—Fyshwick (www.koorong.com), Dymocks Canberra (www.dymocks .com.au), and Paperchain Bookstore (www.paperchainbookstore.com.au) are all found here. Shopping malls include Tuggeranong Hyperdome, Westfield Shopping Town, Woden Plaza, and Canberra Center.

Department stores include Big W, Target, Grace Brothers, and others. There are many supermarkets open every night; Coles is open 24 hours throughout the city, all with varying produce and opening hours. Some specialty grocery stores include Chinese Speciality Food Shop, Coles, and Franklins.

RECREATION AND ENTERTAINMENT

Canberra has prestigious restaurants serving excellent food. There is a good choice of cinemas and theaters. Canberra has many organized sport and leisure facilities that are easily accessible.

Restaurants: Turkish Pide House is a popular spot that offers Turkish cuisine—takeaways are also available. PJ O'Reilly's offers traditional pub meals in an Irish atmosphere. The Chairman and Yip is a trendy and modern Asian cuisine with an emphasis on seafood. Atlantic is a fusion of modern British and French and traditional Australian cuisine. The Boathouse by the lake is an elite upper-class restaurant situated on the shores of Lake Burley Griffin.

Entertainment: Canberra's online *Ecity Guide* (http://canberra.ecityguide .com.au) is a useful resource that is always current with events, concerts, and various performances. Another useful resource is www.thisweekinaustralia.com. For museum and other sources of information check www.museumsandgalleries.act.gov.au. Canberra Theatre Centre (www.canberratheatre.org.au) consists of three theaters—the Canberra Theatre, the Playhouse, and the Courtyard Studio. The theaters seat from 90 to 1,200 patrons and offer shows throughout the year. The Street Theatre is geared towards locally produced plays. A café and a bar are on the premises. Canberra Youth Theatre Company shows include plays, drama, theater, opera, dance, and ballet. Bits Theatre Company is a professional theater company. Cinemas include Manuka Greater Union, Belconnen, Hoyts Tuggeranong Cinema, and Woden.

Museums: The National Museum of Australia (www.nma.gov.au) hosts permanent exhibitions that deal with the themes land, nation, and people, and the Gallery of the First Australians, which conveys the country's indigenous heritage. The museum also houses restaurants, theaters, and a resource center. The Australian War Memorial (www.awm.gov.au) offers an extensive research center and award winning exhibitions based on personal accounts and education. The National Gallery of Australia's special traveling exhibits include renowned national and international art. Old Parliament House is not only the seat of Australia's governing history, but also the National Portrait Gallery is located on the top floor. Solander Gallery is Canberra's oldest, privately owned fine art gallery and houses some of Australia's best native artifacts. Canberra Museum and Gallery, located in the heart of Canberra, houses etchings, collages, lace, and murals. There are also many performances and recitals as well as a museum restaurant.

Entertainment for children: The National Dinosaur Museum (www.national dinosaurmuseum.com.au) exhibits interactive activities and offers a museum shop. The National Science and Technology Centre features a wide variety of interactive displays and exhibitions. At the Canberra Space Dome and Observatory, over 7,000 stars are visible from the observatory, even during rain or during the day. Royal Australian Mint includes entry to the museum and even permits you to mint your own AUD 1 coin. Australian National Botanic Gardens offers entertaining and educational visits; the picnic and rainforest areas are particularly enjoyed by children. Cockington Green is an old English village, built entirely to scale (1/12, with each structure built out of tiny bricks). The trees and gardens are all live but trimmed to size.

Nightlife: Babar Café and Elephant Bar offers outdoor seating in sunny weather—situated close to the theaters, this is perfect for a pre-show drink.

Minque is a grand and modern bar. The Phoenix has a relaxed and friendly bar often with live Irish folk music. Holy Grail Restaurant and Bar is a bustling bar (also part of the club) with a large modern party atmosphere. PJ O'Reilly's offers a warm and cozy traditional Irish feel.

Nightclubs: Mooseheads is a popular nightspot with students and army cadets; the main bar is on the ground floor, and a DJ plays dance music upstairs in the club part of the building. Heaven Nightclub is Canberra's only hard-core dance venue. Gypsy Bar is a diverse and colorful nightspot particularly popular with university students. Club Mombasa features an African rhythm with some Caribbean, Latin, and samba too. Tilley's Devine Café and Gallery is a popular nightclub within the gay community.

Casinos like Canberra Labour Club has over 200 poker machines, lucky badge draws on Wednesdays and Saturdays, and a gala raffle on Fridays.

Sports facilities: There are a number of sports facilities like golf clubs, tennis courts, swimming pools, and fitness centers within the Canberra area. AMF Bowling—Belconnen is a family-friendly bowling center which has "Sunday Funday" specials for families. Canberra Indoor Rock Climbing is for people of all ages and offers "Mums and Bubs" sessions as well as a "Kids Club." Aquatots—O'Connor features the "Black Mountain School Pool." It has a go-karting center which provides adult, junior, and dual karts to cater to all age groups. Belconnen Skate Park is also highly rated. The street skating area is considered to be the best feature of the park while the large vertical bowl and ramp are challenging for even the most experienced skaters. For tourist information, check www.visitcanberra.com.au.

NATURAL ENVIRONMENT

Canberra has a temperate climate with mild winters and hot summers. No natural disasters occur.

HOUSING

There are attractive rental properties available in Canberra, including both apartments and houses. The more prestigious residential districts include Dickson, Kingston, City, and Yarralumla. Domestic appliances and furniture are easily obtainable. Here is a partial list of Canberra real estate agencies: L. J. Hooker, Leader Real Estate, and Darwin Rental Specialists. The online *Yellow Pages* have listings of all available rental agencies (www.yellowpages.com.au). One month's rent as a refundable deposit is required plus references. Garages are usually included in the rental costs. Houses in districts in Canberra: good areas: Dickson, Ainslie; very good areas: Deakin, Kingston; best areas: City, Yarralumla. Apartments in good areas: Dickson, Ainslie; very good areas: Deakin, Kingston, Manuka; best areas: City, Yarralumla, Forrest. There is an adequate amount of furnished apartments available in areas suitable to expatriates; however, unfurnished apartments and houses are easier to find. Large apartments are rare. Accommodation costs can vary considerably, depending on the area and type of housing. The average cost of a two-bedroom, unfurnished apartment in a very good area would be around AUD 1,800 per month; AUD 2,300 a month in the best areas.

INTERNATIONAL SCHOOLS AND EDUCATION

There are several good choices of private schools in Canberra offering primary and secondary levels of education.

- Telopea Park School (French school, www.telopea.act.edu.au) has a harmonized French-Australian curriculum. The French curriculum has been adapted in part to take into account local requirements but still conforms in general to the programs and official instructions of the French Ministry for Education. In the same way the Australian curriculum has been modified to take into account French requirements but also satisfies the broad requirements of the Australian Capital Territory Department of Education and Training. The school applies a uniform policy. A school bus service is available, and there is a canteen for children who wish to eat at school. Before and after school extracurricular activities include tennis, Irish dancing, pottery, drama, and athletics.
- Canberra Anglican Grammar School for boys (www.cgs.act.edu.au) follows the local curriculum. The school serves boys aged preschool to 18 years and girls aged preschool to year 2. A uniform policy is applied. A before- and after-school care service is offered for the younger children.
- Canberra Anglican Girls' Grammar School (www.cggs.act.edu.au) follows the local curriculum. In the senior school, students are prepared for the ACT Year 10 High School Certificate and the ACT Year 12 Certificate. The school serves girls aged preschool to 18 years and boys aged preschool to year 2. A school bus service is available, and a school uniform policy applies. Extracurricular clubs include rowing and friends of music.
- Canberra Japanese Supplementary School (www.canberra-hoshuko.org) is also located here.

MELBOURNE

MEDICAL ISSUES

Few isolated cases of meningococcal disease had been reported in the region.

INFRASTRUCTURE

Utilities and transport: The transport system (known as the Met) within Melbourne is fast and efficient. It is an integrated network of buses, trams, and trains. Trams provide travel between the city and the inner suburbs; trains provide travel between the city and the middle and outer suburbs; and buses cover all areas not served by the tram or train services. New tramlines have been extended in order to reach various suburbs of the city. Traffic is often congested during rush hours.

Air travel: Melbourne Airport (Tullamarine) is situated 22 km from the city center (travel time is 30 minutes) and offers good connections to other cities in Asia and a fair range of flights to Western Europe and North America. The airport is easily accessible, with many public and private transport services available. Melbourne Airport offers passengers a wide range of world-class facilities.

Taxis are available from the ground floor level of the airport. The taxi fare into the city center will cost around AUD 35 to AUD 40, and travel time is 30 minutes. There is an AUD 2 taxi parking fee payable by all passengers leaving Melbourne Airport from a taxi rank, and there is a pre-booked taxi fee of AUD 3 for passengers catching a taxi from the Premium Parking area opposite the International Terminal building.

Skybus offers a shuttle service from the airport to the city center. The service is available 24 hours a day. Buses run every 15 minutes throughout the day, and every 30–60 minutes overnight. Buses leave from the front of the arrivals terminal and run to Spencer Street rail station. There is also a shuttle service to many city hotels. Tickets cost AUD 13 one way and AUD 24 open return. Public bus services operate from the airport terminal to various areas in Melbourne and are run by various local companies. Further information can be obtained from the info desks within the airport.

Car rental companies are located on the ground floor level of the Short-Term Car Park and have offices in the domestic terminal.

Train: Melbourne has an extensive electric train service. All lines radiate from the city center and, apart from the underground city loop, stations are above ground. Train services on most lines are usually frequent. On weekdays there is a train every 15 or 20 minutes and on Saturdays every 20 minutes. On Sundays trains depart mornings, every 30 minutes; afternoons, every 20 minutes; and evenings, every 30 or 40 minutes.

Trains travel in different directions through the City Loop, depending on the time of day and day of the week. On weekdays the direction reverses at approximately 1 P.M., while weekend services run in the same direction day and night. This can be confusing to occasional travelers; however, timetables show the direction the trains will be traveling. The main train station in Melbourne for suburban routes is Flinders Street Station.

Trams provide convenient and frequent travel from the city center to the inner suburbs. Like the train system, most routes provide radial transport towards and away from the city; however, in the inner eastern and southern suburbs, cross-radial routes provide convenient travel to a wide range of destinations.

Tram services on most lines are usually frequent. On weekdays there is a tram every 12 minutes during the day and every 20 minutes in the evening.

Sunday services run every 30 minutes in the morning, every 15 minutes in the afternoon, and every 30 minutes in the evening. Late evening services do not always run their full route. Some routes run more frequently than the intervals mentioned above.

Buses serve suburbs distant from rail lines, act as feeders to railway stations, and provide cross suburban travel not available via train or tram. Most bus routes operate every 20–60 minutes on weekdays and approximately hourly on Saturdays. Very few Melbourne buses run after 7 P.M. or on Sundays. There are night bus services on Fridays and Saturdays.

SHOPPING AND AVAILABILITY OF CONSUMER GOODS

There is a wide choice of consumer goods available in Melbourne. Due to the recent droughts, fruits and vegetables are slightly more expensive. A good selection of alcoholic beverages and cars is also obtainable. A number of shopping malls and supermarkets are located throughout the city.

Bookshops include Angus & Robertson—Melbourne, Koorong—Blackburn, Dymocks—Collins Place, McGills, and The Paperback Bookshop.

RECREATION AND ENTERTAINMENT

Melbourne has an excellent choice of prestigious restaurants serving very good quality food. There is also a very good choice of cinemas and theaters, and many organized sports facilities are easily accessible.

Restaurants: The Moroccan Soup Bar is a very popular restaurant with a Middle-Eastern feel. All dishes are vegetarian. Mario's Café has lots of ambience; dishes include many pasta choices and it is known locally for cakes and its strong Italian coffee. Donovans is a popular restaurant on the St. Kilda beach promenade which offers casual, relaxed fine dining. Warung Agus is a relaxed Bali-inspired restaurant using fresh local produce in its cooking. Finally, Lemongrass Thai is an elite, grand restaurant serving both traditional and modern Thai cuisine.

Events listings can be found in the free magazines *Inpress* and *Beat.* There is an entertainment supplement in *The Age* newspaper on Fridays. The Web site www.melbourne.com.au is a good resource for entertainment in Melbourne as is www.onlymelbourne.com.au.

Culture and entertainment: Theatres and concert halls include Her Majesty's Theatre, which features popular musicals. La Mama features contemporary productions. The Melbourne Theatre Company consists of the Russell Street Theatre which has classical, international, and Australian works; the Princess Theatre, which offers Broadway-style blockbusters; and the Reagent Theater, which offers mainstream productions. The new MTC Theatre opened in

January 2009. Theatreworks offers contemporary Australian plays, and Universal Theatre offers off-Broadway style productions.

Cinemas include Astor Theater, IMAX, and Moonlight Cinema.

Museums: Melbourne Museum has three particular focal points: *Bunjilaka,* focusing on Aboriginal activity in Victoria; the Children's Museum, shaped like a tilted cube; and the open-air Gallery of Life, exhibiting Victoria's flora and fauna. The Arts Centre comprises a series of gallery and theater spaces, including the State Theatre, the George Adams Gallery, and the Performing Arts Museum. There is also Hamer Hall, a venue for major artists and the base for the Melbourne Symphony Orchestra. Immigration Museum is brought to life by true stories from exhibitors. The Customs House is also home to the Hellenic Museum—Australia has the largest population of Greek inhabitants outside Greece. The National Gallery of Victoria has the world's renowned collection of European Masters including Rembrandt, van Dyck, Picasso, Monet, and Turner as well as famous Australian artists such as Sidney Nolan, Arthur Boyd, and Albert Tucker. Chapungu Gallery has the largest selection of modern stone sculpture from Zimbabwe ever shown in Australia; the pieces are available for purchase by private collectors.

Entertainment for children: Puffing Billy Railway is a restored steam railway; the train takes passengers from Belgrave station to Emerald Lake Park. Rare Bears is Melbourne's first indoor play center and is suitable for children up to the age of 10; separate zones are available for children under 3. Jells Park is a huge park in Melbourne's outer east, with exercise circuits for rollerblades, cyclists, and so on and walking tracks that wind their way through the forest. Barbeques in the park are also popular as are picnics. Phoenix Park Community Adventure Playground is an enormous adventure playground with a mock timber castle for exploring as well as sand pits, swings, and slides. Luna Park fairgrounds offers free admission to the park, although there are charges for the rides.

Sports for children: Kingpin Bowling is a funky bowling lounge that features UV bowling (glow in the dark pins and balls). Melbourne Sports and Aquatic Centre offers a program that is focused on four fundamental areas of swimming education. Sidetracked Entertainment Centre features go-karts, laser force, amusement games, tenpin bowling, mini-golf, pinball, and pool tables. River-slide Skate Park is one of the best skating venues in Australia. There is something for all ages and abilities. Wallington Park Equestrian Centre offers specialist, group, and private horseback riding lessons as well as a Saturday school. Five-day intensive camps are offered for children aged 5 to 15.

NATURAL ENVIRONMENT

Melbourne has a temperate climate. Temperatures in the winter can get as low as 0°C and during the summer can sometimes reach 40°C for short periods. Generally free of natural disasters, the Melbourne area was ravaged by fierce wild-fires in early 2009.

HOUSING

Most Australians live in detached or semi-detached houses. High-rise apartment buildings are quite rare. Houses are not as large as those found in the United States, and individual rooms tend to be smaller. Most houses have a patio or terrace.

There are many attractive rental properties available in Melbourne, including both apartments and houses. The more prestigious districts are Toorak, Armadale, Camberwell, and Brighton. Household appliances and furniture are widely available.

Real estate advertisements in the major city newspapers (generally the Saturday editions) list most of what is available for rent or sale in each city and its surrounding suburbs. Placing an advertisement to attract local landlords has given excellent results for some expatriates. Properties are also available through real estate agents (often signposted or advertised as realtors). The agent's fee is usually one month's rent. A garage is sometimes included in apartment rental costs.

INTERNATIONAL SCHOOLS AND EDUCATION

There are International, Japanese, and Swedish schools in Melbourne offering primary and secondary levels of education. There is also a good choice of private schools. International School include the following:

- St. Leonard's College (www.stleonards.vic.edu.au): The curriculum is both local and international in flavor. Exams offered are the Victoria Certificate of Education and the International Baccalaureate Diploma. The school serves children aged between 4–18 years. A school bus service is available. There are many sports available as extra-curricular activities, plus the school runs the Duke of Edinburgh award scheme. A school uniform policy applies.
- Scotch College (English school) (www.scotch.vic.edu.au) offers a varied curriculum. The Victoria Certificate of Education (VCE) is the exam offered in years 11 and 12. The school serves children aged between 5–18 years, and a uniform policy is applied. A canteen is available for children who wish to eat at school. The school is open from 8:40 A.M. to 3:40 P.M.
- Japanese School of Melbourne (www.jsm.vic.edu.au/index.html): There is a school bus service provided, but there is no school canteen. School hours are Monday through Friday, 8:40 A.M. to 3:30 P.M.
- Wesley College (www.wesleycollege.net): The curriculum is both locally and internationally based. Exams offered are the Victoria Certificate of Education and the International Baccalaureate Diploma. The school takes children aged between 3 and 18 years. The school applies a uniform policy, and there are some private bus companies that operate certain routes for pupils traveling to Wesley College. Extra curricular activities include water polo, gymnastics, and rowing.
- Camberwell Girls Grammar School (www.camberwellgirls.net) offers a varied curriculum. The Victoria Certificate of Education is the exam offered. The school serves girls

up to 18 years of age and applies a uniform policy. School hours are 8:30 A.M. to 3:30 P.M. There is no school bus although a shuttle bus provided by the school operates between the senior and junior campuses. Extracurricular activities involve gymnastics, cricket, hockey, diving, skiing, and tae kwon do.

SYDNEY

ENVIRONMENT ISSUES

Travelers to North Queensland and the Northern Territory should use insect repellents. Take sensible precautions against heat and sunstroke, since summer temperatures can reach 40°C. Protect both yourself and your children and be aware of the dangers of sun exposure. You must wear high-factor sun protection cream at all times while in the sun. Sleeping nets need to be used to guard against the risk of contracting mosquito-borne diseases such as dengue fever and Ross River fever. There have also been reports of cases of Murray Valley Encephalitis (MVE), a potentially fatal mosquito-borne disease, in the Northern Territory.

INFRASTRUCTURE

Utilities and transport: The public transport network is comprehensive and well integrated, with buses, metro, and local rail services. Nevertheless, traffic is often congested during rush hour. Sydney has a mass transit system consisting of bus, ferry, and rail services. The system is efficient and cheap.

Bus: The bus services are run by State Transit (www.sydneybuses.nsw.gov.au). Buses run daily between 6 A.M. and midnight. There are night buses, which run on certain routes. Tickets are usually purchased from the driver (correct change is recommended) and cost from AUD 1.60.

Rail: CityRail (www.cityrail.info) operates the train services between the suburbs and the city center. In general trains operate daily between 4:30 A.M. and midnight. Tickets can be purchased from the automatic ticket machines or over the counter at the stations. There are eight stations in the city center: Central, Town Hall, Wynyard, Circular Quay, St. James, Museum, Martin Place, and Kings Cross. If you ask for a ticket to the city, your ticket will allow you to alight or descend at any one of them. After midnight, the NightRide trains operate in Sydney's suburban areas. After 7 P.M. in the suburbs and after 8 P.M. in the city, Nightsafe trains operate, which means only the two carriages nearest the train guard are open to passengers. Animals are not permitted on the rail system.

Metro: The Sydney Metro (www.metrolightrail.com.au) operates the Light Rail and Monorail services. The Metro Light Rail operates between Central Station and Star City, 24 hours daily and between Central Station and Lilyfield, Sunday through Thursday 6 A.M. to 11 P.M. and Friday and Saturday 6 A.M. to midnight. Services operate every 10 minutes between 6 A.M. and midnight and every 30 minutes outside these times. For other times there is a timetable available. There are two zones on the line and fares depend on which zones you wish to take. For Zone 1 or Zone 2 only, a single ticket costs AUD 2.90; to cover both zones a single ticket costs AUD 3.90. Other types of tickets are available; please consult the Web site for further details.

The Monorail operates around the city, Darling Harbor, and Chinatown, Monday through Thursday, 7 A.M. to 10 P.M., Friday and Saturday, 7 A.M. to midnight, and Sunday 8 A.M. to 10 P.M. Services are every 3–5 minutes at any station. A standard fare costs AUD 4 per loop. There are other types of tickets available; full details can be found on the Sydney Metro Web site.

Ferry: The commuter ferry network that crisscrosses Sydney Harbor is one of the best ways to see the harbor. Ferries run from Circular Quay to almost 30 destinations between 6 A.M. and 11:30 P.M. Fares start at AUD 4.80, and ferry/entrance fee passes are available from the ticket office for attractions including Taronga Zoo and Sydney Aquarium. Tickets can be bought either on board or from Circular Quay or Manly. Further information is available from www.sydneyferries.info. Water taxis provide a service on Sydney Harbor (www.watertaxis.com.au).

Taxis can be found at taxi stands outside bus and rail stations and at the larger hotels. The initial meter charge is AUD 2.70, and AUD 1.44 per kilometer thereafter. Surcharges are payable for crossing Harbor Bridge and for using the toll systems in certain areas.

Air travel: Kingsford Smith (Sydney) Airport (SYD; www.sydneyairport.com.au) is situated 8 km from the city center (the travel time is 30 minutes) and offers good connections to other cities in Asia, Western Europe, and North America and to some destinations in Africa and Latin America.

Sydney Airport has three terminals: Terminal 1 is the international terminal, and Terminals 2 and 3 are the domestic terminals. Each terminal has its own taxi rank. Supervisors are on hand in peak hours to ensure a smooth flow of taxis for travelers. Travel time into the city center ranges from 15–30 minutes, depending on traffic.

Taxi fares from the airport are approximately as follows: to Sydney City AUD 25; North Sydney AUD 35; Manly AUD 50; Parramatta AUD 45; Liverpool AUD 40; and Cronulla AUD 35. An AUD 2 supplement is payable by all passengers taking taxis from the airport.

The green and gold Airport Express bus provides fast, comfortable connections between both the domestic and international terminals, the city, and Kings Cross. The service operates daily, along several fixed routes, from approximately 5 A.M. to 11 P.M. Tickets are purchased from the driver and cost AUD 7 one way or AUD 12 return. Although there is a wide range of shuttle bus companies that operate networks in and around the station, most require pre-booking.

The domestic rail station is located between Terminals 2 and 3 and is reached from inside the terminal on the arrivals level. The international rail station is located directly below the international terminal and is reached from inside the terminal on the Arrivals Level.

Airport Link is the fastest and most convenient way to reach the center of Sydney. Trains run every 10 minutes, and the journey into the city takes only 13 minutes. The domestic station links directly to the City Circle, which means that most city destinations (such as offices and hotels) are within a five-minute walk of either Central, Museum, St. James Circular Quay, Wynyard, or Town Hall stations. The cost of a one-way ticket is AUD 11.

Airport Link is also one of the most economical and convenient ways to reach Sydney's suburbs. Tickets can be purchased to all Sydney stations from the international terminal. You need to catch the train from the domestic terminal to Central Station, and there you can change for all suburban services. Passengers can also transfer from the domestic terminals to the international terminal for only AUD 4. Transfer time is two minutes. For further information, Tel: +61 2-8337-8417. All companies provide car rentals in all terminals.

SHOPPING AND AVAILABILITY OF CONSUMER GOODS

Most consumer goods are available in Sydney, and the selection is broad. A good selection of alcoholic beverages as well as cars can be purchased in Sydney. A number of shopping malls, bookstores, and supermarkets are located here.

RECREATION AND ENTERTAINMENT

Sydney has a wide choice of prestigious restaurants serving excellent food. There are numerous cinemas and theaters, not to mention the famous Sydney Opera House. Sydney has many organized sport and leisure facilities that are easily accessible as well.

For listings of events and what's on in the music and pub scene and the like, there are free weekly entertainment guides: *Drum Media, Revolver,* and *3D World.* These guides can be found in bookstores and record shops. On Fridays, the *Sydney Morning Herald* has an entertainment section called the "Metro."

Theatres and concert halls: Capitol Theatre, Her Majesty's Theatre, specializes in Broadway-type shows. Lyric Theatre is where big-budget musicals are performed. Stables Theatre shows up-and-coming performers and plays. The Griffin Theatre Company is the resident theater company, while State Theatre and Sydney Opera House are others.

Cinemas: A number of cinemas, such as IMAX, Cinema on the Square, Hoyts Cinemas, Village Cinemas, Eros Cinema, Cinimagic, and Dendy Cinemas are located here.

Museums: Hyde Park Barracks Museum until 1848 provided accommodation for convicts but has since had many occupants, becoming sequentially an immigration depot for Irish orphans and unprotected females, an asylum, and law courts. Caspian Gallery is one of Sydney's most reputable places to acquire Aboriginal, Melanesian, and Pacific tribal art. Rose Seidler House, managed by the Historic Houses Trust, has been restored to its original, 1950s scheme inside and contains a major collection of furniture inspired by the Bauhaus Movement. Powerhouse Museum houses an immense collection of the old and most modern items; the museum's exhibits range from decorative arts to crafts, social history, science, and technology. Christopher Day Gallery shows regular, changing exhibitions of nineteenth- and twentieth-century traditional and modern Australian paintings, as well as fine European paintings. Art Gallery of New South Wales is the leading museum of art in New South Wales and Sydney, and one of Australia's foremost cultural institutions.

Entertainment for children: Bronte Beach is a body-surfing beach and a 25-meter ocean pool. The large adjoining park offers picnic and barbeque facilities. Rocks Puppet Theatre offers interactive fun for adults and children alike. Bare Island Fort Tours is located in Botany Bay National Park. Built in 1885 as a military fort, the island is connected to the mainland by a 100-year-old wooden bridge. Quarantine Station Ghost Tour is suitable for children over 12; these popular tours are guided by lantern light through the maze of spooky stone cottages, the hospital, mortuary, and cemetery. Quarantine Station was the first port of call for ships suspected of carrying passengers with smallpox, typhoid, and the plague. Aussie Duck offers a 90-minute, fully integrated city and harbor tour aboard its custom-built, amphibious vessel.

Sports facilities: Kartatak is a go-karting center that specializes in kids' parties. AMF Bowling—Randwick is a family-friendly bowling center. Blacktown Ice Arena offers skating lessons and disco skating. Hurstville Aquatic Leisure Centre has three heated swimming pools, two waterslides, a sauna, steam room, three spa pools, and a giant inflatable "water challenge." Karate for Kids is a school for children aged 4 to 16 where self-defense, personal discipline, self-confidence, and personal development are the focus.

NATURAL ENVIRONMENT

Sydney has a temperate climate with mild winters and hot summers. No natural disasters occur, although drought has become a natural feature of the climate.

HOUSING

There are many attractive rental properties available in Sydney, including both apartments and houses. High-rise apartment buildings are quite rare. Houses are not as large as those found in the United States, and individual rooms tend to be smaller. Most houses have a patio or terrace.

The more prestigious districts for those preferring apartments include The City, Edgecliff, Kiaribilli, and Woollahra. Houses can be found in the districts of Lavender Bay, Mossman, Double Bay, McMahon's Point, Neutral Bay, and Kirribilli.

Real estate advertisements in the major city newspapers (generally the Saturday editions) list most of what is available for rent or sale in each city and its surrounding suburbs. Placing an advertisement to attract local landlords has given excellent results for some expatriates. Properties are also available through real estate agents (often signposted or advertised as realtors). Many real estate agents specialize in property management, and the agent's fee is usually one month's rent. House-hunting services are also available in some large cities.

One month's rent, as a refundable deposit, is required as well as three references. A garage is usually included in apartment rental costs. A good choice of unfurnished accommodation is available; however, furnished houses are rare. There is a good choice of furnished apartments in the eastern suburbs and city. Accommodation costs can vary considerably, depending on the area and type of housing. The average cost of a two-bedroom, unfurnished apartment in a very good area would be around AUD 3,500 per month; AUD 4,800 for the best areas.

INTERNATIONAL SCHOOLS AND EDUCATION

Schools in Sydney include the following:

- International Grammar School (www.igssyd.nsw.edu.au) follows the local curriculum. The school serves children aged 3 to 18 years. The school applies a uniform policy, and there is a canteen available for lunch. The Primary School has a bus service provided. An after-school childcare service is available for the younger students. Extracurricular activities include sculpture, cooking, origami, and belly dancing. The senior school day begins at 8:30 A.M. and finishes at 3:15 or 3:55 P.M.

- American International School, Sydney (www.amschool.com.au), is based on the U.S. national curriculum. The students earn a high school diploma. Advanced Placement courses and the International Baccalaureate program are also followed. The school serves children from pre-kindergarten to 18 years of age, and a school bus service is available. The school does not have a uniform policy. The school uses local sports facilities. The American/Northern Hemisphere school holidays are applied, offering summer holidays in the Australian winter and four weeks over the Christmas break.

- Lycée Condorcet (French school, www.condorcet.com.au) follows the French national curriculum, but with a strong Australian influence. The French and International Baccalaureate exams are offered. The school takes children aged 3 to 18 years. There is a school canteen, as well as a café for students and parents alike. No school bus service is provided. Children are taught both French and English. There is no school uniform policy applied.

- Johannes Gutenberg (German school, www.germanschoolsydney.com): The curriculum is based on the German national curriculum with an international input. Students can take the German Abitur exam in year 13 and can also work towards the International Baccalaureate Diploma. A school bus service is available. There is no school uniform policy. Children need to be fluent in German to be admitted.

- Sydney Japanese School (www.sjs.nsw.edu.au): The school follows the New South Wales Board of Studies syllabus. School bus services are provided. School hours are Monday through Friday, 8:30 A.M. to 3:35 P.M. Children receive a bilingual education in Japanese and English.

China

PERSONAL SAFETY AND SECURITY ISSUES

The internal political situation in China is relatively stable; however, there is always potential danger due to strong government control.

Terrorism is rare in China. Overall, the country is relatively safe, with a low crime rate. However, recently, the rate of petty crime has started to increase, as the economic gap among citizens widens. Hence, it is advisable to take common sense precautions with regard to personal safety and safeguarding personal property. Petty theft, mainly pickpocketing, is noticeable around tourist destinations and on the public transport systems. Violent crime against foreigners is very rare; however, incidents do occur. It is recommended that the following safety tips be heeded:

- Never carry large amounts of money around unnecessarily.
- Never exchange money illegally on the streets; always use a bank or official exchange bureau.
- Never walk alone in quiet or dimly lit areas.
- Always carry personal identification with you. It is advisable to make photocopies of passports, visas, permits, and other important documents and keep them in a safe place.

Law enforcement has improved lately with the passage of new laws to improve transparency and implementation—and as China began preparing to host the 2008 Summer Olympics. Corruption and bribery are fairly widespread among officials, despite severe penalties for offenders. All foreign nationals require a passport and a visa for entry into China. Work permits are reasonably easy to obtain.

MEDICAL ISSUES

Chinese medical techniques include Western treatments as well as traditional herbal and acupuncture treatments. Many expatriates tend to use local medical facilities for minor ailments but travel to Hong Kong or Japan for anything more serious. A wide range of medical supplies is available locally and is improving.

Medical care is generally inexpensive when compared with Western costs, but there are limited private or luxury healthcare facilities. Payment in advance is expected for all medical and dental services. Most embassies carry a list of medical centers and hospitals that have high standards of healthcare.

It is essential to have health insurance to cover all medical expenses. Some companies offer employees medical coverage, but it is advisable to have your own private policy, which will cover you in every circumstance. There are many private health insurance companies.

Typhoid, polio, and hepatitis B vaccinations are recommended by many national health authorities, but are not a requirement for entry. Severe acute respiratory syndrome (SARS) has been contained, and there has been no evidence of further outbreaks. The government has made an effort to monitor and control the situation, and the same is true for avian influenza (bird flu). A certificate of vaccination against yellow fever is required by those traveling from an infected area. For persons intending to take up work in China, a health certificate is required. For persons intending to stay in China for longer than one year, an HIV test is mandatory.

ENVIRONMENT ISSUES

In large cities and towns, food and water are for the most part safe to consume. The Chinese themselves, however, will rarely drink straight from the tap and usually boil and store drinking water in a thermos. It is advisable to boil water that is to be used for drinking or brushing teeth. Bottled water is available. Most Chinese food is well cooked, although care should be taken with shellfish or fish and under-cooked meat.

Respiratory infections are very common during the winter months. Travelers often refer to it as the "China syndrome," and it can sometimes be far more serious than a simple flu. Symptoms include fever, chills, weakness, and sore throat. The condition is aggravated by cold weather, changes in diet, and air pollution.

Traveler's diarrhea is often a problem for newcomers to China and is caused principally by the change in diet and different strains of bacteria.

ECONOMIC OVERVIEW, 2008

GDP growth	9.8%
Inflation	6.6%
Unemployment	4.2%

INFRASTRUCTURE

Utilities: Electricity and water supplies are usually reliable, although very rare interruptions may occur. International telephone services are generally fast and reliable. International direct dialing is available from most telephones. Domestic services are improving but calls to some rural areas may prove difficult. Postal services, both domestic and international, are generally very good.

SOCIOCULTURAL ENVIRONMENT

The Chinese government has little tolerance for political opinions other than those of the ruling party. Individuals should be wary of expressing disapproval of the current regime or its leaders. China is officially a secular state. People can still adhere to a variety of religious beliefs, but only through government-controlled channels. There is a Roman Catholic cathedral and a Protestant church in the city. Beijing has several television stations, and broadcasting hours have been extended. International cable television is only available at some of the major hotels. A limited choice of international newspapers is available in Beijing. Many publications are under state control or are censored.

DEMOGRAPHIC/WORKFORCE OVERVIEW

Population	1,313,973,700 (2006 estimate)
Population density	137 inhabitants per km^2
Age structure	0–14 years, 20.8%
	15–64 years, 71.4%
	65 years and over, 7.7%
Life expectancy at birth	
Total population:	72.6 years
Male	70.9 years
Female	74.5 years

WORKPLACE CULTURE

Typical working hours in China are Monday through Friday, 8 A.M. to 6 P.M., with a one-hour break for lunch. Most public offices are open Monday through Friday, 8 A.M. to 5 P.M. Some offices are open on Saturdays until midday. Normal business attire for men is a conservative suit with a shirt and tie. Women should wear conservative suits or dresses. Blouses and tops should have high necklines and sleeves. Colors should be subdued and neutral, as bright colors of any kind are considered inappropriate within the business culture.

The Western custom of shaking hands is spreading within the business circle in China and is often the customary greeting during business dealings; however, sometimes a nod or a slight bow is used. Guests are usually introduced to the most senior Chinese person present first, and then to others in order of rank or importance. Most people should be addressed with a title and their family name. If a person does not have a professional title, use "Mr.," "Ms.," or "Miss" plus the last family name. For business purposes, it is easier to address people using their title and family name (for example, director, chairman, deputy). Do not address someone by their first name unless they have invited you to do so. In the same manner, do not insist that your Chinese associates address you by your first name too soon. Business cards are generally exchanged after the introduction. Business cards should be printed in your own language or English on one side and in Chinese on the other. When you offer a business card or receive one, always use both hands. Never put it into your pocket right away without reading it and never write anything on it. These acts are considered disrespectful and rude. The official policy in Chinese business culture forbids the exchanging of gifts, as this can be considered as bribery. Consequently, if you offer a gift it may be declined. There are certain protocols for gift giving that should always be followed.

Appointments for meetings are essential. Remember to avoid special Chinese holidays when scheduling appointments. Meetings often begin with small talk. It is rude to start business dealings straightaway.

If you are providing written information, it is a good idea to have it translated into Chinese. Always have plenty of copies of your presentation or documents to distribute to everyone. The concept of "face" is essential in Chinese business culture. A person's reputation and social standing rests on this concept. The Chinese regard the respect of their peers and colleagues to be of extreme importance. Causing embarrassment or humiliation would mean the loss of "face," and would be disastrous for business negotiations. Always remain patient and calm during business negotiations.

FINANCIAL ISSUES INCLUDING BANKING SERVICES AND TAXES

Banks: There are restrictions on currency exchange, although some liberalization has occurred in recent years. Currency may be exchanged at the Bank of China and some hotels. As more Chinese banks are becoming commercial banks, the range and quality of banking services are continuously improving.

In general, banking hours are Monday through Friday, 9 A.M. to 5 P.M., and Saturday 8 A.M. to 11:30 A.M. The most common expatriate service bank is the Bank of China, which has branches throughout the country. Full details of services and further information can be found online at www.bank-of-china.com/en/static/index.html. For listings of banks, refer to the following Web sites: www.portalino.it/banks/_cn.htm; www.reserve-bank.com/cnbank.htm; www.escapeartist.com/banks3/banks3.htm; www.chinagate.com.cn/english/179.htm; and www.aaadir.com/countries.jsp?ID=39.

To open a bank account in China, you are required to produce your passport and visa, along with any work or residence papers. Some banks have specific requirements with regard to minimum deposits for new accounts. Local bank accounts can be held by foreigners, including "special" (foreign currency) accounts; however, you are not allowed to withdraw money from such an account unless you have an exit visa stamped on your passport. This regulation has been introduced to curb black market currency exchange. You can, however, wire your money (in foreign currency) from such an account to any country with diplomatic relations with China. The following methods are accepted in China for paying bills: cash, bankcard, credit card, check, or bank transfer.

Currency: Chinese currency is called Renminbi (RMB—"People's money"). The unit of currency is the Yuan (CNY); 1 Yuan = 10 Jiao or 100 Fen. Notes are in denominations of 100, 50, 20, 10, 5, 2, and 1 Yuan. Coins are in denominations of 1 Yuan, and 50, 20, 10, 5, 2, and 1 Fen.

The Yuan is not traded outside China. Foreign bank notes and traveler's checks can be exchanged at branches of the Bank of China, tourist hotels, some friendship stores (state-run stores in larger cities, similar to duty-free shops) and some of the larger department stores, and at the exchange desks at the airport. Hotels and stores usually charge a commission fee; the Bank of China does not. The exchange rate is set by the Bank of China. Most foreign currencies can be exchanged, although the USD is often the most widely accepted for exchange anywhere in China. It is advisable to keep all currency exchange receipts as these are needed to change any Chinese currency back to foreign currency when you leave the country.

There is an active illegal market in the exchange of currency, but expatriates are strongly advised to use only official points of exchange. The punishment for trading currency on the black market is severe. Traveler's checks from most of the world's leading international banks and issuing agencies are acceptable in China in exchange for currency.

Credit cards: Major international credit cards (such as Visa, MasterCard, American Express, and Diners Club) are becoming more widely accepted in establishments frequented by foreigners (for example, appointed shops, hotels, and restaurants). However, this only applies to major cities, and credit cards are rarely accepted in remote areas. Credit cards are generally not accepted for payment when purchasing train and airplane tickets.

The Bank of China allows major credit card holders to withdraw cash against their accounts. There are very few ATMs that will accept foreign cards within China. It is essential that you verify with your bank whether you can get money from your account, and by what method, while in China.

Taxes: The existing PRC Individual Income Tax Law (IIT Law) was last amended in 2005. With minor exceptions, all individual taxpayers (Chinese and expatriates) are treated in a similar manner under this IIT law. The only major difference is that expatriates are entitled to an additional deduction from their taxable income.

The tax year is the calendar year. Tax payments in China are either made through banks or directly to the local tax bureau.

Individuals who are domiciled in China are taxed individually on their worldwide income. Individuals whose domicile is not in China are taxed in accordance with their length of residency in China, as follows:

- Foreign expatriates who travel in China and derive income from an overseas employer with no permanent establishment in China will be exempt from tax if they do not physically stay in China, consecutively or cumulatively, for more than 90 days in a calendar year. The 90-day test is extended to 183 days if the individual is a tax resident of a country that has executed a taxation treaty with China.

- A nonresident individual who resides in China for more than 90 days (or 183 days for treaty country residents) but less than one year will be taxed only on his China-source income.

- Foreign individuals who reside in China for more than one year but not exceeding five years will be subject to tax on both their China-source income and their foreign-source income. However, upon application to and approval from the tax authorities, the taxation of foreign-source income can be limited to that received from Chinese enterprises, Chinese establishments, Chinese economic organizations, and Chinese individuals.

- Foreign individuals who reside in China for more than five consecutive years will be subject to tax on their worldwide income from the sixth year onward.

An additional monthly deduction of CNY 4,000 (over and above the standard deduction of CNY 800) is granted to foreign expatriates in calculating their taxable employment income.

BEIJING

MEDICAL ISSUES

Beijing has plenty of private and public hospitals and clinics. Hospitals in Beijing include the Beijing United Family Hospital, Beijing United Family Clinic, SOS International (medical emergency and evacuation service), Vista Clinic, MEDEX Assistance Corporation (medical evacuation service), Friendship Hospital, and the International Medical Center. Dental clinics include Arrail Dental and Beijing United Family Hospital.

ENVIRONMENT ISSUES

Tap water is not safe to drink, and therefore bottled water, which is widely available, must be purchased. Air pollution in Beijing is a major concern. The condition is aggravated by cold weather, and thus respiratory infections are very common during the winter months.

INFRASTRUCTURE

Air travel: Capital International Airport (www.bcia.com.cn) is located 28 km (18 miles) northeast of Beijing city center and has a good choice of services to Asian destinations and some to Western Europe and North America. Airport facilities include a bank, bureaux de change, ATMs, telephones, a post office, cafés, restaurants, numerous shops, including duty-free, and a 24-hour medical center.

Metered taxis are available outside the terminal building (journey time: 40 to 60 minutes to get downton). The taxi fare costs around CNY 100 to CNY 120. The airport-city shuttle bus departs every 30 minutes from outside the arrivals hall and takes three routes into the city: Xidan, Gongzhufen, and Zhongguancun; the shuttle also stops at major hotels. The main railway stations are Beijing Zhan (Beijing Railway Station) and Beijing Xi Zhan (Beijing West Railway Station). There are ticket windows specially for foreign travelers marked "International Passenger Booking Office." Tickets can also be purchased from the China International Travel Service.

Transport in Beijing: Streets in the central area of Beijing end with the suffix *nei* (meaning "inner"), and in the outer areas of the city, the street suffix is *wai*. Beijing has many long, straight boulevards, although the name may change along its length. The best English language map is the Beijing Tourist Map, which is sold at news stands in large hotels. The best way to travel around Beijing is by taxi or subway. Extensive bus services are also available; however, buses are generally crowded (especially during rush hours, 6:30 to 8:30 A.M. and 5 to 7 P.M.), and knowledge of the Chinese language is necessary.

Taxi: Taxis are plentiful, cheap, and metered. Taxis can be found waiting outside major department stores, hotels, and railway stations and can also be hailed on the street. All taxis have a sticker in the back window indicating the fares/rate per kilometer. The initial meter rate is usually CNY 10 and CNY 1.60 to CNY 2 per kilometer thereafter. There is a 20 percent surcharge after 11 P.M. Taxis can also be pre-booked by telephone. It is advisable to have your destination written in Chinese, as most drivers are unlikely to speak English.

Metro (subway): Beijing has a clean and efficient subway system (www.bjsubway.com) which comprises four lines: Line 1, Line 2, Line 13, and the Batong Line. The subway serves downtown Beijing and its various outlying suburbs and runs regular trains between 5:30 A.M. and 11 P.M. Tickets can be purchased at ticket offices located at all stations and cost CNY 3 regardless of the length of the journey.

Bus: Buses are usually very crowded and can be unsafe. Traffic is often congested, even after rush hour. There are over 650 bus routes covering the whole city and surrounding suburbs. Services generally run between 5:30 A.M. and 11 P.M., with a limited night service operating between 11 P.M. and 5:30 A.M. Bus fares cost CNY 1 to CNY 2 for a journey within the city center, and CNY

2 to CNY 10 for longer journeys to the suburbs. Tickets are purchased on the bus from the conductor. Beijing is flat terrain and perfect for bicycles. Bicycle parking is widely available for minimal costs. Many Chinese use this method of transport.

Car: Expatriates are allowed to drive their own cars in Beijing and on the Beijing-Tianjin highway. Any journey beyond 40 km from Beijing may require special permission. It is advisable to avoid driving in the city center unless you are extremely confident and have good knowledge of the city. Car hire is available, but most companies will insist that foreigners hire the driver as well.

SHOPPING AND AVAILABILITY OF CONSUMER GOODS

A wide range of consumer goods, local and imported, is available in Beijing. Department stores and supermarkets generally stock a wide range of imported goods, and a good selection of alcoholic beverages is available. Several brands and models of cars are available as well. Most larger cities have large bookshops which sell some foreign language books, magazines, and newspapers. The major international/tourist hotels often have a reasonable selection of publications. Bookstores include Beijing Foreign Language Bookstore, China Bookstore, and Yi Friendship Bookshop.

In addition to the many street markets and small shops, there are also large department stores and Western-style shopping malls. The best shopping area in Beijing is downtown on Wangfujing and Dongdan Streets. Jianguomenwai Dajie is also good for shopping.

Most shops are open daily between 8:30 or 9 A.M. and 8 P.M. Some of the larger department stores stay open until 9 P.M. Shopping malls include Lufthansa Centre, Xidan Shopping Centre, Oriental Plaza, China World Shopping Arcade, Guiyou Shopping Mall, and Sun Dong An Market. Department stores include Beijing Department Store, Beijing Friendship Store, Parkson, and PriceSmart membership shopping. Supermarkets include Lido, Scitech Plaza, PriceSmart membership shopping, and Carrefour Supermarket. Among markets are Panjiayuan Market, which is one of Beijing's most popular and sells almost everything. Hongqiao Market (pearl market) is excellent for clothing and jewelry purchases. Silk Alley sells a large variety of merchandise, and Lido Market has reasonably priced goods.

RECREATION AND ENTERTAINMENT

In Beijing, there is a wide choice of restaurants offering Chinese and European food. The city has a fair variety of cultural events including operas, concerts, theaters, and some cinemas.

Social clubs: There is a limited choice of social clubs in Beijing. International associations and clubs in Beijing are The British Council (www.britishcouncil

.org.cn/china.htm), Goethe Institute (www.goethe.de/os/pek/deindex.htm), and the American Club of Beijing.

Restaurants: There are many good restaurants to choose from in Beijing. As well as the various Chinese cuisines, there are also restaurants offering all types of international cuisine. The restaurants in Beijing's major hotels are popular places to entertain, and they usually offer a choice of European and Chinese food. For restaurant listings, see www.travelchinaguide.com/cityguides/beijing/dining.htm and www.fodors.com/world/asia/china/beijing/restaurants-nam.html.

Details of events in Beijing can be found in the city guides *Beijing This Month* (www.cbw.com/btm) and *City Weekend* (www.cityweekend.com.cn) and in the newspaper *China Today* (www.chinatoday.com).

Theatres: Chang'an Da Xiyuan (Grand Theatre) hosts performances of traditional stories and operas. Guanghe Juchang (Guanghe Theatre) stages plays and films as well as operas. Huguang Huiguan (Huguang Guildhall) stages operas in traditional settings. Lao She Chaguan (Lao She Teahouse) hosts performances that include Peking opera and a variety of other folk arts. Beijing Zhanlanguan Juchang (Beijing Exhibition Centre Theatre) stages Chinese and Western plays, operas, and ballets. Tianqiao Le Chaguan (Tianqiao Happy Teahouse) stages a variety of performances including opera and acrobatics. Yinyu Tang (Beijing Concert Hall) is Beijing's main venue for Chinese and Western classical music concerts.

Cinemas include Beijing Theatre, China Cinema, Dongtu Cinema, Star City, UME International Cineplex, Xindong'an Cinema, and Zhonghua Cinema.

Entertainment for children: The National Museum of China has many interesting historical and cultural exhibitions and is home to the National Wax Museum of China. Beijing Zoo (www.beijingzoo.com) is renowned for its giant pandas, but also featured are golden monkeys, Yangtze alligators, and many other animals unique to China. The Great Wall of China is a historic marvel and can be visited at a number of sites near Beijing. For children, Mutianyu is considered the best site, as it is less crowded than Badaling and has a cable car that transports you to and from the Wall. The ride in itself is fun. Beijing Amusement Park covers 400,000 square meters and has over 40 rides. Beijing Aquarium—Blue Zoo is a walk-through aquarium, the largest of its type in Asia.

Clubs and bars: There are an increasing number of clubs and bars in China's major cities. Entertainment such as this tends to focus upon the large international/tourist hotels, many of which have nightclubs and lounge bars. There are more and more bars opening up in Beijing, but most nightlife remains focused upon the bars and clubs in major hotels. Long-term resident expatriates have set about creating their own nightlife focused on the respective national embassies. It is advisable to ask friends and colleagues in Beijing about the current social scene.

Popular bars include Frank's Place, popular among expatriates; Goose and Duck Pub and Restaurant, which has a sports bar with British food;

Henry J. Bean's, with an American-style bar/grill; Jazz Ya, which has jazz music; Minders Café; and the popular Reilly's Irish Pub.

Sports facilities: A number of sports clubs, tennis clubs, swimming pools, and fitness centers are located here. Aside from bowling, the Bowling Centre features ping pong rooms, a few kids' rides, and an arcade. Er Karting Club is an indoor go-karting center, and Di Tan Ice Arena is an ice skating facility.

For more details on tourism, visit China's National Tourism Administration at www.cnta.com/lyen/index.asp.

NATURAL ENVIRONMENT

Beijing has a dry climate with hot summers and cold winters. Heavy rain sometimes causes floods but does not usually affect daily life. The city has been severely damaged by earthquakes in the past, but was not significantly affected by the massive May 2008 earthquake that struck Sichuan, 960 miles to the southwest.

HOUSING

An increasing amount of accommodations are currently being developed for expatriates; most reside either in international hotels or in districts designated specifically for foreigners. The most prestigious residential areas in Beijing include Beijing Riviera, Lufthansa area, the Beijing Business Centre, and Capital Paradise. An excellent selection of good-quality appliances and furniture is usually available.

Until the end of 2002, all foreigners had to live in "authorized" housing, designed for their use. Now, expatriates can rent an apartment or house. However, many prefer to live in accommodations especially for foreigners. A building boom in the early 1990s led to many new villa complexes and high-rise apartment blocks. The result has been higher vacancy rates, more availability, and greater negotiating power for the tenant. It is quite common to try to negotiate a lower rent.

Real estate agencies in Beijing include Elite Realty China (www.eliterealtychina .com), Home 2 Nest (www.home2nest.com), and Cushman & Wakefield (www.cushwakeasia.com).

Once you have found suitable accommodations, it is always advisable to agree on an itinerary and statement as to the condition of the property prior to signing the lease. You may also wish to consult a lawyer before either oral or written agreements are made. When viewing accommodations, you should carry some proof of income or employment, as well as identification. A security deposit is always payable and can be the equivalent of between one and three months' rent, depending on the property. You will usually be requested to pay three months' rent in advance; however, subsequent rent payments may be monthly, quarterly, or half-yearly. Rental costs generally exclude utility costs and management fees.

Houses in districts in Beijing: good areas—River Garden; very good areas—Capital Paradise; best areas—Beijing Riviera. Apartments in good areas—San Li Tun Diplomatic Area, Jianwai Soho; very good areas—Beijing Business Centre; best areas—Beijing Lufthansa Centre.

INTERNATIONAL SCHOOLS AND EDUCATION

There is a relatively good choice of educational possibilities in Beijing, including American, English, French, German, Swedish, and Japanese schools. However, there may be long waiting lists for placement at these schools.

- International School of Beijing (www.isb.bj.edu.cn) offers an international curriculum and the International Baccalaureate program. The school takes children from pre-kindergarten age to grade 12. A school bus service is provided at an additional cost (depending on where students live). A canteen is available for children who wish to eat at school, and a good range of after-school activities is available. Certain documents have to be provided for the admission process. School hours are 8:20 A.M. to 3:20 P.M.

- The Western Academy of Beijing (www.wab.edu) offers an international curriculum and the International Baccalaureate program. The school takes children between the ages of 3 and 18 years. The school provides bus services, and a canteen is available for children who wish to eat at school. A wide range of after-school activities is offered. Admission requirements include an application form and previous school reports. School hours are 9 A.M. to 4:30 P.M.

- The International Academy of Beijing (www.iabchina.net) offers the American core curriculum. As a Christian school, emphasis is placed upon biblical principles and values. The school serves children from kindergarten to the tenth grade (the tenth grade opened in fall 2007). The school's campus is located in the heart of Beijing.

- Beijing BISS International School (www.biss.com.cn) offers the International Baccalaureate program. The school teaches children from kindergarten age to 18 years. A wide variety of after-school activities is offered for children, and a cafeteria is available.

- Beijing French School offers a French curriculum. The school takes children between the ages of 3 and 18 years. Bus services are provided at an additional cost. A canteen is available for children who wish to eat at school (cost EUR 228 per trimester for five meals per week), and a wide variety of after-school activities is offered. Certain documents are necessary for admission. School hours are 9 A.M. to 4:30 P.M.

- Beijing German School (www.dspeking.net.cn) offers a German curriculum. The school provides a bus service. There is no canteen, but a lunch service is available. Certain documents have to be provided for the admission procedure. School hours are 7:55 A.M. to 3:35 P.M.

- Beijing Japanese School (www.jsb.org.cn) offers a Japanese curriculum. There is neither a school bus service nor a canteen available. After-school activities are offered twice weekly. School registration certificate and application form are required for admission. School hours are Monday through Friday, 8:15 A.M. to 4:10 P.M.

SHANGHAI

ENVIRONMENT ISSUES

Air pollution is a major concern in Shanghai, and respiratory infections are very common during the winter months. The local authorities are, however, very strict with certain regulations on pollution control in the industrial areas of Shanghai.

INFRASTRUCTURE

Utilities and transport: The public transport system in Shanghai is extremely crowded, although some improvements have been made. Nevertheless, the best way of getting around Shanghai is by taxis or by the metro system. Buses can sometimes be unsafe; they are extremely crowded (especially during rush hours, 6:30 to 8:30 A.M. and 5 to 7 P.M.) and somewhat unreliable. Traffic is disorderly, and it may be preferable for an expatriate to hire a local driver to reduce the risk of having an accident.

Air travel: Shanghai has two main airports. The domestic airport (Shanghai Hongqiao), situated 15 km from the city center, takes 45 minutes to reach and has an excellent choice of internal flights. Shanghai Pudong International Airport is located 30 km from the city center and has a very good selection of services to Asian destinations, plus some to Western Europe and North America.

Qiao International Airport (www.shanghaiairport.com/en/index.jsp) is located 13 km (8 miles) southwest of the city center. Airport facilities include bureaux de change, banks and ATMs, postal and telecommunication services, restaurants, bars and coffee shops, and duty-free shopping.

Taxis are available from the main taxi stand outside the arrivals hall. The driver should use the meter. The taxi fare into the city center costs around CNY 50 to CNY 65. It is advisable to have the destination written in Chinese or indicated on a map.

Shanghai Airport Bus Co. and the Shanghai Dazhong Bus Corporation operate shuttle buses, which depart every 30 minutes between 6 A.M. and 9 P.M. (journey time is approximately 30 minutes). Luggage space is limited. The fare is CNY 4 to CNY 7, and tickets are sold by the driver.

Transfer buses to Pudong Airport leave from outside domestic arrivals every 30 minutes between 6 A.M. and 9 P.M. (journey time is 60 minutes). The fare is CNY 30.

Public buses run regularly to city destinations: Bus 925 runs to People's Square; Bus 938 runs to Pudong Yangjiadu; Bus 806 runs to Zhong Shan Nan Yi; Bus 807 runs to Shanghai West Railway Station; and airport Bus 1 runs to Shan Xi Lu. There is little space on buses for luggage.

Bus: Reasonable bus and coach services are available between the main cities. Buses are normally crowded but reach parts of the country that trains do not. Bus travel tends to be more uncomfortable than train travel, and journey times can be extremely long. Bus tickets are generally purchased from the ticket offices located in the main bus stations. Fares are usually less expensive than train tickets.

The main stations for long-distance bus services are Hengfeng Lu Bus Station (Tel: +86 21-6371-4966) and Xujiahui Bus Station (Tel: +86 21-6469-7325).

Rail: Railways provide the principal means of travel for people throughout China. The rail network covers every province. China domestic train service is reliable, but quite overcrowded.

The main railway station is Shanghai Railway Station (Tel: +86 21-6317-9090). There are rail services from Shanghai to many major cities throughout China. Foreigners are usually sent to the CITS office, but there are five advance ticket offices in the city. The main ticket office is at 230 Beijing Dong Lu.

Sea and river: All major rivers are served by good ferry networks. Coastal ferries operate between Dalian, Tianjin (Tientsin), Qingdao (Tsingtao), and Shanghai.

Taxis in Shanghai are cheap, safe, and widely available. All taxis have meters, and you should ensure that the driver uses it. Taxi fares are usually CNY 10 for the initial meter charge and then CNY 2 per kilometer thereafter. Rates increase after 11 P.M. to an initial charge of CNY 13 and then CNY 3 per kilometer.

Taxis can be taken from taxi stands, hailed in the street, or pre-booked through taxi companies. The Shanghai Municipal Taxi Association (Tel: +86 21-6368-1055) can provide further information.

Metro: The Shanghai metro system operates between 5 A.M. and 11 P.M., and it is clean and efficient. There are five metro lines at present, and the system is being expanded. Line 1 operates north-south from Gongfu Xincun via Shanghai Railway Station to the southern suburb of Xin Zhuang; Line 2 runs west-east from Zhongshan Park to Zhangjiang; Line 3 runs north-south from North Jiangyang Road to Shanghai South Station; Line 4 currently has 22 out of a planned 26 lines open, and runs in a circle from Damuqiao Road to Lancun Road.

Tickets cost CNY 3 for journeys of up to 13 stops and CNY 4 for longer journeys. Tickets are purchased from the ticket offices above the platforms.

Stations have a red sign resembling an "M," and station announcements in trains are in Mandarin Chinese and English. The Shanghai metro system is run by the Shanghai Shetong Metro Company (www.shtmetro.com).

SHOPPING AND AVAILABILITY OF CONSUMER GOODS

Shanghai offers some of the best shopping in China. All consumer goods are widely available. There is a wide variety of department stores, shopping centers, and markets to choose from. Department stores and supermarkets generally stock a wide range of imported goods. Imported alcoholic beverages are also readily available. Vehicles from international manufactures are in good supply; however, they can be expensive and the purchasing process can be time consuming.

The main shopping streets are Nanjing Lu, Huaihai Zhong Lu, and Xu Jia Hui. Most shops are open daily between 10 A.M. and 9 P.M. Some of the larger department stores stay open until 10 P.M.

RECREATION AND ENTERTAINMENT

Restaurants: The choice of restaurants in Shanghai offering Chinese and international cuisine is good. Many of the major hotels have a selection of excellent continental, Japanese, and Chinese restaurants from which to choose for business and social entertaining. There are also many reputable privately run and joint-venture restaurants offering such a wide range of cuisine that most tastes will be well satisfied. It is advisable to seek recommendations from colleagues and friends regarding good places to eat out, to book well in advance, and to check beforehand whether credit cards are accepted.

Entertainment: The city has a good selection of cultural venues including operas, concerts, and theaters. Local cinemas are increasingly showing the latest international movies. Details of events in Shanghai can be found in the city guides *That's Shanghai* (www.thatsmagazines.com/home/index.asp?location=sh), *Shanghai Talk* (www.shanghai-ed.com), and the *City Weekend* (www.cityweekend.com.cn).

Sports facilities: There is a good choice of sports facilities in Shanghai, the best of which are in sports complexes in larger hotels. Cycling is a popular means of transport for the average Chinese person, and cycle stores can be found almost everywhere. Hiking and trekking facilities are good in China. Popular spectator sports in China include table tennis (ping pong), gymnastics, basketball, and soccer.

Nightlife: Shanghai is renowned for having the best nightlife in China. It revolves around hotel bars and discos, privately run bars, and joint-venture nightclubs.

NATURAL ENVIRONMENT

The city experiences hot summers and cold winters. The extreme humidity in Shanghai can be very unpleasant. Rainfall is frequent and this can sometimes lead to floods, which can have a damaging effect on daily life.

HOUSING

An increasing amount of accommodations are currently being developed for expatriates, and most reside either in international hotels or in districts designated specifically for foreigners. The majority of accommodations is furnished. The most prestigious residential areas include Xu Hui District, Jing An, Shanghai Centre, Lu Wan District, Pudong New Area, and Gubei.

The most popular housing in Shanghai is found in the "expat" communities or "villas." They can be expensive but feature gardens, split-level living, garages, full amenities. and a health club usually located nearby. There are also the "Old Villas," which are much more classy and generally in the old French Concession area. These are residences dating from before the Communist takeover in 1949. For old houses that have been properly renovated, with their electrical systems and plumbing updated, prices can be high, but the location is usually good and comfort guaranteed.

Other popular housing options are the expatriate apartment complexes. These range from luxurious to modest and from the downtown area to Pudong, with prices varying accordingly.

A wide range of household appliances and furniture of excellent quality is available.

INTERNATIONAL SCHOOLS AND EDUCATION

- Yew Chung International School (www.ycef.com) offers an international curriculum and the UK curriculum. The school takes children from pre-kindergarten to grade 12. The school provides bus services at additional fees, depending on the distance traveled. The school applies a uniform policy. A canteen is available for children who wish to eat at school, and a wide range of after-school activities is offered. Certain documents are required for the admission process. School hours are 8 A.M. to 3:30 P.M.

- Shanghai American School (www.saschina.org) offers the U.S. and international curricula. The school takes children from pre-kindergarten to grade 12. The school provides bus services at additional fees. A canteen is available for children who wish to eat at school, and a wide range of after-school activities is offered. Certain documents are required for the admission process. School hours are 8:10 A.M. to 3:30 P.M.

- École Française de Shanghai (French school) (www.chez.com/ecolefrancaiseshanghai) offers the French national curriculum. The school takes children between the ages of 3 and 18 years. The school provides a bus service at an additional cost. A canteen is available for children who wish to eat at school, and a wide range of after-school activities is offered. School hours are 8:15 A.M. to 3:15 P.M.

- Deutsch Schule Shanghai (German school) (www.ds-shanghai.org.cn) offers the German curriculum. The school takes children between the ages of 3 and 18 years. The school provides bus services, and a canteen is available for children who wish to eat at school. A wide range of after-school activities is offered.

- Shanghai Japanese School offers a Japanese curriculum. There is no school bus service, and a canteen is not available. After-school activities are offered to all students. A school registration certificate and an application form are required for admission. School hours are Monday through Friday, 8:30 A.M. to 3:30 P.M.

- Shanghai Community International School (www.scischina.org) is based on the U.S. curriculum and serves children aged preschool through 18 years. Over 40 nationalities are represented throughout the SCIS community. SCIS has four international schools in Shanghai (for different age groups and with varying facilities). See the Web site for in-depth information on each school.

Czech Republic: Prague

PERSONAL SAFETY AND SECURITY ISSUES

Internally, the situation in the Czech Republic is generally stable. Demonstrations occur but usually cause little disruption to daily life. Prague is a relatively safe city, but common sense precautions should be taken at night.

MEDICAL ISSUES

Medical services are generally good, especially in private services in Prague, and the number of private hospitals and clinics is increasing. However, public facilities are not always the most up to date, particularly in rural areas.

Most medical supplies, including a wide range of prescription medicines, are readily available and easily accessible. Free emergency medical care is available to all; however, all other medical treatment must be paid for if you are not insured.

Many doctors and hospitals expect immediate payment for treatment (in general payable in koruna), while some may accept credit cards.

Some private clinics and medical centers advertise themselves as foreign (American, French, Canadian, and so on); this does not necessarily mean that the staff is foreign or that they speak English, and in most cases the doctors and nurses in these clinics are Czech.

ENVIRONMENT ISSUES

Tap water is considered relatively safe to drink but it is usually chlorinated and may cause mild abdominal upsets. Bottled water is widely available and advised for consumption. Milk is generally pasteurized and dairy products are safe to consume. Local meat, poultry, fish, and produce are generally of good quality and safe to eat.

Sewage and waste removal systems are functional throughout the city, but air pollution is a concern in Prague.

ECONOMIC OVERVIEW, 2008

GDP growth	4.4%
Inflation	6.3%
Unemployment	5.0%

INFRASTRUCTURE

Prague has a very good public transport system with a comprehensive metro supported by buses and trams. Traffic is becoming more congested due to the increasing number of vehicles on the roads.

Air travel: Ruzyne International Airport is situated 20 km (12 miles) northwest of Prague and can be reached in 30 minutes by bus. Airport facilities include banks, bureaux de change, a post office, restaurant and bar, shops, car parking, and car rental. The airport has two terminals. For details, see www.csl.cz/en. There is a good choice of direct international flights, but some journeys require a connecting flight.

The number of low-cost airlines flying to and from Prague has increased significantly in recent years. Most low-cost airlines operate flights to London. The main Czech low-cost airlines are Smart Wings (www.smartwings.cz) and Sky Europe (www.skyeurope.com/en).

ČEDAZ shuttle buses offer individual minibus transportation with regular half-hour services between 5:30 A.M. and 9:30 P.M. between V Celnici Street and Prague Ruzyně Airport. The fare is CZK 480 for one to four people. ČEDAZ also provides personal transportation to any place in Prague (hotels, accommodations, and so on). The minibus stand is in front of the arrivals hall.

Taxis can be taken from the stand situated in front of the arrivals hall of both terminals. The trip to the city center will cost approximately CZK 450.

Public transport: Prague has an excellent public transport system operated by Dopravní podnik hlavníhmě ta Prahy (Prague Public Transport Authority, www.dp-praha.cz). The integrated network consists of the metro, trams, buses, certain trains, and a funicular. Services operate between 4:30 or 5 A.M. and midnight; late-night tram and bus services operate between midnight and 5 A.M.

Metro: The metro has three lines. Trains operate every 1–3 minutes between 5 A.M. and 8 P.M., Monday through Friday and at 5- to 10-minute intervals between 8 P.M. and midnight, Monday through Friday, and all day on weekends.

Tram and bus: The tram and bus network covers the whole city. Most services are in operation between 4:30 A.M. and 11:30 P.M. Night services run every 30 minutes between midnight and 5 A.M.

Funicular: There is a funicular railway running from Újezd to the top of Petřín Hill. Services operate every 10–15 minutes daily between 9:15 A.M. and 8:45 P.M.

SHOPPING AND AVAILABILITY OF CONSUMER GOODS

Most products are available in Prague. There are many large, modern shopping centers, department stores, and international supermarket chains, which sell all products required for daily living. There are also open-air markets selling fresh produce, flowers, and groceries.

Opening hours vary between different types of stores; in general, stores are open Monday through Friday, 8 or 9 A.M. to 6 P.M. and Saturday 8 A.M. to 12 or 2 P.M. (grocery stores are usually open all week long, 7 or 8 A.M. to 8 or 9 P.M.).

Some shops are open on Sundays (all shops in downtown Prague are open daily). Large supermarkets and shopping centers usually have longer opening hours. Some supermarkets are open 24 hours a day.

The choice of alcoholic beverages is also wide, and there are almost no restrictions on consumption or purchasing.

The range of brands and models of cars available for purchase in Prague is very good.

The major shopping areas in Prague are Narodní třída running past Můstek to Na Příkopě and the area around Staroměstské náměstí (Old Town Square). There is also a good variety of shops along Celetná, between Staroměstské náměstí and náměstí Republiky. Pařížská ulice and the area just south of Josefov (the Jewish Quarter) are also good places to try for boutiques and antique shops.

RECREATION AND ENTERTAINMENT

Restaurants: The choice of restaurants in the city is good. It is advisable to make reservations in advance (for lunch or dinner), especially in the peak tourist season. Prices are reasonable by Western standards, even in some of the more expensive restaurants. Most restaurants in Prague serve traditional Czech food, although there are a number of new restaurants now, which serve international cuisine. Many of Prague's better restaurants are around the Hradčany and Malá Strana areas of the city. Staré Město probably has the highest concentration of eating places in Prague.

Cinemas are widespread and show all the major international as well as locally produced films. Most foreign films shown in Prague's cinemas are screened in their original language with Czech subtitles and are marked as *titulky;* films that have been dubbed into Czech are marked *dabované.*

Film schedules are listed in the *Downtown* magazine, available from all cinema lobbies. A cinema ticket for the large multi-screen cinemas costs around CZK 120. Most large shopping centers have modern multiplex movie theaters showing the latest feature films and major international productions. Cinema City (www .cinemacity.cz) has four large complexes in Prague including an IMAX screen. Other multiplex cinemas include Palace Cinemas (www.palacecinemas.cz) or Village Cinemas (www.villagecinemas.cz).

Culture and entertainment: Folk songs lie at the heart of all Czech music and are one of the resilient foundations of Czech culture. The style of music can vary depending on the region of the Republic, but the richest tradition of folk music is in Moravia. The great wealth of folk tunes have found their way into much of the country's classical music, of which the Czechs are justifiably proud, having produced at least four composers of fame—Smetana, Dvořák, Janáček, and Martinů. Prague and Brno have music festivals which celebrate both national and international artists. Smaller towns have annual festivals often dedicated to composers. It is easy to catch works by Czech composers throughout the year.

Most opera houses and concert halls are closed in July and August, although the numerous summer concerts held in castles and parks provide some compensation.

The theater is very popular; however, there are very few productions in English. There is also a strong tradition of mime and puppetry.

Entertainment events and venues are listed in the entertainment section of the English-language weekly newspaper *The Prague Post.* The local press also contains cultural listings in the weekend editions.

Classical concerts take place throughout the year in Prague, but by far the largest annual event is the Prague Spring International Music Festival (www .festival.cz), the country's most prestigious international music festival (from May 12 to June 3).

In comparison to other forms of entertainment, tickets for classical music, opera, and ballet performances are expensive. There are central ticket offices, but it is usually cheaper to purchase the tickets for performances at the individual box offices. Performances are often sold out well in advance. Prague has an excellent musical reputation, and there is a large selection of theaters, operas, ballets, and other cultural venues.

Sports: There is a reasonable choice of sports and leisure facilities in the city. The most popular spectator sports in the Czech Republic are ice hockey, soccer, and tennis.

Nightlife: The nightlife is varied and caters to a wide variety of people. Most social life and drinking takes place in pubs (*pivnice* or *hospody*). There are a wide variety of bars, clubs, and casinos located throughout the city. Jazz is extremely popular in Prague, and the city has some great jazz clubs, featuring everything from swing to blues and modern jazz.

For details of cultural and nightlife events, check the English-language newspaper *Prague Post,* or one of the multilingual monthly guides available at hotels, tourist offices, and newsstands.

According to Czech law, every casino visitor must be officially registered. The first time you enter a casino you will need a valid photo ID. The minimum age of entry is usually 18, and there is normally a dress code.

SOCIOCULTURAL ENVIRONMENT

In the Czech Republic there are no limitations on freedom of speech and movement, or on the free practice of religion. There are two state-run television channels and two private channels. Many international newspapers are on sale in Prague.

DEMOGRAPHIC/WORKFORCE OVERVIEW

Population	10,251,000 (2006 estimate)
Population density	130 inhabitants per km^2
Age structure	0–14 years, 14%
	15–64 years, 71%
	65 years and over, 15%
Life expectancy at birth	
Total population:	75.8 years
Male	72.5 years
Female	79.2 years

WORKPLACE CULTURE

Business hours are generally Monday through Friday, 8 or 9 A.M. to 5 or 6 P.M. Government offices are usually open Monday through Friday, 9 A.M. to 5 P.M. Employees usually take an hour off for lunch.

Avoid making important business meetings during the months of July and August, as this is when many Czechs take their summer vacation. Formal business dress is the norm. Men should wear a business suit with a shirt and tie. Women should wear a smart dress or suit. Punctuality is important; if you are going to be late, call in advance. Being more than five minutes late is considered inappropriate. Appointments should be made well in advance and confirmed closer to the time. Avoid making appointments on Friday afternoons as many people leave for the countryside.

Office doors are usually kept closed; it is polite to knock before entering. The decision-making process is quite centralized and hierarchical. Most of the decisions come from higher management levels and are rarely challenged by those of lower rank.

NATURAL ENVIRONMENT

In general, the climate in the Czech Republic is continental, with short, hot summers and cold winters. Spring and autumn can be both pleasantly warm and miserably wet. Winter temperatures have been known to drop as low as −20°C. Prague has witnessed fairly serious flooding in recent years.

HOUSING

Accommodations in the very center of Prague (*Malá Strana*) are often very attractive and gives easy access to Prague's commercial venue and nightlife, but apartments in this area are usually in older buildings and the fittings and fixtures (including the plumbing and heating) are not always in top condition. Nevertheless, more and more apartments are being renovated to very high standards.

Both houses and apartments are available for rent in Prague. In some cases, landlords will agree to provide furniture for an unfurnished property if the terms of the lease justify it.

The most popular districts with expatriates include Josefov, Mala Strana, Stare Mesto, Hanspaulka, Orechovka, Hradcany, and Bubenec. A good selection of accommodations can generally be found in these areas.

Household appliances and furniture of good quality are usually available. Maintenance and repair services, while on the whole are of a reasonable standard, can sometimes be time consuming.

Many expatriate business people find property through private rental agencies. The usual commission fee is the equivalent of one or two months' rent if accommodations are found. It is also advisable to ask fellow expatriates and Czech colleagues for any advice regarding finding accommodations within the city. Agencies are listed in the local newspapers.

FINANCIAL ISSUES INCLUDING BANKING SERVICES AND TAXES

Foreign banks have been quick to establish themselves in Prague. Most of the country's leading banks have been privatized, and the range of banking services available in the city is wide.

Currency: The unit of currency of the Czech Republic is the koruna (CZK; Crown); 1 koruna = 100 haléř. Notes are in denominations of CZK 5,000, 2,000, 1,000, 500, 200, 100, and 50. Coins are in denominations of CZK 50, 20, 10, 5, 2, 1, and 50 haléřů.

Cash, traveler's checks, and credit cards: Currency can be exchanged at banks, private exchange offices (*Směnárna*), some travel agencies, and major hotels. Currency exchange offices generally charge over 2 percent commission fees. Banks usually charge only 2 percent commission and give better exchange rates, but their hours are shorter than the exchange offices and service is generally slower. There is a 24-hour exchange bureau at Ruzyně, Prague's international airport.

Many ATMs are available in Prague and are connected to the Cirrus, Maestro, Eurocard, MasterCard, and Visa systems.

Traveler's checks are widely accepted, the most popular being U.S. dollars, British pounds and Euros, and can be exchanged in banks and exchange offices.

Credit cards such as Visa, MasterCard, and American Express are accepted in most hotels, restaurants, and shops; Visa and MasterCard are more widely accepted than American Express.

Banks: The supervisor of the Czech financial market is the central bank of the Czech Republic—ČNB (www.cnb.cz). The ČNB also supports the general economic policies of the government.

In terms of the number of banks and their ownership, the Czech banking sector has been stable for the last few years. More than 96 percent of the sector's total assets are directly or indirectly controlled by foreign banks. The sector is characterized by continuing growth in household lending and a significant increase in electronic banking.

Banking hours are generally 8 or 9 A.M. to 5 or 6 P.M., Monday through Thursday, and 8 or 9 A.M. to 4 or 5 P.M. on Fridays.

To open a bank account in the Czech Republic, you need to provide means of identification, usually your passport. Different banks may have differing regulations and services.

Taxes: The tax year for individuals is the calendar year. A resident of the Czech Republic is subject to tax on worldwide income, regardless of whether the income is remitted to the Czech Republic.

An individual who spends more than 183 days in a calendar year or has a permanent place of abode in the Czech Republic is a resident for tax purposes. A nonresident is liable to tax on Czech-source income only, subject to double taxation treaties.

Czech-source income includes income from work performed in the territory of the Czech Republic even of just one day's duration, regardless of the place of payment if the employer is a Czech resident or has a permanent establishment in the Czech Republic. A nonresident is exempt from Czech tax on employment income resulting from work performed for a foreign employer resident abroad and no permanent establishment or deemed place of business in the Czech Republic.

INTERNATIONAL SCHOOLS AND EDUCATION

- International School of Prague (www.isp.cz) offers the International Baccalaureate Diploma; the school takes children between the ages of 3 and 19 years. The school does not apply a uniform policy. A canteen is available for children who wish to eat at school, and a wide range of after-school activities is offered. Certain documents have to be provided for the admission process. A personal interview is also required.

- The Prague British School (www.pbschool.cz) takes children between the ages of 18 months and 18 years. Pupils up to year 9 (aged 14) follow the National Curriculum for England and Wales. Pupils in years 10 and 11 (aged 15 and 16) follow the International General Certificate of Secondary Education (IGCSE), governed by the University of Cambridge Board. This is followed by the International Baccalaureate Diploma (IB) in years 12 and 13. School bus services are provided. The school does not apply a uniform policy. There is no canteen available, but a wide range of after-school activities are offered. Certain documents have to be provided for the admission process. A personal interview is also required.

- Lycée Française de Prague (www.lfp.cz) offers the French national curriculum; the school takes children between the ages of 2 and 18 years. The school does not apply a uniform policy. A canteen is available for children who wish to eat at school, and a wide range of after-school activities is offered. Certain documents have to be provided for the admission process. A personal interview may also be required.

- Deutsche Schule Prague (www.dsp-praha.cz) offers the German national curriculum; the school takes children between the ages of 2 and 18 years. The school does not apply a uniform policy. There is no canteen available. A wide range of after-school activities is offered. Certain documents have to be provided for the admission process. A personal interview may also be required.

- Japonská Škola Prague offers a Japanese curriculum. The school does not apply a uniform policy. There is no canteen available. A wide range of after-school activities is offered on Wednesdays. Certain documents have to be provided for the admission process.

Egypt: Cairo

PERSONAL SAFETY AND SECURITY ISSUES

Egypt has a relatively stable association with most countries. Nevertheless, the relationship with Israel has worsened since violence in the Palestinian Territory has increased. Although radical Islamic groups have discontinued their campaign against the Egyptian government, occasional violent incidents cannot be ruled out. Apart from incidents such as these, Cairo is generally a fairly safe city for visitors. Egyptian law enforcement and security officials have increased their counterterrorism activities and security presence throughout the country. It is essential to be vigilant while on public transport in Egypt—theft and pickpocketing are uncommon, but you should keep an eye on your belongings at all times.

All foreign nationals require a passport and a visa for entry into Egypt. Business visas and work permits are reasonably easy to obtain.

MEDICAL ISSUES

Cairo's public health facilities do not always reach the standards of Western nations, but in general, Egyptian hospitals offer a good standard of emergency care and simple procedures. Private medical practitioners and private hospitals are preferable to the public facilities. Cholera, typhoid, and polio vaccinations are advisable. It is important to take prompt care of cuts and skin irritations, since flies can quickly spread infection. Bilharzia infects the Nile waters, and it is strongly advised not to bathe or walk barefoot in the river. There is a very limited risk of malaria in Egypt; the only location being highlighted at present is in the El Faiyum governorate (50 miles southwest of Cairo), although no cases have been reported since 1998. Prophylaxis is not necessary, as the medication can have unpleasant side effects.

Many doctors in Egypt are trained in the West and speak English. Medical facilities in Cairo and Alexandria are adequate for routine problems, but emergency services can prove limited. Facilities elsewhere are inadequate or nonexistent. Hospital equipment may not be up to date. Most doctors and hospitals will expect payment in cash, regardless of whether you have travel health insurance. Serious medical problems will require air evacuation to a country with state-of-the-art medical facilities.

Cairo has been established as Egypt's main center for medical treatment, and in general, has the most advanced level of medical care in the country. Some of Cairo's most famous hospitals are El Nozha International Hospital, Anglo American Hospital, El Salam International Hospital (Egypt's largest private hospital with 350 beds), Ain Shams University Hospital, and Qasr El Ainy General Hospital. Dental care has been cited as being very good in Cairo—facilities are of a high quality, with well-qualified and highly trained doctors. Many dentists speak English.

Pharmaceuticals are, in general, reasonably priced, although if a certain drug must be imported, it can end up being quite expensive. You will have no difficulties finding a pharmacy; they are usually open until 9 P.M. or later. You need to ask for an *ag-zakhana* or *sigh-daliyya,* or look for signs depicting a snake coiled around an apothecary's cup. For minor complaints, you should go to your nearest pharmacy; there are a number of 24-hour pharmacies in Cairo. Poisoning of feral cats and dogs is an issue in Cairo; dogs can pick up poisoned food, so you have to be careful not to let your dog snack indiscriminately from the ground. Some strays can be aggressive and it is worth bearing in mind that walkers carry sticks to fend off strays.

ENVIRONMENT ISSUES

Bilharzia infects the Nile waters, and it is strongly advised not to bathe or walk barefoot in the river to avoid schistosomiasis, a parasitic disease that can lead to serious chronic illness. It is advisable to drink only bottled water, as tap water is heavily chlorinated and might not be properly filtered. Air pollution is a major concern in Cairo.

ECONOMIC OVERVIEW, 2008

GDP growth	7.2%
Inflation	11.7%
Unemployment	8.7%

INFRASTRUCTURE

Utilities and traffic: The Cairo metro is simple to use (although crowded in rush hour), and bus and minibus services reach all parts of the city. Traffic is congested during rush hours, and occasionally at other times as well. Driving can be hazardous in some parts of the city.

Air travel: The Cairo International Airport (www.cairo-airport.com) is situated 22.5 km from the city center. There is a good choice of flights to destinations in Europe and the Middle East, and a fair range of departures to North America, Africa, and Asia. With the completion of a third terminal in early 2007, Cairo has excellent facilities for passengers. There is a free shuttle bus linking the terminals. Getting to and from the airport by taxi from Cairo Center takes around 30 minutes. Taxis leave from outside the arrivals hall—it is recommended to haggle to get the best price for the journey. Limousines are available from the airport to central Cairo for a flat rate fare. Black Mercedes limousines leave from outside the arrivals hall. Buses are available from the airport to central Cairo as well. An airport bus service operates from Terminal 1. Bus No. 400

leaves every 30 minutes during the day and every hour at night. The Super Jet Coach Company operates a bus service to Alexandria from Cairo Airport. Buses between Cairo and Alexandria depart every hour. Reservations should be made at least one day in advance. Ticket costs vary depending on the type of bus; some buses are more comfortable than others. Sleeper trains are also available; see Cairo-Luxor-Aswan, www.sleepingtrains.com. Trains run almost hourly from Cairo to Alexandria. All trains leaving Cairo depart from Ramses Station (Mahattit Ramsis or Mahattit Misr). Others are the overnight sleeper train Cairo-Luxor-Aswan and daytime air-conditioned express trains.

Bus: Cairo has a public bus system that offers several lines of service in different classes and prices: standard bus service; air-conditioned service, known as CTA (short for Cairo Transport Authority), for a higher price; and mini-buses (smaller buses with a more extensive network). Other transport services include the traditional micro-buses, privately run by individuals. Micro-buses are the cheapest form of transport in Cairo; however, they do not have a good reputation for reliability. Buses and mini-buses are a good option to get around the city, as they cover a good network of routes. You will need to be able to speak and read Arabic, however. Tickets can be bought on board. You should be prepared for a delay at peak times on the buses.

Metro: Cairo boasts the only metro system in Africa. In Cairo the metro system is identified by circular signs with a big red M. The first two carriages are reserved for women only (although women can also sit wherever they like on the rest of the train). The trains not only run until midnight every night but also they are reliable, on time, and excellent value for your money. You should buy your tickets at the departure station and hold on to them until you exit at your destination station. Tickets are currently EGP 1 for each journey regardless of distance. The system currently consists of two operational lines, with a third in an advanced stage of planning. The existing routes connect Helwan in the South of the city to Heliopolis in the North, with various branches to Shubra, Ataba, and Abdin. Cairo also has tram systems and Heliopolis is served by six tram lines.

Taxi: The traditional Cairo taxi is being replaced by the Cairo cab for a more modern look in the city. The introduction of a new organized private taxi service finally began in March 2006. The new yellow taxis offer a more reliable and luxurious taxi service in modern air-conditioned cars through privately run companies operating in Cairo. They are introducing designated ranks for the cabs, and there is a free number from which you can order a taxi. The drivers can generally speak English. There are many taxis in Cairo—they can be hailed easily from any corner of any street. However, it can be difficult to get a fair price, and the driving in Cairo may not suit passengers with a nervous disposition. Generally taxi meters do not work, so you should agree on a price before you get into the taxi. However, do not be surprised if the driver stops to pick up additional passengers on the way—this happens quite often. You should remember that single men should sit in the front of the taxi and single women should sit in the back. It is also important to keep small notes handy so you can pay the exact amount when you get out of the cab.

SHOPPING AND AVAILABILITY OF CONSUMER GOODS

Cairo has a wide variety of bazaars, shops, boutiques, and department stores, and a reasonable choice of most Western consumer goods is available, with the exception of high-tech items. There is a reasonable selection of foods, but fruit and vegetables should be disinfected and meat thoroughly cooked before consumption. Alcoholic beverages are obtainable in the market. It is possible to purchase most models of cars in Cairo, but it can be time consuming.

Bookstores include Cairo Anglo-Egyptian Bookshop, International Language Bookshop (ILB), Everyman's Bookshop, and Lehnert and Landrock.

Shopping: Particularly good buys from Egypt are spices, perfume, gold, silver, carpets, brass and copperware, leather work, glass, ceramics, and mashrabiya (a distinctive type of wood carving particular to the Arab East mainly used for windows). Many supermarkets will deliver goods to your home for a small fee. Children's clothes, in particular, are expensive, and some expatriates have difficulty finding clothes or shoes larger than a size 12 or size 45.

Cairo offers an incredible mixture of shopping and culture. Shopping ranges from the famous Khan el-Khalili souk (largely unchanged since the fourteenth century) to modern air-conditioned centers home to the latest designs and fashions. Some of the well-known street markets are worth visiting, such as Wekala al-Balaq for fabrics, including Egyptian cotton, the Tentmakers Bazaar for appliqué work, and Mohammed Ali Street for musical instruments. Cairo is considered to be the fashion center of the Arab world. Many new and trendy boutiques have been set up in Heliopolis (in particular around Horreya Street).

Shopping malls: Arkadia Shopping Mall is the largest shopping mall in Egypt, with over 500 stores. Most of the shops accept all major credit cards, although there may be additional charges for this. City Stars is a huge complex with hundreds of shops and restaurants. Alongside the international chain stores such as Mango and Virgin Megastores, there are luxury boutiques such as Tiffany's and Givenchy. Dandy Mega Mall consists of many boutiques plus a huge Carrefour hypermarket, department stores, and a cinema complex, as well as a number of food outlets and restaurants. El Boustan is situated in the heart of Cairo; there are nine floors and underground parking. The mall is not known for its fashion; however, for cheap casual wear this mall is ideal. There are also airline offices, an optician, and a small bookstore. Nile Hilton Mall has high-quality goods available at moderate prices. There is also an Internet café and a childcare center. The main clientele are upper-middle class locals and tourists.

Department stores: There are many Omar Effendi stores in and around Cairo, although the one in Adly Street is the newest and has by far the best selection of international goods; other branches have received varying reviews from expatriates. Sednaoui, although selling few international brands, is a popular department store that was once one of the finest stores in Cairo (cosmetics, luggage, and kitchenware, for example, are available at reasonably competitive prices). Although Rivoli is a fairly plain department store with an unspectacular selection of goods, its main benefit is that unlike most other department stores, prices here are highly negotiable. Fouad Hayek Sons is small, dusty, and cramped but houses a surprising selection of goods, particularly household appliances. Alfa Market has an excellent selection of unique and quality products as well as many international goods. Each branch has a deli, sports department, cosmetics counter, and extensive selection of food and housewares products. Prices are slightly higher than elsewhere, but the convenience factor of having everything one could need in a single store often wins shoppers. Branches are found at Maadi, Giza, and Nasr City. Supermarkets, such as Carrefour, are located here.

RECREATION AND ENTERTAINMENT

Cairo offers most kinds of local and international cuisine. The restaurants in the major hotels are among the more prestigious and safe places to go. The choice of cultural events is improving, with quarterly opera and theater performances. The number of cinemas has extensively increased in Cairo, although many films shown are still censored. The annual film festival helps to add to the variety. There is a fair selection of sports clubs in Cairo and the surrounding area, and a number of new sports facilities (for example, riding and water sports) have opened in recent years.

International associations and clubs: The American Chamber of Commerce in Egypt meets monthly for lunch at the Cairo Marriott Hotel. This is open to members and their guests. The Baladi Association meets the first Sunday of every month at 5 P.M., mainly for the preservation of nature and the improvement of the environment. The Bridge Club and the British Community Association are others.

Restaurants: Cortigiano, an Italian restaurant, is a favorite among the locals, due to its good food and even better atmosphere. Fish Market is one of the best seafood restaurants in the city. Andrea is a family-oriented restaurant with an indoor dining room and a popular garden terrace. Roast chicken, kebabs, and kofta are some of the more popular dishes on the menu. The restaurant serves local beer and wine, but no desserts. Kandahar is an elegant restaurant serving authentic Indian food. Live singing performances are presented after 9:30 P.M. Raoucha is an upscale restaurant overlooking Sphinx Square. The restaurant serves authentic Lebanese dishes in an elegantly styled dining room.

Theatres and concert halls: Cairo Opera House has two opera houses, of which one is highly formal and the other more casual. Check the local press for performances and times. Howard Theatre stages short plays, stand-up comedy acts, and dance, as well as poetry events. You should call to obtain a schedule. Hashad Theatre, one of the oldest buildings on the campus of Cairo University, is equipped with state-of-the-art audio/visual equipment.

Museums: The Egyptian museum is one of the greatest collections of Egyptian artifacts in the world. Military Museum houses more about the military ceremony than war, and more British military history than Egyptian. This museum nevertheless frequently ranks among the top attractions in the city. Abdeen Palace Museum, once a royal palace, is now a weapons and medals museum. Gayer-Anderson Museum has two houses now joined together, exquisitely decorated and full of authentic Egyptian items and artifacts. The house was once used in the filming of the James Bond film *The Spy Who Loved Me* (1977). Arabesque is an impressively decorated art gallery with contemporary exhibits that change each month.

Cinemas: Metro is situated in a classic building in downtown Cairo. They have midnight shows on Thursdays and Fridays. Odeon is one of the best cinemas in Cairo, with three screens and a good selection of films. Midnight shows are on Thursdays, Fridays, and Saturdays. Normandi has midnight showings every day. Watch for the open air Normandi in summer. El Shorouq City Drive In is a new cinema in Cairo. The film audio is carried by the FM radio in your auto, though you may also rent a radio.

Entertainment for children: Dr. Ragab's Pharaonic Village is a living museum simulating life and work in ancient Egypt. The museum is situated on an island in the Nile and is accessible only by boat. Dream Park is one of the largest parks in the Middle East, and there are many rides and attractions for young children, teenagers, and adults. There are also 22 restaurants on the 150-acre site. Sayyed Zeinab Cultural Park is a park where children can explore the village or play with paint, computers, and so on. Park and Aquarium is located in the vibrant area of Zamalek, a peaceful park with an interesting aquarium. Al Fustat Garden is a theme park with huge green areas, children's slides, and roundabouts.

Nightlife: La Bodega is one of the most popular bar/lounge venues in the city with a belle époque-styled location and different areas such as a cigar room and bistro areas. Piano Bar is elegant and ideal for a quiet drink with an upscale clientele. Harry's Pub is a busy and vibrant bar, with many foreigners who enjoy the eclectic mix of jazz nights and karaoke; limited but popular bar snacks are served. Deals is a very popular bar with young locals and expatriates; the bar food has gotten good reviews. Sherlock Holmes Pub is a delightful tribute to the fictional detective with a warm atmosphere and a good selection of imported drinks.

Nightclubs: Cairo Jazz Club is an Über-cool venue for the young and rich. Crazy House disco is not the most stylish place in the city but has some die-hard fans who love the loud music and "anything goes" atmosphere. Coco Jungle is a tropical jungle theme with live DJs from 11 P.M. Absolute is a favored spot for Cairo's young professionals, with the right decor and mix of music although the drinks can be expensive. Taverne du Champs de Mars is a very popular bar and nightspot (particularly on weekends) in a warm and charming European-style venue.

Casinos: Casino d'Egypt is a top-quality casino for the serious gambler. Ramses Hilton Casino is ideal for all, whether a novice or a highly experienced gambler. Casino Libnan El Salam is a very plush and quality casino, with a wide choice of slot machines and tables. Casino Sheraton Cairo has all the usual roulette, blackjack, and slot machines.

Sports facilities: Games are conducted using U.S. dollars. Egypt's most popular sport is undoubtedly soccer, both as a spectator sport and for participation. Al Ahly and Al Zamalek are Egypt's top clubs and are also revered throughout other Arab countries and across Africa. The Egyptian handball team, football, and racket sports, such as squash and tennis, are also strong spectator sports. Horse racing is a common sport as well. The *Egyptian Gazette* carries full details of the events. The Cairo Cyclists have regular Friday and Saturday cycle rides from 8 A.M., which begin outside the Cairo American College. There are a couple of rowing clubs in Cairo, which meet on the east bank of the River Nile between Giza and Embaba. Cairo has a number of diving clubs. They organize regular excursions and meet on the first Monday of each month at the Semiramis Intercontinental Hotel. The Cairo branch of the international network, The Hash House Harriers, meets each Friday afternoon/evening for noncompetitive runs around the city. There are four golf courses in and around Cairo, as well as a number of tennis clubs, swimming pools, and fitness centers. Sports for children in Cairo include Crazy Water, which has waterslides and a wave pool. The Katameya Heights resort has plenty of sports available for children as well as its own clubhouse (www.katameyaheights.com).

SOCIOCULTURAL ENVIRONMENT

Egypt is a limited democracy in which the president may rule by decree. The National Democratic Party has been in power since 1978 and is expected to continue indefinitely. Political parties have been banned in the past. Free practice of religion is guaranteed by national law, but anti-Semitism is widespread. Unescorted women are vulnerable to sexual harassment and various verbal abuses. Although a diverse press is tolerated, the government retains and exercises the right of censorship. Television in Egypt is state-owned. Cable and satellite television are widely available in Cairo, and a good choice of international newspapers is on sale in the city.

DEMOGRAPHIC/WORKFORCE OVERVIEW

Population	80,335,036 (2007 estimate)
Population density	80.7 inhabitants per km^2
Age structure	0–14 years, 32.2%
	15–64 years, 63.2%
	65 years and over, 4.6%
Life expectancy at birth	
Total population:	71.57 years
Male	Male, 69.04 years
Female	Female, 74.22 years

WORKPLACE CULTURE

Egyptians often consider their country to be a bridge between the European West and the Arab East; therefore, you will often find that business practices resemble European or Arab practices or anything in between. Nearly all Egyptians speak Arabic; however, most international business people will also speak English, French, or both. Friday is the Muslim holy day, when all commercial activities are closed. Many companies also close operations on Thursday; hence the Egyptian "weekend" is Thursday and Friday.

During the holy month of Ramadan, all Muslims fast from dawn to dusk and cannot work more than six hours each day. Foreigners are not required to fast, although they should be respectful of the local customs at this time and not eat or drink while in public. Fasting includes chewing gum and smoking. Once the sun has set, Muslim families come together to celebrate the breaking of the fast (*iftar*), which often goes on until late in the night. During this month, most businesses operate on a reduced schedule and open and close at unusual times.

Foreigners are expected to abide by local standards of modesty; however, it can be offensive for a non-native to adopt native clothing. A jacket and tie are usually required for men at business meetings. Men should wear long pants (never short pants) and a shirt, and with the exception of a wedding ring never have visible jewelry, especially a necklace or earrings. Women should always wear modest clothing in public and take care to cover themselves up appropriately. Sleeves should cover most of the arm, shoulders should not be exposed and skirts and dresses should come to below the knee.

You should take time to develop a personal relationship with your Egyptian counterpart before doing business, as Egyptians prefer to work with those they know and respect. Networking is also very important in establishing yourself in the Egyptian business circle. Be prepared to answer extensive questions about you and your family (health, etc.) before getting down to business talks.

Rank and hierarchy are very important in Egypt; therefore, you should always show ultimate respect to the senior person in the group. Usually this person will also act as the spokesperson. The senior person will make the decision, but only after obtaining group consensus. Direct eye contact is a sign of honesty; therefore, you may find that you are regarded quite intensely at times by your counterparts—you should make sure that you are able to hold someone's eye to show your sincerity.

Egyptians judge people on appearances, hence it is very important to be well dressed and presented at all times. If you are offered tea or coffee by your business associates, you should always accept (even if you do not actually drink it); saying "no" to hospitality is akin to saying "no" to the person. You should always make appointments to see an Egyptian business person in advance, and confirm both a week and a day before either in writing or by telephone. Egyptian meetings are rarely private and you may experience frequent interruptions. If someone enters the room and discusses a different subject, you may join in the conversation but not return to your original discussion until this person has exited the room.

It is wise to have all foreign agendas, presentations, and business cards translated into English and Egyptian Arabic. You should be aware that business in Egypt moves at a slow pace and that it may take a number of visits to achieve what seems like a simple task. Do not forget that during this time your Egyptian counterpart will be assessing your personal relationship for long-term business prospects. Egyptians hate to say no and thus tend to not reply or give any response. Egyptians rarely see an offer as being final, and haggling may continue beyond the "final" deal. Egyptians are tough negotiators. Names can often be confusing. It is best to meet, speak to, or correspond with them so that you can find out both their full names and how they are to be addressed in person. Arabic magazines are read from right to left, and books start at what would be the last page in the United States and Europe, for example. Printed literature should have an impressive back cover, even if printed in English.

NATURAL ENVIRONMENT

Cairo has hot and dry summers, with mild winters and cold nights throughout the year. The climate is hot from May to September. Egypt has experienced mild earthquakes.

HOUSING

There is no shortage of either furnished or unfurnished accommodations; however, finding good accommodations is difficult. Beware that Egyptian landlords are quick to raise the price of property rental to non-Egyptians—often as much as two or three times the local price. Many landlords will tell you that they have rented the apartment out before and give you a fantastical price. Unless it was to another foreigner, it was most definitely not rented at this price. You should be aware that many Egyptian landlords are not honest. This makes a private search for accommodations very difficult. Some expatriates take over properties that are currently rented by other internationals.

A local classifieds board is available at www.expatriates.com/classifieds/egt/hs. Furnished properties often overflow with the landlord's tired or gaudy rejects. They may try to convince you that the appliances and furniture are new when advertising, but it is very rarely the case. However, new furniture is a bargain and you can have anything made to your specifications at a reasonable cost.

Mosques dot every neighborhood in Cairo. Five times each day (from predawn to night), the followers of Islam are summoned for prayer from loudspeakers positioned at the top of each mosque. During the month of Ramadan, they are turned up to full capacity. To avoid signing a lease on a property where you are blasted out of bed each morning by the sound, it is strongly advised that you go by the property at a time that coincides with the duration of a prayer call to check the sound level from inside the property. As the streets are quiet at this time, it is worth remembering that it will be even louder at dawn.

Regardless of what the real estate agent or owner tells you about completion dates, do not lease a property that is unfinished or in a building containing units that have not been finished. Everything is made of cinderblock. To create living space, workmen are using sledge hammers from dawn until the early hours of the next morning. Not only noise, but vibrations and construction debris will also find their way into your home. It is also advisable to ask about your neighbors—particularly who live above you if you will be in an apartment. Egyptian children tend to stay up much later than many other nationalities, and the boys in particular are disciplined less than perhaps some cultures would expect.

Air conditioning in Egypt is not a luxury; the oppressive heat makes it a must in every bedroom and the living room. It is strongly advised to check the air conditioning before signing a lease, as many landlords do not ensure regular servicing of the units. If you have a dog and your budget does not allow for a villa, you might want to consider leasing an apartment on the ground floor with a private yard. There are few places to walk a dog, and some domesticated animals have been poisoned by tainted food left out by those intent upon eradicating the homeless dog and cat population.

Real estate agencies include Trenta Real Estate, Coldwell Banker, Paradise Real Estate, Alexandria, Egyrents, and Betna.

Lease and rental conditions: Garages are not usually included in rents, and it is usual to put down a deposit of one month's rent. However, this deposit is rarely returned at the end of your lease, as the landlord will give you a string of excuses as to why you cannot have it and there are no worthwhile legal avenues. It is advisable to avoid fixed-term contracts. You should ensure your contract clearly states that it can be cancelled if you give a 30-day notice regardless of the reasons or circumstances—a "get out" clause is essential. Despite this, the value of a contract in Egypt is questionable—bribes and corruption are much more common than abiding by contracts.

Districts in Cairo: The neighborhood you live in will usually be determined by your family situation. Couples and singles who work downtown usually prefer living close to work in Zamalek or Mohandssen. Those with children generally prefer to live in the El Maadi/Digla area where American, British, and German schools are located, or in Kattameya or Mirage City gated communities.

Houses in good areas include Dokki; very good areas: Mohandssen, Zamalek, Helio polis; best areas: Maadi, Kattameya Heights. Apartments in good areas: Dokki, Garden City; very good areas: Mohandssen, Zamalek, Heliopolis; best areas: Maadi, Kattameya Heights, Rehab.

Availability and costs: Depending on the area, charges for a garage range from EGP 200 to 250. A two-bedroom unfurnished apartment in a very good area is approximately USD 2,000; a furnished apartment is approximately USD 2,100.

FINANCIAL ISSUES INCLUDING BANKING SERVICES AND TAXES

Currency can be exchanged at banks and with authorized money changers. The local currency is the Egyptian pound (EGP). EGP 1 = 100 piastres. The currency is often written as LE (short for French *livre égyptienne*) or by using the pound sign, £. In Arabic the pound is called *gunaih* from English "guinea," and piastres are known as *qirsh*.

Cash, traveler's checks, and credit cards: Bank notes are available in all denominations ranging from 100 pounds to 5 piastres. In 2006 new 50-piastre and 1-pound coins were introduced. It is rare that you would find any counterfeit notes, but exchanging Egyptian pounds outside the country can be difficult. American Express, Diners Club, MasterCard, and Visa are accepted, but only at larger hotels or restaurants in Cairo and restaurants in tourist areas. It is recommended to bring traveler's checks in U.S. dollars, Euros, or pounds sterling to avoid additional exchange rate charges. Banks are usually closed on Friday and Saturday, but private exchange bureaus, called "Forex," are open daily and banks in major hotels are often open 24 hours. Cairo branches of HSBC (formerly the Egyptian British Bank) and Banque Misr now have ATMs that accept Visa, MasterCard, and Cirrus and are quite common in the main tourist areas.

Banks: Bank hours are Sunday through Thursday, 8:30 A.M. to 2 P.M. The issuing of bank notes and the setting of monetary policy objectives are the responsibility of the Central Bank of Egypt (www.cbe.org.eg). Some major international banks are represented in Cairo. Sophisticated banking services are available, including international services, but are time consuming. Bank commission charges are somewhat high by international standards.

Opening an account:
• Barclays (www.barclays.com/africa/egypt/pers_bank.htm): You need a minimum monthly salary of EGP 1,500 to be able to open a current account with Barclays, although there are no minimum balance requirements.

- HSBC (www.egypt.hsbc.com/hsbc/egypt_per/account-services): A current account can be opened in any major currency.
- Banque du Caire (www.bdc.com.eg) is Cairo's principal bank. An account can be opened with just a piece of personal identification and the completion of a form. If you are outside Egypt, you can contact any Banque du Caire branches in Egypt, and the branch will reply to you with all the needed documentation to be completed. Otherwise you can make the request via the Egyptian Embassy in the country you are in.
- Bank of Alexandria (www.alexbank.com): Established in 1957 with a domestic network of 184 branches covering all parts of Egypt, the bank offers multiple savings schemes and loans.
- Credit Agricole Egypt (www.ca-egypt.com): Current accounts can be opened with a minimum balance of EGP 2,500 or USD 1,000 or equivalent. Noninterest-bearing checking accounts may be opened in local or major foreign currencies.
- National Bank of Egypt (www.nbe.com.eg/en/main.aspx): This is one of the oldest established commercial banks in Egypt. All banks offer telephone banking and online banking services

Taxes: The Egyptian tax year is the calendar year. Employers based in Egypt must withhold taxes at the source on a monthly basis and submit the money to the Tax Department within 15 days of the subsequent month following the date of payment. The employee is responsible for the payment of tax in the following cases: (1) the employer has no permanent establishment in Egypt; (2) the employer is a nonresident. Salary tax returns including details of gross accounts withheld will be required to be filled on a quarterly basis, that is, January, April, July, and October of each year. Payments made to nonresident individuals for employment services will be subject to a 10 percent fee to be deducted at the source without any tax exemptions.

Individuals are resident of Egypt if Egypt is their "place of habitual abode." The place of habitual abode is defined as follows: If the taxpayer is present in Egypt most of the year whether in an owned or leased residence; if the taxpayer has a commercial, professional, or industrial place of business or any other place of business; individuals resident in Egypt for a period more than 183 days whether continuously or noncontinuously in a 12-month period; and Egyptians who perform their services overseas and receive their income from an Egyptian treasury (public or private).

INTERNATIONAL SCHOOLS AND EDUCATION

There is a good choice of educational possibilities for children of expatriates in Cairo, with international, American, British, German, French, and Japanese schools offering all levels of education.

- The American International School in Egypt (www.aisegypt.com) offers an American curriculum as well as the International Baccalaureate Diploma program. The school is accredited by the Middle States Association of Colleges and Schools. The school is located in new Cairo (a suburban development outside the old city limits) and has excellent, modern, purpose-built sport facilities. The language of instruction is English. The elementary school is for children from pre-kindergarten age to grade 5. The Middle School is for grades 6 to 8. High school children can take the American diploma or the IB diploma. AIS Egypt has over 1,000 pupils representing over 30 nationalities. A strong emphasis is placed on extracurricular activities.

- Cairo American College (www.cacegypt.org) has an American curriculum. The International Baccalaureate and Advanced Placement courses are offered in high school. A private coeducational day school offers an American curriculum for pre-kindergarten through to grade 12. School instruction is in English.

- Cairo American College is accredited by the Middle States Association of Colleges and Schools. There is no religious instruction in the school. The school has over 1,300 pupils.

- British International School (www.bisc.edu.eg) offers the British national curriculum (fourth- and fifth-year students study for GCSEs) and the International Baccalaureate Diploma. The school takes children from age 3 (foundation stage) to 18 years (upper sixth). The school has over 600 pupils representing over 50 nationalities. The school is located on the island of Zama lek. A bus service is available. An online registration form must be completed and is followed by an interview and examination.

- Lycée Français du Caire (www.lfcaire.com) is spread over three sites. The school follows the French curriculum. Secondary school hours are from Sunday through Thursday, 7:45 A.M. to 2:25 P.M. (with a break from 9:40 A.M. to 10 A.M. and 11:55 A.M. to 12:30 P.M.) and 2:40 P.M. to 4:35 P.M. The school has a cafeteria, and pupils are only allowed to leave the school at lunch times with written permission from their parents. A school bus is available.

- Deutsche Evangelische Oberschule Kairo (www.deokairo.de) follows the German national curriculum, with an international flavor. School hours are from 7:15 A.M. to 3 P.M. The school takes children from kindergarten to Sekundarstufe II. The school has over 1,200 pupils representing 20 different nationalities.

- Cairo Japanese School is also located here.

Hong Kong

PERSONAL SAFETY AND SECURITY ISSUES

Hong Kong is a Special Administrative Region of the People's Republic of China. A policy of "one country, two systems" has been implemented, whereby Hong Kong operates its own economic system, theoretically without interference from Beijing. Unlike many Western cities of similar size, Hong Kong is relatively safe. Organized gangs, known as Triads, run drugs, gambling, prostitution, and money-lending services; however, they have little impact on foreigners.

Strikes are rare and hardly disturb day-to-day life. Political demonstrations occur from time to time. Due to the economic difficulties encountered in Asia, street demonstrations are increasing.

The heavy police presence makes it unlikely that you will encounter any problems. The biggest problems are pickpocketing and occasional purse snatchings. Avoid carrying too much cash. Take basic common sense precautions. Avoid flashy displays of wealth; dress and behave conservatively.

MEDICAL ISSUES

Hong Kong's medical facilities are among the finest in the world, and many of the territory's registered doctors and dentists are trained or have undergone postgraduate training overseas. Pharmacists, too, are registered; their dispensing hours are usually from 10 A.M. until 7 P.M. All hotels have a list of recommended medical services.

Medical treatment is generally of a good standard in both public and private hospitals, and medicines are widely available.

Severe acute respiratory syndrome (SARS) has been contained, and there has been no evidence of further outbreaks. The government has made an effort to monitor and control the situation, and the same is true for avian influenza (bird flu).

ENVIRONMENT ISSUES

Waste and sewage removal systems are a problem in some areas, and many visitors find the local habit of spitting in the streets unpleasant. Air pollution is a serious concern in Hong Kong.

ECONOMIC OVERVIEW, 2008

GDP growth	3.8%
Inflation	4.5%
Unemployment	3.8%

INFRASTRUCTURE

Hong Kong has an extensive, reliable public transport system, with good bus, underground, and ferry networks.

Air travel: Hong Kong International Airport (HKG) (www.hongkongairport .com) is located 34 km (21 miles) from central Hong Kong on Lantau Island and is considered one of the best airports in the world. The trip takes 23 minutes with the Airport Express Line or approximately 60 minutes by bus. Airport facilities include banks, money exchange offices, gift shops, duty-free shops, a wide range of car rental companies, 24-hour bars and restaurants, a police station, post office, and tourist information centers.

Hong Kong International Airport is served by a highly efficient, comprehensive transportation network. Connected to the passenger terminal, the four-level Ground Transportation Centre houses the station for the Airport Express trains and an extensive public transport interchange with facilities for taxis, franchised buses, tour coaches, hotels, limousines, and private cars.

The Airport Express is a dedicated airport railway line, providing fast and reliable service operating daily from 5:50 to 1:15 A.M. (the last train departs from the airport and Hong Kong stations at 12:48 A.M.) at 12-minute intervals. The train journey to or from downtown Hong Kong takes approximately 24 minutes. An adult single-journey ticket costs HKD 100 to Hong Kong Station, HKD 90 to Kowloon Station, and HKD 60 to Tsing Yi Station.

Free services of scheduled shuttle buses are available at Hong Kong and Kowloon stations for Airport Express passengers. They can take the shuttle bus to and from major hotels plus key transport interchanges at these stations.

Bus services are available from the airport to various destinations throughout Hong Kong. Taxi stands are located on the north side of the Ground Transportation Centre (the left-hand ramp if you are leaving from the arrivals hall). Separate aisles are designated for different taxis.

Taxis are plentiful, inexpensive, and often the best choice for traveling short distances. Taxis are easily hailed from the street, although areas marked with double yellow lines are restricted for pick-ups and drop-offs. At peak periods, you may opt for a hotel taxi queue. All taxis are regulated and drivers are required to clearly display their name and car number on the dashboard. Many drivers speak some English, but it is wise to have your destination written in Chinese characters.

Taxis come in different colors depending on the area they are allowed to service. Red taxis serve all destinations throughout Hong Kong, except Tung Chung Road and roads in south Lantau. Green taxis serve the New Territories and specified roads on Lantau, and blue taxis serve Lantau Island. All three may serve the Hong Kong International Airport at Chek Lap Kok on Lantau Island.

Taxi fares are charged by metered tariff. When crossing the harbor by the cross-harbor tunnel, the two-way tunnel toll is added to the fare. With the other tunnels, only the one-way toll is added. There is an extra charge per piece of luggage (a list displaying extra charges is posted in the taxi). Meter rates are also displayed. Tipping is usually confined to small change. Only Hong Kong dollars are accepted. Receipts are available upon request.

Metro: The Mass Transit Railway (MTR) (www.mtr.com.hk) has six lines: the Kwun Tong, Tsuen Wan, Island, Tung Chung, Tseung Kwan O, and Disneyland Resort Lines, running through 51 stations. Trains run regularly between 6 A.M. and 1 A.M.

SHOPPING AND AVAILABILITY OF CONSUMER GOODS

There is a full variety of excellent quality consumer goods (both native and imported). A broad choice of alcoholic beverages is available without restrictions, and the selection of automobiles is likewise very wide, with an extensive choice of brands and models.

RECREATION AND ENTERTAINMENT

Restaurants: Hong Kong's multicultural society has created one of the world's greatest dining capitals. Apart from the different Chinese cuisines, practically all other Asian and Western cuisine is available. There is a wide choice of restaurants serving excellent food. Chinese restaurants are generally open daily from 8 A.M. to 10 P.M. and Western restaurants from midday to 11 P.M. As well as the thousands of restaurants, pubs are a popular place to eat lunch and many clubs and national associations have excellent restaurants.

There are more than 6,000 Chinese restaurants offering a unique chance to sample almost every variety of Chinese fare. The predominant cuisine is Cantonese but the cuisine of Peking, Szechuan, northern China, Shanghai, Chiu Chow, and Hakka are all represented and each has its own distinct character and specialties.

Cinemas are plentiful and show a variety of international and Chinese films. Festivals and cultural events of international reputation are regularly organized.

There are almost 200 cinemas in Hong Kong, and it is possible to see the latest British and American films. Programs are advertised in the *South China Morning Post*. There are three categories of film: Class 1—for all ages; Class 2—parental guidance; and Class 3—over 18 years of age. All films in English have Chinese subtitles and all locally produced Mandarin-language films have English subtitles.

There are also a number of private cinema clubs, such as Studio One. Films are also shown at the Alliance Française, the British Council, and the Goethe Institute. The Film Culture Center of Hong Kong shows original local works.

The Hong Kong International Film Festival takes place during March and April each year. Further information on this event can be obtained from the Hong Kong Tourist Association.

Hong Kong has four main cinema chains:

- Broadway circuit (12 cinemas); www2.cinema.com.hk
- UA Cinemas (9 cinemas); www.cityline.com.hk
- Golden Harvest (6 cinemas); www.goldenharvest.com
- MCL (4 cinemas); www.ticketsuper.com

For details on cinemas in Hong Kong, please visit www.hkfilms.com

Culture and entertainment: Western music, dance, and art coexist easily with Cantonese opera and time-honored festivals, especially the Chinese Lunar New Year. Lunar cycles determine the dates of many of these festivals. A series of special events, including the Hong Kong Fashion Week fashion show, the Hong Kong International Arts Festival, and such sporting events as Sevens Rugby, International Horse Races, and World Wushu Championships (martial arts) add excitement to the Hong Kong events calendar.

There is a wide range of Chinese and Western cultural events in Hong Kong. The best listings of events are in the *South China Morning Post,* which has a daily arts and culture page, the *Hong Kong Standard,* and the *TV and Entertainment Times.* There is also a "Hong Kong Today" program on radio station RTHK 3 (567 AM) between 7 A.M. and 10 A.M., which advertises events.

For information on events and venues, you can check the Leisure and Cultural Department's Web site at www.lcsd.gov.hk.

Events take place at the many stadiums and halls around the territory. The City Hall (5 Edinburgh Place, Central, Hong Kong; Tel: +852 2921-2840) is one of the major venues for events and there are always posters and listings of events on the bulletin boards as well as free copies of the monthly newspaper *City News Urban Council.* Cultural events also take place at the Hong Kong Cultural Center (L5, Auditoria Building, Hong Kong Cultural Centre, 10 Salisbury Road, Tsim Sha Tsui, Kowloon, Hong Kong; Tel: +852 2734-2009). The Hong Kong Philharmonic Orchestra and the Hong Kong Chinese Orchestra are both renowned for their excellent musical productions and hold regular performances at the Hong Kong Cultural Center.

The Hong Kong Arts Festival takes place in January and offers Western dance, drama, and music. This festival is very popular and performances are booked well in advance. The Hong Kong Fringe Festival runs simultaneously.

A wide range of events takes place at the Hong Kong Arts Center (2 Harbour Road; Tel: +852 2582-0232) where there are 15 floors of auditoriums, rehearsal halls, and recital rooms. It is particularly well known for its encouragement of local artists and performers. There is a monthly magazine, which advertises all forthcoming events, and it is worth subscribing to their mailing list. Across the road from the Hong Kong Arts Center is the Hong Kong Academy for the Performing Arts (1 Gloucester Road; Tel: +852 2584-8500), which is another important center for cultural events.

The Koshan Theatre in Kowloon (Ko Shan Road Park in Hung Hom) is the venue for Chinese opera troupes, but many neighborhood groups erect temporary theaters for local performances. The Hong Kong Dance Company has a good reputation for performances of classical Chinese and Chinese folk dance. The Modern Dance Theatre of Hong Kong integrates jazz, modern, and Chinese styles of dance. The Hong Kong Ballet presents traditional ballet performances.

Big events such as rock concerts are held at the Hong Kong Coliseum (9 Cheong Wan Road, Hung Hom, Kowloon; Tel: +852 2355-7261).

There are professional and amateur drama groups, including the Chung Ying Theatre Company, the Garrison Players, the Hong Kong Stage Club, the Hong Kong Repertory Theatre, and the American Community Theatre.

There is a wide choice of museums in Hong Kong, as well. There are no casinos in Hong Kong, as gambling is illegal, except for betting on horse races.

Sports: There is a good variety of high-quality sports facilities available in Hong Kong and an impressive variety of sporting activities, both for those who like to watch as well as for those who like to participate.

The most popular spectator sport is horse racing. The Hong Kong Jockey Club supervises meetings at the Happy Valley and Sha Tin Racecourse. The horse racing season runs from late September to June. Races are usually held on Wednesday evenings from 7 to 11 P.M. and on Saturdays from 1 to 6 P.M. Other sporting events which provide excellent entertainment are the Hong Kong Annual Open Golf Championship, the Windsurfing Open Championship, and the Hong Kong Tennis Classic.

You can find a variety of water sports, including good deep-sea fishing. Sailing is very popular amongst expatriates, and secondhand crafts are often listed for sale in the classified advertisements in the newspapers. The Hong Kong Yacht Club at Kellett Island and the Aberdeen Boat Club offer mooring and supervision. Licenses and certificates are issued by the Marine Department.

Hong Kong has some beautiful beaches, although these can get quite crowded (and polluted) during the summer months and especially on Sundays. Snorkeling and scuba diving are popular, particularly on the eastern side of the eastern islands of Mirs Bay, Clear Water Bay, and the Ninepin Group of Islands.

Walking through the 172 square miles of countryside is another popular way to get away from the crowds in the city. The MacLehose Trail stretches 100 km (60 miles) and links eight of the areas' most beautiful parks. There is also an impressive 70 km trail on Lantau Island. Running and jogging are best in the parks around Hong Kong, as the streets get crowded. Victoria Park on Hong Kong Island and Kowloon Park in Tsim Sha Tsui are popular spots.

Nightlife: There are a number of popular bars and night clubs in and around Hong Kong city. You can find an extensive list of bars, clubs, and discos at www.hkclubbing.com.

SOCIOCULTURAL ENVIRONMENT

Hong Kong is a Special Administrative Region of the People's Republic of China. Hong Kong maintains its own legal system, police force, monetary system, customs policy, immigration policy, and delegates to international organizations and events.

Historically, personal freedom and the free practice of religion have been guaranteed, and opposition to the government could be freely voiced. However, it is feared that the situation might deteriorate due to China's interference in how Hong Kong is run. Currently a partially democratic region, the government plans to introduce full democracy, and China is clearly against this move.

The local media sometimes refrains from publishing controversial material to avoid government reprisals but international newspapers are widely available. Hong Kong enjoys both satellite and cable television.

DEMOGRAPHIC/WORKFORCE OVERVIEW

Population	6,940,432 (2006 estimate)
Population density	6,294.65 inhabitants per km^2
Age structure	0–14 years, 14%
	15–64 years, 74%
	65 years and over, 13%
Life expectancy at birth	
Total population:	81.59 years
Male	78.9 years
Female	84.5 years

WORKPLACE CULTURE

Large businesses are generally open from 9 A.M. to 5 P.M. on weekdays and 9 A.M. to 1 P.M. on Saturdays. However, some Chinese businesses open at 10 A.M. and close around 6 P.M. or later. Generally, expatriate staff arrive in the office around 8:30 A.M. and remain until at least 6 P.M., with a lunch break between 1 and 2 P.M. Chinese staff generally work from around 7:30 A.M. to 6 or 7 P.M. There is a strong work ethic in Hong Kong and the Chinese have earned a reputation for being strong and hard-working people. Business attire is Western in style and relatively formal. In general, the Hong Kong Chinese are more formal than many Westerners with regard to both their professional and social dress, and they set the tone for Westerners in Hong Kong.

NATURAL ENVIRONMENT

Hong Kong's climate is very wet and humid. The city is often affected by typhoons and tropical storms, which frequently cause damage to property and sometimes cause loss of life.

HOUSING

There is a good choice of unfurnished accommodations currently available in Hong Kong; however, furnished accommodations are more difficult to find.

Most apartments are managed by agents who can make arrangements for you to view the properties and provide you with necessary details.

Hotels and serviced apartments: These are usually quite small and fully furnished. Some hotels have rooms that are available for rent on a monthly or even quarterly basis. Most of these will have laundry and maid services but may not have cooking facilities.

High rises: These are by far the most common type of rental accommodation in Hong Kong. Flats come in all sizes and variety, from the very small and basic to the large and luxurious, with fantastic harbor views. There are older 6-storied walk-up buildings to modern 45-storied high rises located throughout Hong Kong.

Town houses and houses are considered luxurious accommodations and are more commonly found in The Peak, Repulse Bay, and the southern part of Hong Kong Island, and Sai Kung and Tai Po of the New Territories. Their sizes are generally larger and the rental rates are higher than those of the high-rise flats.

Housing prices have dropped slightly in the past few years. Luxury houses and apartments are available, and the most popular areas include Tai Tam, Chung Hom Kok, The Peak, Upper Mid-Levels, Repulse Bay, Stanley, Lookout, and Jardines.

Many people find accommodations through agencies, house-hunting services, or relocation specialists. There are no multiple listings, so it is necessary to contact different agents for a better choice of properties. It is advisable to clarify the fees before proceeding with any arrangements. Generally, most agents receive 50–100 percent of the first month's rent as their commission fee.

FINANCIAL ISSUES INCLUDING BANKING SERVICES AND TAXES

Hong Kong is a financial capital, and banking services are extremely efficient. The vast majority of foreign currencies can be exchanged at competitive rates at any time. There are no restrictions on the import or export of either local or foreign currency.

Currency: The currency of Hong Kong is the Hong Kong Dollar (HKD). 1 dollar = 100 cents. Notes are in denominations of HKD 1000, 500, 100, 50, 20, and 10. Coins are in denominations of HKD 10, 5, 2, and 1, and 50, 20, and 10 cents.

Cash, traveler's checks, and credit cards: Hong Kong's position as Asia's leading financial center means that it is very easy to exchange money and to have money wired or transferred. Traveler's checks can be cashed at banks, hotels, and exchange kiosks throughout the city.

In Hong Kong, almost any foreign currency may be bought and sold in the open market. Commission fees vary considerably and can run as high as 5 percent at the airport. Hotels generally give the poorest exchange rate, while foreign exchange offices and banks will offer the most favorable rates.

Many shops accept payments with U.S. dollars or other major currencies for large purchases, although you probably will not get the official exchange rate.

Major credit cards (for example, Visa, MasterCard, American Express, and Diners Club) are accepted almost everywhere, except at very small shops and street vendors.

Automatic teller machines (ATMs) can be found almost everywhere; some Hong Kong bank "electronic money" machines provide 24-hour cash withdrawal (HKD) facilities for Visa and MasterCard holders. American Express cardholders have access to Jetco ATMs and can withdraw local currency and traveler's checks at the Express Cash ATMs in town. EA$YCHANGE is a 24-hour automatic currency exchange service available in Hong Kong.

Banks: Major banks are open from 9 A.M. to 4:30 P.M., Monday through Friday, and 9 A.M. to 12:30 P.M. on Saturday; they are closed on Sunday and public holidays. Some banks and branches are open slightly longer hours; however, some banking services are not available an hour before closing.

Hong Kong has one of the largest representations of international banks in the world. Opening a local bank account is advisable. Required documentation for opening an account includes your passport and Hong Kong ID card.

Taxes: The tax year runs from April 1 to March 31. Employers usually do not withhold taxes on wages and salaries but are obliged to do so in case the employee is about to leave Hong Kong for a month or more until the taxpayer has cleared his tax obligations.

Employees are required to pay a provisional salaries tax based on salaries payable for the previous year. The payment is credited against the salaries tax for the current year, which becomes payable on assessment. There is no set date when provisional payments are due. Due dates for final returns and final payments are determined on a case-by-case basis.

Residence, domicile, and citizenship are not relevant to tax liability where the term "resident" is used, except for the purpose of the Mainland China double-taxation arrangement. All individuals, resident or nonresident, are subject to tax on Hong Kong source employment income, Hong Kong income from an office, and Hong Kong pensions.

The determination of the situs of employment income depends on various factors, such as the place where the employment contract negotiated was concluded and is enforceable; the residence of the employer; and the territory where the remuneration was paid. If the source of employment income is in Hong Kong, it is all taxable unless all services were rendered outside Hong Kong. However, to provide unilateral relief for Hong Kong-source employment, income referable to services rendered outside Hong Kong will not be taxed in Hong Kong if the employee is liable to and has paid tax similar in nature to Hong Kong tax in the territory where the services are rendered.

Non-Hong Kong employment income is apportioned so that only the part attributable to services rendered in Hong Kong is taxable. When deciding whether or not all employment services are rendered outside Hong Kong, no account is taken of services rendered in Hong Kong during visits not exceeding a total of 60 days in a tax year ending March 31. Income from an office and pensions does not rank for the apportionment basis and exclusion of income under the 60-day rule.

Income from an office (for example, directors' fees): The source of such fees is determined by reference to the place where the company is managed and controlled.

Pensions are taxable if the funds out of which the payment is made are situated in Hong Kong. There are no specific tax concessions for expatriates, but Hong Kong tax rates remain very reasonable. In addition, following a decision in the courts in 1986, income earned by an individual who spends part of his time outside Hong Kong is taxable only on the amount of income apportioned to Hong Kong on a time basis provided that the individual has "non-Hong Kong employment."

Where the individual is a visitor to Hong Kong (that is not based in Hong Kong) and visits to Hong Kong do not exceed 60 days in a tax year (that is to March 31), the individual is not subject to salaries tax for that tax year.

Employment income from a Hong Kong employer is exempt from Hong Kong tax if such income is derived by a person who renders all services in connection with his or her employment outside Hong Kong.

If an individual has overseas duties (and is employed by a Hong Kong company for these duties) and must pay tax in another country on the income received, the income may be excluded for Hong Kong tax purposes, provided certain conditions are met.

INTERNATIONAL SCHOOLS AND EDUCATION

There is a wide variety of schools that serve expatriate children. There are international, British, French, German, Swiss, Korean, and Japanese schools, offering both primary and secondary education.

- The Hong Kong International School (www.hkis.edu.hk) is based on the U.S. curriculum. Examinations offered are ACT, AP, PSAT, SAT, and Stanford. The school takes children between the ages of 4 and 18 years. School bus services are available. The school applies a uniform policy, and a canteen is available for children who wish to eat at school. There is no special admissions policy. The school offers various after-school activities. The school is open between 7:50 A.M. and 2:50 P.M.

- English Schools Foundation (ESF) (www.esf.edu.hk) is based on the English national curriculum. Exams offered are GCSE, GCE "A" Level, "AS" Level, and Special Level, and GNVQ. A bus service is available. There is no uniform policy. A canteen is available for children who wish to eat at school. Certain documents have to be provided to the school for the application process. A personal interview is also part of the admission process. The school is open from 8:45 A.M. until 3:30 P.M. The ESF runs 18 schools: five secondary schools, ten primary schools, two kindergartens, and a special school.

- Lycée Français International "Victor Segalan" (French school) (www.lfis.edu.hk) has two "streams" available: French and international. The French stream is based on the French national curriculum and exams offered are the Baccalaureate E, ES, and L. The international stream offers the International Baccalaureate Diploma and International General Certificate of Secondary Education. The school takes children between the ages of 4 and 17 years. School bus services are provided by private companies. There is no uniform policy, and a canteen is available for children who wish to eat at school. School hours are 8:30 A.M. to 3:30 P.M. (primary) and 8:30 A.M. to 5:30 P.M. (secondary).

- German Swiss International School (http://mygsis.gsis.edu.hk) has two "streams" available: German and international. The German stream is based on the German national curriculum and offers German exams. The international stream is based on the English national curriculum and offers exams GCSE and GCE "A" Level and "AS" Level. The school takes children between the ages of 3 and 18 years. School bus services are provided. There is a canteen available for children who wish to eat at school, and books are included in the tuition fee. There is no uniform policy, and the school offers a wide range of extracurricular activities. Certain documents have to be provided to the school for application process. A personal interview is also part of the admission process.

- Hong Kong Japanese School and Japanese International School (www.hkjs.edu.hk) offer streams in Japanese and English. There are school bus services provided, but there is no canteen available. There are a number of athletic clubs, and a playground is available for students during break time. Student registration certificate and application forms are needed for admission. School hours are from 8:20 A.M. to 3:40 P.M., Monday through Friday.

- The Australian International School (www.aishk.edu.hk) follows the Australian (NSW) curriculum. A private company provides bus services. The school applies a uniform policy. Students from the preparatory year upwards have their lunch at school.

- The Canadian International School of Hong Kong Limited (www.cdnis.edu.hk) follows the Canadian curriculum. School bus service is provided, and two canteens are available for students. There are two gymnasiums, three playgrounds, and one swimming pool inside the campus.

Hungary: Budapest

PERSONAL SAFETY AND SECURITY ISSUES

The relationship between Hungary and other countries is generally stable. Hungary is a member of NATO and the European Union. There are occasional minor differences with neighboring countries, usually over the status of minority Hungarian populations there. The internal political situation is stable, although some demonstrations and strikes may occur.

There are increasing safety problems in Budapest. Street crime (some of which is violent), including pickpocketing and bag snatching, has risen in the capital. Law enforcement is usually reasonably efficient, although there is some corruption in the police force. Most foreign nationals may enter Hungary without a visa, and work permits are reasonably easy to obtain.

MEDICAL ISSUES

General health facilities and sanitation conditions are good. The private health sector is small but expanding, and a full range of medical supplies is available. Hospitals in Budapest include First Med Center (www.firstmedcenters.com), International Medical Services, Medicover West End Clinic (www.medicover .com/hu), and the Rózsakert Medical Center. Public hospitals in Budapest include the Central State Hospital.

Dental practitioners tend to have set costs for dental care. Dental clinics in Budapest include Professional Dental Associates, SOS Dental Service, Vital Center, Profident, and Bakáts Dentál.

Medicines can only be bought in pharmacies in Hungary. Most medicines require a prescription, with the exception of common drugs, such as certain painkillers. Pharmacies are generally open 8 A.M. to 6 or 8 P.M. on weekdays. There is always a pharmacy open late and on weekends and the name and address of this pharmacy is posted on the door of all pharmacies. Twenty-four-hour pharmacies in Budapest include Szent Margit Pharmacie, Óbuda Pharmacie, Teréz Pharmacie, Déli Pharmacie, and Mária Pharmacie.

ENVIRONMENT ISSUES

Tap water is palatable and safe to drink; nevertheless, it is advisable to drink bottled water, which is widely available. The quality of sewage and waste removal services is reasonable. Air pollution is sometimes a problem.

ECONOMIC OVERVIEW, 2008

GDP growth	1.1%
Inflation	6.3%
Unemployment	8.0%

INFRASTRUCTURE

Utilities and transport: Budapest has a well-developed public transport system, including buses, trams, and a metro. There is often traffic congestion during the rush hour, but it is not a major problem at other times.

Air travel: The airport (Budapest Ferihegy International Airport, www.bud.hu) is located 17 km southeast of the city center and can be reached in 30 to 45 minutes, depending on traffic conditions. The airport offers a good choice of flights to other European cities, and the range of services to other international destinations has improved considerably in recent years. The airport has three terminals: Terminal 1 is used only for cargo, and Terminals 2A and 2B are for passengers. Malév Hungarian Airlines uses Terminal 2A, and all other airlines use Terminal 2B.

Airport facilities include a bank, bureau de change, shops, restaurants and snack bars, and car rental desks. There are also conference and business facilities. The Air Traffic and Airport Administration (LRI) operate an airport minibus service to any address in Budapest for HUF 2,300 (single) or HUF 3,900 (return). Tickets need to be purchased at the welcome desk in the arrivals hall prior to departure. Centrum minibuses run a shuttle bus to the city center bus station every 30 minutes between the hours of 5:30 A.M. and 10 P.M. The journey takes approximately 40 minutes and tickets cost HUF 800 and are purchased on the bus. Number 93 bus service goes to the Kobánya-Kispest metro station. Tickets cost HUF 250 and have to be purchased at the vending machines or kiosks in the airport. This ticket is also valid for the metro journey into the city center. There is also the public airport bus, which is the cheapest option. The bus stops at the airport every 15 minutes, from 4:55 A.M. to 11:20 P.M. The bus goes to Kobanya-Kispest metro station, 20 minutes away. From there you have to take the metro into town (it takes 20 to 25 minutes to reach Deakter in downtown Pest). Bus tickets (HUF 185–USD 0.9) are available from the orange vending machines outside Terminal A or next to the stop, or the newsstand inside Terminal B.

There are taxis available at all times from the taxi stand outside the terminal building. Official airport taxis have fixed rates according to the zone of your destination. You should make sure that the driver uses the meter. A taxi ride to the city center will take about 40 minutes and costs around HUF 5,500 to HUF 8,000. It is advisable to avoid unofficial taxis as they often overcharge, and you should definitely avoid drivers inside the terminal who are looking for business. Car rental companies are represented at the airport and include Avis, Budget, National, and Hertz. The car rental desks are located in the Arrivals Hall of Terminals 2A and 2B.

Inter-city bus travel: International coach services are available from Budapest to a large selection of European destinations. There is a good domestic coach service operating between all towns and cities throughout Hungary. There are three coach stations in Budapest and each has coaches departing to specific regions within Hungary. It is advisable to reserve tickets in advance to ensure a seat is available; however, tickets can be purchased from the driver up until 20 minutes prior to departure. There are direct rail links that connect Hungary to 16 European cities.

Rail: There is also an extensive and efficient domestic rail service throughout the country. Services are operated by the Hungarian State Railways (www .mav.hu). There are three railway stations in Budapest: Déli Train Station: South: Alkotásu; Keleti Train Station, Nyugati Train Station, West: Nyugatitér. There are also domestic lines that connect Budapest with other resorts along the Danube. For information see www.mahartpassnave.hu.

Public transport: Public transport in Budapest is excellent and is run by Budapesti Kozlekedési Vállalat (www.bkv.hu/english/home/index.html). There are 200 bus routes, 14 trolley bus routes, 34 tram routes, and 3 metro lines. The HÉV suburban railway has 4 train lines. There is also a cogwheel railway, chair lift, funicular, and boat service. Bus, tram, train, and metro services operate approximately between 4:30 A.M. and 11 P.M. Beyond these hours there is a night bus service.

Bus: Trolley buses are red and their stops are marked by red signs. Regular buses are blue and their stops are marked by blue signs. Tram stops are marked by blue or yellow signs. A route map and timetable is usually posted at each bus stop.

Metro stations are identified by a large "M" inside a circle. The three metro lines all meet at Deák tér station. Line M1 (yellow line) starts in the city center at Vörösmartytér and follows Andrássyu to Mexikóiu. Line M2 (red line) runs from ÖrsVezértér in the eastern suburbs, past the Keleti station through the city to the Déli station. Line M3 (blue line) runs from Árpád híd to Deák tér through the city to the Nyugati station and Köbánya-Kispest. Metro Line 4 is currently being built and the plans for Line 5 are ready for implementation. Both lines are estimated to be operational by 2010. Trains run frequently between 6:30 A.M. and 8 P.M.: every three to six minutes on weekdays and every five to eight minutes on weekends; there are still services outside these times (4:30 A.M. to 11 P.M.) but trains are less frequent.

Train: The suburban railway service operates on four routes: Csepeli HÉV, o Gödöll i HÉV, Ráckevei HÉV, and Szentendrei HÉV. The cogwheel railway runs between Városm ajor utca and Szëchenyi Hill. Services operate daily, every 15 minutes between 5:20 A.M. and 11:30 P.M. The funicular runs from Clark Adam tër to the Castle District, daily between 7:30 A.M. and 1:30 P.M. Tickets cost HUF 2. Information on services, timetables, tickets, and prices can be found on the BKV Web site.

Taxi: All taxis must have a yellow number plate and a yellow taxi sign. Also, they must use a meter and display a price list on the dashboard. Taxis not complying with these rules should be avoided as they are not licensed and may overcharge for their services. Taxis can be hailed on the street, but it is worth calling one in advance as you will be charged a slightly lower rate. In Budapest there is an official ceiling price applied to taxi fares. There are two tariffs: daytime tariff between 6 A.M. and 10 P.M. and a night tariff between 10 P.M. and 6 A.M. In the day, the initial meter charge is HUF 300 and the rate per kilometer is

HUF 260; at night, the initial meter charge is HUF 420 and the rate per kilometer is HUF 336. Taxi companies in Budapest include City Taxi (www .citytaxi.hu), Buda Taxi (www.taxi2000.hu), Fötaxi (www.fotaxi.hu), and Radio Taxi.

Car: If you do decide to drive into Budapest, be prepared to get stuck in traffic queues. Trams and buses have priority over private vehicles. There are also certain routes that private cars are not permitted to use. The main problem with taking your car is parking. There are parking meters or parking attendants for all street parking and there is a maximum parking period of two hours. Meters take coins and cost around HUF 150 to 500 per hour. Cars will be "booted" if no parking fee is paid or has expired. Car rental companies are widely represented throughout Hungary. To rent a car, you may need an international driving permit (depending on your country of origin) and must have had a driver's license for over 12 months. Rental companies include Avis (www.avis.hu), Budget (www .budget.hu), and Europcar.

SHOPPING AND AVAILABILITY OF CONSUMER GOODS

The supermarkets in Budapest are usually well stocked and most goods can be obtained. Local car dealers sell an excellent variety of locally manufactured and imported vehicles. Almost all major international publications can be purchased in large hotels, some bookstores, and most newsstands. The following is a selection of bookstores in Budapest that sell foreign language books (including English and French): Bestsellers (www.bestsellers.hu) bookstore orders books from the UK and the United States every week. They also deal in French books and act as a newsagent, with a wide selection of English and French language newspapers and magazines. CEU (Central European University) Academic Bookshop (www .ceu.hu/student_services.html#book) is the best academic English language bookshop. Király Books has two floors of books in English and French, from the same owner of Bestsellers Books. Libri Könyvpalota and Libri Studium are others.

Hungarian shops offer a wide range of products. Prices tend to be higher in the larger cities but there are still lots of bargains available. Hungarian crafts include embroideries, national dolls, woven rugs, Herend China and Zsolnay porcelain, and crystal. The main, more upmarket shopping district in Pest is the pedestrian area in and around Váiutca, between the Erzsébet and Széchenyi Chain Bridge. Another good shopping area is Rakocziutca, a major shopping street where almost anything can be purchased. Some of the malls have a variety of shops and supermarkets. There has also been an increase in large stores and these can be found in the outskirts of the city.

Shopping malls include Duna Plaza, Europark (www.europark.hu), Pólus Center (www.polus.com/hu), Westend City Center (www.westend.hu), and Mammut (www.mammut.hu).

Department stores include Corvin Áruház (http://wikimapia.org/57459/
Corvin-Department-Store), which is a traditional Hungarian department store.
Marks and Spencer (www.marksandspencer.com) has six stores in Budapest
including one in each major shopping mall. IKEA (www.ikea.hu), Luxus is a per-
fectly located and recently revamped department store housed in a beautiful
secessionist building. Skála Metro Divatáruház (www.skala.hu) is a good local
department store for bargain hunting. Supermarkets are located in shopping centers as well as in most districts throughout the city. Ecseri Piac, Petofi Csarnok,
and Vasarcsarnok are a few of them.

RECREATION AND ENTERTAINMENT

Budapest has a number of good restaurants and a relatively good selection of
cultural events and cinemas. Sporting clubs and facilities are numerous and
accessible.

International associations and clubs include the Austrian Cultural Institute,
the British Council Hungary, the French Institute, the Italian Cultural Institute,
and the Professional Women's Association. Language courses can be sought at the
Hungarian Language School.

Restaurants: There is also a huge variety of ethnic cuisines to choose from.
The following is only a very small selection of what is available: Arnyas Restaurant and Garden offers excellent Hungarian wines and delicious traditional
Hungarian food. Gundel offers masterful cuisine; Remiz has excellent salads
and one of the best and healthiest lunch menues in town. Hungarian Empire
has a grand old world style decoration and a very good selection of game dishes.
Karpatia offers a tempting range of medieval recipes.

Entertainment: The Hungarians are famous for their love of music, and this is
certainly reflected in the wealth of musical entertainment and performing arts
available in Budapest. Hungary has many cultural events and festivals throughout
the year. In addition to world-class operas, operettas, classical and modern musical concerts, there are also rock and jazz evenings, circuses, and theater. Budapest
is the cultural center of Hungary. *The Budapest Week* and *The Budapest Sun* (www
.budapestsun.com) have sections listing forthcoming events around the country,
including a list of English language films showing in Budapest cinemas. In the
hotels, you can find the *Where Magazine,* which gives information on cultural
and social events. Information on all types of events is available at www
.kulturinfo.hu. There are several music events to choose form each evening.
Listings of musical events are given in the English language papers. A monthly
Koncert Kalendarium lists all concerts and the Budapest Müsorkalauz (program)
lists theater productions.

Theatres and concert halls: Hungarian State Opera House (Magyar Allami
Operaház) presents programs of classical and modern Hungarian and
international works; the season is from mid-September to mid-June. Erkel

Színház has opera and ballet performances; the season is from mid-September to mid-June. Madách Theatre (www.madachszinhaz.hu) has very original and high-quality performances. Merlin Theatre stages English-language dramas. Budai Vigadó (Buda Concert Hall) stages the Hungarian State Folk Ensemble, established in 1951 and regarded as one of the best in Hungary.

Museums include the Budapest History Museum—Castle Museum, housed in one of the wings of the palace, the exhibitions retell the city's history. Ethnographical Museum gives an overview of the Hungarian people through regional folk costumes and depictions of daily life. The Hungarian Natural History Museum presents the history of mankind housed in a beautiful historical building. War History Museum has models, battle scenes, uniforms, medals, weapons, and military art. Holocaust Memorial Center (www.hdke.hu) has temporary and permanent exhibitions which enlighten the public about the Holocaust in Hungary.

Cinemas: There are around 30 cinemas in Budapest. Many show the latest Hollywood blockbusters. Films are often shown in the original language with Hungarian subtitles; however, some are dubbed. Cinema listings are advertised in the local press. Corvin, Campona, Atrium, and Muvész are some of them.

Entertainment for children in Budapest includes Vidam Amusement Park which features two museums, a huge park, thermal baths, a circus, and much more. Children's Railway has 11 kilometers of narrow gauge line running through the woods and hills of the city. Budapest Zoo has a lovely park featuring all the classic favorites along with ancient Hungarian livestock. Budapesti Planetárium is worth seeing, and Budapest Puppet Theatre (Budapest BábszínházNemcsak) is very famous and highly professional.

Nightlife: Budapest has a lively and varied nightlife. There are many nightclubs, bars, cafés, and casinos. *Bars:* Harry J. Bean's Bar & Grill offers a wide range of drinks and delightful dishes. Darshan Udvar has live music performances, interesting décor, and exciting drinks. For Sale Pub is a country-style pub with an extensive dining area and menu. Pertu Station is a cozy bar decorated as a subway station; it attracts a young crowd and offers live music. Leroy's Beach Club has a good selection of Hungarian wines and cocktails along with an interesting menu. *Nightclubs:* Kameleon Club is a Latin club on the fourth floor of the Mammut II shopping mall. E-Klub has renowned DJs, exotic performances, and fantastic drinks. Bahnhof Music Club (www.bahnhof.hu) is a trendy club boasting two dance floors, friendly service, and cheap beer. Troca dero is a lively Latin club. Home is one of Budapest's trendiest and most famous places.

Casinos include Las Vegas Casino, Casino Budapest Hilton, Tropicana Casino, and Várkert Casino. A huge variety of sports and sporting activities is available throughout Hungary, including water sports, fishing, horseback riding, diving, golf, hiking, cycling, and swimming. The Tourist Information Offices can help you plan a sports outing or holiday. If you want to go fishing, you will need to apply for a state license and regional permit. Information and advice is provided by the National Association of Hungarian Anglers (MOHOSZ), Budapest. One of Hungary's natural gifts is geothermally heated mineral water and there are 154 thermal bath and spa facilities throughout the country. Hungary also has five national parks and almost 1,000 protected areas. Soccer is a popular spectator sport. One of the most important annual sporting events is the Hungarian Grand Prix (Formula One).

Sports facilities: Golf is very popular in Hungary. For a list of clubs and courses see www.golfcourses.hu/palyak.php. Most of the larger hotels have tennis courts where nonresidents can play on a pay per court basis. There are also plenty of swimming pools and fitness centers available. Sports for children in Budapest include an ice skating rink, built in 1875, which is the largest open-air ice rink in Europe. A swimming pool on Margaret Island, open since 1919, has eight swimming pools, including a children's pool heated to 30°C. Aquarena is a water park featuring a mile-long slide, pools, a lazy river, caves, and much more. Görzenál Gör korcsolya és Szabadidőpark (skating park) has ramps and areas for skateboarding and rollerblading. They also offer lessons and skate clubs for young children. Budaring Go-karting includes a children's playground and a special track for kids.

SOCIOCULTURAL ENVIRONMENT

In Hungary, there are no limitations on the freedom of speech and movement or on the free practice of religion. There is a variety of national television channels, and cable television is available in some areas.

DEMOGRAPHIC/WORKFORCE OVERVIEW

Population	10,076,600 (2006 estimate)
Population density	109 inhabitants per km^2
Age structure	0–14 years, 17%
	15–64 years, 68%
	65 years and over, 15%
Life expectancy at birth	
Total population:	72.7 years
Male	68.4 years
Female	77.1 years

WORKPLACE CULTURE

Hungary has a very formal culture, and formality and the correct way to do things are considered important. It is essential to adhere to established protocol and etiquette. Rank, status, and age should also be respected. Hungarians are often very direct and will say exactly what they think. They are generally clear and decisive.

Office hours are generally Monday through Friday, 8 A.M. to 5 P.M. Some offices may finish earlier on Fridays at 3 P.M. Government offices are usually open Monday through Friday, 8 A.M. to 4:30 P.M. Business clothing should be smart and conservative. Men are expected to wear suits and ties. Women should wear suits or smart dresses. Hungarians, in general, tend to dress casually unless the occasion dictates otherwise. Smart, formal wear should be worn for business meals or special occasions. The form of dress should always match the occasion.

Appointments should be made well in advance and should be confirmed. Punctuality is very important as it is considered rude to arrive late for meetings. Shaking hands on meeting is customary, but men should wait for women to offer their hand first. Shake hands again on departing. Always address others formally, using Mr., Mrs., or Miss and the surname. It is advisable not to schedule meetings for July and August or mid-December to mid-January, as these are the main vacation periods in Hungary. Business cards are widely exchanged and it is polite to have cards printed in Hungarian as well as your own language. Many business meetings are conducted in German or English if all parties cannot speak Hungarian. It is considered not a good practice to ask a colleague to translate. Translation services are widely available. Hungarians expect you to remain calm and courteous throughout the duration of the meeting.

NATURAL ENVIRONMENT

Budapest has an average continental climate, although the temperature in winter occasionally drops below -10°C for short periods. Spring and autumn are usually pleasant. In the summer, the temperature can rise above 25°C.

HOUSING

Most expatriates live in the Buda Hills region, which is within easy reach of the city center. The most prestigious areas are Rozsadomb, Svábhegy, Pasaret, Huvosvolgy, Zuglò, Vizivaros, and Lipotvaros. A good variety of quality household appliances and furniture is on sale, and acceptable repair and maintenance services are usually available.

Houses and apartments that are available for rent are often advertised in the rental section of the *Budapest Sun* and the *Budapest Business Journal* as well as on the Internet. The Hungarian real estate database (http://ingatlan.com/index _en.php) is one of the most complete online resources that includes not only listings, but also statistics, articles, and real estate trends. Budapest Rent (www .budapestrent.com) is also a good online source of high-standard rental properties. There is a wide range of accommodation agencies and estate agents. The easiest way to find accommodations if you have little time is to go through a reputable agency. Depending on your family situation, your daily commute, and your personal preferences, you might be inclined to live in the inner city on the *Pest* side of Budapest or in the more residential and quiet *Buda* side of the city. The Buda or western side of the city is home to Districts 1, 2, 3, 11, and 12, which tend to be the most popular neighborhoods for expat families. This part of the city offers family homes, townhouses, and apartments and is also home to international schools. The downside of this area is the commute during rush hour, which gets most difficult at the bridges crossing from the Buda side to the Pest side and vice versa.

The Pest or eastern side of the city offers proximity to the city center and its amenities; most of the housing here is in apartments, with the preferred districts being 5, 6, 7 and part of District 13. The convenience of this location can be offset by the smaller size of the properties and the more urban, thus noisier, setting.

Fully furnished, partially furnished, and unfurnished properties are available. Fitted kitchens including all major appliances (stove, oven, fridge, and dishwasher) are standard equipment whether a property is furnished or not. There may or may not be a washing machine and cloth dryers are not widely used. There are a number of apartments in old buildings with plenty of character, but it is important to take into account the standard of renovation.

Real estate agencies in Budapest include At Home Budapest (www .athomebudapest.com) and Move One Relocations (www.moveonerelo.com). A full list of real estate agencies can be found online at http://virtualhungary .com/lists/realesta.htm. In general, the equivalent of two months' rent is required as a refundable deposit and one month's rent paid in advance. Prices are often quoted in Euros, but payment is usually made in the local currency. Most lease agreements are signed for a year but you can negotiate a shorter or longer lease. In any case, it is important to include the possibility of extending the lease period in the contract. The standard notice period is one month by either party. Make sure the lease agreement specifies who pays the building maintenance fees.

Building maintenance fees include heating and lighting in the stairwell, cleaning of common areas, chimney sweep, general house maintenance costs, and garbage disposal. A small portion of it also includes a renovation fund. It is also important to specify which utilities (if any) are included in the rent. The cost of water and heating are sometimes included in the building maintenance fees, so disagreements on this issue may arise unless clarified from the very beginning. Tenants should ask the landlord for complete information about other people who may have keys to the property. If you have any doubts, have the locks changed. Make sure to discuss any unannounced visits from the landlord beforehand. By law, it is not accepted that anyone enters the tenant's apartment; however, it is better to make this clear and to have your privacy respected. Houses in districts in Budapest include: good areas: Vizivaros, Lipotvaros; very good areas: Pasaret, Huvosvolgy, Zuglò; best areas: Rozsadomb, Svabhegy. Apartments in good areas: Vizivaros, Lipotvaros; very good areas: Pasaret, Huvosvolgy, Zuglò; best areas: Rozsadomb, Svabhegy.

Rental costs in Budapest are stable at present and there are plenty of accommodations to choose from, especially apartments. Rental costs generally vary depending on the type of accommodation and the location. The average cost of a two-bedroom unfurnished apartment in a very good area is EUR 1,800 per month (USD 2,304).

FINANCIAL ISSUES INCLUDING BANKING SERVICES AND TAXES

Currency, traveler's checks, and credit cards: There are no restrictions on the import of foreign currency. Money can be exchanged at banks and exchange offices. There is a good choice of banks, which are mainly privately-owned foreign banks. Most banking services are available and credit cards are widely accepted. The Hungarian currency is the Forint (HUF or Ft) (1 Forint = 100 Fillér; however, fillér is no longer in use). Notes are in denominations of HUF 200, 500, 1,000, 2,000, 5,000, 10,000, and 20,000; coins are in denominations of HUF 1, 2, 5, 10, 20, 50, and 100. Currency can be exchanged at official exchange offices at banks, hotels, some restaurants, and travel agencies. All currency exchange receipts should be retained as they are needed to "re-exchange" any HUF back into foreign currency; however, this is often a difficult procedure and the exchange rate will be very poor, resulting in money loss. The rate of exchange will be the same throughout Hungary but commission charges vary depending on where you go. Travel agencies usually charge 1 percent commission. There are ATMs available throughout Hungary and they are generally compatible with the Visa, MasterCard, Maestro, Cirrus, and EuroCard networks. Traveler's checks can be exchanged at most exchange offices. Main post offices will usually change traveler's checks without charging commission. Credit cards (for example, American Express, Visa, MasterCard, and Diners Club) are accepted at selected shops, restaurants, and hotels, and the card sign will be displayed at the entrance.

Banks: Different banks and branches often have varying opening hours. In general, the banking hours are Monday through Thursday, 9 A.M. to 4 P.M., and Friday, 9 A.M. to 1 or 2 P.M. Some banks may open on Saturday mornings. There are local and international banks in Hungary with nationwide branch coverage.

Opening a bank account is relatively easy in Hungary. Most banks will request to see your passport for identification purposes and you will just have to fill in the forms. Some banks request a minimum sum of money to open an account; however, other banks do not. Foreigners may open a forint bank account (*forint számla*) or a hard-currency bank account (*deviza számla*). There are many services and accounts to choose from and banks will advise you on the best service for you. It is best to shop around to find the best deals available. Many banks offer telephone and Internet banking services and have Internet banking facilities, and bills can sometimes be paid using this method.

Taxes: Resident individuals are taxed on total worldwide income, while non-residents are only taxed on Hungarian source income, subject to possible Double Tax Treaty relief. The tax year for individuals is the calendar year. Income tax is withheld from salaries and investment income. Individuals who only have income derived from a single employer are not required to file a tax return, although the employer must submit a declaration instead. If an individual is required to file a tax return, the deadline is March 20 of the following year. Income tax is withheld from locally provided salaries and some dividends. Where no withholding occurs, taxes are due either quarterly or by the filing date of the tax return (on capital gains or other income).

Hungarian personal income tax is assessed in the following ways: domestic-source income and foreign-source income, provided the resident is in Hungary. In case the income originates from abroad, income tax will be due regardless of whether this income has been transferred or brought into the country.

INTERNATIONAL SCHOOLS AND EDUCATION

There are English, American, French, German, Japanese, and international schools in Budapest, most of which offer education at kindergarten, primary, and secondary levels.

- International School of Budapest (www.isb.hu) has an international curriculum based on British, Australian, and American core texts. The school takes children between the ages of 4 and 11 years (kindergarten to grade 6). The school provides a bus service at an additional cost depending on the distance traveled. The school does not have a uniform policy. Hot lunch is provided at an additional cost, and after-school activities are offered to all students. Certain documents have to be provided for the admission process. School hours are 8 A.M. to 3 P.M.

- American International School of Budapest (www.aisb.hu) offers curriculum based on the best practices in American and international education. The school takes children between the ages of 3 and 18 years (pre-kindergarten to grade 12). Bus services are provided. The school does not have a uniform policy. A canteen is available for children who wish to eat at school, and after-school activities are offered to all students. Certain documents have to be provided for the admission process. School hours are 8 A.M. to 3 P.M.

- The British International School, Budapest (www.bisb.hu), offers an international curriculum based on the national curriculum of England and Wales, for children aged 3 to 16 years, and the International Baccalaureate program for students over 16 years. Bus services are provided. The school applies a uniform policy. A canteen is available for children who wish to eat at school, and after-school activities are offered to all students. Certain documents have to be provided for the admission process. School hours are 8 A.M. to 3:30 P.M.

- Lycée Française de Budapest (French school) (http://web.axelero.hu/lfb) offers the French national curriculum. Students work towards the Baccalaureate Diploma. The school takes children between the ages of 3 to 18 years. There is a school bus service provided. The school does not apply a uniform policy. A canteen is available for children who wish to eat at school, and after-school activities are offered to all students. Certain documents have to be provided for the admission process. School hours are 8:30 A.M. to 4 P.M.
- Deutsche Schule Budapest (German school) (www.deutscheschule.hu) offers the German national curriculum. Students work towards the German Abitur. The school takes children between the ages of 5 and 18 years. Certain documents have to be provided for the admission process.
- Budapest Japanese Supplementary School (www.hoshuko.hu) offers a Japanese curriculum. School bus services are provided.

India

PERSONAL SAFETY AND SECURITY ISSUES

Religious and communal tensions can occur in some regions of India. New Delhi, as the national capital, attracts many demonstrations and protests and also terrorist attacks related to the insurgence in Punjab and Kashmir. Foreign companies occasionally become the focus of protests, and thus many are given police protection during demonstrations.

The crime rate has increased, partly because of the growth in the urban populations due to migration. Caution is advised, especially at night. Law enforcement is often inefficient, due to corruption and political interference.

Some terrorist groups are active in India. Although they have not targeted foreign nationals specifically in the past, civilians have been killed or injured in blasts and explosions that have taken place in public places such as markets or on public transport. Mumbai was the site of a vicious terrorist attack in November 2008 that killed more than 100 people, some at the main train station. Demonstrations can occur spontaneously and can on occasion be violent. Foreigners are also requested to be extra vigilant around festival times when large crowds ensure petty theft and minor injuries are rife.

MEDICAL ISSUES

Although improvements are being made, Indian healthcare is likely to be different from what one may be used to in ways of hospital standards. Nevertheless, medical standards are high, and increasing numbers of Westerners are seeking medical treatment in India due to its high quality and comparatively low cost.

State-run hospitals are overcrowded and understaffed, but private hospitals in the major cities offer a good standard of care. Most expatriates choose to leave the country for operations. A range of medical supplies is generally available.

It is highly recommended that you find doctors and hospital facilities upon arriving and before you actually need one. Recommendations from colleagues or friends are very useful.

The main dangers to health in India are cholera, malaria, typhoid, polio, and hepatitis; it is essential to be inoculated against these diseases. Cases of dengue fever have been reported in recent years. There is also a fairly high incidence of AIDS.

ENVIRONMENT ISSUES

Tap water is drinkable only after boiling and filtering. Contaminated drinking water is a serious problem. To be safe, stay away from ice, uncooked food, and unpasteurized milk and milk products, and drink only water that has been boiled for at least 20 minutes or bottled. Also turn down offers of "filtered" water; water is often filtered to take out particles, but this does not mean it has been purified to kill parasites. Check the caps of water bottles to make sure they have not been tampered with, as bottles are sometimes refilled with tap water.

You should avoid raw vegetables and fruit that have been peeled before they are brought to you. Peel your own fruit, and choose varieties with thick skins. Pork products should be avoided; make certain that other meats are thoroughly cooked. Stomach upsets may be caused due to both the richness of Indian food and a lack of hygiene.

ECONOMIC OVERVIEW, 2008

GDP growth	6.2%
Inflation	8.3%
Unemployment	7.2%

SHOPPING AND AVAILABILITY OF CONSUMER GOODS

Meat is in good supply, and the most widely available variety is mutton. Beef is rarely seen, because cows are considered sacred by many Indians. At seaports such as Mumbai, there is a good supply of fresh fish. All meat and fish should be carefully cleaned and thoroughly cooked before eating.

Fruits and vegetables are easily available. Most goods for daily consumption are available, and imported items are becoming more common, as multinational firms enter the local marketplace.

Supermarkets stock goods to meet most requirements. Alcoholic beverages are fairly easy to obtain, but outlets and hours of purchase are restricted, and alcohol may not be consumed in public places. Most hotels are licensed to sell alcohol.

The range of vehicles available has improved, with manufacturers entering the local market. Importing a car can be time consuming.

SOCIOCULTURAL ENVIRONMENT

Freedom of speech is guaranteed by the constitution, and India has a wide range of political parties and groups. Religious freedom is also guaranteed. Due to the diverse and sometimes volatile mixture of religions in the country, it is advisable for visitors to think carefully before expressing strong opinions on religious topics. The caste system still exists in India, and many people have conservative opinions on this subject. Adapting to life in India may be difficult for many expatriates due to cultural differences.

International newspapers, magazines, and television channels are available. Movies are censored for cultural reasons, and scenes of excessive violence (or sex scenes) are not permitted. Political comment in the media is not subject to censorship, although most publications follow the guidelines of the Press Council of India. The government is reluctant to allow foreign media into the Indian market.

DEMOGRAPHIC/WORKFORCE OVERVIEW

Population	1,095,351,995 (2006 estimate)
Population growth rate	1.38% (2006 estimate)
Age structure	0–14 years, 31%
	15–64 years, 64%
	65 years and over, 5%
Life expectancy at birth	
Total population:	64.7 years
Male	63.9 years
Female	65.6 years

WORKPLACE CULTURE

Office hours are usually 9:30 A.M. to 5:30 P.M., Monday throgh Friday and sometimes on Saturday from 9:30 A.M. to 1 P.M. Lunch is usually taken from 1 to 2 P.M. Schedule appointments in advance and reconfirm arrangements a couple of days before. Indian executives generally prefer to meet late mornings or early afternoons. If you are traveling to India for a series of business meetings, it is worth considering allowing an extra couple of days for any unexpected problems with cancelled meetings or travel delays.

When working, men should wear a suit and tie, although the jacket may be removed during the summer. Businesswomen should wear conservative dresses or pantsuits.

Most meetings begin with small talk over a cup of tea. It is customary to refuse the first offer when refreshments are offered but to accept the second or the third. You may be asked questions about your family and personal background, which may seem intrusive. However, this is usually part of polite conversation, and polite responses are appreciated. It is important in business, as in social relations, to be sensitive to particular religions as well as differences in customs, attitude, and behavior.

Decisions are made slowly, as Indians prefer to take their time and discuss every aspect of a proposal. Remember to remain patient, as impatience is considered rude and high-pressure attempts to speed matters along will be resisted and resented. The word "no" has harsh implications in India. Evasive refusals are more common and are considered more polite. Never directly refuse an invitation or proposal; remain vague and avoid a time commitment. Saying "I'll try" is an acceptable refusal.

FINANCIAL ISSUES INCLUDING BANKING SERVICES AND TAXES

The Foreign Exchange Regulation Act (FERA) has been relaxed, and currency can now be exchanged at authorized agencies. Mumbai is the financial capital of India, and many major international banks are represented locally. Service levels are fairly high but could improve in some areas. Credit cards are accepted at most large establishments.

Currency: The unit of currency is the rupee (INR). Each rupee is divided into 100 paise. Notes are in denominations of 1,000, 500, 100, 50, 20, 10, 5, 2, and 1 rupee. Coins are in denominations of 5, 2, and 1 rupee, and 50, 25, 20, 10, and 5 paise.

Cash, traveler's checks, and credit cards: India has strict rules against importing or exporting its currency. International airports have currency exchange booths that are always open for arriving or departing overseas flights. When changing money, remember to get a certain amount in small denominations and do not accept torn bills. Many merchants, hotels, and restaurants do not accept worn or tattered bills; exchanging them for new notes is a hassle.

There is a black market in currency exchange, but it is common for those risking such transactions to be cheated or robbed. Always change money from an authorized exchange office or bank, and insist on receiving an encashment slip. Some banks now charge a nominal fee for this slip, but the slip is necessary if you plan to pay hotel bills or travel expenses in rupees. The encashment slip is also required if you need to reconvert rupees into your own currency at departure.

Traveler's checks are widely accepted and may be changed at banks. Banks offer the most favorable exchange rates, but it can take a while to cash traveler's checks. You can save time by using American Express Traveler's Service or Thomas Cook. Otherwise, cash the check at the foreign exchange counter at your hotel, although rates will be slightly lower. Fees charged for ATM transactions may be higher than at home, but Cirrus and Plus exchange rates are excellent since they are based on wholesale rates offered only by major banks.

Major international credit cards are widely accepted at upmarket establishments in large towns and cities, but not outside of these establishments. It is advisable to check with your credit card company for details of merchant acceptability and other services, which may be available in different destinations in India. The most widely accepted credit cards in India are MasterCard, Visa, American Express, and Diners Club.

Foreign nationals are often expected to pay hotel bills in foreign currency.

Banks: Banking hours are 10 A.M. to 2 P.M., Monday through Friday, and 10 A.M. to midday on Saturday. Some foreign banks have extended hours. International airports, some domestic airports, and a few luxury hotels have 24-hour money changing facilities.

Before leaving home, make sure that your credit cards have been programmed for ATM use in India and that your credit card is widely accepted in India.

Foreign nationals living and working in India usually open a rupee account at a local bank. Savings and checking accounts are both available, although the latter are not interest bearing. To open an account, you will need to provide the following:

- the name and address of your employer,
- the name and address of your overseas bank,
- a copy of the reserve Bank of India's letter granting permission for you to open an account (this is usually obtainable through your employer),
- your passport with a non-tourist visa.

Taxes: The Indian tax year runs from April 1 to March 31.

Taxation is primarily based on the residential status of the individual concerned. The following types of residential status are envisaged for an individual:

- Residents in India: Resident and Ordinarily Resident (ROR) or Resident but Not Ordinarily Resident (RNOR)
- Nonresident in India (NR)

An individual is said to be a resident in a particular year if he or she

- stays in India for a period of 182 days or more in any tax year or
- was in India for a period of 365 days or more in aggregate in the four preceding tax years, and in the current tax year, he or she has been in India for 60 or more days.

It is not essential that the stay in India be continuous or at the same place. If these conditions are not met, the individual is said to be a nonresident in India.

A resident individual is treated as a ROR in India if he or she satisfies the following conditions:

- he or she has been in India for more than 182 days during at least 9 out of 10 tax years preceding the tax year for which the residential status is being determined; and

- he or she has been in India for a period of 730 days or more days during 7 tax years preceding the tax year for which residential status is being determined.

A residential individual not satisfying any of these conditions is classified as a RNOR.

A ROR is subject to tax in India on the whole of his or her world income, wherever received. A RNOR is subject to tax in India only with respect to income that accrues in India or is received in India or is from a business or profession set up in India.

A nonresident is subject to tax in India only with respect to income that accrues or is received in India. A RNOR and a NR are not subject to tax with respect to their income earned and received outside of India.

MUMBAI

ENVIRONMENT ISSUES

Waste removal is becoming a serious problem for Mumbai, with the result that the city almost always appears dirty except for a few upmarket areas. Numerous campaigns by the local authorities have failed to improve matters. Sewage systems are normally functional in the more affluent areas of the city, although breakdowns in the service are becoming frequent. Monsoon rains sometimes cause problems with the sewage system.

Air pollution is an increasing problem, due to the rapid industrialization of the city and the growth in traffic. Mosquitoes, cockroaches, and rats are a severe problem in Mumbai due to the humid climate and inadequate sanitation.

INFRASTRUCTURE

Utilities and transport: The public transport network in Mumbai is more comprehensive than in most other Indian cities and includes an electric railway system, buses, and taxis. However, these tend to be very crowded, and are generally not used by anyone who can afford alternative means of transport.

Buses and trains should definitely be avoided during the rush hour, when congestion reaches dangerous levels. Traffic is fairly heavy, but less chaotic than elsewhere in the country. The narrow roads contribute to delays and are sometimes flooded during the monsoon season.

Air travel: Chhatrapati Shivaji International Airport (BOM) (www.mumbai airport.com), formerly known as Sahar Airport, is situated approximately 35 km north of Mumbai at Sahar and at Santa Cruz, 25 km north of Mumbai. The airport is thus spread over two locations with Terminal I in Santa Cruz dealing with domestic flights and Terminal II in Sahar for international traffic.

Both terminals have telephones, hotel reservation counters, bureaux de change, ATMs, and a postal service. Several shops and restaurants sell food and beverages. There are also tourist information counters, a visitor's lounge, an executive lounge, TV, first aid, and medical services.

Many car rental companies are represented at the airport, including Avis (www.avis.com; Tel: +91 22-2285-7419).

Taxis, buses, and motor rickshaws are available at the airport. The journey time to the city greatly varies with the time of day; allow up to three hours during peak hours.

A railway reservation counter is also in Terminal 2 for connections to the metro rail system; trains run to the nearby airport Mumbai CST Terminus (previously known as the Victoria Terminus) and Churchgate for connections to Mumbai and destinations throughout India.

Rail: In Mumbai, further information regarding rail services may be obtained from the Western Railways, Tel: +91 22-2300-5959; www.westernrailway india.com, and from the Central Railways, Tel: +91 22-2265-6565. These two companies carry over five million rail passengers each day.

Sea and river travel: An air-conditioned catamaran with places for 400 passengers runs between Mumbai (leaves from the New Ferry Wharf/Bhaucha Dhakka in Mumbai) and Goa. The service operates on Tuesdays and Thursdays, leaving Mumbai at 10:30 P.M. and arriving in Panaji at 6 A.M. (passengers are requested to board the ship two hours before departure).

Bicycle and scooter hire: Scooters and bicycles are popular forms of transport on the crowded streets of Mumbai, and there does not seem to be any requirement for cyclists to wear helmets. Scooters are available for short- and long-term buyback options. There are also various places, usually small, that hire bicycles cheaply, and visitors keen to do so should inquire at a garage.

Bus: There are a large number of bus routes run by Brihanmumbai Electric Supply and Transport (BEST) (Tel: +91 22-2414-3611, for 24-hour inquiries; www.bestundertaking.com), which provide transport within the city and suburbs. The buses are extremely cheap, but it is difficult to determine where the buses go since the route maps (available at newspaper stands) are virtually indecipherable. They are often very crowded and seats hard to come by. Some routes operate a round-the-clock service. A small minority of buses are fitted with air conditioning. Tickets are best purchased from the conductor, and although concession fares are offered, no passes are currently available.

Taxis: Mumbai has a huge number of taxis. For the foreign visitor, they represent the best way of getting around the city, especially as motor rickshaws (a staple form of urban travel elsewhere in India) are banned from the center of Mumbai. Taxis can be hailed on the street, and drivers are reasonably knowledgeable of the geography of the city. All taxis have a meter. These are, however, out of date, so each driver carries a conversion table with which to compute the correct fare. It is important to ensure that the meter is zeroed before starting a journey. Fares are inexpensive, and taxis will rarely cost more than INR 1,000 for a full day. For those who prefer a higher degree of luxury, Cool Cabs

(Tel: +91 22-2613-1111) provides more modern, air-conditioned taxis. These are metered and charge a minimum fare of INR 170; a full-day hire costs in the region of INR 1,000. In general, a 10 percent tip is acceptable.

RECREATION AND ENTERTAINMENT

Restaurants: The city has a good range of restaurants offering a variety of cuisines. Nearly all the acceptable restaurants are in major hotels.

Culture and entertainment: There is a fairly small range of theater and opera performances to choose from. Mumbai has many facilities for entertainment and claims to be the liveliest city in India. Bars, nightclubs, and restaurants are busy every night of the week, with revellers or those who take advantage of the cultural events on offer or are just enjoying the more sedate side of Mumbai's entertainment. Regular local events mix eclectic with major international festivals, shows, and concerts. Western rock bands can often be found giving concerts at the Mumbai Stadium.

Cinema: There are many cinemas in Mumbai, though few show films in English.

Sports: The city has a good number of sports and leisure centers, but most sports facilities are available to club members only, and fees are expensive. Most of Mumbai's sporting facilities are restricted to private clubs such as the Willingdon, Bombay Gymkhana, Otters Club, and Khar Gymkhana. Some of them, such as the Breach Candy Club, offer temporary membership for a visitor, although this is discretionary.

Cricket is a hugely popular spectator sport in India. The Cricket Club of India, Church Gate (Tel: +91 22-2282-0262) can provide information on upcoming matches. Most international hotels have swimming pools. Beaches in town tend to be dirty; suburban beaches are cleaner.

Nightlife: Mumbai claims to be the capital of Indian nightlife; catering to 15 million people, clearly, there is something in the city for every taste and preference. Being home to the "Bollywood" film industry—the largest film industry in the world—ensures that essential glamour ingredient in a city that claims to never sleep.

Clubs and discos are found largely in two areas—adjoining the business district and the western suburban area of Bandra and Juhu. Those situated in South Mumbai have mostly a business-type clientele, apart from the rich and famous crowd. The bars in the suburbs are visited by the city's younger party-goers.

NATURAL ENVIRONMENT

Mumbai has a warm climate for most of the year, but the high humidity can make it somewhat unpleasant. The monsoon brings torrential rains, with the possibility of localized flooding (particularly since drainage is a problem). Such floods can lead to casualties and damages.

HOUSING

Housing in Mumbai is scarce. Experts estimate an annual housing deficit of 59,000 units in Mumbai by 2021. The acute shortage of housing has pushed up prices considerably over the last 15 years.

Mumbai is a big city (around 15 million inhabitants) and almost without exception everyone lives in apartments, even the most affluent of Mumbai residents. Apartments cover a wide range, from studios to luxury penthouse suites and duplexes. Although most modern apartments have balconies, there is very limited external space.

The easiest apartments to source are in the two- to three-bedroom categories. It can be difficult to find four-bedroom apartments, as space is at such a premium. There has been a significant price increase over the last six months across the range of three- and four-bedroom apartments.

The Nariman Point and Fort areas have traditionally been home to most multinational corporations and the head offices of virtually all major Indian companies with offices in Mumbai. However, transport difficulties in the city (poor public transport and overcrowded and badly maintained roads) and a lack of commercial land for expansion has led to significant development in other areas, in particular the Bandra district and environs.

Advertisements in newspapers and with agencies will refer to BHK. This stands for bedroom, hall, and kitchen. Thus, 2BHK means a two-bedroom apartment with a hall and kitchen. Most modern apartments will have a layout similar to those most commonly found in cities such as New York and London: master bedroom with an adjoining bathroom; open lounge and dining area; separate kitchen and balcony; and an entrance hall area.

As Mumbai builders try to maximize living space, in most apartments the storage is very limited, as is the area on the balcony. Also, many slightly older buildings have awkward, small stairwells and lifts.

INTERNATIONAL SCHOOLS AND EDUCATION

There are a number of good international schools in Mumbai: American, German, French, and Japanese. There is also a good choice of reputable English language private schools, and a number of professional colleges and management institutes.

- The American School of Mumbai (www.isbi.com/istd-viewschool/3463-Bombay _Japanese_School.html) offers the American curriculum. The school does not apply a uniform policy. There is a cafeteria available for children who wish to eat at school, and a wide range of after-school activities is offered: tennis, drama, dance, cooking, piano, tae kwon do, table tennis courts, basketball courts, a playground area, and a swimming pool. Certain documents have to be provided as admission requirements. School hours are 8 A.M. to 2:50 P.M.

- Bombay Japanese School (www.geocities.cojp/HeartLand-Namiki/6682): A bus service is available, for which additional fees are paid. There is no canteen available. There is a brass band activity every Tuesday and Saturday, and a playground is available. School hours are 8:20 A.M. to 3:30 P.M.

- Deutsche Schule Bombay International School (www.dsbindia.com) offers English and German curricula. School buses are available. There is no school uniform policy. There is no canteen available; children bring packed snacks or they have their meals upon returning home. A wide range of after-school activities is offered, and a playground is available. School hours are 8:30 A.M. to midday (for kindergarten) or 2 P.M. (primary and secondary).

- Ecole Française Internationale de Bombay (www.efi-bombay.org) offers the French curriculum. The school does not provide a bus service. There is no uniform policy. The school offers a wide range of after-school activities including sports, yoga, dance, and tae kwon do. A playground is available as well. School hours are 8 A.M. to 2:30 or 3 P.M. The school takes children from the age of 3 up to and including Lycée age (15).

NEW DELHI

ENVIRONMENT ISSUES

Waste removal services are inadequate in New Delhi, and large areas of the city remain dirty for long periods.

Many hotel restaurants tend to cook Indian dishes especially with a large amount of oil, which can trigger "Delhi belly" (diarrhea). Ask the chef to use less oil. Fried foods from street vendors often look delicious, but check the oil: if it looks as old as the pot, it could be rancid and lead to trouble. It is safest to resist the temptation. Remember to wash your hands before you eat anything, even snacks. A useful tip is to carry pre-moistened towelettes to use when soap and water are not available.

Sewage systems are generally functional in the more affluent areas. Many parts of the city, however, still have open drains, and there tends to be an increased risk of malaria in such areas.

Air pollution is a severe problem, due to the rapid industrialization of the city and the growth in traffic. Factory fires and domestic heating also contribute to the problem. The level of pollutants may cause breathing difficulties for some people.

Mosquitoes, cockroaches, and rats are a severe problem in New Delhi due to the humid climate and inadequate sanitation.

INFRASTRUCTURE

Public transport is inefficient and very crowded and is generally not used by anyone who can afford alternative means of transport. Some private companies have entered the market, but safety standards remain low.

New Delhi has a metro system comprising three lines. Traffic is a severe problem, exacerbated by poor road planning, uncontrolled crossings, and stray animals in the streets. The accident rate is high.

Air travel: Indira Gandhi International Airport (www.delhiairport.com) is situated 20 km south of New Delhi. The airport's two terminals, one for international and one for domestic flights, are 5 km apart. An air-conditioned shuttle service is available. Airport facilities include banks, bureaux de change, a post office, snack bars, restaurants, several (duty-free) shops, and a pharmacy.

Chauffeur-driven car hire is available at both terminals. However, self-drive cars are not available. Prepaid taxi vouchers can be obtained from the Delhi Traffic Police booth in the arrivals areas. Metered taxis as well as motor rickshaws are also available outside the airport. It is recommended to pre-book a taxi in the arrivals area; the Delhi Traffic Police Pre-Paid Taxi booth issues a ticket, which is given to the allocated driver in lieu of a cash payment. There are two 24-hour bus services available, but allow 50 minutes to get into town.

There are a fair range of services to major cities in Asia, Western Europe, and the Middle East.

Rail travel: The Indian internal railway system is the largest in Asia and the second largest in the world. Delhi is the main hub of the Indian Railways (Tel: +91 11-2334-8787; www.indianrail.gov.in). The city has two major railway stations, in New Delhi and Old Delhi. New Delhi station, east of Pahar Ganj (Main Bazaar), is within walking distance of Connaught Place. Main Delhi station (Old Delhi), west of Red Fort, is about 7 km (4 miles) from Connaught Place. Express trains run from Delhi to all parts of the country.

One of the most popular lines is the Shatabdi Express, which travels to Agra, Lucknow, and Chandigarh. Tickets are available for purchase at the International Tourist Bureau (Tel: +91 11-2334-6804), located at New Delhi station. This service is for foreigners only, and payment can be made in U.S. dollars, Euros, or pounds sterling. Otherwise, the main ticket office is at the IRCA building on Chelmsford Road, Pahar Ganj. You can also book tickets over the Internet. Delhi, Mumbai, and Bangalore have facilities for home delivery of tickets booked over the Internet.

Bicycle: Cycling is an excellent way of getting around, especially in New Delhi. The roads are, by Indian standards, uncrowded, wide, and in good condition.

Bus: Delhi Transport Corporation runs a large fleet of buses operating throughout the city. Some of them on certain routes are available at all the railway stations and the interstate bus terminals. Peak hours are from 7 A.M. to 10 P.M., with the frequency being slightly lower from 1 to 2:30 P.M. Night service buses are also available on selected routes and are also operated from the railway stations, from 11 P.M. to 5 A.M. For confirmation of exact bus fare, contact the nearest bus booth. Buses tend to be extremely crowded.

Car rental: There are several private operators who offer this facility and if one has a valid driver's license, there are several outlets from which to choose.

Rickshaws: A more economical option that renting a car or hiring a taxi is to hire a three-wheeler auto rickshaw, which carries two passengers, runs on a meter, and costs roughly half the equivalent taxi fare. These are found all over the city. Auto rickshaws are generally faster than taxis on short trips. Always negotiate a fare before you board. Six-seated motorcycle rickshaws run fixed routes at fixed prices and are a good value during rush hours. Cycle rickshaws are banned from New Delhi itself, but can be handy for traveling around "Old" Delhi.

Metro: There are currently three lines that are fully operational: Shahdara-Rithala, Vishwa Vidyalaya-Central Secretariat, and Indraprastha-Dwarka (Sub City). Extensions to these lines are currently underway. All Delhi Metro stations have the logo prominently displayed. For further information on network and fares visit the Web site www.delhimetrorail.com. Feeder buses enabling commuters to conveniently reach Metro stations are available.

Taxis are available at all hotels and in almost all commercial and residential areas. Black and yellow taxis are metered. Ensure the meter is turned back before starting the trip. There is a surcharge over the meter, and you are advised to check the rate list available from the driver before payment. There are plenty of metered yellow and black taxis, but invariably the meters are out of date, not working, or the drivers will simply refuse to use them. If this happens, hail another taxi and do not forget to negotiate a fare before you set out.

Taxi scooter: These are metered. Ensure that the driver flags down the meter before he starts. Revised meter reading fare charts should be available with all public transport drivers.

RECREATION AND ENTERTAINMENT

Restaurants: The city has a wide range of restaurants, offering mainly Indian, continental, and Chinese cuisine. In addition, a number of multinational fast-food chains have recently entered the local market.

Cinema: There are a number of cinemas in the city, and the choice of English-language films is fair. Top international movies, however, are generally only screened some time after release. A comprehensive listing of cinemas in the city is available at www.delhigate.com/@delhi/cinema.htm.

Culture and entertainment: There is a fair range of theater and opera performances to choose from. Few international performers visit the city, except for occasional pop music acts. Gambling is illegal in India, with the exception of betting on horse races.

Sports: The city has a good number of sports and leisure centers, but most sports facilities are only available to club members, and fees are expensive. After the IX Asian Games in New Delhi in 1982, the capital city now boasts of some very modern sports facilities.

India holds eight Olympic gold medals in field hockey, and the sport has now been hailed as the country's official national sport. Cricket is a hugely popular spectator sport in India. Other popular games are soccer, basketball, volleyball, and badminton.

Nightlife: Delhi has a number of bars and nightclubs in and around the city.

NATURAL ENVIRONMENT

New Delhi's climate experiences extremes, with temperatures ranging from 0°C to 46°C during the course of the year. Summer lasts for up to six months and is extremely hot. The unreliable local power supply means that air conditioning is not as useful as it could be. The region has no history of natural disasters.

The sun can be intense in India. Beware of overexposure even on overcast days. To avoid sunburn, use a sunscreen with a sun protection factor of at least 30. To be safe, also wear a wide-brimmed hat and be sure to drink plenty of water.

HOUSING

The recent building boom has improved the possibilities of finding appropriate housing in India. The possibilities range from large colonial houses to city apartments, both furnished and unfurnished. When you are looking for a place to stay it is advisable to pay close attention to the surroundings as well. Traffic may go on all night, and a river may turn out to be a smelly discomfort.

Housing is a major problem in New Delhi. Furnished accommodations and smaller-sized apartments are rare in New Delhi, as are houses in general.

Housing is mainly apartment style in residential "gated" colonies. Apartment living is becoming increasingly the norm, particularly in Gurgaon, where much accommodation is located in modern, architectural high-rise blocks. A number of duplex apartments are available. In South Delhi, you may find more colonial-style houses, but it is rare to find one with a traditional garden as they mostly have "yards." You will often find that in the case of independent houses, the landlord and his family occupy one floor, while the tenant (and his/her family) occupies the other floor.

Some expatriates opt for "farm houses." These houses usually comprise four to five bedrooms, and are built on between two and five acres of land. Most of them have their own generators or power backup systems. Other facilities may include a swimming pool and tennis court.

For South Delhi accommodations, expect older units, with occasional problems with plumbing, leaks, and bugs. Most apartments are totally unfurnished, which means that there is no furniture, no domestic appliances, or air conditioning. Houses are generally designed to stay cool, so in the winter you should buy some portable heaters as no insulation is used within the properties. Mosquitoes in India are a general problem, and it is worth looking for accommodations with built-in mosquito repellent facilities.

Properties in Gurgaon tend to be newer and of a more modern design, with better facilities, as many are purposely built for the expatriate population.

New Delhi is still experiencing many problems with water and power outages. Water shortages in the summer in South Delhi are acute. South Delhi's neighborhoods of Golf Links and Jor Bagh have fewer problems than other areas, but they do occur from time to time, despite the premium paid to live in those areas.

Generally, South Delhi suffers more with power and water supplies than Gurgaon, although this may be because the newer housing of Gurgaon is equipped with modern power backup systems and large water reservoir tanks. Nevertheless, it is not uncommon in either district to hear generators running night and day.

Summertime can be particularly problematic for power and water supplies.

The neighboring state of Uttar Pradesh has witnessed a spurt in crime, and hence residential colonies in border areas are not very popular. There is an increased burden on the housing supply due to the continued influx of population from rural areas. The most prestigious residential areas are Chanakyapuri, Jor Bagh, Golf Links, and Sunder Nagar.

Household appliances of acceptable quality can be found. It is advisable to use a reputable dealer and ascertain the quality and functionality of the goods before paying for them.

Leases are usually for two to three years, and it is not unusual for landlords to expect up to one year's rent in advance or as a security deposit. It is also advisable to check on any extra charges, as these are often suddenly added on, for such things as redecoration, extra furniture, and fittings, which may or may not appear. It is advisable to seek the advice of a lawyer before signing a lease agreement and parting with large sums of money.

Lease agreements typically include an escalation clause of 10 to 15 percent. The rent increase will usually become effective after the first term (generally 11 months) and is applicable every term thereafter.

INTERNATIONAL SCHOOLS AND EDUCATION

There is a good choice of international educational facilities in New Delhi, including American, British, French, and Japanese schools. The choice of reputable English language private schools is also good.

- American Embassy School (www.aes.ac.in) offers the American program, Advanced Placement program, and the International Baccalaureate. The school provides a bus service at additional fees. There is no uniform policy. A canteen is available for children who wish to eat at school. The school offers a wide range of after-school activities such as arts, electronics, tennis, computer, chess, and photography. A playground is available. Certain documents have to be provided as admission requirements. School hours are 8:30 A.M. to 2:30 or 3:35 P.M. for the primary and secondary schools.

- British School, Chanakyapuri (www.british-school.org), offers the English curriculum. The school provides a bus service. The school has no uniform for regular wear, but for outings students are expected to wear white shirts and black trousers or skirts. A canteen is available for children wishing to eat at school, and a wide range of after-school activities is offered. A playground is available as well. There is a soccer field, a cricket field, and a basketball court. Certain documents have to be provided for the admission process. School hours are 7:55 A.M. until 2 P.M. After-school activities take place from 2:15 to 3:45 P.M. and include sports, drama, modern languages, and environment-related activities.

- Deutsche Schule (www.dsnd.de) offers the German curriculum. The school provides a bus service to and from home. There is no dress code policy. A wide range of after-school activities is offered such as basketball, volleyball, table tennis, tennis, crafts, and pottery. A playground is available. School hours are 8 A.M. to 1:15 or 3:15 P.M. Children are accepted from the age of 18 months at the Sternschnuppen toddlers group. This group is bilingual and is designed to prepare the child for kindergarten at age 3.

- Ecole Française (www.ac-toulouse.fr/eco-francaise-delhi) offers the French curriculum. The school does not apply a dress code policy. A canteen is available for children wishing to eat at school. School hours for kindergarten and primary school are 8:30 A.M. to 1 P.M. and 3 to 5 P.M. only on Mondays and Thursdays; for secondary school hours are 8:30 A.M. to 1 P.M., and 3 to 5 P.M. every day.

- G. D. Goenka Public School (www.gdgoenka.com) offers CBSE and NCERT programs. The school provides a wide range of after-school activities including sports, music, and dance. Certain documents have to be provided as admission requirements. A canteen is available for children who wish to eat at school. There are school bus facilities. A uniform policy is in place—children may be measured for and purchase their uniform at the school shop.

- Japanese School (www.ndjs.org) offers the Japanese curriculum. The school provides children with a school bus service. A canteen is not available. The school provides a wide range of after-school activities such as an athletic club. A playground is available as well. Certain documents have to be provided as admission requirements. School hours are 8:30 A.M. to 4 P.M.

- Pathways World School follows the IGCSE and the IB programs. The school has boarding facilities. A uniform policy is applied. School meals and snacks are provided, although only vegetarian food is available. The school provides full- and half-day childcare facilities for children up to grade 1.

Indonesia: Jakarta

PERSONAL SAFETY AND SECURITY ISSUES

Demonstrations occur, but less frequently than in the past and have seldom led to violent riots and other acts of civil disorder. Bombings are increasingly common in Jakarta.

Crimes happen regularly, and one should take precautions at all times. Some areas should be avoided, especially at night. Foreigners have often been the victims of violent crimes. Although law enforcement has become more democratic, civil laws are incomplete and one cannot always rely on the police to enforce them. Corruption and racism are prevalent.

The September 9, 2004, terrorist bombing of the Australian Embassy in Jakarta, the previous bombing of the JW Marriott hotel in August 2003, and the 2005 Bali bombings have exacerbated concerns in the area over security initiated by the bombing of a Bali nightclub in October 2002. These targets were all identifiably Western. Expatriates and visitors are advised to be extra vigilant in areas where Westerners, particularly Americans, British, and Australians, have traditionally congregated, such as hotels, restaurants, schools, places of worship, and clubs. Travelers are advised to maintain a low profile, to vary routines, and to avoid any large crowds or demonstrations. Embassies strongly advise foreign nationals to register with the country's embassy or consulate on arrival in Indonesia, to facilitate any evacuation plans that may be required. Travelers are encouraged to read local newspapers and keep an update of current regional political affairs.

Sectarian and ethnic attacks also put foreigners at risk in various parts of the island. Religious, political, and business targets have been affected by domestic attacks. Jakarta International Airport and Indonesian government buildings have suffered bombing attacks since 2003.

MEDICAL ISSUES

The standard of medical care in Indonesia falls below the standard that most Western expatriates would be used to. Limitations are found with the availability of drugs and medicines.

Blood, although screened for HIV and Hepatitis B, is not checked for the presence of Hepatitis C. Ambulances are slow to arrive at medical emergencies and often do not have a qualified paramedic crew. Hospital attendance times fall short of international standards. Ambulance drivers will only take you to the nearest hospital in the event of an emergency, rather than to the hospital of your choice. Cardiac and intensive care facilities are generally inadequate as are pediatric and maternity care.

Several new private hospitals have been established in recent years. Medical facilities and services in private hospitals are good for most major treatments; however, some expatriates and wealthy locals still prefer to be treated overseas for major operations. Basic medical supplies, including the most common prescription medicines, are available and easily accessible.

A number of serious infectious diseases such as dengue fever, typhoid, malaria, and Japanese encephalitis occur locally and visitors should obtain inoculations before traveling. Less serious diseases are also widespread and it is essential to take precautions and cook food thoroughly and boil drinking water. Bottled water is also available for drinking.

ENVIRONMENT ISSUES

It is advised to avoid drinking tap water and to use boiled water for brushing teeth. Expatriates sometimes have water coolers installed at home. To avoid incidences of gastroenteric illnesses, it is recommended to drink only bottled water.

Waste removal and sewage services are functional in some parts of the city. The level of air pollution in Central Jakarta is very high. Mosquitoes are common in some areas, especially at night, and some species transmit serious illnesses.

ECONOMIC OVERVIEW, 2008

GDP growth	6.1%
Inflation	11.2%
Unemployment	8.5%

INFRASTRUCTURE

Utilities and traffic: Local transport includes a variety of small motor, pedal, or animal-powered vehicles. The public transport system is unreliable and crowded, but taxis are widely available. Traffic is congested during the rush hours and road conditions may be hazardous, especially near construction sites.

Air travel: The airport (Soekarno-Hatta) is situated 13 km from the city center and can be reached in approximately 20 minutes from the business center. The airport offers excellent connections to other Asian cities and Australia, and a fair range of flights to Western Europe.

The Damri shuttle bus runs from the airport to Blok M Plaza, Bekasi, Rawamangun, Gambir, Depok, and Bogor. Buses leave approximately every 30 minutes; the journey takes approximately one hour and will cost between IDR 10,000 and IDR 12,000. Buses run from 6 A.M. until 8 P.M. There is a free shuttle bus that runs frequently between Terminals 1 (sub-terminals A, B, and C) and 2 (sub-terminals D, E, and F). International flights depart from and arrive at Terminal 2. Terminal 1 currently only serves domestic and special flights. Terminal 2 has four VIP first- and business-class lounges, nursery rooms, prayer rooms, and a shopping arcade; both terminals provide snack bars, cafeterias, restaurants, bureaux de change, banks, bookstores, and newsstands. The Terminal 2 Information Centre is open 24 hours a day.

Taxi companies operate from the ranks outside arrivals at the airport. Make sure you use a licensed metered taxi. Blue Bird taxis are the most popular local company. Most drivers speak English and the cars are air conditioned.

Taxi: Taxis can be hailed from the street (*pangkalan*—taxi rank) or ordered by phone. Although a taxi ordered by phone can sometimes take a while to arrive, it is the safest way, as your name, location, and the taxi number are recorded in the taxi headquarters. All taxis in Jakarta are air conditioned, although the air conditioning may not function well. If you get into a taxi and the driver tells you the meter is broken or if the meter seems to be giving erratic readings, you should get out of the taxi. Depending on the quality of your taxi, the initial meter charge should be between IDR 3,000 and IDR 4,500. Rates per kilometer are between IDR 1,500 and IDR 2,500. Not all drivers speak English, so it is advisable to have your destination with directions written in Bahasa Indonesian.

Bus: There are a number of bus companies that operate in Jakarta. There is a set price for buses that should be posted in the bus. Prices are usually between IDR 1,300 and IDR 3,500 for a journey in the city. Students in uniform will pay less. The conductor will usually walk back and fro to collect bus fares. Although the routes and fares should be rigid, in practice they are not. You can pay less for shorter distances. Drivers occasionally deviate from set routes; there are no timetables to adhere to; passengers are picked up and dropped off other than at designated stops; and sometimes the buses just slow down rather than come to a complete halt to pick up passengers. The points of departure and destination are written on the front of the buses. The route number is also noted on the front.

Jakarta's city bus stations are found at Pulogadung, Pasar Senen, Tanjung Priok, Kalideres, Kampung Rambutan, Blok M, Kota, and Lebak Bulus.

The Transjakarta Busway opened in 2004 and reduced, to some degree, the overcrowded traffic in the city by providing professionals with a fast, reliable, and safe—including from pickpockets—public means of transportation. There are currently seven routes. The construction of a monorail system was in progress for many years but was abandoned in March 2008 due to financial and technical problems.

SHOPPING AND AVAILABILITY OF CONSUMER GOODS

A good variety of local food products and consumer goods is available and can be obtained easily. The selection of imported items has improved following the economic recovery. A wide range of alcoholic beverages is available in special duty-free shops for members, but supermarkets have a more limited selection. Vehicles from local dealers are of good quality and import restrictions on luxury cars have been lifted.

Shopping hours in Jakarta are generally from 10 A.M. until 9 or 10 P.M., seven days a week. Throughout the city, a full range from designer goods to local crafts can be purchased.

There is a wealth of choice for grocery shoppers in Jakarta. An influx of foreign hypermarkets during the last 20 years meant that a wide range of international brands could be imported on a large scale.

RECREATION AND ENTERTAINMENT

Restaurants: Indonesian cuisine is generally hot and spicy; *chillies,* garlic, cumin, turmeric, lime, lemon, shallots, ginger, coconut, lemongrass, and soy sauce are all staples of local cooking. Rice and fried rice are the most popular base foods; rice table (*rijsttafel*) is a buffet-style method of eating that is served in many Indonesian restaurants. Similar to this is the *Padang* food, originating from the island of *Sumatera.* You are served a selection of meat, fish, and vegetable dishes with rice, and your bill is calculated on how many empty bowls you leave on the table. Satay (*sate*) and soups (*soto*) are also well-known popular dishes. Fresh tropical fruit is the most popular choice for dessert.

Jakarta has a huge selection of restaurants, from top-quality international cuisine (found in the restaurants of top hotels) to the *warung* (street stalls) that sell local "fast food," which is excellent.

Jakarta has a Hotel and Restaurant Association. All establishments which are members of this association are obliged to charge all customers a 10 percent sales tax, plus an additional 10 percent service charge. It is important to be aware of this when assessing the price of dishes on the menu. If the restaurant does not charge this tax, then it is recommended that you leave a small tip as a token of your appreciation of the meal. This is not obligatory, but will always ensure excellent service next time you eat there.

Cinemas: Jakarta has over 40 cinemas and some show English language and subtitled films. The number of European film festivals held in Jakarta is increasing. There are currently a handful of luxurious cinemas in Jakarta, which provide reclining seats and even serve refreshments inside the theaters. Links www.indoindians.com and www.21cineplex.com have up-to-date lists of all the movie theaters and films currently showing. The "21" chain of cinemas has the monopoly over good and high-quality cinemas in the major cities of Java.

Casinos are banned in Indonesia (the Muslim religion forbids the practice of gambling or betting), although there are many underground casinos in Jakarta and Batam.

Culture and entertainment: Entertainment in Jakarta is plentiful, with a good selection of nightclubs, associations, stage performances, and cinemas.

The *Jakarta Kini* magazine is an English language guide to what's on in Jakarta; where to go, places to see, and reviews. The magazine is freely distributed in top hotels and throughout the community in shops, restaurants, bars, and schools.

The *Jakarta Program* and *Jakarta Week* are both periodicals listing attractions and events in the city. Newspapers such as the *Jakarta Post* and the *Indonesian Observer* have a "What's On" section, with reviews and entertainment listings.

The availability of international-style operas is minimal, but there is an increasing number of interesting local classical concerts, theaters, and other performances.

The center of cultural activity in Jakarta is at the Jakarta Art Center; the Taman Ismail Marzukior TIM as it is known as, is Jakarta's largest cinema, theater, and entertainment complex, featuring live performances across the cultural spectrum from ballet to rock.

Sports: There are over 150 sports and fitness centers in Jakarta alone. To find the best for your needs, it is advisable to speak with other expatriates in your area and your colleagues to find out which ones they recommend. Your office may have a corporate membership to a certain gym or your local expatriate social group may be able to recommend their favorite. A good Web site with listings of all activities offered is www.expat.or.id/orgs/sports.html.

Nightlife: Jakarta has a number of night clubs and bars around the city. Tanamor is probably Jakarta's most popular nightclub, particularly amongst the expatriate crowd. The principal theme is techno music. There is an admission fee on weekends. The bar is expensive, but there is an excellent variety of drinks offered.

SOCIOCULTURAL ENVIRONMENT

The situation regarding human rights in the country has improved, and freedom of speech and movement is now generally upheld. There is a growing number of local television channels. International newspapers, satellite, and cable television are available. The local media faces some censorship for cultural reasons and tends to present a favorable image of the government.

DEMOGRAPHIC/WORKFORCE OVERVIEW

Population	234,693,997 (2007 estimate)
Population growth rate	1.213% (2007 estimate)
Age structure	0–14 years, 29%
	15–64 years, 66%
	65 years and over, 6%
Life expectancy at birth	
Total population:	Total population 70.16 years
Male	67.69 years
Female	72.76 years

WORKPLACE CULTURE

Business hours are generally Monday through Friday, 8 A.M. until 4 or 5 P.M. Some businesses work Saturday mornings; if so, it is rare that they will work past 1 P.M. On Friday, Muslims will be permitted time off to pray at noon. Occasionally businesses will have half days on Fridays and Saturdays instead of a full day on Friday.

Lunch breaks are taken between 12 and 12:30 P.M. until 1:30 P.M. Retail establishments are normally open from 9 A.M. until 9 P.M. seven days a week.

The principal dress code in Indonesia is influenced by Muslim customs. Women do not normally wear low necklines, bare their arms, or wear miniskirts in public places, especially offices.

Shirt and tie are the usual business attire for Western men. It is considered both disrespectful and impolite to dress in a casual manner at work.

NATURAL ENVIRONMENT

The climate is tropical, hot, and humid for most of the year. Jakarta is not normally subject to severe natural disasters. However, localized floods do occur in some parts of the city during the monsoon season. The risk of undersea earthquakes is thought to be a concern.

HOUSING

There is a wide choice of accommodations. Apartments (both serviced and nonserviced) and houses are available within a reasonable distance from the business center.

Rents, which are usually payable in U.S. dollars, must be paid in advance for the full term of the lease. The most popular residential areas are Kebayoran Baru, Senayan, Kuningan, Permata, Hilton Residence, Simpruk Cilandak, and Pondok Indah.

Rental costs vary greatly depending on the area, although generally rental prices are stable. A furnished three-bedroom house will cost between USD 2,800 and USD 4,300 depending on the area. Unfurnished houses are 10 percent less than furnished houses. Furnished three-bedroom apartments begin at around USD 3,600 for a good area up to USD 5,400 in the best areas. Unfurnished apartments are between USD 3,300 and USD 4,300.

FINANCIAL ISSUES INCLUDING BANKING SERVICES AND TAXES

Although there are no restrictions on currency exchange, there are often difficulties in exchanging large amounts of local currency.

A number of international banks offer a good range of services, although the credibility of some institutions has suffered and some banks have limited liquid funds.

Currency: The unit of currency in Indonesia is the Rupiah (IDR). Notes are issued in denominations of IDR 100, 500, 1,000, 5,000, 10,000, 20,000, 50,000, and 100,000. 1 Rupiah = 100 Sen. Coins are issued in values of IDR 25, 50, 100, 500, and 1,000.

Although there are a variety of coins, it is rare that you will purchase any items or pay for any services less than IDR 1,000. Even a small tip for a porter will amount to several thousand Rupiah per case.

Cash, traveler's checks, and credit cards: The best way to carry currency in Indonesia is with traveler's checks and cash (preferably in U.S. dollars). Credit cards are accepted by the more expensive hotels, restaurants, and shops, but not for general daily purchases. In major city centers, you can always find a bank that will advance cash on Visa or MasterCard. ATMs in city centers are connected to the Alto, Cirrus, Maestro, Plus, MasterCard, and Visa networks. The Citibank Branch ATM is the only distributor of U.S. dollars. ATMs are located in shopping malls and offices throughout the city.

The easiest currency to exchange is the U.S. dollar, but traveler's checks in either U.S. dollars or UK pounds sterling are always easy to exchange and normally without additional exchange rate charges. Licensed money changers generally offer the best rate for U.S. dollars and do not charge a commission. Traveler's checks can be exchanged at banks and hotels (although hotels will offer a favorable exchange rate, they are often open from 7 A.M. until 7 P.M.). Traveler's checks are recommended in Indonesia for security purposes, as pickpocketing and theft are on the increase.

Credit card fraud in Indonesia is a problem. Banks advise you to use cash for purchases and to only use your debit card while withdrawing cash at your own branch. MasterCard, Visa, and American Express are the most widely accepted credit cards.

There are no restrictions on the import or export of foreign currency, although amounts over IDR 5,000,000 must be declared when leaving the country.

The Bank of Indonesia and the Central Bank ensure that the stability of the Indonesian Rupiah is maintained and the exchange rate in terms of other currencies is reviewed on a daily basis. It is worth noting that Bank Negara Indonesia and Bank Rakyat Indonesia are the only state-owned banks permitted to exchange foreign currency.

Banks are open from 8 A.M. until 3 P.M. on weekdays and closed on the weekends. Money changers are open later in the weekdays until the evening, and you may find some open on Saturdays. They are located in most shopping malls, hotels, and some department stores. Money changers frequently reject marked notes, so it is advisable to bring new notes when changing money.

Account services vary greatly from bank to bank in Indonesia. It is highly advised that you make thorough inquiries before committing to a particular account and bank. It is possible to open a U.S. dollar account, but you will invariably be required to maintain a minimum balance. Some expatriates have most of their wages deposited into a local Rupiah account and ask for the remainder of their salary to be given to them in cash.

Opening an account in Indonesia is fairly straightforward. You will need to bring the following to your chosen bank:

- Completed application form, if supplied in advance.
- Copy of passport plus original.
- Copy of KITAS card (work permit) plus original.

Taxes: The tax year is the calendar year for individuals. Residents in Indonesia are required to pay tax on not only income received in Indonesia, but also on all global income, A resident tax payer is determined by whether they reside in Indonesia for more than 183 days in a 12-month period or is in Indonesia for part of a year with intention to become a resident. A nonresident is taxed on work carried out for an Indonesian company in Indonesia at a rate of 20 percent. A nonresident who works short-term for a company that does not pay taxes in Indonesia (and who is part of the Indonesian Tax Treaty) may be exempt from Indonesian tax.

Individuals who earn over the tax threshold are required to register with the Indonesian Tax Authorities in order to obtain a personal tax identification number (NPWP).

Tax credits are applicable for employees, spouses, and children:

- A standard deduction of IDR 2,880,000 for all resident taxpayers.
- IDR 1,440,000 for a spouse.
- IDR 1,440,000 for each dependent child (up to a maximum of three children).

Company cars, medical expenses, housing allowance, and pension and Social Security contributions are generally nontaxable. A tax-free allowance of 5 percent of the gross income is given to cover business expenses to a maximum of IDR 25,920,000. If you make contributions to approved pension schemes or make obligatory Social Security contributions, these are also deductible.

Expatriate employees are not required to participate in the Indonesian Social Security system (*Jamsostek*).

INTERNATIONAL SCHOOLS AND EDUCATION

There are international, British, French, German, and Japanese schools in Jakarta. All offer kindergarten, primary, and secondary levels of education. There is also a reasonable choice of local private schools affiliated with various Australian private schools, where the language of instruction is English.

- The Australian Intnernational School (www.ais-indonesia.com) follows the Australian national curriculum. It offers a fully accredited Australian Senior Secondary program. Instruction is in English; students are offered the opportunity to learn the Bahasa Indonesian language from kindergarten onwards. It also offers the Gifted and Talented Program. The school provides special needs educational programs as well. School hours are from 8 A.M. until 2 P.M.
- British International School (www.bis.or.id) is based on the national curriculum for England and Wales; Key Stages 1 to 4 from Infant School through to General Certificate of Secondary Education level (years 10 and 11). The International Baccalaureate is offered for years 12 and 13. Instruction is in English. A school bus is provided. The school operates a uniform policy. The school has student boarding facilities for families who do not live in Jakarta. A wide choice of extracurricular activities is offered.

- Deutsche Internationale Schule (German school) (www.dis.or.id) offers the German national curriculum and follows the German government's international standard for overseas schools. The school takes students from kindergarten to abitur ages (3 to 19 years), with small class sizes between 15 and 20 pupils per class. The school offers a wide range of extracurricular activities. There is a bus service provided. Language of instruction is German, and students are also taught English from preschool age. There is a canteen if children wish to eat at school. The school does not have a uniform policy. School hours are from 7:30 A.M. until 2 P.M.

- Jakarta International School (www.jisedu.org) is based primarily on the North American system. Secondary students can study either the Advanced Placement Program and/or study for the International Baccalaureate. The school is open to all expatriate children living in Jakarta. Classes are in English. The school consists of prep reception (three-year-old children), prep junior (four-year-old children), and prep senior (five-year-old children) through grade 5; a middle school consisting of grades 6 to 8; and a high school with grades 9 to 12. The school has no uniform policy. A bus service is provided and a canteen is available. School begins at 7:30 A.M., with the kindergarten and primary schools finishing at 1:55 P.M. and the secondary finishing at 2:40 P.M.

- The Jakarta Japanese School (www.jjs.or.id) is for Japanese levels, elementary and junior high school. The school provides a bus service at an additional charge. No canteen is available. School hours are 7 A.M. to 2:20 P.M.

- Lycée International Français de Jakarta (French school) (www.lifdejakarta.org) is based on the French national curriculum. The International Baccalaureate program is offered. The school provides instruction in French to students from the ages of 4 to 18 years. After-school activities are available.

- New Zealand School (www.nzis.net) is based on primary, secondary, and kindergarten classes, based on the New Zealand education system. This school opened in 2002. Instruction is in English. Students are accepted from the age of 3 up to the age of 18 years.

Israel: Tel Aviv

PERSONAL SAFETY AND SECURITY ISSUES

It is strongly advised that foreign nationals living in Israel take particular care to maintain personal security arrangements and remain vigilant against indiscriminate attacks. Most foreign embassies advise their expatriates to register with them on arrival in Israel.

Consulates and embassies advise against travel along Israel's borders with Lebanon. Visits to the occupied territories are strongly discouraged, especially at night, and visits to the Gaza Strip should be for essential purposes only, as there is still a risk of kidnapping in the area.

The Israeli government often imposes travel restrictions during periods of unrest. Despite Israel's reputation as a high-risk country, it is a relatively safe place to live. Muggings and other forms of street crime are very uncommon; however, car thefts and burglaries do occur. All the usual common sense precautions should be exercised with regard to personal safety; for example do not carry excessive amounts of money around unnecessarily, and do not walk alone on unlit streets at night. If you are a victim of crime, you should report the incident immediately to the local police and your embassy or consulate. Security is generally high around government buildings and public places. Your bags may be regularly searched when entering buildings, cinemas, restaurants, and so on. This is common practice to ensure higher safety standards and should not be alarming or taken as an insult.

Tel Aviv is a fairly safe city to live. The rate of violent crime is reasonably low, and the chance of being caught up in a terrorist incident has decreased recently. Israeli police and security forces are generally efficient.

MEDICAL ISSUES

Hospital services are good and capable of dealing with all but the most sophisticated procedures. Most daily medical supplies are plentiful.

There are both private and public healthcare facilities in the country. It is usual to pay for health services as you receive treatment. Many hospitals will accept credit card or cash payments. You can then claim payments from your health insurance. In some circumstances, you can send the bills straight to the insurance fund.

Health insurance is compulsory in Israel. There are four sick funds (health funds) that you can choose from. The funds are mainly financed by the government through taxes and health fund payments collected by the National Insurance Institute from employees' wages. The employer also contributes to the fund. The amount you have to pay depends on your income level and family status (up to 4.8 percent of income). The largest health fund is Kupat Holim Clalit, which has its own hospitals. The other funds are Macabbi Health Services, Mehuhedet, and Leumit.

You can find information in English about emergency medical facilities and after-hours pharmacies in the *Jerusalem Post* and English language *Ha'aretz* newspapers.

ENVIRONMENT ISSUES

Serious infectious diseases are rare, and visitors are more likely to experience minor intestinal problems.

Tap water is safe to drink, and the sewage and waste removal services are effective. Air pollution is a problem in Tel Aviv. Some insects such as sand flies are present, but are more of a nuisance than a threat to health.

There are no particular health precautions to be taken in Israel. All persons traveling to Israel should ensure they have up-to-date routine immunizations, such as tetanus-diphtheria, measles, and varicella (chickenpox). An outbreak of the West Nile virus infection in 2000 led to 452 cases and 29 deaths, mainly in the central and northern parts of the country. Subsequent years have seen up to 72 deaths caused by the mosquito-borne diseases. Travelers in these areas of the country are advised to take precautions against mosquito bites between August and November.

Water is generally safe to drink; however, it is normally chlorinated and may cause mild abdominal upsets, hence it is advisable to initially purchase bottled water, which is widely available. In rural areas it is essential to sterilize all tap water. Local meat, produce, and dairy products are usually of good standards and are safe to consume.

ECONOMIC OVERVIEW, 2008

GDP growth	4.1%
Inflation	3.8%
Unemployment	6.0%

INFRASTRUCTURE

Utilities and transport: Electricity and water services are efficient, and disruptions are rare.

The telephone service has improved in recent years and is now of an excellent standard. The mail service is reliable but occasionally slow. The public transport system (buses and trains) is fairly comprehensive and efficient. Traffic congestion has become more severe recently, and delays may be experienced outside peak periods.

The Ben Gurion Airport, which is located within one hour of the city, offers a good choice of flights to Europe, some to other destinations in the Middle East, and major cities in North America and Asia.

Air travel: The cities of Eilat, Haifa, Jerusalem, Kiryat Shmona, Masada, Rosh Pina, and Tel Aviv are all linked by Israel's two domestic airlines: Arkia Israel Airlines and Israir. Many domestic flights depart from Tel Aviv's Sde Dov Airport, which is close to Midtown in the northern part of the city, as well as from Ben Gurion International Airport. Flights operate daily, except from Friday evening to Saturday evening.

Buses: Within Tel Aviv city, the bus system is very efficient, with the Dan Bus Cooperative and Egged being the primary operators. The fare in the city center is around ILS 4, which is a fixed price for travel within that zone. Tickets are purchased on the bus. By buying books of 25 tickets, you only pay the equivalent cost of 20. This is called a Kartisia. It is important to remember that although the tickets can be used in any city, they cannot be interchanged among operators. Two of the major lines, 4 (Ben Yehuda and Allenby Streets) and 5 (Dizengoff

Street and Rothschild Boulevard), are serviced by red minibuses. These have to be hailed from the roadside, but one can request to be dropped off at any point along the route, even between stops. The fare is the same as on the buses. Regular bus companies do not run on Saturday; however, privately run minibuses do.

Taxis: All taxis are now clearly marked by uniform signs. Within the metropolitan area, you must ensure that the driver turns on the meter when you get into the car, as this is a legal requirement. For journeys that take you outside the city, you should agree on a price with the driver beforehand. Should you be in any doubt that the amount quoted is not correct, you can ask to see the tariff booklet that each driver should carry. After 9 P.M. the rates go up and are normally 25 percent higher than in the day. It is not normal to tip taxi drivers when in Israel. Taxi fares are ILS 9.10 for the initial meter charge and then ILS 4.5 per kilometer thereafter. An additional NIS 2.7 is applicable for each piece of luggage.

Operating from the Central Bus station are a fleet of stretch Mercedes-Benz limousines called *Sherut,* which are taxis operating along the same routes as the local and intercity buses (prices are about 30 percent higher than for the buses). There is no definite schedule followed; the limousines simply depart when all seven seats are filled. Sheruts run on Saturday.

SHOPPING AND AVAILABILITY OF CONSUMER GOODS

Nearly all food items and consumer goods are freely available with no shortages (pork is still difficult to obtain for religious reasons, but the situation has improved due to relatively new large food stores). A few imported items may be hard to obtain. Alcoholic beverages are also widely available, with plenty of choice. It is possible to purchase almost any model of car.

Shops are normally open from 8 A.M. to 7 P.M., Sunday through Thursday, and from 8 A.M. to 2 P.M. on Friday. You will find most stores closed on Saturday, with the exception of restaurants, bars, and shopping centers within the vicinity of large cities. There is a wide choice for shoppers in Israel; you should expect to bargain, especially in the Arab markets. Most larger stores take credit cards; MasterCard and Visa are almost universally accepted, with American Express and Diners Club becoming increasingly popular.

RECREATION AND ENTERTAINMENT

Restaurants: There is a very good range of restaurants in Tel Aviv; food from most parts of the world is available (such as Asian, Arabic, and South American), as well as excellent restaurants serving local Jewish cuisine. Tel Aviv citizens have a tendency to eat out much later than others in the country; it is not uncommon for people to go to a restaurant at 9 or 10 P.M. to have a meal. Many restaurants stay open until 2 A.M. Tel Aviv is less strict on observing religious practices than Jerusalem, so you will be able to find many restaurants that are open on Friday evenings and Saturday that would not otherwise be open in Jerusalem. This also filters through to the type of food available; there is a far greater selection of non-kosher food in Tel Aviv than you would find in Jerusalem.

In keeping with Tel Aviv's casual nature, bistro dining is the most popular form of eating out; it is generally less expensive than restaurants, and diners like to sit outside and watch the world pass by as they eat. Portion sizes are often very generous, and some find that sharing a main meal between two is quite adequate. Markets are also popular places for grabbing a snack at very little cost, and ideal when you are on the run. Some of the major hotels in the city are home to the most exclusive and upmarket restaurants.

Many new visitors in Tel Aviv head towards the annual food festival in the city. Every June, the Ta'am Ha'Ir Food Festivalat Hayarkon Park is an excellent way to get to know the kind of food that is available in Tel Aviv; many restaurants set up booths and allow you to sample their dishes for a very reasonable price.

Cinemas: There is an excellent choice of cinemas, and new films are shown not long after release in the United States. Sports facilities are fairly plentiful. For lists of festivals and events in Tel Aviv, there are several main guides; for Hebrew speakers *Achaber Ha'Ir* (meaning City Mouse) provides good listings of Tel Aviv events, as does the Israeli "Timeout" Web site (www.timeout.co.il). English speakers should pick up a Friday edition of *Ha'aretz/Herald Tribune International,* which contains "The Guide." For cinema and film listings, refer to *The Jerusalem Post* and *Ha'aretz* newspapers. Foreign films are always shown in their original soundtrack with subtitles in Hebrew; therefore, all the Hollywood blockbusters are shown in English.

For other information on events and features in the city, buy a copy of *The Jerusalem Post* on Friday to get the weekend "What's On" section. There is also a free tourist booklet called "Events in the Tel Aviv Region" available from bookstores, hotels, and tourist outlets.

Culture and entertainment: Local cultural productions are of a fairly high standard and international productions sometimes visit the city. But with the security problems, there are less international performers willing to visit Israel.

Tel Aviv is home to the Israel Philharmonic Orchestra, based at the Mann Auditorium, and the Israel Chamber Music Orchestra. The Israel Philharmonic Orchestra was established 60 years ago and is famous worldwide. The New Israel Opera was established in 1985 and in October 1994 was moved to its permanent home at the Tel Aviv Performing Arts Centre (Mishkan Ha'Omanuyot) located next to the Tel Aviv Museum of Art.

Tel Aviv has many museums and art galleries. Major ones include the Eretz Israel Museum ("Land of Israel Museum"; www.eretzmuseum.org.il), which is actually a collection of museums featuring ceramics, coins, and folklore; the Tel Aviv Museum of Art (www.tamuseum.com), featuring Israeli painting and sculpture but also including a good French Impressionist collection; and The Jewish Diaspora Museum (www.bh.org.il), focused on the history of the Jewish people and their contribution to human culture over more than 2,000 years.

Sports: Tennis courts and swimming pools can usually be found at most larger hotels. Golf is not yet a popular sport in Israel, although interest is steadily mounting. The best-known golf course at present is The Caesarea Golf Club, located at the Dan Caesarea Hotel in the seaside town of Caesarea, about 45 minutes north of Tel Aviv (Tel: +972 4-626-6911). There is also a relatively new golf course located in the Kibbutz Ga'ash area, just north of Kfar-Shmaryahu (Tel: +972 9-951-5111; www.golfgaash.co.il).

Horseback riding is a common pastime and is available throughout the country, as is cycling where riders prefer to avoid the busy and congested towns.

With Israel's long coastline, it is no surprise that all manner of water sports such as swimming, surfing, sailing, water skiing, yachting, and fishing are available. There are marinas in Tel Aviv and some other cities of Israel.

In recent years, country clubs have sprung up in many of the more exclusive neighborhoods, including Bavli, Ramat Aviv-Gimmel, Ramat Hasharon, Herzlia, Kfar Shmaryahu, and Ra'anana. These clubs always have swimming pools and generally tennis courts, as well as other sporting facilities.

Nightlife: There are no casinos in Israel, as gambling is not permitted within the country. But there are nightclubs and discotheques in most Israeli cities, with Tel Aviv being no exception. Tel Aviv has a wealth of entertainment with rock, jazz, folk, and pop music clubs throughout the city.

SOCIOCULTURAL ENVIRONMENT

Israeli law allows detention without trial of suspected activists. Freedom of religion is available to all groups. However, Palestinians and Jews are sometimes refused access to places of worship, particularly in East Jerusalem in order to prevent religious riots. Orthodox Jewish groups have a strong influence on government policy, and this imposes some restrictions on other residents.

Israel has a free press, radio, and TV. The government has limited powers of censorship.

DEMOGRAPHIC/WORKFORCE OVERVIEW

Population	6,352,117 (2006 estimate)
Population density	312 inhabitants per km^2
Age structure	0–14 years, 26%
	15–64 years, 64%
	65 years and over, 10%
Life expectancy at birth	
Total population:	79.5 years
Male	77.3 years
Female	81.7 years

WORKPLACE CULTURE

Israel comprises many cultures and many diverse groups. Within each of these cultural layers lies a different code of conduct. Within Israel, you may find that the majority of international level Israeli business people are largely secular and generally operate according to Western business etiquette norms. However, you may also meet companies and representatives who follow Middle Eastern customs. Israel has a large Arab population, so it is advisable to be aware of the various cultures you may encounter and let your counterpart determine the code of conduct.

Israeli business hours vary widely, but are normally defined by religion. Business hours will depend on the religion of the proprietor. Jewish businesses are usually open from 8 A.M. to 4 P.M., Sunday through Thursday, and 8 A.M. to 1 P.M. on Friday. Businesses will very rarely open on a Saturday (*Shabbat*). The Sabbath runs from sunset on Friday until sunset on Saturday and is the Jewish holy day.

An Arab business will most likely follow the Middle Eastern practice of opening from Saturday to Thursday and closing for the holy day on Friday. Christian-owned businesses are normally open Monday through Saturday and closed on Sundays. Offices are generally open 8 A.M. to 7 P.M. (lunch is taken by employees, but offices do not close) from Sunday through Thursday.

Punctuality is not seen as a priority in the Middle East; however, as many businesses take their code of practice from Western cultures, you may find that some of your business partners are on time for meetings.

Business dress in Israel is very similar to what you would wear in a business setting in Western Europe or the United States.

NATURAL ENVIRONMENT

Tel Aviv has a temperate climate, with hot and humid summers; you should ensure that sun protection is used at all times to avoid damage to the skin.

HOUSING

It is quite easy to obtain suitable housing in Tel Aviv. Popular areas for expatriates include Herzlia Pituach, Kfar Shmaryahu, Neve Tzedek, Ramat-Aviv, Tel Aviv Sea Promenade, and Sea and Sun.

Although there is a very limited choice of furnished accommodations in Israel, unfurnished accommodations are easier to find. The easiest and most convenient way to find housing in Tel Aviv is through a rental or real estate agency or relocation companies. *The Jerusalem Post* has a real estate classified section that covers the whole of Israel.

Guarantees of up to six months' rent are usual, sometimes more, but not normally. The financial or security guarantees that must be paid to a landlord vary greatly in both amount and method, and it is up to the tenant to negotiate with the landlord. Rents are negotiable, although trends show that rents are on the increase.

The standard rental agreements in Israel are very much biased towards the landlord and give the tenant few rights. It is strongly advised for the tenant to employ a lawyer or notary to handle the contract from your side; contracts are always negotiable with landlords. Legal advice should cost you the equivalent of between one and two months' rent. It is also strongly advised that you do not give the landlord a series of forward dated checks; you will be unable to cancel these in the event of not seeing out your lease or wishing to withhold some money when repairs have not been carried out for example.

A garage is usually included in rents. Bills such as utilities, *arnona* (municipal taxes), and *va'ad bayit* (building maintenance) are usually the obligation of the tenant. Beware that landlords frequently ask the tenant to pay half of the costs for his notary to draft the rental agreement. It is advised against agreeing to this as the landlord's notary does not represent the tenant.

A three-bedroom unfurnished house will cost between USD 4,400 and USD 7,100 per month depending on the area; a three-bedroom unfurnished apartment will cost from USD 4,100 up to USD 7,000 again. In most Israeli apartment buildings, tenants elect from among themselves a syndicate or committee, which is responsible for upkeep of the general property (landscaping, intercom, third-party insurance, and so on). The tenants, at periodic meetings, decide on a monthly fee to be paid by all residents for the above services. This is not a voluntary payment and is protected by law. The fee can range from USD 20 per month for buildings without elevators or intercoms, up to USD 100 and more for more luxurious properties (especially if the building employs a doorman or permanent maintenance person).

You should always ensure there is a clause in your contract that obliges the landlord to carry out essential maintenance and repairs to the building within a certain time frame; otherwise there is little in law that you can fall back on to have crucial damages (to the central heating or hot water boiler, for example) repaired.

FINANCIAL ISSUES INCLUDING BANKING SERVICES AND TAXES

There are no major restrictions on the import or export of currency, but large amounts should be declared. Most currencies are available for exchange at banks and bureaux de change in Tel Aviv. Most banking services are available in the city.

Currency: Israel's currency is known as the New Israeli Shekel (can be abbreviated NIS, although most businesses use the international standard of ILS). One ILS is divided into 100 agorot. Bank notes are in denominations of

20, 100, and 200 ILS. Coins are in denominations of 10, 5, and 1 New Israeli Shekels, and 50, 10, and 5 agorot.

Cash, traveler's checks, and credit cards: Only Israeli banks are currently authorized to change foreign currency. It is also possible to change foreign currency to Shekels at hotels and bureaux de change. You will find many street traders operating as money changers; foreigners have frequently been charged exorbitant exchange rates or short changed with their Israeli currency; therefore the general advice is to avoid unlicensed street traders. It is advisable to change the minimum amount for your currency needs as you are only permitted to exchange a maximum ILS 2,000 back into foreign currency when leaving the country.

The export of foreign currency is limited to the amount imported.

All credit cards are widely accepted within Israel (especially in larger shops, hotels, and restaurants), and traveler's checks are also widely accepted. It is recommended that you bring traveler's checks in U.S. dollars, therefore avoiding additional exchange rate charges.

It is recommended to carry small amounts of local currency with you to pay for taxis, tipping, and purchases in smaller shops and markets.

Banks: In general, banking hours are Sunday through Friday, 8:30 A.M. to midday, and Sunday, Tuesday, and Thursday, 4 to 6 P.M. Some banks may follow different hours but are always closed on Friday afternoon and Saturday. The majority of banks have 24-hour ATMs from which cash can be obtained using the stated debit or credit cards.

Every foreign worker in Israel has the right to open a checking account in Shekels with an Israeli bank on presentation of their passport. There may be certain restrictions imposed on a foreign national's account. It is possible with some banks to open an account in U.S. dollars.

It is not advisable to open an account with an overseas branch of an Israeli bank before arriving in the country, as the banks in Israel do not have access to information held abroad.

When opening an account in Israel, you must have a deposit of at least USD 2,000 before you are permitted to have a credit card. Some banks use Visa; Isracard, Diners Club, and American Express are becoming more popular. It is important to note that these credit cards are only valid for Israel. If you wish to use your Israeli credit card outside of Israel, you will have to request this, and there is an additional charge for its issue.

Taxes: The tax year is the calendar year. A resident taxpayer whose income consists solely of earnings from employment is not required to file a tax return where tax is withheld at the source from his wages, which do not exceed ILS 490,000. If applicable, tax returns should be filed by April 30, although it is usually possible to obtain an extension of a few months from the assessing officer.

Foreign experts invited to provide services in Israel by a resident employer and approved by the government or by teaching institutions are entitled to a tax deduction for accommodation expenses and a daily living allowance for a period not exceeding 12 months. The maximum daily allowance is restricted to ILS 250. If the nonresident is no longer entitled to the deductions or otherwise does not qualify; he or she is not entitled to the credit points for single individuals.

Other individuals who qualify as "approved specialists" are taxed at a maximum rate of 25 percent on their employment income for up to three years (which may be extendable for a further five years). They are also entitled to the foreign experts' deductions mentioned above. Approval is normally given on income up to USD 75,000 per annum, but only if the individuals are experts who possess skills not readily available locally.

INTERNATIONAL SCHOOLS AND EDUCATION

- Walworth Barbour American International School in Israel (www.wbais.org): Tuition is based on the American national curriculum and advanced placement program. Lessons are conducted in English. The school accepts children from kindergarten to grade 12. A school bus service is provided at an additional charge, depending on the distance. (Kfar Shmaryahu is a residential area approximately 15 km from the center of Tel Aviv.) The school does not apply a uniform or dress code policy. School hours are 8:10 A.M. to 3 P.M.

- Collège Marc Chagall (French school; www.isbi.com/istd-viewschool/3645-College _Marc_Chagall.html): The curriculum is based on the French national curriculum. The school serves children from kindergarten to grade 12 (ages 3–18 years). Lessons are conducted in French. There is no school bus service available. The school does not apply a uniform or dress code policy. School hours are 8 A.M. to 1:15 P.M. The school runs a combination of lessons in class and by correspondence.

- In Tel Aviv there are German "Saturday schools," which offer German as a supplementary subject for students who visit schools that provide general education in Israel. The project is recognized by the German Federal Office of Administration.

- Verein Deutsche Schule, Tel Aviv (www.tel-aviv.diplo.de/Vertretung/telaviv/de/06/ Intern__schulen/Internationale_20Schulen_20in_20Israel.html); Tel: +972 9-9571374. Contact also the Goethe Institut, Tel Aviv; Tel: +972 3-6917266.

Japan: Tokyo

PERSONAL SAFETY AND SECURITY ISSUES

In general, the Japanese are honest and law-abiding people. Japan has one of the lowest crime rates in the world, so personal safety is not much of a concern; theft and drug-related crimes are relatively rare. Bicycle theft, however, is extremely common. To discourage petty crime, there is a police box (*koban*) in every neighborhood.

Demonstrations and strikes are very unusual. Tokyo is considered to be a safe city, and there are virtually no safety problems for expatriates. Police work is competent, and laws are strictly enforced.

You must carry a piece of identification at all times, such as your passport or permit. The police have the right to arrest anyone who fails to do so. They rarely stop foreigners, but car drivers are frequently checked. If you are found without a valid ID, the police will accompany you to your home to collect it.

MEDICAL ISSUES

Tokyo has a very good health service, and hospitals are modern and well equipped. However, few doctors speak a language other than Japanese. Medicines often include instructions in Japanese only.

Healthcare is expensive, and it is advisable to purchase comprehensive medical and dental insurance. Western medicine is the most common form of treatment, although alternatives such as Chinese medicine, acupuncture, and Japanese acupressure massage are available.

Procedures for medical care may be different from that in your home country. In general, people line up to see medical staff at hospitals and clinics. You can visit a hospital clinic as an outpatient, but it is unwise to do so unless you speak Japanese well, you are with a Japanese speaker, or you have been referred by an English-speaking doctor. Your company or organization may recommend particular doctors/clinics with English-speaking staff, or your national embassy may also be able to provide a list of recommended practitioners. Private specialist clinics are of a high standard.

ENVIRONMENT ISSUES

Food and water are safe to consume, and there is very little risk of serious infectious diseases in Japan. It is advisable to take the usual personal care while traveling from a different climate to Japan's seasonal weather conditions.

Tap water is safe to drink throughout Japan, but you should avoid drinking directly from streams or rivers. It is also not a good idea to walk barefoot through flooded paddy fields, due to the danger of waterborne parasites. With regard to food, you should have no fears of eating raw seafood or fish, including the notorious *fugu* (globefish). However, raw meat and river fish are best avoided.

Japan has high standards of health and hygiene, and there are no significant diseases to worry about. Air pollution is a common problem in many large cities, and Tokyo is no exception.

ECONOMIC OVERVIEW, 2008

GDP growth   0.3%
Inflation   1.6%
Unemployment   4.1%

INFRASTRUCTURE

Utilities and traffic: Telephone, mail, water, and electricity services are of the highest standards. The authorities of Tokyo provide very good public transport facilities, which include buses and one of the most advanced metro systems in the world. A quarter of all Japanese workers live in Tokyo or the surrounding areas, and this often results in severe traffic congestion, despite the well-organized public transport system.

Air travel: The airport (Narita International Airport) offers an excellent choice of services to most destinations worldwide, but journey time to and from the airport is usually over one hour as it is situated 66 km from the city center.

Tokyo has a large comprehensive public transport system of buses, tramways, two underground railway systems (subway), and many private rail services. It is among one of the most efficient systems in the world. The Japan National Tourist Office (www.jnto.go.jp) in Tokyo produces a bilingual Tourist Map of Tokyo that is invaluable for understanding the transport system.

A map of the metro system can be found online at www.tokyometro.jp. There are 13 metro lines, and each has a number and is color coded. Tokyo Metro operates the following lines: Ginza (orange), Marunouchi (red), Hibiya (grey), Tozai (pale blue), Chiyoda (green), Yurakucho (yellow and new brown line), Hanzomon (purple), and Namboku (turquoise). The Transportation Bureau of Tokyo Metropolitan Government (Toei) (www.kotsu.metro.tokyo.jp) operates the remaining lines: Asakusa (pale pink), Mita (blue), Shinjuku (pale green), and O-edo (dark pink). The Metro operates between 5 A.M. and 12:15 A.M. (rush hours are 7:30 to 9:30 A.M. and 5 to 7 P.M.).Tokyo's Metro is considered to be very foreigner-friendly. All stations are announced in both Japanese and English, and ticket machines can switch between Japanese and English user-faces.

Rail: There is an extensive rail network that provides services to the suburbs. Most of the major train services finish at either Tokyo or Ueno stations, both of which are on the JR Yamanote line. The Yamanote line runs in a loop around central Tokyo, and most other trains run from major points on this loop to outlying areas. Electric commuter trains run above the ground and are color coded, with fares charged depending on the distance traveled. Tickets can be purchased at the embarking station, after which you will run it through the entrance wicket, then again at the exit wicket at your destination. If you are unsure of the correct fare for your destination, buy the cheapest ticket, then go to a "fare correction" machine near the exit wickets, insert your ticket, pay the extra fare and the ticket will then be coded to let you out.

Bus: There are two types of buses you can use in Tokyo. One type lets passengers board the bus using the front door; the other lets you board using the rear door. You need to check in advance which route you should take to go to your destination, since the routes of bus services are complicated a large PDF file showing major bus stations can be found at www.kotsu.metro.tokyo.jp/english/ images/pdf/bus_guide_english.pdf. Most bus routes in the 23 wards of Tokyo use a fixed fare regardless of your destination. These types of buses are called "front-boarding" buses.

When you take one of these buses, you will board the bus from the front entrance, put the fare into the fare box beside the driver's seat, and then take a seat. Exit when you reach your destination. Buses that operate outside of the 23 wards are "rear-boarding." You have to take a ticket when you board towards the rear of the bus. When you reach your destination, you have to pay the fare indicated for your ticket, which is shown on the electric signboard at the front of the bus. You then exit from the front door.

Taxis are widely available. They can be hailed on the street or taken from taxi ranks, usually by major hotels and train stations. Taxis are for hire if there is a red sign lit in the window in front of the passenger seat. A green light means there is an additional nighttime surcharge and a yellow light means that the taxi is on call. Taxi drivers control the opening and closing of the doors by remote control so let the driver handle this. The taxi should be entered from the curb side. You can also call and reserve a taxi in advance. There is usually a surcharge for this service (around JPY 500).

All taxis are metered, and fares vary little across the country. The initial meter charge is JPY 660, which covers the first 2 km; after this it is around JPY 275 per kilometer (or JPY 80 per 275 m). There is a time charge if the speed drops below 10 km/h (JPY 90 every two minutes). Drivers do not expect a tip unless they have provided a special service, your destination has been particularly difficult to find, or they have carried your luggage. There is a 30 percent surcharge between 11 P.M. and 5 A.M.

Most taxi drivers will not speak English, and so it is advisable to carry a note with your destination written in Japanese, as well as your return destination, office and/or home address. Tokyo is so complicated that even taxi drivers may not know a certain area, although they have detailed maps. However, if a driver does not understand your final destination, he may refuse the trip. Cars can be hired with English-speaking drivers, but the cost is much higher.

Car: Traffic congestion and scarce parking places are normal in Tokyo, so it is advisable not to drive in the city. The public transport system is so efficient that you really do not need to drive downtown.

SHOPPING AND AVAILABILITY OF CONSUMER GOODS

Tokyo has extensive shopping facilities including a number of supermarket chains, and an excellent selection of both Japanese and imported goods are available, although prices can be high. A good choice of alcoholic beverages is obtainable, and any model of car can be purchased.

Most shopping areas in and around Tokyo are a mixture of traditional shops, boutiques, and department stores. The main shopping areas in Tokyo are in Shinjuku, Shibuya, Ikebukuro, and the Ginza. The Ginza is Japan's most famous shopping district, full of expensive shops, famous department stores and restaurants, as well as art galleries, theaters, and cinemas. It is also the best area for quality arts and crafts.

Generally, most stores are open daily between 10 A.M. and 8 P.M. Department stores close around 7 to 9 P.M. and are usually closed one weekday each month (they alternate days, so one store may be open when another is closed).

RECREATION AND ENTERTAINMENT

Restaurants: Tokyo has an excellent choice of high-quality restaurants. In Tokyo you will be spoiled for choice of places to eat. For entertaining, top foreign executives use the grand French restaurants in the Okura and New Otani hotels or in the Ginza, while Japanese executives choose amongst the exclusive *ryotei* (dining clubs) in Akasaka. Nishi Azabu is an area with some of Tokyo's most stylish and fashionable bars and restaurants. The restaurants in Aoyama are also considered fashionable.

Cinema: There are many cinemas in Tokyo, and foreign films are usually shown with the original soundtrack and Japanese subtitles. At one or two cinemas, you can see Japanese films by internationally famous directors, such as Kurosawa, with English subtitles. Screenings are listed in the local newspapers.

Culture and entertainment: Tokyo is Japan's center for entertainment and particularly the performing arts. A sizeable proportion of productions are in English, or accessible to the Western visitor. High levels of demand, however, can sometimes make it difficult to get tickets for performances.

The National Noh Theatre opened in 1983, but each school of Noh also has its own theater in Tokyo. The Kanze, the oldest and most popular school, is based at Kanze Nohgakudo. The other main schools are Hosho, at Hosho Nohgakudo, and Kita, at Kita Nohgakudo.

The traditional arts, such as Kabuki, continue to flourish in Tokyo, and Western artists of all kinds from ballet companies and orchestras to rock stars are frequent visitors. Tokyo is the home of Kabuki and the spectacular combinations of costume, makeup, scenery, action and music make this very popular amongst visitors to Japan. There are English language programs and earphone guides.

The choice of music in Tokyo is immense. There are excellent local orchestras. There is the music of internationally acclaimed Toru Takemitsu and the synthesizer musicians Ryuichi Sakamoto and Kitaro. Several international rock bands have made their name in Japan and regularly perform in Tokyo, as do Japanese rock artists. There are also concerts of traditional Japanese music, including the popular *enka,* as well as the more familiar classical *koto* and *shamizen* music.

Sports: There are many sports clubs in the city, but they are often crowded. Private fitness clubs are also available.

Nightlife: In Tokyo there are three main areas for after-office-hours entertainment. Both Ginza and Akasaka have elite and expensive clubs, although the Akasaka district is an area of high-class entertainment of all varieties. The small, exclusive *ryotei,* where politicians and company directors dine to the accompaniment of geisha entertainment, are concentrated here, and Akasaka's cabarets, nightclubs, discos, bars, and restaurants are among the smartest in town.

At night, the Roppongi's neon-lit main street is packed with pleasure seekers. You can eat, drink, and dance in its restaurants and discos until morning. The crowds here are younger and more international than in Akasaka. Nishi Azabu also has some fashionable and stylish bars. Shinjuku is for very late night drinking. Most bars stay open until 1 or 2 A.M.; some are open later.

The *Tokyo Journal* publishes a list of events ranging from department store sales to photography exhibitions, restaurants and bars, and so on.

The *Tokyo Journal* is published monthly and is available from bookstores, restaurants, and bars. It can also be consulted online at www.tokyo.to. Additionally, *The Japan Times* and *The Daily Yomiuri* carry information on theater, films, and special events. *The Tokyo Weekender,* a free weekly journal for expatriates, is also a good guide to entertainment in Tokyo. It can be found at www.weekender.co.jp.

SOCIOCULTURAL ENVIRONMENT

Under the Constitution of Japan, freedom of speech, personal freedom, and freedom of religion are protected. However, foreigners may have difficulty adjusting to the Japanese society. The conservative nature of Japanese people can sometimes be hard for foreigners to understand. National television is broadcast in Japanese, but international cable television is widely available. Many international newspapers can be purchased in Tokyo.

DEMOGRAPHIC/WORKFORCE OVERVIEW

Population	127,463,600 (2006 estimate)
Population growth rate	0.02% (2006 estimate)
Age structure (2006 estimate)	0–14 years, 14%
	15–64 years, 66%
	65 years and over, 20%
Life expectancy at birth (2006 estimate)	
Total population:	81.2 years
Male	78.0 years
Female	84.7 years

WORKPLACE CULTURE

The normal business hours are 9 A.M. to 5 P.M., Monday through Friday. Some offices may open on Saturday from 9 A.M. until midday.

The Japanese tend to avoid loud colors and flashy styles in their dress. Following are some points to remember while working in Japan:

- Punctuality is essential.
- Never address a Japanese person by their first name.
- The usual form of greeting is a low bow; however, the handshake may be used if you are non-Japanese.

The business language in Japan is almost always Japanese.

NATURAL ENVIRONMENT

Tokyo has a four-season climate, with annual temperatures ranging from 0°C to 35°C.

All of Japan's main cities lie within a major earthquake zone, and several minor tremors usually occur every year.

Tokyo is an earthquake-prone city. The worst natural disaster ever known in Tokyo during modern times was the great earthquake of 1923, which struck the Kanto district. Severe earthquakes causing serious damage and loss of life can also occur, but are less frequent. The area is affected by typhoons as well.

HOUSING

Most of Tokyo's residential areas lie outside the city center, and many people commute long distances to work each day, although some expatriates find it more convenient to live in the city center. Some of the most prestigious areas of Tokyo are Komazawa, Sakura Shin-Machi, Yoyogi Uehara, Nakameguro, Aoyama,

Hiroo, Azabu, and Fukasawa. Setagaya and Mejiro are traditionally the places where Tokyo's elite reside.

Domestic appliances and furniture of excellent quality are widely available.

Most expatriates rent their accommodations through agencies (*fudosan*). Agencies generally charge the equivalent of one month's rent as a fee. Housing for expatriates is becoming scarce in Tokyo in certain areas such as Aoyama and Hiroo. Two- and three-bedroom properties make up 60 percent of the market, and the selection of more than four-bedroom properties is quite limited.

Accommodation costs in Japan are relatively high. The cost of accommodations varies depending on the type of housing and its location. The average monthly rental cost for a two-bedroom unfurnished apartment, in a very good area is JPY 680,000 in Tokyo.

Garages and parking spaces in Tokyo are scarce and expensive. A parking space in a prime location in Tokyo costs around JPY 40,000–50,000 per month.

FINANCIAL ISSUES INCLUDING BANKING SERVICES AND TAXES

Currency can be exchanged at major banks and hotels. Banks sometimes do not hold a wide range of foreign currencies in cash, but bank transfers in most currencies are usually available. Major credit cards are widely accepted.

Tokyo is a major international financial center, thus financial and banking services are very well organized and efficient.

The Japanese unit of currency is the Yen (JPY). Notes are in denominations of JPY 10,000, 5,000, 2,000, and 1,000. Coins are in denominations of JPY 500, 100, 50, 10, and 1.

Cash, traveler's checks, and credit cards: Japan has a strong cash economy; however, credit cards are becoming more widely accepted.

Exchange rates are listed daily in the English language newspapers and are posted at all banks and major hotels. Cash and traveler's checks can be changed at major hotels, some large shops, authorized exchange offices and at "authorized foreign exchange banks."

In Japan, traveler's checks attract a slightly better exchange rate than currency. Banks usually offer the best rates, with little variation between them, and no commission fees. A valid passport and lots of time are needed, since a simple transaction can take 30 minutes or more. All foreign exchange banks accept American dollars and most of them will take British pounds; other currencies can be a problem, even in Tokyo. Cash or traveler's checks can also be changed in main post offices, with rates close to those of the banks'. Some big department stores also have an exchange desk, although a small commission fee might be charged.

All major international credit cards are widely accepted in large establishments in the cities, but may not be so readily accepted in smaller towns and rural areas. However, some shops will only accept Japan-issued cards.

ATMs can be found at the entrance of most of the banks. They are available from 9 A.M. to 9 P.M., Monday through Friday and 9 A.M. to 5 P.M. on Saturday and Sunday. A small commission fee is charged from 5 P.M. to 9 A.M. on weekdays, from 2 P.M. to 5 P.M. on Saturday, and all day on Sunday. ATMs can be found in department stores and shopping malls, but relatively few accept non-Japanese cards. Some Citibank machines allow international access, and local ATMs operated by JCB, UC, DC, Sumitomo, or Million are the most likely to accept foreign cards. These machines usually have instructions in English and a help line with English-speaking staff.

It is safe to carry cash in Japan. A certain amount of cash is necessary in Japan, for most forms of public transportation and some restaurants and shops do not accept credit cards or traveler's checks. Personal checks are usually not for general daily use. Yen traveler's checks can be purchased at many overseas banks. Credit cards are widely used in urban areas. Shops and restaurants that accept credit cards have stickers at their entrance or signs posted elsewhere to designate which cards are accepted.

Banks: Japanese banks are usually open Monday through Friday, 9 A.M. to 3 P.M.

In order to open an account at a Japanese bank, a foreigner needs to present his/her Alien Registration Card, the document any foreigner needs to apply for when staying in Japan for more than 90 days. An *inkan* (personal stamp) or signature is also needed. If you are not fluent in Japanese, it is advisable to take a Japanese-speaker along to open an account. The banks will be able to advise you on the best account for your needs. Main branches of large banks often have English-speaking staff, but this cannot be guaranteed.

When transferring funds to Japan, it is advisable not to depend upon cashier's checks as these can sometimes take as long as a month to clear through a Japanese bank.

Taxes: The tax year is the calendar year. Taxpayers normally file a national tax return by March 15. National and local taxes are withheld by the employer on salaries and bonuses paid in Japan. No withholding is required if the employee is both employed and paid by an offshore (non-Japanese) entity.

Nonresident taxpayers are taxed only on their Japan-source income. Non-permanent resident taxpayers are taxed on Japan-source income plus that part of non-Japan-source income that is paid in or remitted to Japan. Permanent resident taxpayers are taxed on their worldwide income. Expatriate taxpayers are generally classified as non-permanent resident taxpayers for the initial 60 months of residency unless their Japan assignment period is limited to less than 12 months (if limited to less than 12 months, they are classified as nonresident). After the first 60-month period, the expatriate becomes a permanent resident tax payer.

There are no formal tax concessions for expatriates in the tax law. Expatriates, however, are typically classified as non-permanent residents and are thus taxed only on Japan sourced income, or income paid or remitted to Japan. In addition, certain tax treaties provide concessions for expatriates from certain countries.

INTERNATIONAL SCHOOLS AND EDUCATION

- AJIS Aoba-Japan International School (www.a-jis.com/eng) offers an international curriculum. The school takes children between the ages of 4 and 16 years. School bus services are provided. The school applies a uniform policy, and there is a canteen available for children who wish to eat at school. There are also Saturday lessons for certain students.

- The American School in Japan (www.asij.ac.jp) offers an American curriculum. The school takes children between the ages of 3 and 18 years. School bus services are provided at additional costs. The school applies a uniform policy, and there is a canteen available for children who wish to eat at school.

- The British School in Tokyo (www.bst.ac.jp) offers the English national curriculum. The school takes children between the ages of 3 and 13 years. No school bus services are provided. The school applies a uniform policy; there is no canteen available. School hours are 9 A.M. to 3:30 P.M.

- Lycée Franco-Japonais (French school) (www.lfjt.or.jp) offers the French national curriculum. The school takes children between the ages of 3 and 18 years. A canteen is available for children who wish to eat at school.

- Deutsche Schule Tokyo (German school) (www.dsty.jp) offers the German national curriculum. The school takes children between the ages of 3 and 18 years. A school bus service is provided at an additional cost. The school does not apply a uniform policy. School hours are 8 A.M. to 4 P.M.

- Tokyo International School (www.tokyois.com) offers the International Baccalaureate Primary Years Program and Middle Years Program. The school is located in the center of Tokyo, and transportation by school buses is available. There is no cafeteria; students bring their own lunch and eat in the classrooms. A number of after-school clubs are available, such as aikido, tennis, soccer, computers, science, pottery, and photography. The school facilities include two spacious playgrounds, a full-size gym, and an open-air swimming pool.

Malaysia: Kuala Lumpur

PERSONAL SAFETY AND SECURITY ISSUES

Strikes are unusual in Kuala Lumpur. The general crime rate is increasing; however, cases of petty theft have decreased. Malaysia has a high rate of credit card fraud.

MEDICAL ISSUES

The general standard of hospital services and medical supplies is good, but expatriates usually travel to Singapore for major treatment or to fill more esoteric prescriptions.

Health standards in Malaysia are generally good, and Kuala Lumpur has the highest concentration of private hospitals and clinics in the country. Malaysia has about 14,500 doctors and 1,900 dentists, a quarter of them serving in the capital. Many health professionals are trained overseas and can speak English. Doctors and hospitals often prefer to be paid immediately in cash, although major credit cards are also accepted.

Infectious diseases are typical of those in tropical/subtropical climates and can be prevented if normal precautions are taken. There have been cases of dengue fever reported in Malaysia; therefore, it is advisable to take precautions against insects. The outbreak of avian influenza (bird flu) is currently being closely monitored by the government.

Your embassy or consulate can usually provide a list of doctors who speak your language.

ENVIRONMENT ISSUES

Food and water are mostly safe, although care should be taken if there is an abrupt change in diet and climatic conditions from one's country of origin. Care should also be taken away from the more commercial areas. Water rationing may occur due to failure of distribution networks. The government advises that water be boiled prior to drinking.

Milk is sometimes unpasteurized and should be boiled before drinking. Nevertheless, pasteurized milk is also available. Fruit and vegetables should be thoroughly washed and peeled prior to consumption. All meat and fish should be cooked well.

Air pollution is moderate. The unrestricted burning of forests in neighboring Indonesia periodically causes atmospheric pollution to rise to unhealthy levels.

ECONOMIC OVERVIEW, 2008

GDP growth	5.3%
Inflation	6.0%
Unemployment	3.2%

INFRASTRUCTURE

Utilities and transport: Kuala Lumpur has an efficient, inexpensive public transport service, which includes buses, trains, the Light Railway System and a new Monorail system. In recent years, traffic congestion during rush hour has increased, mainly due to ongoing roadwork.

Air travel: The Kuala Lumpur International Airport is located in Sepang, over 60 minutes from the city center. It provides excellent connections to other Asian cities and a fair range to Western Europe and North America.

The airport is located 55 km (34 miles) south of Kuala Lumpur, near Putra-jaya. Airport facilities include duty-free shops, bank/currency exchange, lounges, a fitness center, a post office, a business center, several car rental companies, restaurants, and bars.

The KLIA Ekspres is a direct express rail service between the airport and KL City Air Terminal in Kuala Lumpur Central Station. The service runs every 15 minutes during peak hours and every 20 minutes during off-peak hours between 5 A.M. and midnight. The nonstop journey takes 28 minutes. Tickets can be purchased from the airport ticket counter or the ticket machines in the station. The KLIA Transit runs every 30 minutes between 5:52 and 1 A.M., and stops at Salak Tinggi, Putrajaya, and Bandar Tasik Selatan.

Express bus services are available from the airport to Kuala Lumpur. Bus services leave from the bus station located on the ground floor of Block C. The Express Coach to Kuala Lumpur runs regularly between 6:15 A.M. and 12:30 A.M. Tickets are purchased in the arrivals hall or the bus station.

The taxi service uses a coupon system from the airport to destinations within the city or its suburbs. Vouchers, at fixed prices depending on destinations, must be purchased at the start of the journey. There are four types of taxis. The fare to Kuala Lumpur Central costs MYR 67.40 (budget), MYR 92.40 (premier), and MYR 180.40 (luxury and family). The journey time is 30 to 45 minutes or longer in heavy traffic.

Car hire companies are represented at the airport. They operate 24-hour desks in the arrivals hall.

Train services: Malaysian Railways (Keretapi Tanah Malayu: KTM) operates two KTM commuter lines: the Blue Line runs from Rawang to Seremban, and the Red Line runs between Sentul and Pelabuhan Klang. Both lines pass through Kuala Lumpur Central Station. Services operate daily between 5 A.M. and midnight.

Fares depend on the distance traveled and cost between MYR 1 to MYR 8.60 for a single journey. Return tickets as well as weekly and monthly tickets are also available. There are discounts for youths, students, and senior citizens.

Light Railway Transit (LRT): There are two lines: Kelana Jaya Line (officially called PUTRA Line) comprising 24 stations between Kelana Jaya and Gombak; and Ampang and Sri Petaling Line (officially called STAR Line) comprising 25 stations, between Sri Petaling/Ampang and Sentul Timur.

Route and fare maps are displayed at all stations. One-way fares range from MYR 1 to MYR 2.80, depending on the distance traveled.

Monorail: The elevated Monorail has been fully operational since 2003. There are 11 stations on the line, which runs between Titiwangsa to Kuala Lumpur Central. The fare ranges between MYR 1.20 and MYR 2:50, depending on the distance traveled. Information can be found at www.monorail.com.my.

Buses: Bus services are provided by Cityliner, RapidKL, and Metrobus. In general, main services run between 5 A.M. and midnight. Tickets are purchased on board the bus and fares depend on the distance traveled. The two major bus stations are Pudu Raya on Jalan Pudu and the Kelang terminal on Jalan Sultan Mohammed.

Taxis: Taxis are inexpensive and air conditioned. Long-distance taxis carry four passengers, unless you commission the whole car. Taxis can be pre-booked or hailed on the street. Taxi stands are conveniently located throughout the city.

All taxis are metered, and you should ensure that the meters are used. The initial meter rate varies between MYR 2 and MYR 4, with a charge of MYR 0.40 for each subsequent kilometer. Surcharges are payable for each piece of luggage (MYR 1) and for journeys made between midnight and 6 A.M. (50 percent).

Cars: Driving around the city may be quite challenging for some. In some places, there are one-way systems and traffic can get quite heavy at times, especially during rush hours.

SHOPPING AND AVAILABILITY OF CONSUMER GOODS

A good choice of food and daily consumption items is available in Kuala Lumpur.

There is a broad selection of brands and models of cars, and delivery does not usually take long.

In Kuala Lumpur, the Karyaneka Handicraft Centre sells crafts from the different states in Malaysia (open on Monday between 9:30 A.M. and 5 P.M. and from Tuesday to Sunday between 9:30 A.M. and 6 P.M.).

Most daily requirements and luxury goods can be bought in Kuala Lumpur. There are numerous shopping centers, street markets, and specialty stores. Some street markets set up one night each week in residential areas, and others, such as the large markets on Petaling Street and Chow Kit (on upper Jalan Tunku Abdul Rahman), are open most nights. On Saturday night (between 6 and 11 P.M.), lower Jalan Tunku Abdul Rahman is closed for the market. On Sunday there is another open-air market (*pasar minggu*) in the Kampong Baru area, which offers Malay crafts and local food.

RECREATION AND ENTERTAINMENT

Restaurants: The choice of restaurants in Kuala Lumpur is very good, and most international cuisine can be found. Although restaurants and food stalls are numerous in Kuala Lumpur, there is a relative lack of purely Malay restaurants. The hotels usually offer Malay buffets and à la carte dishes. There are frequent food festivals in the city featuring regional specialties.

Many Chinese restaurants offer a variety of different styles of Chinese fare, from Cantonese to Szechuan and Nonya. Three main styles of Indian cuisine are available: south Indian, Mogul, and Indian Muslim. There are an increasing number of European restaurants, which are popular with both locals and expatriates. The major hotels also offer a range of Continental and Southeast Asian cuisine. The many food stalls (Hawkers) located throughout the city offer good food at excellent values.

Cinema: The city's cinemas often show Malay and Chinese films with English subtitles and also a fair range of international films.

Culture and entertainment: Theatres, operas, and other cultural events are primarily focused on local cultures. The Malaysian Philharmonic Orchestra is based in Kuala Lumpur.

Traditional cultural programs are presented on Fridays between 8 and 9 P.M. on Level 2 of the Putra World Trade Centre. There are also free performances every evening from 7:45 P.M. at the Central Market.

From time to time, organizations such as the British Council host touring dance and musical performances, and British theatrical groups occasionally perform at the Park Royal Hotel. The National Theatre (Jalan Tun Razak), Tel: +60 3-425-2525, is home to the National Theatre Company and the National Symphony Orchestra. Alternatively, the Malaysian Philharmonic Orchestra (MPO) plays regularly at the philharmonic hall at the Petronas Twin Towers, and occasionally, international artistes perform with the MPO. Drama, dance, and musical performances are shown on a regular basis at the Actor's Studio and the Kuala Lumpur Performing Arts Centre. There are regular international artistes, drama, dance, and musical performances held in the Genting Arena of the Stars as well.

For details of events going on in Kuala Lumpur, check the free monthly *Malaysia Now* guide, available at hotels and Malaysian Tourism Promotion Board offices. The "Time Out" pages in Thursday's *Sun* newspaper include an excellent calendar of all that is going on in town as well as restaurant reviews. The "Metro Diary" column in the daily *Star* also lists cultural events, including films, seminars, and clubs.

Sports: Sports facilities, for example tennis, squash, and swimming, are available in private clubs, which are plentiful throughout the city. There are many private clubs in Kuala Lumpur, offering swimming, tennis, cricket and rugby; they generally do not allow non-members to use their sports facilities.

In Kuala Lumpur, two popular places to jog are the trails in Lake Gardens, around the KLCC Park where the Petronas Twin Towers are located, and the Bukit Kiara area heading to Sri Hartamas.

The city's major hotels have comprehensive sports and fitness facilities, which are open to nonresident members as well. The Hilton, Shangri-La, and Pan Pacific Hotels are amongst the best known. Carcosa Seri Negara at the Lake Gardens, Hotel Nikko on Jalan Ampang, and The Regent on Jalan Bukit Bintang also have gym, massage, and sauna facilities, as well as swimming pools and tennis courts. There are quite a few fitness centers, where gym memberships are required, in and around the city center.

Nightlife: At dusk, a new facet of Malaysia reveals itself. Hotel lounges and clubs, frequently found within the larger hotels, are active at night. These clubs usually have entertainment on a nightly basis, excluding Sunday. Performances and styles range from jazz to piano/singer acts to popular music and singers.

Pubs and bars can also be found. Major hotels also have pubs, but these are more expensive than their counterparts. Music, often live, is played on a nightly basis. Pubs close around 1 to 2 A.M. Discos begin to warm up just as the pubs start closing their doors, and often stay open until 2 to 3 A.M. Some have live bands and light shows, but often require cover charges or drink minimums.

Kuala Lumpur has a busy and varied nightlife. The area called Bangsar, a short taxi ride from Kuala Lumpur city center, is an excellent place for pubs and night-clubs. This area is also extremely popular with the expatriate community.

SOCIOCULTURAL ENVIRONMENT

Malaysia has conceptual freedom of speech and movement, and free practice of religion. Nevertheless, racial, religious, and political tensions occur from time to time.

The national television is state-owned and broadcasts in a variety of languages (including English). Some international newspapers are on sale locally. Some movies have been banned in the past for their sexual content, and the executive branches sometimes exert pressure on the media.

DEMOGRAPHIC/WORKFORCE OVERVIEW

Population	24,821,300 (2007 estimate)
Population density	73 inhabitants per km^2
Age structure	0–14 years, 32%
	15–64 years, 63%
	65 years and over, 5%
Life expectancy at birth	
Total population:	72.7 years
Male	70.1 years
Female	75.6 years

WORKPLACE CULTURE

There is a hierarchical social and family structure, which encourages authoritarian styles of management and deference to people in authority. However, when it comes to decisions being made, a collective approach is often favored (amongst people of similar "rank").

When doing business in Malaysia, you should never assume, as you might in North America, that a signed contract is a final agreement. Understand that in Malaysian business culture, it is commonplace for negotiations to continue after a contract has been signed especially if it involves variations to the contract signed.

Standard business hours are 8:30 A.M. to 5:30 P.M. Monday through Friday. However, offices are sometimes open half a day on Saturday, usually in the morning. Government offices are usually open Monday through Friday, 8 A.M. to 12:45 P.M. and 2 to 4:15 P.M. and on Saturday from 8 A.M. to 12:30 P.M. (except for the first and third Saturdays of the month). On Friday there is an extended lunch break between 11:15 A.M. and 2:15 P.M. (due to Friday prayers).

Comfortable and informal clothing is the norm during the day and is recommended all year round because of the tropical climate.

NATURAL ENVIRONMENT

The climate in Malaysia is warm and humid throughout the year. There is no distinct wet or dry season. Major natural disasters are rare, but heavy rains sometimes cause localized flooding and landslides.

HOUSING

Both apartments and houses of good quality are currently available for rent in Kuala Lumpur, especially unfurnished apartments and houses. There is a variety of suitable districts to choose from. Accommodation costs can vary considerably, depending on the area and the type of housing. The average cost of a two-bedroom, unfurnished apartment in a very good area is around MYR 10,000 per month.

A few of the areas popular with expatriates are Kenny Hills, Ampang, Duta, Country Heights, Embassy Row, and Bangsar.

Accommodations are usually found through the numerous accommodation agencies or house-hunting agencies operating in Kuala Lumpur and in major cities. The landlord generally pays the accommodation agencies' commission (as a finders' fee). Accommodation agencies and details of accommodations available for rent are advertised in the local newspapers and in publications such as *The Star, Malay Mail* and the *New Straits Times*.

FINANCIAL ISSUES INCLUDING BANKING SERVICES AND TAXES

Currency: Currency may be exchanged at all banks, exchange offices, most hotels, and some restaurants. Some restrictions apply to currency transfers. All travelers must complete a Traveler's Declaration Form on arrival and departure and have it signed by a customs officer.

Malaysia has a modern banking system, and most services are available. Many foreign banks have offices in Kuala Lumpur.

The unit of currency in Malaysia is the Ringgit (MYR), which is sometimes referred to as the Malaysian dollar. 1 ringgit = 100 sen. Notes are issued in denominations of MYR 1, 2, 5, 10, 50, and 100. (MYR 500 and 1,000 notes are no longer valid.) Coins are in denominations of 1, 5, 10, 20, and 50 sen. (MYR 1 coins are no longer valid.)

Cash, traveler's checks, and credit cards: Major foreign currencies and traveler's checks can be freely exchanged in major cities and tourist resorts. There is usually a fixed handling charge for traveler's checks.

Authorized money changers generally give the best rate of exchange, followed by commercial banks. Hotels usually offer a poorer rate of exchange. In Kuala Lumpur, there are many banks in the city center and numerous money changers, particularly around Jalan Ampang, Jalan Sultan, and Jalan Bukit Bintang.

Banks: In general, banking hours are Monday through Friday, 9:30 A.M. to 4 P.M., and Saturday 9:30 A.M. to 12 noon. Hours may vary between different states, for example, in Sabah banks open at 8 A.M. and close for an hour over lunch. Banks are closed Sundays, public holidays, and the first and third Saturdays of the month.

Foreign and local currency savings, investment, and checking accounts are available. Minimum deposits are usually required but vary depending on the bank and account type. To open an account, you will need to show your passport and a letter of guarantee or formal bank credit reference.

Taxes: The tax year in Malaysia is the calendar year. Employers withhold tax on employment income under the Scheduler Tax Deduction Scheme (STD), which is similar to a pay-as-you-earn scheme (PAYE). In practice, annual returns are generally required to be filed by April 30 for income earned in the previous calendar year, and any balance of taxes due must generally be paid by April 30, together with the filing of the annual tax return.

Income tax is imposed on a territorial basis. Individuals, whether resident or nonresident in Malaysia, are taxed on income accruing in or derived from Malaysia. Nonresident individuals are exempt from tax on foreign income remitted into Malaysia. Resident individuals are also exempt from tax on foreign income remitted into Malaysia.

The income of a resident individual is subject to income tax at rates varying from 0 percent to 28 percent after personal relief, while the income of a nonresident individual is subject to income tax at 28 percent without entitlement to claim personal relief.

Nonresident individuals may claim tax exemption on their Malaysian employment income if they exercise employment in Malaysia for a period or periods of 60 days or less in a calendar year or for a period of not more than 60 days if such a period overlaps two calendar years. However, if the individuals are employed in Malaysia for more than 60 days but less than 183 days and are tax residents of a country in which Malaysia has double taxation agreement, exemption may be available provided other conditions as stipulated in the taxation agreement are met.

There are no significant tax concessions provided to expatriates in Malaysia. However, where an expatriate is employed in an approved Operational Head Quarters status or Regional Office status in Malaysia there are tax concessions.

INTERNATIONAL SCHOOLS AND EDUCATION

A number of international schools are available in Kuala Lumpur, each offering all levels of education. They include international, English, French, Japanese, and German schools.

- The International School of Kuala Lumpur (www.iskl.edu.my) is based on the U.S. curriculum. Exams offered include Advanced Placement, International Baccalaureate Diploma, and SAT. The school takes children between the ages of 3 and 18 years. School bus services are provided. The school applies a uniform policy, and there is a canteen available for children who wish to eat at school. Hours are for kindergarten, 8 A.M. to midday; primary, 8 A.M. to 2:35 P.M.; and secondary, 8 A.M. to 2:45 P.M.
- Garden International School (www.gardenschool.edu.my) is based on the UK curriculum. Exams offered are GCSE, GCE A Level, and IGCSE. The school takes children between the ages of 3 and 18 years. School bus services are provided. The school applies a uniform policy except for sixth form (the final two years of secondary school). There is a canteen available for children who wish to eat at school. Hours are 7:45 A.M. to 1:45 P.M.
- Lycée Français de Kuala Lumpur (www.lfkl.edu.my) is based on the French curriculum. Exams offered include French Baccalaureate L, S, ES, and Brevet des Collèges. The school takes children between the ages of 3 and 17 years. School bus services are provided. The school does not apply a uniform policy. There is a canteen available for children who wish to eat at school. Children have to be fluent in French to be admitted. Hours are primary, 8 A.M. to 2:30 P.M. and secondary, 8 A.M. to 4 P.M.
- Deutsche Schule Kuala Lumpur (www.dskl.edu.my) is based on the German curriculum. The German national exams are offered. School bus services are provided. The school does not apply a uniform policy. There is a canteen available for children who wish to eat at school. Children have to be fluent in German to be admitted. Hours are primary, 8 A.M. to 1:20 P.M. and secondary, 8:30 A.M. to 3:30 P.M.
- Japanese School of Kuala Lumpur (www.jskl.edu.my) is based on the Japanese curriculum. Japanese exams are offered. School bus services are provided. The school does not apply a uniform policy, and there is no canteen available. Hours are 8:30 A.M. to 4:20 P.M.

New Zealand: Auckland

PERSONAL SAFETY AND SECURITY ISSUES

New Zealand's relations with other countries is good. Demonstrations and strikes are unusual. Auckland is generally a safe place, but violent crimes occur occasionally, and common sense precautions should be taken when venturing out at night.

It is recommended that items of value should be kept in a safety deposit box. Do not leave valuable items on view inside a car, but lock them in the boot/trunk instead. Pickpocketing and purse snatching do occur, especially around public parks and tourist areas. Do not display jewelry or large amounts of cash in public.

Foreign nationals must hold a valid passport and a visa before entering New Zealand. Work permits are reasonably easy to obtain. Crime in New Zealand is relatively low, although there has been an increase in property crime over the past few years (mostly vehicle theft). The New Zealand Police Service Web site address is www.police.govt.nz.

MEDICAL ISSUES

Both public and private health services are of a high standard. Medical treatment is excellent, and almost all treatment can be done in the city, although there is a waiting list for public hospital treatment. Medicines are widely available, but some new and high-priced medicines might be difficult to obtain, as they are not subsidized. Hospitals in Auckland include the Auckland City Hospital (www.adhb.govt.nz /ACH/ach.htm); Starship Children's Hospital (www.starship.org.nz); Mercy Ascot Hospital (private) (www.mercyascot.com); and National Women's Hospital.

ENVIRONMENT ISSUES

Food and water are safe to eat and drink. Air pollution is not a major concern in Auckland. Sand flies, ants, and cockroaches are common in New Zealand but are considered a nuisance rather than a health hazard.

ECONOMIC OVERVIEW, 2008

GDP growth	0.7%
Inflation	4.2%
Unemployment	4.0%

INFRASTRUCTURE

Utilities and traffic: The telephone system in New Zealand is very good. The mail service is efficient and reliable, as are the utilities. The electricity supply is efficient and interruptions are rare. Public transport is efficient and comprehensive. Traffic is often congested during rush hours.

Air travel: The airport is situated 22 km from the city center and offers a good choice of flights to Western Europe, North America, and to other destinations in Asia. The Auckland International Airport (AKL) (www.auckland-airport.co.nz)

is located 21 km (14 miles) south of central Auckland, in the suburb of Mangere. It is the main international gateway to New Zealand. Facilities at the airport include a bank, tourist information center, bureau de change, snack bars, newsstand, duty-free shops, a restaurant, courtesy telephones, Internet access terminals, left luggage, and car rentals. Rental car offices are all located in the ground floor arrivals area. A few are Avis (www.avis.co.nz), Budget (www.budget.co.nz), and Hertz (www.hertz.com). The airport is well connected to the public transport network. It has an airbus service that connects all three terminals with the Downtown Airline Terminal. Buses run every 20–30 minutes every day from 6:20 A.M. to 10 P.M.

Bus: The main bus provider in Auckland is Stagecoach Auckland. The service runs on weekdays from 6 A.M. to 10 P.M. (11:30 P.M. on Fridays) and weekends from 7 A.M. to 11 P.M. The fares operate on a zone system. The basic fare is NZD 1.50 for travel in the city center and is an additional NZD 1.50 for each addition zone traveled. Day passes are available for NZD 13 and are valid for use on all buses, trains, and harbor ferries. A ticket for the city center circular route bus is a flat fee of NZD 1.50. Further details on fares and networks are available in the *Auckland Busabout Guide.* This guide can be found at news agencies and in visitor centers and is free of charge.

Metro: This service serves mainly commuters as it links the residential suburbs with the city center. Connex Auckland (www.connexauckland.co.nz) has three main lines; fares are charged according to the length of the journey. A short fare is NZD 1.10; the fare from the city center to the end of the line is up to NZD 8. Day passes are available (valid after 9 A.M. only) as well as multiple-trip tickets and monthly passes. All tickets and passes can be bought on the train although by purchasing them at the Britomart, you will normally receive a discount. Purchasing tickets on the train normally requires that you have the exact change.

Taxi: There are plenty of taxis available in Auckland. Either you can hail a taxi on the street or book one in advance by telephone. All taxis should be metered. The initial meter charge approximately is for one hour. Tickets cost NZD 15 for one way and should be purchased directly from the driver. Private shuttle services into the city are also available at the airport. A taxi to the city center will cost NZD 45. Principal Auckland taxi companies are as follows: Auckland Co-op (www.cooptaxi.co.nz), Alert (www.alerttaxis.co.nz), and Corporate (www.corporatecabs.co.nz).

SHOPPING AND AVAILABILITY OF CONSUMER GOODS

Good-quality food, including fresh fruit and vegetables, is widely available. Most daily consumer goods are also available in Auckland. A wide range of alcoholic beverages can be obtained, although retail liquor outlets may not operate on Sundays and some residential suburbs are self-elected "dry" areas, which do not allow retail liquor outlets and pubs/bar to operate. All models of car are readily available.

It is possible to buy almost everything that you can imagine in New Zealand. Shops open normally from 9 A.M. to 5 P.M., Monday through Saturday; however, many stores are also open on Sunday mornings from 10 A.M. to 1 P.M. In larger cities and in various resorts, the opening hours are much longer.

The Thursday *Auckland Tourist Times* is a free newspaper with the latest information on tours, exhibitions, and shopping and is available from hotels and visitor centers. The main shopping precincts for clothes and shoes are Queen Street and Newmarket. Ponsonby is known in the Auckland area for its design stores and fashion boutiques. Popular flea markets include the atmospheric Victoria Park Market and Otara, which is supposedly the largest Polynesian market in the world.

Shopping malls include St. Lukes Shopping Centre, which is probably the principal shopping center in Auckland which houses over 100 specialty shops, including fashion and clothing boutiques, shoes, sports gear, pharmacies, food, books, gifts, housewares, and photography shops, plus department stores and supermarkets. The Queens Arcade has a delightful collection of exclusive boutiques in a quaint wrought-iron decorated arcade. Manakau Shopping Centre has over 100 different shops, spread over north, south, and west wings. There is a department store, supermarket, and numerous brasseries/snack bars. Dressmart was the first of the factory outlet malls, with boutiques selling seconds and reduced designer and label goods. Shore City Galleria has made a name for itself locally in fashion retail, with well-known brands and designer names. There is a Farmers department store and many eateries as well as household and electrical goods' shops.

Department stores include Smith and Caughey Ltd. (www.smithandcaugheys .co.nz), which is the oldest established department store in Auckland and quite possibly the most prestigious. DFS Galleria Custom House is a renaissance style store that has some of the best international products in the world, particularly interesting to the duty-free shopper. In all, there are shops over four floors for those who love brand names such as Louis Vuitton, Gucci, Christian Dior, Prada, Hermes, Oroton, Adidas, Burberry, and Tiffany. Rendells Ltd. has inexpensive goods, particularly clothing. Briscoes is a departmental store specializing in soft furnishings. The Warehouse Ltd. is a warehouse full of bargains from electrical goods to household items.

Supermarkets include the Midtown Food Centre, Newmart, Food Town Supermarkets, and Star Mart (with numerous branches).

RECREATION AND ENTERTAINMENT

Auckland has an excellent range of restaurants serving good-quality food. There is also a good choice of entertainment with operas, cinemas, and theaters.

Restaurants: Auckland is renowned for its sport and leisure activities. A number of restaurants are located here. Andiamo has a highly sophisticated ambience, décor, and menu. Bolliwood has high-end Indian cuisine, very popular with business people. Fusion has a great atmosphere in this light and airy bistro/restaurant. You can enjoy the fresh air outside or stay in the cosy interior by the fire. It is a good family-friendly restaurant. Cin Cin is one of the oldest established restaurants in the city. Cuisine is Italian and Asian influenced. Caluzzi is a restaurant with a difference. Alongside the excellent wide ranging menu is a cabaret and show as kitsch as it is popular.

Culture and entertainment: A number of theaters and concert halls are found in Auckland:

- the Edge Theatre (www.the-edge.co.nz),
- the Silo Theatre (www.silotheatre.co.nz),
- the Auckland Theatre Company (www.atc.co.nz),
- Maidment Theatre (www.maidment.auckland.ac.nz), and
- Howick Little Theatre (www.hlt.org.nz).

Museums and galleries include Auckland War Memorial Museum (www.aucklandmuseum.com), which has a stunning setting and has many interactive displays for the family. Particularly popular is the Maori cultural performance (which is about 20 minutes long) that involves songs, dancing, games, display of weapons, and haka. Auckland Art Gallery Toio Tamaki has free guided tours every day at 2 P.M. The Auckland Art Gallery contains the largest collection of both domestic and international art in the country. New Zealand National Maritime Museum has maritime history displays as well as restored ships in the harbor. Anna Bibby Gallery has free admission. Avant garde artists are particularly represented at this independently run dealer-gallery. Museum of Transport and Technology (www.motat.org.nz) is home to one of only three working beam engines in the world. It provides a variety of vintage vehicles as well as tram rides around the museum. Cinemas located here include Rialto Cinemas, Academy Cinema, Capitol Cinemas, The Bridgeway, and Sky Village Cinemas.

Entertainment for children can be found at the Howick Historical Village, which is a living museum, where people and property are exactly as they were during Auckland's colonial days. Auckland Zoo is New Zealand's largest collection of native and non-native species. It has a café and picnic areas. The Sky Tower is the tallest building and has a restaurant and snack bar at the top. Sheep World shows involve a sheepdog rounding up sheep—one of the most popular features of this children's park. It also includes a small animal farm and an adventure playground. Picnics and camping are permitted. Waitomo Caves has caves where you can float through on boats and see millions of glowworms suspended from the ceilings.

Bars such as Spy is the epitome of cool, and the clientele are well-dressed, successful professionals. Khuja Lounge has a relaxed laid-back music lounge, playing jazz and soul. The Classic Comedy and Bar is a very popular bar with stand-up comedians. Shakespeare Tavern and Brewery is a very typical English style pub. Beers are brewed on the premises and are very popular in this lively and casual pub. Lime provides a very comprehensive selection of drinks; this casual bar is as unpretentious as it is friendly. Nightclubs include Roots Bar Café and Cabaret and The Powerstation.

Casinos: SkyCity Auckland is a mega complex, boasting two casinos. It admits people aged 20 and over only. For further details, visit www.skycityauckland .co.nz.

Sports facilities: There are a great number of golf clubs around Auckland to suit all preferences and abilities. For a full listing, visit www.nzga.co.nz/SITE _Default/play_golf/Clubs/auckland.asp. Clubs include the Auckland Golf Club, Whitford Park, the Grange, Formosa Auckland Country Club, Titirangi, and Gulf Harbour Country Club.

For a complete listing of tennis courts and clubs in the Auckland area, see www.aucklandtennis.co.nz. Clbus include Blockhouse Bay Tennis Club, Campbell Park Tennis Club, Mission Bay Tennis, Royal Oak, and Orakei. Olympic Pool, Parnell Baths and Lagoon Leisure, Cameron Pool, Point Erin Fun Pool and Fitness are swimming pools in the area. A number of fitness centers are also located here.

SOCIOCULTURAL ENVIRONMENT

In New Zealand, there are no limitations on freedom of movement and on the free practice of religion. New Zealand has censorship regulations for television and other media governing the broadcasting or publishing material of an offensive nature (that is, explicit sexual content or excessive violence). International cable television is available. Most international newspapers are available in Auckland.

DEMOGRAPHIC/WORKFORCE OVERVIEW

Population	4,035,500 (2005 estimate)
Population growth rate	1.02% (2005 estimate)
Age structure	0–14 years, 21.4%
	15–64 years, 66.9%
	65 years and over, 11.7%
Life expectancy at birth	
Total population:	78.7 years
Male	75.7 years
Female	81.8 years

WORKPLACE CULTURE

When conducting high-level business in New Zealand, you should dress conservatively and work towards a formal look. Women should wear a suit, dress, or skirt and blouse with a jacket. The wardrobe should incorporate classic styles and neutral colors (navy and grey). Men should wear dark suits with a conservative tie and a white shirt to maintain the level of formality.

Talking is minimal while you are eating a meal. Dinners are reserved for social interactions, and business matters are not discussed. Lunch is used for business conversations. New Zealanders are generally more reserved than in other cultures as is the case in business. It is important to earn the trust and respect of your New Zealand counterpart before business deals can be achieved. New Zealanders have an inherent dislike for those they see as "tall poppies" (overtly ambitious and ostentatiously clever). When meeting or saying goodbye to someone, use a firm handshake and make good eye contact. Show a genuine interest in meeting or seeing the person. Men generally wait for a woman to be the first to extend her hand for a handshake. The Maori greeting, of rubbing noses, will frequently be witnessed in New Zealand.

When you are meeting someone, it is best to say "How do you do?" A more relaxed greeting, such as "Hello," is reserved for the meetings after you've had the opportunity to get to know the person. You should always address a person using his or her title (that is, Sir or Dr.), or Mr., Mrs., Miss plus the full name. Do not use first names unless the other person has invited you to do so. You should expect to be addressed in an equal manner by others. Your demeanor, particularly when meeting someone for the first time should be reserved and formal, but warm. Punctuality is part of the culture.

You should try at all times to maintain a reserved and polite behavior. Cover your mouth if you must yawn, and do not chew gum or toothpicks in public. Do not confuse or compare New Zealand with Australia, as they are two distinct countries. Politics, sports, and weather are good conversational topics. To be a good conversationalist, stay current and informed on critical topics. Being overly demonstrative with another man is taboo for men in New Zealand. The stereotypical greeting of "G'day, mate" is more likely to result in offense than anything else when spoken by a non-native.

NATURAL ENVIRONMENT

Auckland has a temperate climate with mild winters and hot summers. No natural disasters occur, although tropical cyclones and earthquakes are a risk.

HOUSING

There are many attractive rental properties available in Auckland, including both apartments and houses. The more prestigious districts are Mission Bay,

Paraitai Drive, Herne Bay, and Remuera. Domestic appliances and furniture are widely available. Demand is quite high, and potential tenants should make a quick decision when viewing property. Wednesday and Saturday's newspaper editions are best for accommodation advertisements. Should you encounter any difficulties as a tenant or have a general question, visit www.tenancy.govt.nz. Foreign nationals generally have the right to purchase property in New Zealand, depending on several factors, including residence status. Real estate agencies include Barfoot & Thompson and L. J. Hooker Papakura.

Most rental properties are unfurnished, apart from an oven, a laundry facility, curtains, and carpet. The landlord does not provide a heater in the property, so be prepared to buy your own. Some parts of New Zealand are cold and do not have much sunlight; as a result, these properties are usually damp.

A tenancy agreement form should be signed by both the landlord and tenant. There are three main types of tenancy, and you should be sure you are signing the correct one for your requirements:

- Periodic tenancy: Any tenancy that is not for a fixed time and continues until the landlord or the tenant ends it by giving notice. This is the most common form of tenancy.
- Fixed-term tenancy: These finish on a date recorded in the agreement, and neither the landlord nor the tenant can end the tenancy earlier.
- Fixed-term tenancies not fully covered by the Residential Tenancies Act of 1986: These include tenancies of less than 120 days and tenancies of five years or more, in which the Tenancy Agreement states that the Residential Tenancies Act does not apply.

A refundable deposit of two to four weeks is normally required. The payment of rent is paid in advance, usually bimonthly. One week's rent plus GST (goods and services tax) are paid to the real estate agent once the rental contract is completed. Garages and parking spaces are usually included in the rental cost of properties.

Houses and apartments in districts in Auckland—good areas: Mt. Eden, Herne Bay; very good areas: Epsom, Remuera; best areas: Mission Bay and Waterfront.

Furnished houses and apartments are very rare and are usually available only for short-term rentals. There is a good choice of unfurnished accommodations. In Auckland, three-bedroom furnished apartments range from NZD 2100 to NZD 4200 according to their location. Furnished three-bedroom houses vary from NZD 2400 in a good area to NZD 4300 in best areas.

FINANCIAL ISSUES INCLUDING BANKING SERVICES AND TAXES

Currency: The unit of currency in New Zealand is the New Zealand Dollar (NZD). 1 NZD = 100 cents. Notes are in denominations of NZD 100, 50,

20, 10, and 5. Coins are in denominations of NZD 2 and 1 and 50, 20, and 10 cents. The New Zealand Dollar was introduced in 1967 to replace the New Zealand Pound, when the country decimalized its currency. The Reserve Bank is the sole supplier of New Zealand bank notes and coins.

Nearly all currencies, including traveler's checks, may be exchanged at all New Zealand banks, bureaux de change, and most hotels. Banks may impose a fee for exchanging currency. Banks generally offer better exchange rates on traveler's checks. Credit cards are widely used. Payment by major credit cards, including MasterCard, Visa, American Express, Diners Club, JCB, and Bankcard (Australia) are widely accepted throughout New Zealand. International credit cards may be used to obtain cash from automatic teller machines for which a PIN number is required. EFTPOS cash cards may also be used in the ATMs provided the international symbols displayed on the back of the card match those displayed on the ATM. There are over 1,500 ATMs throughout New Zealand.

Banks: New Zealand banks are connected to the Cirrus network. Banking hours are 9 A.M. to 4:30 P.M., Monday through Friday and are closed on public holidays. The Reserve Bank of New Zealand provides consumers with a list of all banks registered in New Zealand and their credit ratings.

Some banks specify that you will be living in New Zealand for at least six months in order to open a local bank account. It is often possible for you to set up your bank account in advance of arriving in New Zealand, provided you fulfil the necessary requirements. Banking services are modern and efficient. Account holders have access to account information and management online, telephone banking, direct debit facilities, and are entitled to check and credit cards. A valid passport, proof of work and residence in New Zealand, and a guarantee of monthly income into the account is normally required in order to open an account. Some banks do offer foreign accounts, although it is advisable to seek further information from the bank regarding these accounts.

Taxes: Individuals are subject to income tax on worldwide income while resident in New Zealand. All worldwide income of a resident in New Zealand is taken into account in determining their effective rates of tax. A nonresident is only taxable on New Zealand-source income. Any individual who is present in New Zealand for more than 183 days in aggregate over a 12-month period is deemed to be a resident. However, where a person is absent for a period or periods exceeding 325 days in any 12-month period, nonresident status may be claimed, provided that person has no permanent place of abode in New Zealand. The tax year runs from April 1 to March 31.

No special exclusions from taxable income are available to expatriates residing in New Zealand apart from certain relocation allowances. A tax credit, not exceeding the equivalent of the New Zealand tax, is allowed for foreign tax which is paid on any foreign source income where such tax is similar in nature to New Zealand income tax. New Zealand as of 2005 has agreements for the avoidance of double taxation concluded with most of New Zealand's major trading partners.

INTERNATIONAL SCHOOLS AND EDUCATION

There are international and French schools in Auckland. In addition, a good choice of private schools offering all levels of education is available.

- Saint Kentigern School (www.saintkentigern.com) is an international school, where pupils follow the New Zealand NCEA curriculum. The school offers boarding facilities for boys, available at the college hostel, Bruce House, either as full-term boarding or weekly boarding. An extensive range of sports are available at the college, from cricket to fencing, squash and yachting. The school has a uniform policy.
- Auckland Japanese Supplementary School (http://homepage.ihug.co.nz/~ajss) provides Japanese curriculum.
- Auckland International College (www.aic.ac.nz) provides a preparation program for IB Diploma in the first year, followed by the two-year IB Diploma. The college is a three-year senior secondary school for international and New Zealand students who wish to gain entry to universities in New Zealand as well as in other countries. This school accepts students from the age of 15 to 19 years. Boarding facilities are also available here.

Philippines: Manila

PERSONAL SAFETY AND SECURITY ISSUES

Strikes and demonstrations are common, and crime is a serious concern in Manila. There has been an increase in kidnappings. Common sense precautions should always be observed. In 2007, an explosion occurred at a shopping center in Makati City in Manila.

You should always remain vigilant with regard to personal safety and possessions. Pickpocketing and credit card fraud are common. As in many major cities, drug-related crimes, robbery, and assault are prevalent in Manila. It is better to avoid wearing large amounts of jewelry and carrying large amounts of money around.

Do not walk alone in dark or unpopulated areas. When driving, the car doors should be kept locked. Children should never be left unsupervised. House alarms are highly recommended, and some expatriate families hire security guards.

Many rural areas are not safe to travel to, because of risks of kidnapping and general harm. Therefore, before visiting any unknown areas, it would be wise to check with the tourist information services or the Philippine embassy.

MEDICAL ISSUES

There are both public and private hospitals throughout the Philippines, and the standard of medical care is generally good in larger cities; however, in rural areas healthcare facilities are limited. Information is available at the Department of Health Web site, www.doh.gov.ph.

There are 33 hospitals in the city of Manila; 23 are licensed private hospitals and 6 are national government hospitals. There are 46 health centers in the city.

Medical facilities have improved considerably, and major hospitals now offer much better services. Some individuals, however, still travel to Hong Kong or Singapore for major medical treatment. Most medical supplies, including a wide range of prescription medicines, are readily available and easily accessible.

All visitors are advised to be inoculated against cholera, typhoid, and polio. Precautions against malaria and hepatitis are also recommended. In 2007, an alert of dengue fever was issued for the country. The government has made efforts to monitor and control avian influenza (bird flu).

ENVIRONMENT ISSUES

Waste management is a problem in certain areas, and the sewage system is not completely effective. Tap water is safe to drink but can taste of chlorine, which may take foreigners some time to become accustomed to. Bottled water is widely available and is recommended for drinking.

Water used for drinking, brushing teeth, or making ice should always be boiled or sterilized first. Unpasteurized milk should also be boiled; however, it is advisable to use powdered or tinned milk that is reconstituted with pure water. Try to avoid any dairy products that are likely to have been made from unsterilized or unboiled milk. Meat and fish should be thoroughly cooked and served hot. Vegetables should be washed and well cooked, and fruit should always be washed and peeled.

Air pollution is a severe concern in Manila.

ECONOMIC OVERVIEW, 2008

GDP growth	4.4%
Inflation	9.6%
Unemployment	7.6%

INFRASTRUCTURE

Utilities and traffic: Manila's public transport is fairly comprehensive, but it is often crowded and uncomfortable. Taxis are widely available. Traffic is still a major concern in Manila, although construction of new roads has helped to slightly curb this problem.

Air travel: The airport (Ninoy Aquino International Airport) is situated 7 km from the city center, and has a good selection of flights to cities in Asia, plus some major destinations in Western Europe and North America. Other journeys require a connecting flight. Airport facilities include banks, bureaux de change, a post office, shops, restaurants, bars, a pharmacy, and car rental desks.

Manila's domestic terminal is only five minutes from the international terminals. Telephone information service is available (Tel: +63 2-877-1109). Flying is the preferred method of transport between the islands.

It takes around 30 minutes to travel into the city center, although in the rush hour it can take over one hour. Hotel transport is one of the easiest ways to get into the city. Taxis are available 24 hours. It is highly recommended that you use only taxis that have Department of Tourism accreditation (for personal safety reasons and for cost). Taxis can be booked at the taxi desk in the arrivals hall. An airport shuttle bus operates regularly to Metro Manila between 5 A.M. and 11 P.M.

Bus: Bus services are available between major towns, are usually inexpensive and fairly reliable, and mostly run by various private companies. There are 20 major bus companies covering the entire archipelago. Services between major destinations are often on an hourly basis. Bus companies serving major routes have coaches with or without air conditioning.

Buses are not allowed into the streets in the city center, but do service the surrounding areas. Buses run from 5:30 A.M. to 11:30 P.M. daily, and fares differ depending on the destination and if air conditioning is provided. In general, the minimum fare on an air-conditioned bus is PHP 9 (plus PHP 2 per kilometer) and on a regular bus is PHP 5.50 (plus PHP 1 per kilometer). No unified bus passes or ticket schemes are available.

Rail: The only railway is on Luzon Island, from Legaspi to San Fernando. Rail services are operated by the Philippine National Railways (PNR; Tel: +63 2-743-9644). Services on this network include three trains daily to and from Manila, and one overnight train with sleeper facilities and a dining car. There are air-conditioned carriages on all trains. Travel by air or even by bus is quicker and more reliable.

Sea and river travel: Inter-island ferries with first-class, air-conditioned accommodations connect the major island ports. Information can be obtained from the local ship lines. The hub of the shipping services is Cebu.

In Manila, the port area is called Pier Port and it is divided into the North and South Harbours. Both international and domestic services are available. Information is available from the Philippines Port Authority (Tel: +63 2-527-4856).

Metro: The elevated Light Rail Transit (LRT; www.lrta.gov.ph) operates two lines: LRT 1 (yellow line) and MRT 2 (purple line). LRT 1 is 15 km long and provides a fast and efficient service from Baclaran in the South to Kalookan City in the North. Eighteen stations are spread at almost every kilometer from the main terminals. The service operates daily from 5 A.M. to 10 P.M. MRT 2 provides a service from the Manila in the West to Pasig in the East, passing through Quezon City. There are 10 stations along the line, and services operate Monday through Friday, 5 A.M. to 10 P.M. and on weekdays from 6 A.M. to 8 P.M.

The MRT 3 line, commonly referred to as Metrostar, runs along the EDSA ring road, connecting North Avenue in Quezon City to Taft Avenue in Pasay City, passing through the Makati financial district.

Taxis: Taxis are a convenient method of travel and are normally inexpensive. Always ensure that you use a taxi with a meter installed and that the driver uses it. Initial meter charges are normally PHP 30, and the rate per kilometer thereafter is PHP 12.5. It is always advisable to have small denominations of money, as often drivers have no change. Taxis can be hailed in the street or called for in advance.

Some hotels run their own fleets of taxis and generally charge 50 percent above the normal taxi rates.

Jeepneys: The other popular means of travel are the Jeepneys (brightly colored jeeps), which are very cheap and widely available in Manila and run 24 hours a day. The destination is normally posted on the front of the vehicle, and they can be hailed from anywhere in the street. Costs are generally around PHP 5.50–10 per trip.

SHOPPING AND AVAILABILITY OF CONSUMER GOODS

Manila is the commercial capital of the Philippines and most goods are readily available here. Street markets are found in the older parts of central Manila, and shopping centers are located in the newer areas of the city.

The largest market district is north of Binondo, where everything from fresh produce to handicrafts is available. Ready-to-wear clothing can be found at the street stalls on Roxas Boulevard near Baclaran Church. The San Andres Market, renowned for its fruits, is located in the Tourist Belt.

A wide selection of good-quality meat and fish, including imported items, is always available. Fruit and vegetables are also easily obtainable. A variety of alcoholic drinks are available, and there are no restrictions on purchasing and consumption.

European and American-made cars have managed to penetrate the automobile market, which was previously dominated by Japanese manufacturers. Importing cars can be time consuming.

In Manila, most shops are open six days a week. Opening hours vary from 9 or 10 A.M. to 7–10 P.M. Most shopping centers, supermarkets, and large department stores are open from 9 or 10 A.M. to 7 or 9 P.M. daily.

RECREATION AND ENTERTAINMENT

Restaurants: Most traditional and regional specialties of Philippine cuisine can be found in Manila, as well as an array of different international cuisines. Manila's finest restaurants are often inexpensive and casual by Western standards. Some of the best snack foods can be bought from the street stalls.

Some of the most popular restaurants in Manila can be found in the major hotels. These are particularly popular for business entertaining or reciprocating hospitality.

Popular restaurant chains have opened in and around Manila, offering a wide choice of cuisine.

Cinemas: There is an excellent choice of cinemas (many located in shopping malls and major hotels), and top international movies are screened, although they may not appear until a few weeks after release.

Every December there is a two-week film festival held in Manila, during which the cinemas of Metro Manila show only Philippine films.

Culture and entertainment: International cultural events are becoming more frequent, and the standard of local productions has improved.

Manila has a diverse choice of entertainment to suit all tastes. Current and forthcoming cultural events and other entertainment are listed in the daily papers. The *Manila Bulletin City Guide* is a good source, as are the free magazines *What's On in Manila* and *Expat Weekly* (available in major hotels and tourist information centers).

The Cultural Center of the Philippines is the venue for a wide variety of entertainment events including music, dance, and theater productions (www.cultural center.gov.ph; located at the CCP Building, Roxas Boulevard, Pasay City; Tel: +63 2-832-1125). Both local and international artists appear here. The Center has a resident dance company, Ballet Philippines (Tel: +63 2-551-1003), and also provides a base for the Bayanihan National Folk Dance Company (Tel: +63 2-832-3688). It also houses the Philippine Philharmonic Orchestra (Tel: +63 2-832-1125) and the Manila Chamber Orchestra. The Center publishes a monthly listing of forthcoming events, which is available in the lobby.

During the summer season, often free concerts are offered on Fridays at 6 P.M. in Paco Park, on Saturdays at 6 P.M. at the Puerto Real in Intramuros, and on Sundays at 5 P.M. in Rizal Park.

Sports: Good-quality sport and leisure activities are available through private clubs. Golf is very popular within the local business and expatriate community. Most golf clubs require membership, but some courses are also available in Manila for non-members. Tennis is a popular sport, and there are numerous private and public tennis courts in Manila. All the major hotels have swimming pools, which are open to nonresidents upon payment of a fee. Many sports centers also have swimming pools. The gymnasiums at the Philippine Plaza Hotel and the Manila Hotel are open to nonresidents. Other major hotels also have well-equipped gyms and offer membership programs.

Nightlife: There is a vast array of nightlife in Manila to suit most entertainment tastes. There are many bars offering shows and the company of a "hostess" across Manila and Quezon City. However, there is a more cultured side to the city's nightlife, with music lounges located throughout Makati and several places in Quezon City.

SOCIOCULTURAL ENVIRONMENT

The law guarantees freedom of speech and religion, and opposition to the government can generally be vocal. However, when a week-long state of emergency was declared in 2006 following a failed coup attempt, freedom of the press was temporarily suppressed.

International newspapers and publications are readily available. Cable television services, with more than 60 channels, are generally easy to obtain.

DEMOGRAPHIC/WORKFORCE OVERVIEW

Population	89,468,677 (2006 estimate)
Population density	300.06 inhabitants per km^2
Age structure	0–14 years, 35%
	15–64 years, 61%
	65 years and over, 4.1%
Life expectancy at birth	
Total population:	70.21 years
Male	67.32 years
Female	73.24 years

WORKPLACE CULTURE

To a large extent, Filipinos have adopted Western (particularly American) business and financial management methods and styles.

Business and office hours are generally 8 or 9 A.M. to 5 or 6 P.M., Monday through Friday. Some private companies are open on Saturdays from 9 A.M. to 12 P.M., but it is unusual to arrange business meetings on a Saturday. Most government offices are open Monday through Friday between 9 A.M. and 5 P.M. and close for lunch from 12 to 1 P.M.

Business wear tends to be formal and after-office wear is generally designer casual. Businessmen should wear lightweight business suits with a shirt and tie. Businesswomen should wear smart dresses or suits.

NATURAL ENVIRONMENT

The Philippines has a tropical climate tempered by constant sea breezes. In an average year, it is fairly common for Manila to experience one or more typhoons between July and October. These may cause disruption and damage to property, and sometimes loss of life. Earthquakes and volcanic eruptions sometimes occur elsewhere in the Philippines, but these rarely have any impact on Manila.

HOUSING

The choice of housing is varied and ranges from luxury apartments in high-rise buildings to large single-family homes in self-sufficient, gated communities or "villages"—self-contained gated communities that are usually administered by the village association.

Both houses and apartments are available for rent in Manila. Districts popular with expatriates include Ayala Alabang, Fort Bonifacio, Pacific Plaza Towers, Essensa, One Roxas, Ortigas, San Lorenzo, Bel-Air, and Makati City.

Several large retail establishments carry a wide range of good-quality appliances that are always available. Locally made furniture is also in good supply. In terms of household maintenance and repair, it sometimes takes time to obtain a quality service.

Rented accommodations are generally advertised in the local newspapers. The easiest method of finding suitable accommodations is through real estate agencies. Most agencies usually charge one month's rent as a commission fee.

FINANCIAL ISSUES INCLUDING BANKING SERVICES AND TAXES

The import and export of local currency is limited, whereas the import and export of foreign currency is unlimited. Currency may be exchanged at all banks and in most hotels.

Banking services in Manila are adequate, particularly since the opening of more foreign banks. Major credit cards are widely accepted in Manila.

The unit of currency of the Philippines is the Philippine Peso (PHP). 1 PHP = 100 centavos. Notes are in denominations of PHP 1,000, 500, 100, 50, 20, 10, and 5. Coins are in denominations of PHP 5, 2, and 1, and 25, 10, and 5 centavos.

Cash, traveler's checks, and credit cards: Foreign currency and traveler's checks can be exchanged at hotels, most department stores, banks, and at shops accredited by the Central Bank of the Philippines. Varying rates of exchange may be offered, so it is advisable to shop around for the best deal. The official exchange rate is listed daily in Manila newspapers. Commission charges are also payable and are sometimes very high when changing traveler's checks.

International credit cards (American Express, Visa, MasterCard) are accepted in hotels, restaurants, and shops; however, sometimes a surcharge is added when payment is made by a credit card. There are many local credit card companies and banks offering credit card services.

Banks: There are a wide variety of banks to choose from in the Philippines, each offering competitive rates and services.

To open a bank account, you will need to provide proof of identification, for example, a passport, current driver's license, or other legal documentation. For some banks you may need to provide your Tax Identification Number or Social Security number. Most bank accounts can be opened free of charge. The bank will give advice on which is the best account for your needs, as a wide variety of accounts are available.

Taxes: The tax year is the calendar year. Income tax is withheld from salaries by the employer source. This is considered a creditable withholding tax. Any additional tax due must be paid at the time of filing the annual return (on or before April 15 of the following year). Married couples are generally required to file joint returns; however, they are required to compute their income tax liabilities separately.

The Philippines taxes its citizens and residents on their worldwide income. A nonresident citizen is taxed only on income from sources within the Philippines. A nonresident alien individual who comes to the Philippines and remains there for more than 180 days during any calendar year will be deemed a nonresident alien doing business in the Philippines. If the aggregate stay in the Philippines during any calendar year does not exceed 180 days, then the individual is deemed a nonresident alien not doing business in the Philippines.

Expatriate tax concessions: Expatriate personnel employed by regional headquarters companies, offshore banking units, and petroleum service contractors and subcontractors are subject to tax at a flat rate of 15 percent on gross compensation income earned in the Philippines. The compensation of a regional executive should not be less than the gross equivalent of USD 1,000 per month.

Expatriate staff employed by regional headquarters are also permitted tax and duty-free importation of personal and household effects. They may also import motor vehicles but must pay the corresponding import taxes and duties.

INTERNATIONAL SCHOOLS AND EDUCATION

There are international, American, Japanese, British, French, and other European schools offering all levels of education. A number of local schools also offer a high standard of education in Manila, and some expatriates choose to enrol their children in these schools.

- International School Manila (www.ismanila.com) is based on the American curriculum. Advanced placement and International Baccalaureate Diplomas are offered in the high school. The school takes children from pre-kindergarten to grade 12 (ages 3–18 years). A canteen is available for children attending the elementary school only (cost PHP 3,620 per quarter.)

- Brent International School Manila (www.brent.edu.ph) offers the International Baccalaureate program. The school takes children from kindergarten to grade 12 (ages 4–18 years). School bus services are available. The school applies a uniform policy. There is a canteen for children who wish to eat at school. A personal interview is part of the admission process.

- The British School Manila (www.britishschoolmanila.org) offers the English national curriculum. Children are prepared for national curriculum tests at 7, 11, and 14 years of age; the GCSE at 16 years; and the International Baccalaureate at 18 years. The school takes children from nursery to year 13 (ages 4–18 years). School bus services are available. The school applies a uniform policy, and there is a canteen for children who wish to eat at school. Specific documents are required for the admission process.

- The French School of Manila (www.eis-manila.org/International-School) offers the French national curriculum and the French Baccalaureate. The school takes children between the ages of 3 and 18 years. Bus services are available. The school does not apply a uniform policy. Certain documents have to be provided for the admission process. A family interview is also required.

- The German School of Manila (www.gesm.org) offers the German national curriculum. The school takes children between the ages of 3 and 18 years. Bus services are available. The school does not apply a uniform policy. Students have to be fluent in German to be admitted.

- Manila Japanese School (www.mjs.org.ph) offers the Japanese curriculum. The school provides bus services at additional costs. Certain documents are required for the admission process.

Poland: Warsaw

PERSONAL SAFETY AND SECURITY ISSUES

Crime rates in Poland vary in different areas. Warsaw has high rates of crime against residents and foreign visitors. Organized groups of thieves and pickpockets often operate in major tourist destinations, railway and bus stations, and on public transport. In Warsaw, it is advisable to avoid the central railway station at night.

Poland is a member of NATO and the European Union. Internally, the situation is fairly stable. Strikes and demonstrations happen from time to time, but usually do not seriously affect daily life.

Crime is on the increase, and common sense precautions should be taken when walking around at night. Civil laws are democratic, but police work is not always efficient.

MEDICAL ISSUES

The healthcare system consists of public hospitals and outpatient clinics and a growing private sector. State-provided healthcare services are improving, but are still not up to Western European standards. Private healthcare, on the other hand, is generally of very high quality.

In private establishments, the staff is more likely to be able to speak another language. Medical care of a good standard is available for most major treatments in private hospitals. A few of the most recently established public hospitals also have adequate facilities. There are approximately 13 public clinics, 7 medical institutes, 23 hospitals, and many private clinics and small hospitals.

It is advisable to obtain information on private medical care when treatment is needed. National embassies can provide advice on hospitals or clinics providing care in your language. Private medical companies offer special healthcare programs for both companies and individuals in Poland.

Common prescription medicines are available in pharmacies, and other items can usually be imported without delay.

ENVIRONMENT ISSUES

Water is officially potable, but many people prefer to drink bottled water because the water in Poland tends to be chlorinated and may cause slight stomach upsets. It is advisable to boil all drinking water or to buy bottled water, which is widely available.

Sewage and waste removal systems are functional. Air quality is poor in commercial and industrial areas.

ECONOMIC OVERVIEW, 2008

GDP growth	4.8%
Inflation	4.2%
Unemployment	9.5%

INFRASTRUCTURE

Utilities and transport: The electricity and water supplies are reliable, and interruptions are rare. The telephone service has improved, and the mobile telephone network is growing rapidly. Postal services are fairly slow and sometimes unreliable.

The public transport system in Warsaw includes buses, trams, and a north-south metro line, which is being extended. The network is reliable and fairly extensive. Traffic is very congested during the rush hour, and this has worsened with ongoing road work.

Air travel: Poland's national airline is LOT Polish Airlines (www.lot.com). Many other major international airlines fly to Poland, including Air France, British Airways, SAS, and Lufthansa.

A number of budget airlines also operate in Poland and usually fly to and from Krakow and to and from Warsaw Terminal Etiuda. Budget airlines in Poland include Easy Jet, Sky Europe, Central Wings, Wizz Air, and German Wings.

Warsaw Frederic Chopin Airport, formerly Okecie International Airport, is situated 10 km from the city center. It offers a good choice of flights to other European destinations, and the selection of other international flights is improving. Several international airlines operate flights to and from Warsaw.

Bus/tram/metro: The public transport system in Warsaw is operated by the Municipal Transport Board.

There is a bus, tram, and metro network. The system is divided into two zones: a city zone and a metropolitan zone.

Buses and trams run between 5 A.M. and 11 P.M., and there is a night bus service that runs at half-hour intervals between 11:15 P.M. and 4:45 A.M. The one-line metro operates between 5 A.M. and midnight, and trains run every 3 to 8 minutes depending on the time of day.

Tickets (*bilety*) should be purchased before boarding all types of public transport. Tickets can be purchased from *Ruch* kiosks, post offices, vending machines at metro stations, and some hotels and restaurants. On trams and buses, tickets can be bought from the driver, but you must have exact change, and there is a surcharge of PLN 0.60. On night buses, tickets can also be purchased from the driver and cost PLN 5.40.

A single-fare ticket during the day costs PLN 2.40 for the city zone. A full-fare ticket must be purchased for every large piece of luggage (e.g. suitcase or backpack). Tickets need to be validated in the box inside the bus or tram and at the turnstiles on entry to the underground. Inspectors will issue a fine if you are caught traveling without a ticket. Fines are PLN 120.

Taxis: There are plenty of taxis in Warsaw. They can be ordered, taken from taxi ranks, or hailed in the street; however, it may be safer and cheaper to order one by telephone. Taxi fares range from PLN 5 to PLN 6 as an initial meter charge, and then PLN 1.20–2 for every kilometer traveled, depending on the taxi company. Rates increase between 10 P.M. and 6 A.M. If you are traveling longer distances, it is advisable to negotiate the price prior to departing.

All taxis have a sticker on one of the rear windows showing the rate per kilometer. Private taxis that do not belong to any taxi company can charge as much as PLN 5 per kilometer. They are usually parked outside the railway station or on street corners. Before getting into a taxi on the street, check the rate to avoid being overcharged.

Taxi companies in Warsaw include

- MPT: Tel: 0 22 91 91;
- Halo Taxi: Tel: 0 22 96 23;
- Wawa Taxi: Tel: 0 22 96 44 ;
- Super Taxi: Tel: 0 22 96 22;
- Ele Taxi: Tel: 0 22 811 11 11; and
- Euro Lux Taxi: Tel: 0 22 96 62.

Car rental: All of the major car rental companies have agencies in Poland. The minimum age to hire a car varies from company to company; however, in general the minimum age is 23 years. The documentation required to hire a car is a passport (with visa, if applicable), valid driver's license, and an international driving permit. An international insurance certificate may also be necessary. Prices vary depending on the type of car hired.

SHOPPING AND AVAILABILITY OF CONSUMER GOODS

There is a good choice of food items and consumer goods in Warsaw, and the supply is improving. A wide range of alcoholic beverages is available, and there are almost no restrictions on purchasing. Almost any brand and model of car can be purchased, and many popular models are produced locally. Importing certain models of vehicles is possible, although it may take time.

RECREATION AND ENTERTAINMENT

Restaurants: Warsaw offers a good choice of restaurants serving traditional food and international cuisine. Restaurants in Warsaw are multiplying very quickly. There are restaurants for every type of ethnic cuisine you can think of. Prices have increased, making it significantly more expensive to eat out in Warsaw than in any other Polish town or city. The restaurants in the major hotels offer a full menu and good quality food; however, if you prefer not to eat at hotels, the restaurants around the Old Town and the Main Market Square are among the best in Warsaw.

A comprehensive list of restaurants in Warsaw can be found online at www. warsaw-life.com/eat/restaurants.php.

Cinemas: Although Poland has a strong history of film making, very few cinemas in Warsaw show Polish films. Cinemas usually show U.S. and international box office hits in the original version, with Polish subtitles. Ticket prices vary from PLN 12 to PLN 25.

The selection of cinemas is good, and the latest American releases are generally screened. The city also holds several film festivals to promote films from other countries.

Sports: The choice of sports and leisure facilities is reasonable. Popular sports in Poland include cycling, hiking, and skiing. Water sports, boating, and sailing are popular in the Mazurian Lake District (Mazury). The main centers offering leisure and sporting facilities in the region are Gizycko, Mragowo, and Wilkasy. Soccer is a popular spectator sport in Poland, with most cities having a soccer team. In Warsaw, Legia (Warsaw's most popular team) plays at Legia Stadium. A comprehensive list of tennis courts in Warsaw can be found online at www.korty.pl/nr.asp?p=34,8,2.

Warsaw has many high-quality swimming facilities. Every district has a least one fully equipped recreation center with a swimming pool. A comprehensive list of swimming pools can be found online at www.ewarszawa.com/uslugi/miejsca/baseny/index.html. The major hotels in Warsaw all have good health and fitness facilities that invite membership from nonresidents.

Jogging is discouraged in Warsaw's largest and most beautiful park, Lazienki. But popular jogging routes include the trail through parkland from the Ujazdowskie Park to Mariensztat (9.5 km), the Vistula embankment (12 km), around the Pilsudski Park (4.5 km), and the pathways of the Saski Gardens (Ogrod Sask).

Culture and entertainment: The city has an excellent reputation for musical performances, and there are many theaters, operas, ballets, and other cultural events and venues in Warsaw. Poland has very strong musical and theatrical traditions, which reflect in the country's culture and entertainment.

The performing arts scene in Warsaw is a busy one. There are 17 theaters and three opera companies offering a variety of performances. The listings of events and performances can be found in the daily newspapers: *Gazeta Wyborcza* and *Dziennik*. Both newspapers have a cultural supplement on Fridays, with very comprehensive information for the following week. The weekly *Warsaw Voice* also has information on performances and events. The Warsaw Tourist Information Bureau has an online calendar of cultural events (www.warsawtour.pl). In addition to the venues themselves, tickets can be purchased at the ZASP ticket office located at Al. Jerozolimskie 25; Tel: +48 22-621-9454.

In the summer, free Chopin concerts take place at the Chopin monument in Lazienki Park and every Sunday at *Zelazowa Wola* (Chopin's birthplace), 58 km outside Warsaw.

Nightlife: Nightlife in Poland has evolved over time with the introduction of more upmarket clubs and pubs. There is now a much wider variety of venues in the larger cities.

The minimum age for buying alcohol is 18 years. There are no licensing laws so many pubs and clubs stay open until the last client leaves.

As in any other city, there are some pubs that visitors or foreigners should avoid; however, nightlife in Warsaw is constantly improving. Venues in Warsaw are spread throughout the city, and there are many nice establishments on the city outskirts as well as in the city center. The Old Town in particular has many pleasant pubs.

A comprehensive list of bars and nightclubs can be found online at www.warsawtour.pl.

SOCIOCULTURAL ENVIRONMENT

In Poland, there are no limitations on the freedom of speech and movement or on the free practice of religion. There are, however, some restrictions on the rights of trade unions. The Catholic Church holds a dominant position in Polish society and at one point forced the government to ban abortions, although the situation has again been liberalized slightly in recent years.

Cable and satellite television are widely available. There are two nationwide public television channels and seven nationwide private television channels. It is possible to find most international newspapers on sale in Warsaw.

DEMOGRAPHIC/WORKFORCE OVERVIEW

Population	38,132,277 (2006 estimate)
Population density	121 inhabitants per km^2
Age structure	0–14 years, 16%
	15–64 years, 71%
	65 years and over, 13%
Life expectancy at birth	
Total population:	75.0 years
Male	71.0 years
Female	79.2 years

WORKPLACE CULTURE

Shaking hands is the normal form of greeting. Polish men generally have a firm, enthusiastic handshake. Women also shake hands with men, but the man should always wait until the woman extends her hand first. It is considered bad luck to shake hands while standing in a doorway.

The traditional and polite way for a man to greet a woman is to kiss the back of her hand; however, this is considered somewhat old-fashioned. It is normal for relatives and close friends to greet with three kisses given alternating between cheeks.

People do not ask, "How are you?" when they greet others. When asked this question, a person in Poland will not understand it as a simple courtesy, but as a serious concern and may find themselves at a loss for an appropriate yet honest answer. It is better to avoid the question altogether.

Polish business culture is quite formal, and it is necessary to make appointments well in advance and to reconfirm closer to the date. Punctuality is essential. Business negotiations and proceedings may take longer than anticipated, as Poles are very thorough in their business dealings. It is important to remain patient and calm and not show frustration.

NATURAL ENVIRONMENT

The climate in Warsaw is temperate, with warm summers and cold winters. Spring and autumn can be both pleasantly warm and very wet. Winters in Poland are long and with very little sun/daylight. Common colds, flu, seasonal disorders, and depression can become quite frequent. Be prepared for unpredictable weather, which can shift in very little time.

Serious floods have occurred in the southern and western regions of Poland. Although these did not directly affect the city of Warsaw, they had a severe impact on the national economy (for example, on food prices).

HOUSING

A good selection of apartments is available for rent in Warsaw, and many new apartment blocks are under construction. Houses can also be found, though they are generally not as widely available as apartments. Good-quality household appliances and furniture are usually available. Maintenance and repair services can be time consuming.

Accommodations can be found through advertisements in the local newspapers (such as GazetaWyborcza, Rzeczpospolita), through estate agents, or via the Internet. Estate agents will charge a commission fee, usually the equivalent of one month's rent. Properties are advertised according to the number of rooms, a room being any living area excluding the kitchen and bathroom(s). Apartments are generally small by Western standards, and typically consist of one or two bedrooms, a living/dining area, and one or two bathrooms. En-suite bathrooms are rare.

Rental prices are generally quoted in PLN but can also be quoted in EURO or USD. Payment is usually made in PLN.

FINANCIAL ISSUES INCLUDING BANKING SERVICES AND TAXES

Currency: The Polish currency is the Zloty (PLN); 1 zloty = 100 groszy (gr).

Currency can be exchanged at banks, exchange offices, and at some hotels. Rates can vary considerably between places. A number of foreign banks have opened in Warsaw, and banking services are becoming more extensive and efficient.

Foreign currency can be exchanged for zloty at banks, major hotels, and bureaux de change, called *Kantor* in Polish. Hotels generally offer a lower exchange rate than Kantors, but neither charges a commission. Kantors usually offer a higher exchange rate than banks, and the service is normally faster. Kantors only exchange cash and accept most of the major world currencies. It is advisable not to exchange money "on the street," as it is illegal and it is common for people to be cheated in such transactions.

Kantors are usually open on weekdays between 9 A.M. and 6 P.M. and on Saturday between 9 A.M. and 2 P.M. Some are open longer and a few stay open for 24 hours. Kantors in small provincial towns may offer up to 5 percent less on the exchange rate, so it is advisable to change money in large urban areas. It is also common for banks to offer up to 5 percent less than the rates offered by Kantors.

Credit cards: Major international credit cards (American Express, Visa, MasterCard, Diners Club, and Eurocard) are widely accepted in hotels, restaurants, cafés, well-established shops, and car rental agencies. It is possible to obtain cash from credit cards in most banks.

Euro checks can be changed at most post offices and banks, but not in Kantors. Traveler's checks are readily exchanged at banks, although the rates of commission tend to be higher. In general, it is easier and quicker to change cash.

Banks: Banking hours are generally Monday through Friday, 9 A.M. to 5 P.M. and Saturday, 9 A.M. to 2 P.M. Most banks have branches that stay open until 8 P.M.; 24-hour ATM machines are available throughout the country.

The Polish banking system is considered to be strong and stable. After the political transformation in 1989, Poland managed to avoid most of the serious shocks experienced by other countries within the region.

Banks in Warsaw include the following:

- Bank PEKAO: www.pekao.com.pl
- PKO Bank Polski: www.pkobp.pl
- Citibank: www.citibank.pl
- Deutsche Bank: www.deutsche-bank-pbc.pl
- Millennium Bank: www.millenet.pl

To open an account in Poland, you will need to have your passport and a valid Polish residence permit or work visa. However, requirements may vary from bank to bank. A wide variety of accounts and services is available.

Taxes: The tax year for individuals is the calendar year. Taxpayers are required to submit tax returns by April 30 of the following tax year.

An individual who is a resident of the Republic of Poland, or whose temporary stay in the Republic of Poland is longer than 183 days in a given tax year, is liable to tax on worldwide income, regardless of the origin of the income. A nonresident who stays in the Republic of Poland for less than 184 days in a given tax year is liable to tax only on income from work performed in the territory of the Republic of Poland on the basis of a service agreement or an employment contract, regardless of the place of payment or of other income arising in the territory of the Republic of Poland.

A special tax regime applies to certain specified sources of income for individuals who come to Poland for a temporary stay in order to undertake employment in Polish companies or branches formed with foreign ownership. These employees are subject to Polish taxation only on income resulting from work carried out on the territory of Poland despite where they receive the payment and other income source in Poland. They may take advantage of a preferential tax rate of 20 percent on certain Polish source income (e.g. income in respect of formal management board duties or the provision of "know-how"). Other Polish source income of expatriates is taxed at normal rates.

The preferential tax rate of 20 percent on certain Polish sourced income for expatriates is subject to Polish Tax Authority approval. The above percentage should be considered only as informative, as it has not yet been confirmed. For an exact tax rate for expatriates, local tax specialists should be consulted.

INTERNATIONAL SCHOOLS AND EDUCATION

- The American School of Warsaw (www.asw.waw.pl) offers the American and international curricula, Advanced Placement, and the International Baccalaureate Diploma. The school accepts children between the ages of 3 and 18 years. A school bus service is provided. The school does not apply a uniform policy. A canteen is available for children who wish to eat at school. Certain documents have to be provided for the admission process. School hours are 8 A.M. to 3 P.M.

- The British School (www.thebritishschool.pl) offers the British and international curricula, GCSE, IGCSE, and IB Diploma. The school accepts children between the ages of 3 and 18 years. School bus services are provided. The school applies a uniform policy. A canteen is available for children who wish to eat at school. Certain documents have to be provided as part of the admission process. School hours are 9 A.M. to 2:45 P.M. for kindergarten; 8 A.M. to 3 P.M. for primary and secondary school.

- International American School (www.ias.edu.pl) offers an international curriculum. The school accepts children between the ages of 3 and 18 years. No bus service is provided. The school does not apply a uniform policy. A canteen is available for children who wish to eat at school. A personal interview is part of the admission process. School hours are 8:30 A.M. to 3 P.M.

- The Japanese School at the Japanese Embassy (www.japoland.pl/gakko) offers a Japanese curriculum. There is no school bus service, canteen, or dress code policy. Children must be fluent in Japanese. Certain documents have to be provided as admission requirements. A personal interview is also part of the admission process. School hours are Monday through Friday, 8:30 A.M. to 4:05 P.M.

- Lycée Française de Varsovie (French school) (www.lfv.pl) offers the French national curriculum and French and International Baccalaureate programs. The school accepts children between the ages of 3 and 18 years. Transport services are available. The school does not apply a uniform policy. A canteen is available for children who wish to eat at school. Certain documents have to be provided as admission requirements. A personal interview is also part of the admission process. School hours are 8:15 A.M. to 5:15 P.M.

- St. Paul's (The British International School of Warsaw) (www.stpaulswarsaw.tripod.com) offers the British national curriculum. The school accepts children between the ages of 3 and 18 years. School bus services are provided at an additional fee. The school does not apply a uniform policy. A canteen is available for children who wish to eat at school. Certain documents have to be provided as admission requirements. A personal interview is also part of the admission process. School hours are 8 A.M. to 3:30 P.M.

- Willy-Brandt Schule (German school) (www.gi.shuttle.de/gi/wbbs/frameset.htm) offers the German national curriculum. The school provides bus services. The school does not apply a uniform policy. A canteen is located in the neighboring school, which children can use if they wish to eat at school. Certain documents have to be provided as admission requirements. All applicants must be fluent in German. School hours are 8:30 A.M. to 4 P.M.

Romania: Bucharest

PERSONAL SAFETY AND SECURITY ISSUES

Romania's relationships with other nations are generally good. The country is a member of NATO and recently joined the European Union. Romania has minor disputes with Ukraine over Snake Island in the Black Sea and the construction of the Bastroe Channel, as well as an unresolved issue with Russia regarding the Romanian Treasure.

Relations with Hungary have significantly improved in recent years. The internal political situation is fairly stable, although labor unrest among miners and industrial workers is a regular occurrence. Strikes and demonstrations against the privatization of state industries take place, but have little effect on daily life. Bucharest is a relatively safe city, but common sense precautions should be taken when walking around at night. Law enforcement still retains elements of corruption, but this does not usually interfere with everyday life. Entry and exit regulations are fairly relaxed.

Stray dogs are a widespread problem in the city.

MEDICAL ISSUES

Medical care is provided by general and specialized hospitals and territorial polyclinics. General healthcare facilities and sanitation conditions are poor when compared to international standards. Many expatriates go to Germany or Austria for major treatments.

The private healthcare sector is small but expanding. Public medical care in Romania has not yet reached Western standards; basic medical supplies are often limited and modern technology is still lacking, especially outside major cities. However, medical care in many of the private clinics and hospitals in Bucharest, and other main towns and cities, is of good standards. Embassies/consulates often keep lists of appropriate medical practitioners and medical facilities.

Further information on the health service structure is available at the Ministry of Health (www.ms.ro). A complete list of public hospitals in Bucharest can be found online at www.travelworld.ro/romania/bucuresti/spitale_bucuresti.php. Private hospitals and medical centers in Bucharest include Rombus Medical Center, Medsana Bucharest Medical Center, and Medicover.

Often, the best way to find a reliable dentist is by recommendations or referrals by colleagues or friends. In Bucharest and in most towns there are many private dentists who offer good and inexpensive treatment. Dental treatment usually has to be paid for at the time of administration. Dental clinics in Bucharest include Novident (www.novident.bizcity.ro) and The Clinic.

The supply of medicines (both prescription and over-the-counter drugs) has improved in recent years with the opening of new pharmacies (*farmacia*), which are widely available throughout the country. The pharmacy chain Sensiblu has branches throughout the city, which offer a complete range of medications and products. Most of these stores are open 24 hours. Other 24-hour pharmacies in Bucharest include Farmacia, Nos. 20 and 26.

ENVIRONMENT ISSUES

Tap water is not safe to drink, and therefore bottled water should be purchased, particularly in the summer. Sewage and waste removal services are functional and have improved in recent years but can still be described as fairly poor by international standards. Air pollution is a concern in Bucharest.

ECONOMIC OVERVIEW, 2008

GDP growth   8.2%
Inflation   7.9%
Unemployment   4.6%

INFRASTRUCTURE

Utilities and transport: Bucharest has a well-developed public transport system including the metro, trams, and buses. Public transport is, however, extremely crowded during rush hours.

Air travel: The city's main airport (Henri Coanda International Airport) is situated 16 km from the city center and can be reached within 30 minutes. There is a good choice of flights to Western European destinations, but most other journeys require a connecting flight. Bucharest's second airport is the Aurel Vlaicu International Airport, which is currently undergoing renovation. It is expected to offer a limited range of flights to European destinations using primarily low-cost airlines. The airport is clean and modern and has numerous facilities, including banks, bureaux de change, shops, bars, restaurants, business lounges, a mother and infant room, and car rentals.

Taxis are available from the stand outside the arrivals terminal. There is only one official taxi company that can service the airport: Fly Taxi. Fly Taxi is slightly more expensive than other taxi companies in Bucharest, but its service is reliable and the cars are safe and clean. A taxi ride from the airport to the center costs about USD 20 (about RON 50), but you must firmly agree on the price with the driver before setting off. This will help avoid being overcharged. There are taxi drivers in the arrivals hall who will offer their services, but they are usually not from any official company and have been known to charge up to 50 USD for a drive to the city center.

The Express 783 bus connects the airport with Bucharest city center. The journey time is approximately 40 minutes. The bus operates Monday through Friday, 5:30 A.M. to 11:40 P.M., every 15 minutes, and Saturday, Sunday, and public holidays every 30 minutes. The bus stop is located in front of the terminal building. The stops on the way to the city are Henri Coanda Airport, Baneasa Airport, Piata Presei Libere, Piata Victoriei (subway links between Piata Victoriei and North Railway Station), Piata Romana, Piata Universitatii, and Piata Unirii. The bus fare is RON 4 (magnetic card/return trip). The cards can be purchased from the kiosk located in front of the arrivals terminal, open daily 6 A.M. to 8:30 P.M.

Sky Services operates a shuttle bus service between the airport and any hotel in Bucharest or, by arrangement, any address in Bucharest. Return tickets are valid for a 30-day period. Car rentals include Avis, Budget, Europcar, and Hertz. The main hub for domestic flights is Bucharest's Baneasa Airport (BBU), located 20 minutes from the international airport. Tarom offers an extensive network of domestic flights from Baneasa Airport to most parts of the country accessible by air.

Metro: Bucharest has an efficient and reliable metro system; it provides the easiest way to get around the city. The metro is operated by Metrorex, between 5 A.M. and 11:30 P.M. Trains run every 3 to 12 minutes depending on the time of day. Metro stations are indicated by a white sign with a blue "M." There are four metro lines and 45 stations in the network: M1: Red line (Pantelimon-Republica; Eroilor-Gara de Nord); M2: Blue line (IMGB-Pipera); M3: Yellow line (Eroilor-Industriilor); M4: Green line (Gara de Nord-1 Mai). Tickets come in the form of magnetic strip cards and are purchased from the "Casa." Four types of tickets are available: two-journey tickets, ten-journey tickets, one-day tickets, and monthly passes. Further information can be found at www.metrorex.ro.

Buses and trams are operated as an integrated system by The Bucharest Surface Transport Operator "*RATB*" (www.ratb.ro). The system runs between 5 A.M. and midnight, and tickets are interchangeable between all three modes of transport. Tickets are available from kiosks and tobacconists and must be validated in the machine on board. A single-journey ticket costs RON 1.10. One-day tickets, weekly tickets, 15-day tickets, and monthly tickets are also available.

Taxis are widely available, and can be taken from taxi stands, hailed on the street, or called for in advance. It is recommended that you use only the official yellow taxis that have meters installed and display the fares on one of the rear windows in both new and old Lei. In general, the initial meter charge is between RON 7 and RON 10, and the rate per kilometer is between RON 0.8 and RON 1.5 depending on the company. There is a small surcharge for night journeys. It is customary to round up the fare. Taxi drivers rarely have change, so ensure that you have smaller denominations of notes. Beware of taxis parked outside railway stations and large shopping malls. Unscrupulous taxi drivers in Bucharest are plentiful, and private taxis that do not belong to a reputable company are likely to overcharge you. Reputable taxi companies include Alfa Taxi, Cris Taxi, Meridian, EuroFly Taxi, OK Taxi, and Taxi RO. Maxitaxis are also available. These are minibuses that drive from Piata Romana to Piata Unirii and from the Opera Romana to Bulevardul Carol I, every 10 minutes between

6 A.M. and 9 P.M., and can be hailed anywhere along the route and cost around RON 1.5–2.0.

SHOPPING AND AVAILABILITY OF CONSUMER GOODS

With the opening of new stores, the availability of food items and consumer goods has markedly improved. Most vegetables are available all year round, with seasonal variations in prices. Alcoholic beverages are in good supply, and some international brands such as Stella Artois and Tuborg are produced locally. A fairly limited variety of cars is available in Bucharest, and delays in delivery should be expected. The services offered by major automobile companies have improved with the introduction of leasing options.

Shops are generally open Monday through Friday from 9 A.M. to 6 P.M. and Saturday from 9 A.M. to 2 P.M.; however, many large department stores and super-markets remain open until 8 P.M. on weekdays. Some convenience stores are open on Sunday mornings. In Romania, VAT is 19 percent and is included in all bills and transactions.

Malls: The main streets/areas where shops are located include Calea Victoriei, Bulevard ul G. Magheru, Balcescu, Piata Unirii, and Calea Dorobantilor. The following are all large, modern, Western-style shopping malls, with restaurants, underground parking, and children's facilities: Bucuresti Mall (www.bucuresti mall.com.ro) has more than 70 stores, 20 restaurants, a supermarket, a children's play area, and a 10-screen cinema; it is open daily from 10 A.M. to 10 P.M. Unirea Shopping Center, World Trade Plaza Shopping Center, and Mario Plaza, are others.

Department stores include Cocor and Bricostore. Bucharest has many super-markets and hypermarkets. Large supermarket chains such as Carrefour, Fourmi, Selgros, Billa, Mega Image, and Metro Cash and Carry have numerous locations throughout the city. The largest stores can usually be found in large shopping cen-ters in the outskirts of the city. Supermarkets are well stocked and sell most well-known international brands of groceries and personal care products. Nevertheless, if you have the need for a very particular brand of item or for local specialties of your home country, make sure you bring some with you until you can get them in Bucharest. Baby products are generally quite expensive. Because more tradi-tional farming methods are still used, produce is generally very healthy, flavorful, and of high quality. The same applies to dairy products and poultry.

Markets include Piata Amzei, the most central outdoor market in the city. Piata Bazar Dorobanti is Bucharest's largest, liveliest, and best outdoor market.

RECREATION AND ENTERTAINMENT

Restaurants: Many new restaurants have opened in recent years, and the qual-ity of food has improved. The quality of service remains variable in some of the older restaurants. There are many restaurants and eating places to choose from in Bucharest, including food kiosks, cafés, grills, and fast-food chains; almost any type of international cuisine is available, as well as different classes of restaurants. The standard or level is not consistent, but it is improving.

Restaurants include Heart Rock Café (a reasonably priced American restaurant with a sense of humor), Mesogios (a consistently good seafood restaurant), Barka Saffron (Indian cuisine, an expat favorite), Casa Doina (traditional Romanian food in a classy setting offering impeccable service), and Balthazar (the one truly original fusion restaurant in the city).

Culture and entertainment: Theatres, operas, ballets and other cultural institutions are plentiful, although international talent rarely performs locally except during the annual Georg Enescu festival.

Concert halls such as Opera National (Romanian National Opera) have a wide repertoire, with internationally renowned performances. Ateneul Roman hosts concerts with the Romanian National and International Philharmonic Orchestras. Sala Radio (Romanian Radio Society) organizes concerts in its two halls starting at 7 P.M. Teatrul de Opereta (Musical Comedy Theatre) concerts usually start around 6 P.M., except for Musical Comedy matinees that start at 11 A.M. The Museum of Natural History is one of the first natural history museums established in the world. National Cotroceni Museum reconstructs the atmosphere of the Mediavale Cotroceni Church (seventeenth century), and the ancient Royal Residence of King Ferdinand, Cotroceni Museum, is a valuable architectural and historical site. "George Enescu" Museum houses collections illustrating the history of music composition and documents from the life of eminent Romanian musician, George Enescu. The National Museum of Art has a large collection of European art with numerous Romanian and foreign masterpieces, housed in what was once the Royal Palace. The Art Collections Museum exhibits art genres, including Romania's famous glass-painted icons. These once private collections were donated posthumously for public exhibition.

Cinemas: Cinemas are located throughout the city. Foreign films are shown in the original language, with Romanian subtitles. Most malls have a multiplex cinema. Some of the city's cinemas have been renovated, resulting in higher standards. The films shown include all major releases, although these may take time to reach the city.

Hollywood Multiplex (www.hmultiplex.ro) has a 10-screen cinema showing all the latest movies. Corso is a one-screen cinema showing mainly Hollywood blockbusters. Movieplex Cinema Plaza Romania (www.plazaromania.ro) has 11 screens and shows a mixture of blockbusters and independent films. Cotroceni/Glendale Studio is a small and exclusive art house cinema. Europa is a small cinema, showing mainly European films.

Entertainment for children: The Village Museum (www.muzeul-satului.ro) is an outdoor museum, covering 30 hectares and displaying over 70 exhibits of traditional techniques and devices (water and windmills, oil presses, etc.) from all the country's provinces. Insula Copiilor (Children's Island) is a true gold mine of a children's playground, full of bouncy castles, slides, rides, and the like. The City Astronomic Observatory is a small museum on the history of Romanian astronomy and holds both a science fiction and an astronomic club. Globus Circus has daily performances at 6:30 P.M. and a matinee on Sundays. Kid's Planet has a wonderful indoor playground where children can play in a safe environment and parents can relax.

Sports: There is a limited range of good sports clubs, which are usually attached to hotels and charge high membership fees. The sea offers a wide variety of opportunities for swimming, windsurfing, sailing, and other water sports. Romania's most popular winter sport is skiing, and its most famous ski resorts are Sinaia, Bus teni, Predeal, and Poiana Brasov in the Carpathian Mountains between Bucharest and Brasov. Downhill and cross-country skiing are both very popular. The most popular spectator sport in Romania is soccer. Other popular team sports are volleyball and basketball. Golf facilities, tennis clubs, and swimming pools are plentiful. Water Park is a complete water park with all kinds of activities for children and adults. Patinoarul Floreasca has a large outdoor skating rink. Good Time Texas has eight modern bowling lanes for the whole family. Hipocan is one of Romania's most respected riding centers, offering lessons for children and adults.

Nightlife: Bucharest has a wide variety of entertainment and nightlife venues. Most major hotels have nightclubs, and there are also several Parisian-style cafés. There are around 16 casinos located throughout the city, including Casino Palace, Casino Astoria, Casino Bucharest, Cesar Casino, and Grand Casino.

Bars include Jukebox (a busy, enjoyable and unpretentious venue that attracts large groups of young foreigners), Klein Bar and Bistro (which has a bar and bistro inside the Rembrandt hotel), Laptaria Enache (located at the top of the National Theatre; houses a famous live music bar, especially popular with students), Deja-vu (considered one of the best cocktail bars in Bucharest), and Amsterdam (a popular expat bar and grill by day and a lively drink venue by night). Bonsai is a tasteful and trendy nightspot club. Exit offers smooth music from the Amsterdam Bar. It caters to a groovy and mature crowd. The Office attracts an expensive and exclusive crowd dancing to the sound of top DJs. Club A has an unpretentious crowd listening to all-time classic tunes. Studio Martin is a nightspot with incredible music played by top European DJs.

For more information, visit the Romanian National Tourist Office (www.romaniatourism.com).

SOCIOCULTURAL ENVIRONMENT

In Romania there are few limitations on the freedom of speech and on the free practice of religion. The media is limited, but relatively free of state control. There are seven national television channels, and cable television is now widely available, with programs in English, German, French, Italian, and Spanish. A good range of international newspapers and magazines are available.

DEMOGRAPHIC/WORKFORCE OVERVIEW

Population	22,303,552 (2006 estimate)
Population density	94 inhabitants per km^2
Age structure	0–14 years, 16%
	15–64 years, 70%
	65 years and over, 15%
Life expectancy at birth	
Total population:	71.6 years
Male	68.1 years
Female	75.3 years

WORKPLACE CULTURE

Like other Eastern Europeans, Romanians are a hospitable and friendly people who are overcoming a difficult past. Romania has a long, proud tradition of culture, letters, and music, which is evident throughout the country but which was heavily suppressed under an oppressive regime.

The economic growth that the country is experiencing has created marked differences between people in large urban settings and the more rural population. Foreigners visiting Romania will find that the younger generation in Bucharest has embraced Western culture in its attitudes and ways, while older generations still conserve many of the traits and beliefs they were brought up with. This contrast of the old and the new gives Romania much of its paradoxical flavor and can be both a challenging and a thrilling environment for first-time visitors.

International business travelers have become very common in Bucharest and other major business centers. Romanian business people are well versed in Western business ways, and English and French are widely spoken as second languages. Despite the rather traditional gender roles in Romania, women hold high positions in business. This does not detract from the men's traditionally chivalrous role, and businesswomen visiting Romania should not be surprised at hand-kissing and flattering yet harmless remarks. Handshakes are the standard greeting among both men and women. Kissing on the cheek is common among close friends.

Romanian business culture is based on civil law, originating in the late 1800s and based on the Napoleonic Code, supplemented by recent legislation post Ceausescu. As in any country, there can be frustration in doing business (the failure to progress to a Western European transaction timetable is often criticized), so having a sense of humor is highly recommended. Business hours are usually Monday through Friday, 8 A.M. to 5 P.M. Government offices are generally open Monday through Friday, 8 A.M. to 4 P.M. Business dress is conservative and smart.

Businessmen should wear a suit with a shirt and tie, and businesswomen should wear suits or smart dresses. Avoid wearing loud or flashy colors and accessories.

NATURAL ENVIRONMENT

Bucharest has a warm continental climate, although there is snow in the winter and modest rainfall throughout the year. Temperatures vary between −10°C and 30°C. The city has been severely affected by earthquakes in the past and more recently by serious floods, causing extensive damage.

HOUSING

The availability and quality of housing have improved in recent years, yet it can still sometimes be difficult to find acceptable accommodations at a reasonable price. The quality and availability of locally produced furniture have improved. Many international brands of household appliances can be purchased locally. Maintenance and repair services can sometimes be unreliable. Real estate agencies are listed in the *Yellow Pages* telephone directory, which is also available online at www.yellowpages.ro (over 650 real estate agencies are listed). The following are a selection of agencies with Web sites in English: www.atlasq.ro, www.cagead.ro, and www.colliers.com/Markets/Bucharest.

Once you have found suitable accommodations, it is recommended that you perform a full inventory and fill out a statement as to the condition of the property prior to signing the lease. You may wish to consult with a lawyer before either oral or written agreements are made. Lease agreements are usually signed for one to two years and rental prices can be renegotiated on a yearly basis subject to inflation. A refundable deposit equivalent to between three and six months' rent is usually required. Rents are usually quoted in Euros, and are usually paid monthly in advance.

Real estate agents often charge one month's rent as a commission fee, which will be paid by the tenant. Rental prices do not usually include utilities, but in some cases may include water. Many higher-end properties will include a guard for the building.

Houses in districts in Bucharest: good areas: Baneasa, Floreasca; very good areas: Aviatorilor, Herastrau, Dorobanti; best areas: Primaverii, French Village. Apartments: good areas: Floreasca, Dobrobanti; very good areas: Aviatorilor, Herastrau; best areas: Primaverii. Over the last couple of years, the cost of rented property in Romania, particularly in Bucharest, has rapidly increased. Unfurnished properties tend to be easier to source than furnished. Accommodation costs can vary considerably depending on the type of housing and location. The average cost of a two-bedroom unfurnished apartment in a very good area is EUR 1,600 per month.

FINANCIAL ISSUES INCLUDING BANKING SERVICES AND TAXES

Exchanging currency has become easier, as there are now numerous exchange offices in the city. Romania is expected to adopt the Euro within the next decade. Credit cards have become more widely accepted, and ATMs that accept international credit cards are now available. Major Romanian banks have been privatized, and a number of foreign banks are represented in Bucharest. It is reasonably easy to withdraw funds, and most banking services are available.

Currency: Romania's currency is the Leu (plural "Lei"—RON). As of July 1, 2005, Romania has dropped four zeros from its national currency; 10,000 st (old) Romanian lei (ROL) now equals 1 (new) leu (RON). Both old and new coins and bank notes were only permitted in circulation until December 31, 2006. The old currency is no longer legal tender. New bank notes have been issued in 1, 5, 10, 50, 100, and 500 lei denominations, and coins in 1, 5, 10, and 50 bani coins; 1 leu = 100 bani.

Checks and credit cards: Romania has traditionally been a "cash-only" economy. While an increasing number of establishments do accept major credit cards and debit cards, travelers are advised to use cash where possible due to an increase in credit card fraud. If you are visiting rural areas, make sure you have enough cash to cover all your basic expenses—do not rely on cards in these instances. Foreign currency can be exchanged at banks and official exchange offices. The exchange rate is generally posted in the window. You will usually need your passport to exchange money. Traveler's checks cannot be used to pay for goods or services. A commission fee is usually payable for this service. Some hotels and travel agencies also offer currency exchange facilities. You should always retain your exchange receipts for future reference. Never attempt to exchange currency on the "black market"; it is illegal and you run the risk of being cheated. Many ATM machines are located throughout the major cities.

Banks: Since 1990, the Romanian banking system has undergone a major restructuring in accordance with the European Union banking directives and based on the Western European banking model. This process resulted in the organization of a two-tier banking system, which consists of the National Bank of Romania, on the one hand, and credit institutions, on the other hand. Since that time, the banking sector in Romania has seen a clear development marked by the establishment of many foreign bank branches and an increased participation of foreign capital in Romanian banks. Electronic banking has also advanced considerably, but electronic banking fraud still remains an issue. Banking hours are generally Monday through Friday, 9 A.M. to 12 P.M., and 1 to 3 P.M.; opening hours may vary between banks and branches. To open a current account, you should have a valid passport. There is usually a minimum deposit.

Taxes: The tax year for individuals is the calendar year. An individual is deemed a Romanian tax resident if he or she meets at least one of the following conditions: The individual has their domicile in Romania; the individual has a center of vital interest in Romania; the individual is present in Romania for a period or periods exceeding 183 days during any 12 months, ending during the corresponding calendar year. As a general rule, Romanian tax residents are liable for Romanian income tax on their worldwide income, whereas nonresidents are liable for Romanian income tax on their Romanian-source income.

Expatriate tax concessions: Consultants (non-Romanian nationals) working on projects financed by international governmental or nongovernmental organizations (not the Romanian government) are exempt from the tax on salary. Romanian nationals domiciled outside Romania and non-Romanian nationals earning income from activities carried out in Romania must apply for a taxpayer number within 30 days from the date they earn their first income for the activities carried out in Romania.

INTERNATIONAL SCHOOLS AND EDUCATION

French, American, British, Japanese, Italian, and German schools are available in Bucharest, offering a high standard of education at both primary and secondary levels.

- Aldo Moro Scuola Italiana (Italian school) (www.scuolaitaliana.go.ro) offers the Italian curriculum. No school bus services are provided. The school does not apply a uniform policy. There is no canteen available. Certain documents have to be provided for the application process.
- American International School of Bucharest (www.aisb.ro) offers the International Baccalaureate program. The school takes children between the ages of 3 and 18 years. School bus services are provided. The school does not apply a uniform policy. No canteen is available. A wide range of after-school activities is offered. Certain documents have to be provided for the application process.
- British School of Bucharest (www.britishschool.ro) offers the British national curriculum. The school takes children between the ages of 4 and 12 years. School bus services are provided. The school applies a uniform policy. A canteen is available for children who wish to eat at school. A wide range of after-school activities is offered. Certain documents have to be provided for the application process.
- Deutsche Schule Bukarest (German school) (www.lic21.de) offers the German national curriculum. The school has kindergarten, primary, and secondary schools. No school bus services are provided. The school does not apply a uniform policy. There is no canteen available. The school offers a wide range of after-school activities. Certain documents have to be provided for the application process.
- International School of Bucharest (www.isb.ro) takes children between the ages of 3 and 18 years. It has kindergarten and primary school sections, which offer the English national curriculum. The secondary school section takes children aged 11–14 years and offers the National Curriculum for England; for children aged 14–16 years, the IGCSE curriculum is followed; for those aged 16–18 years, the International A-level curriculum is offered. School bus services are provided. The school does not apply a uniform policy. A canteen

is available for children who wish to eat at school. A wide range of after-school activities is offered. Certain documents have to be provided for the application process.

- Japanese School in Bucharest (www.jpschool.ro) offers the Japanese curriculum. School bus services are provided. A canteen is available for children who wish to eat at school. A range of after-school activities is offered. Certain documents have to be provided for the application process.

- Lycée Français Anna De Noailles (French school) (www.lyfrabuc.ro) has the French national curriculum. The school takes children between the ages of 3 and 18 years. No school bus services are provided. The school does not apply a uniform policy. There is no canteen available. The school offers a wide range of after-school activities. Certain documents have to be provided for the application process.

Russia: Moscow

PERSONAL SAFETY AND SECURITY ISSUES

Demonstrations and strikes are still frequent. A number of serious terrorist attacks have occurred in Russia in recent years, many due to the war in Chechnya, including the Beslan school hostage crisis, aircraft bombings, and car bombings. Many people have been killed in military clashes in North Caucasus.

Organized crime and violent crime are on the increase throughout Russia, and particularly in Moscow. Muggings and pickpockets are prevalent in the city. Extreme caution should be exercised at all times. Entering Russia can sometimes be difficult, but should not present a major problem provided formalities are in order.

MEDICAL ISSUES

The state medical service is free. However, the general standard of public medical care is poor, and basic supplies are often limited; on the other hand, the number of private healthcare facilities is growing. It is advisable to get a complete medical check up before leaving home and to take a copy of your medical records.

There is an increasing selection of joint-venture private medical and dental practices offering services to foreign nationals. It is important to ensure that any health insurance is fully comprehensive and includes repatriation or transportation to a Scandinavian or Western European capital in the event of suitable treatment being unavailable in Russia. You should also ensure that health insurance covers both European and Asian Russia. Private medical care in Russia is expensive.

Many consulates have a list of medical and dental practitioners that offer services to the expatriate community. It is also advisable to ask friends and colleagues for recommendations regarding local practitioners.

A few international private clinics exist where a relatively good level of treatment can be received. Most medical supplies are available, but the number of pharmacies in the city is quite limited.

ENVIRONMENT ISSUES

The main risk to health is diphtheria, and it is recommended that foreigners be vaccinated against this disease before traveling to Moscow. Tap water is not drinkable, and bottled water must be purchased instead. Local mineral water may taste unpleasant, but imported brands are also available.

Sewage and waste removal systems are not completely functional in some areas of the city, making them unpleasant to visit. The air is heavily polluted, though much of the industrial activity of the suburbs has been shut down in recent years. Troublesome insects like flies and mosquitoes sometimes appear during the summer, but are a nuisance rather than a health hazard.

ECONOMIC OVERVIEW, 2008

GDP growth	6.0%
Inflation	13.5%
Unemployment	6.1%

INFRASTRUCTURE

Utilities and transport: Public transport in Moscow is cheap and efficient. The metro network is one of the most extensive in the world. Traveling by bus or tram, however, can be extremely slow at times due to traffic congestion. On weekends, traffic is less of a problem.

At the heart of Moscow is the Kremlin. Red Square lies along its East Side and the Moskva River flows past its south side. The rest of Moscow comprises four rings, spreading out from the center:

- The first is a semicircular ring in the northern half of the Kremlin, formed by Mokhovaya ulitsa, Okhotny ryad, Teatralny proezd, Novaya Ploshchad, and Staraya Ploshchad. Manezhnaya Ploshchad and Lubyanskaya Ploshchad, two large traffic-dominated squares, are located in this ring.
- The second is the Boulevard Ring (Bulvarnoe Koltso).
- The third is the Garden Ring (Sadovoe Koltso).
- The fourth ring, much further out, is Moscow's outer ring road, the Moskovskaya Koltsevaya Avtomobilnaya Doroga or MKAD.

Moscow's main radial roads cut across these rings, and the Moskva River runs across the city from northwest to southeast.

Air travel: Sheremetyevo International Airport is Moscow's main air facility. It is located 35 km from the city center and requires a journey time of approximately 50 minutes. The airport offers a good selection of flights to European destinations, plus a fair range of departures to other parts of the world. Moscow's other international airport, Domodedovo International Airport, provides mainly domestic and European flights.

Metro: The easiest way to travel around Moscow is by using the efficient Metro network (www.metro.ru) (in Russian only). Information in English and a metro map can be found online at www.wtr.ru/moscow/eng/metro/metro.html.

The Metro operates between 6 and 1 A.M. During rush hours (8 to 10 A.M. and 5 to 7 P.M.), stations and trains are extremely crowded. Eleven metro lines give the city extensive coverage. Lines are color coded for simplicity. There is one circular line, which links to the other 10 lines. Metro stations are indicated by a red letter "M," and the names of the stations are in Cyrillic alphabet only.

Tickets come in the form of a magnetic-strip card. Metro fares are as follows:

- single-journey ticket: RUB 15;
- 5-trip card: RUB 70;
- 10-trip card: RUB 125;
- 20-trip card: RUB 230;
- monthly metro pass: RUB 450; and
- monthly all-urban transport pass: RUB 900.

When accessing the platform you need to swipe the ticket at the turnstile machine. Tickets can be purchased in vending machines and ticket booths located in every station. A fine is payable if you are caught riding on public transportation without a valid ticket.

Bus and tram: There is a vast network of buses, trolley buses, and trams covering the city, but they are generally very overcrowded (especially during peak hours). General hours of operation are 5:30 until 12:30 A.M. Services operate every 5 to 40 minutes depending on the route and the time of day. There are no late-night services.

Bus stops are indicated by a yellow sign with "A," trolley bus stops by a white sign with "T," and tram stops by a white sign with "Tp."

Tickets can be purchased from the driver or a conductor, but preferably in advance from kiosks located next to Metro stations. A single-journey ticket costs RUB 13 in a kiosk and RUB 15 on the bus or tram. Tickets can also be purchased in strips of 10. Tickets must be validated in the ticket machines located inside the bus, trolley, or tram.

A fine of RUB 100 is payable if you are caught riding a bus or tram without a valid ticket.

Taxi: Official taxis are yellow cars with a checked pattern on the door. All official taxis have meters and must display a fare table inside the vehicle. Many drivers will negotiate the fare instead of using the meter. Fares will vary between taxi companies, but initial meter charges are usually RUB 35, with an average of RUB 15 per kilometer. You will also have to pay a surcharge if you are traveling outside of certain districts.

Many private cars will also stop if flagged down in the street. You must always negotiate a price in advance. You should never share a taxi with a stranger, or get into a car that has passengers already. It is advisable to only use official taxis.

Marshrutki (route-taxis) are minibuses that follow a set route. They can be taken from most metro stations or flagged down at a bus stop. The fare is paid to the driver and costs around twice as much as a normal bus ticket, but in general this depends on where you are going. When you want to get off you need to tell the driver. Marshrutki generally run between 8 A.M. and 10 P.M.

SHOPPING AND AVAILABILITY OF CONSUMER GOODS

A good variety of meat, fruit, and vegetables of high quality is available in major supermarkets. Shopkeepers in Russia generally know little of customer service and may seem unfriendly and unhelpful, although this is starting to improve. There are very few restrictions on the purchase and consumption of alcoholic beverages, and the range of brands available is wide.

A fair selection of brands and models of cars can be purchased in Moscow. Both buying a car and acquiring replacement parts for an imported car can, however, be time consuming.

Shops are generally open Monday through Saturday, 9 A.M. to 6 P.M. Supermarkets are usually open daily from 8 A.M. to 8 P.M., except Sundays when they close at 6 P.M. The large department stores are open daily between 10 A.M. and 9 or 10 P.M.

Popular shopping streets include Novy Arbat, Arbat ulitsa, Tverskaya ulitsa, and Kutuzovsky prospect. There is also an IKEA store in Moscow.

RECREATION AND ENTERTAINMENT

Restaurants: There is a good choice of restaurants in Moscow, serving both Russian and international cuisine. Many Japanese restaurants have recently opened. The quality of food served differs greatly from one place to the next, as does the price. Moscow's present-day restaurant scene is nothing like it was 15 years ago. Since the beginning of the 1990s, an entire range of restaurants has appeared. For those who can afford it, the selection of Moscow's top-class restaurants is unparalleled. There is also a thriving fast-food scene, including all the major chains as well as a large selection of cafés and snack bars.

It is always advisable to make reservations at restaurants; if you want to be sure of a table, it is best to make the reservation in person and to leave a deposit.

A good Web site for information on restaurants in Moscow is www.moscow city.com/restaurants/restaurants.htm.

Cinemas: In recent years, several modern cinemas have opened in Moscow, with modern sound equipment, and showing international films shortly after release. Many cinemas show films in the original language with Russian subtitles (*sub'titry*), but sometimes the films are dubbed into Russian; when they are, the film advertisement is usually marked "dubbed" (*dub'lirovan*).

Cinema tickets generally cost from RUB 50 to RUB 300 (more expensive in the evenings and on weekends).

Culture and entertainment: Opera, ballet, and theater companies in Moscow are world famous and of the highest quality. Tickets for cultural events have become very expensive. A wide variety of cultural events such as theater, circus, concerts, and variety performances is available in Russia.

Information on upcoming events is available from the "Moscow Out" Web site: http://eng.moscowout.ru; *The Moscow Times* Web site www.themoscow times.com also has event listings.

It is advisable to purchase tickets in advance. If you purchase tickets on the night of the show, they will be very expensive. Tickets can be purchased at the individual box offices or special ticket-selling kiosks located throughout the city.

Moscow has literally hundreds of museums, which cover history, science, art, and many other areas of Russia's rich cultural life.

A comprehensive list of museums in Moscow can be found online at www .moscow-taxi.com/museums/index.asp.

Sports: Sports clubs and other leisure facilities have improved; however, they are still fairly limited in number and their quality is not always high.

The spectator sport that comes a close second to soccer is ice hockey. Both Moscow and St. Petersburg have good ice hockey teams. Other popular sports are volleyball, basketball, and weight lifting. Tennis also enjoys a great deal of popularity mainly due to the international success of Russian players. Indeed, Russia is home to some of the world's greatest sports personalities.

For those who wish to participate in sports, Russia has an increasing number of activities to offer, including skiing, water sports, horseback riding, hiking, ice skating, tennis, and golf.

Alpine skiing is becoming increasingly popular, with a new center that recently opened outside of Moscow. Volen Sport Park is a comfortable resort with a well-developed infrastructure to alpine ski or to snowboard, and it is situated 60 km outside Moscow (travel time: 1 hour, 20 minutes by car or by local train). Usually there is good snow coverage in the Moscow area from mid-December until mid-March. Volen Park has six slopes up to 400-meters long. For details, contact Tel: +7 495-578-3502; www.volen.ru. More information and listings are available at www.waytorussia.net /Moscow/Activities.html and www.infoservices.com/moscow/2533.htm.

Nightlife: Moscow's nightlife is world class. There are bars, pub, clubs, and casinos to cater for all tastes and budgets and available 24 hours a day. Moscow alone has more casinos than the whole of Europe, many of them meeting international standards.

Comprehensive nightlife information can be found online at www.world66. com/europe/russia/moscow/nightlife or www.moscow-life.com/moscow/ nightlife.

SOCIOCULTURAL ENVIRONMENT

The law on the whole guarantees personal freedom, although it is not universally upheld. There are restrictions on mass demonstrations and protests, and some media censorship still exists.

Russia's last independent television channels have all been shut down in recent years. Cable television is widely available in Moscow, and international newspapers can readily be obtained.

DEMOGRAPHIC/WORKFORCE OVERVIEW

Population	142,893,500 (2006 estimate)
Population growth rate	-0.4% (2006 estimate)
Age structure	0–14 years, 14%
	15–64 years, 71%
	65 years and over, 14%
Life expectancy at birth	
Total population:	67.1 years
Male	60.45years
Female	74.1 years

WORKPLACE CULTURE

In general, business hours are Monday through Friday, 9 A.M. to 5 P.M.; many employees work 10 A.M. to 6 P.M. Usually, an hour is taken off for lunch, around 1 to 2 P.M.

Men usually wear smart business suits with a shirt and tie. Women usually wear smart suits or dresses. The standard business greeting is a firm handshake. Russians often state their name while giving a handshake. You should always address business colleagues and associates with the appropriate title and their family name.

NATURAL ENVIRONMENT

Winters in Moscow are bitterly cold and last from November to March, when the average temperature is 10°C below freezing. Summers, on the other hand, are usually warm and pleasant. There is no record of natural disasters affecting the city.

HOUSING

In general, finding good accommodations in Russia can be difficult and expensive. Most of Russia's urban accommodations are apartment based, with apartments being relatively small by Western standards. Some rental properties can be in very nice historical buildings that have been refurbished to Western standards; others can be in modern apartment buildings with 24-hour security and sports facilities. Apartments are owned by the city authorities, by a cooperative, or by a private landlord. Most accommodations are rented furnished.

Houses are usually found in the outskirts of the city. They can be Western-style homes formerly used as summer homes, large country houses (cottages) with gardens (*dacha*) or houses in gated communities.

Apartments are usually rented according to the number of rooms. Kitchens do not usually count as a room, but living areas do. Ads and agencies will use the term *Euro-remont* or European renovation; this refers to the fact that a property has been renovated to "Western standards," with a fitted kitchen, tiled bathrooms with modern fixtures, wood-panelled parquet floors, and so on.

There are many accommodation and private rental agencies where English is spoken, and it is advisable to seek their services when trying to find accommodations. Agencies generally charge the equivalent of one month's rent as a commission fee. Many expatriates find accommodations simply by asking friends and colleagues for information. Accommodations for rent are published in the print and online versions of English language newspapers; the largest is the Real Estate section of *The Moscow Times* at www.realestate.moscowtimes.ru; more general real estate reporting can be found in *The Moscow News Weekly* at www.mnweekly.ru/estate.

Historically, expatriates have preferred to stay in the common expatriate areas, normally around the embassy and near the metro, for security reasons. Nowadays, good-quality accommodations are becoming more widely available, and some expatriates are moving into more mixed areas. However, quality housing generally comes at a high price in Moscow. The most prestigious residential areas of the city include Ostozhenka, Prechistenka, Patriarchy Ponds, Chistie Ponds, Serebriany Bor, Chaika, Nakhabino, and Pokrovskie Hills.

The selection of household appliances and furniture available is reasonable, and some international brands can be purchased. The quality of household maintenance and repair services is acceptable, but there can be a waiting time for such services.

FINANCIAL ISSUES INCLUDING BANKING SERVICES AND TAXES

Currency: Major currencies such as U.S. dollars and the Euro are usually available for exchange.

Other currencies can be found at a limited number of banks and exchange offices. It is recommended that only official points of exchange be used. A few foreign banks have subsidiaries in Moscow, and, in general, international banking services are average. Credit cards are widely accepted.

The Russian currency is the Ruble (RUB). 1 ruble = 100 kopeks. Notes are in denominations of RUB 1,000, 500, 100, 50, 10, and 5. Coins are in denominations of RUB 5, 2, and 1, and 50, 10, 5, and 1 kopeks. Only notes and coins dated after 1997 are valid.

According to the law, all financial transactions in Russia are to be made in rubles. Foreign currency should only be exchanged at official bureaus, banks, or at exchange outlets, which are widely found in the city centers. Sometimes it is a problem in the smaller cities to find a currency exchange. In view of this, you should ensure that you have sufficient cash to provide for minimal needs before traveling around the country. Banks and exchange bureaus are very particular about the condition of foreign currency bills. Bills that have marks or are fairly worn may be rejected even if they are legitimate.

Avoid using the black market to change money as this is illegal, and if you are caught you will be in serious trouble with the police. It is essential to keep all currency exchange receipts, and all transactions need to be recorded on the currency declaration form, which is given on arrival. Hotel exchange offices usually offer the same exchange rate as the banks, but often have more convenient opening hours.

Credit cards: Credit cards are widely accepted in establishments that cater to foreign visitors and expatriates in larger towns and cities. Visa, MasterCard, and American Express are the most widely accepted. Nevertheless, if you are traveling around the country do not assume you will be able to use a credit card. Always carry some cash with you. Cash can be advanced with major credit cards in most large banks. Credit card theft is on the increase, and you may be asked to produce your passport whenever you use your credit card.

Traveler's checks are accepted in banks and official foreign currency exchange bureaus in exchange for currency but cannot be used to pay for goods or services in retail outlets, etc.

There are many ATM machines in Moscow and St. Petersburg, operated by a variety of financial institutions. There are some ATM machines that dispense U.S. dollars and Euros, but they are not widespread.

Banks: Banking hours are generally Monday through Friday, 9:30 A.M. to 5:30 P.M. Russia's banking system is not yet up to Western standards. As a result of the 1998 financial crisis, the sector suffered heavily, and many people who lost their savings lost trust in the system. Although banks are experiencing strong growth, the sector is still relatively small and poorly regulated. Most banks have an ATM at every branch, and some banks have started to offer Internet banking.

There are a number of foreign banks with branches in Moscow and St. Petersburg. A comprehensive list of Russia's largest banks can be found online at www.portalino.it/banks/_ru.htm.

Foreign citizens may open ruble and foreign currency accounts in foreign and/or Russian banks. You will need to do this especially if you are paid locally. When opening an account, you will receive a debit card (with a four-digit pin) but not a checkbook, since checks are hardly ever used in Russia. Debit cards can be used to withdraw money from ATMs and to pay in many shops. The required documents to open an account vary, but in general you will have to show your passport, visa, and employment contract. You do not need any cash to open the account. Fees vary from bank to bank, but you can expect to pay a monthly management fee, debit card insurance, and fees for using ATMs different from your bank's own.

Taxes: Residents of Russia are taxed on income received from Russian and foreign sources, in cash or kind, in a calendar year. Persons not resident in Russia are taxed on income received from sources in Russia, regardless of their place of residence or customary place of abode.

An individual who is present in Russia for 183 days or more in a calendar year, excluding days of arrival and including days of departure, is considered to be a Russian tax resident in that calendar year and is subject to Russian tax on his or her worldwide income (subject to the availability of relief under the terms of a double tax treaty). Individuals who spend 182 days or less in Russia in a calendar year are subject to personal income tax on their Russian-source income only.

INTERNATIONAL SCHOOLS AND EDUCATION

There are French, German, British, American, Canadian-American, Italian, Swedish, and Japanese schools in Moscow, all of which offer both primary and secondary levels of education. Local schools are mostly private, and the standard of education offered is questionable.

- The International English School (www.englishedmoscow.com) offers the British national curriculum. The school adheres to a uniform policy. For additional fees, a canteen and a school bus service are available for students. The school serves children aged between 3 and 16 years.

- The Anglo-American School of Moscow (www.aas.ru) follows the International Baccalaureate program; the school has lower, middle, and upper school departments (kindergarten, and grades 1 to 12). The school takes children between the ages of 3 and 18 years. School bus services are provided. The school applies a uniform/dress code policy, and a canteen is available for children who wish to eat at school. A wide range of after-school activities is offered. Certain documents have to be provided for the admission process.

- The British International School Moscow (www.bismoscow.com) offers the British national curriculum, IGCSE exams (the International General Certificate of Secondary Education), and the International Baccalaureate Diploma. The school takes children between the ages of 3 and 18 years. There is also a Russian section following the Russian national curriculum. The school has seven buildings on different sites (see Web site for addresses and contact details). School bus services are provided. The school applies a uniform/dress code policy, and a canteen is available for children who wish to eat at school. A wide range of after-school activities is offered. Certain documents have to be provided for the admission process.

South Africa: Johannesburg

PERSONAL SAFETY AND SECURITY ISSUES

Internally, the level of political violence has diminished, although there still might be a few pockets of conflict. Strikes and protests are common. Violent crime in Johannesburg has increased to epidemic levels, and visitors should exercise caution at all times. It is not safe to walk through the city center at any time, and many businesses have relocated to the safer northern suburbs. Carjacking, burglaries, and other violent crimes occur frequently. Overall, although criminality is high in Johannesburg, security has improved slightly, with closed-circuit video cameras and continuous police patrols. Morale in the police force is very low, and law enforcement is inefficient.

MEDICAL ISSUES

The standard of healthcare in South Africa is generally good. However, in recent years, public hospital budgets have been cut to provide primary healthcare in rural areas, and this has led to deterioration in standards. Excellent private hospital facilities are available at a high price.

Bilharzia may be encountered in some local water sources. Malaria is still a health concern in South Africa. AIDS is a growing concern in South Africa, although it has not yet reached the level seen in some other African countries.

Medical and dental care is generally of a high standard. The majority of South Africans are covered by the large public sector; this healthcare is free albeit extremely rudimentary and basic, in brief under-resourced and over-used. Around 18 percent of South Africans (usually the higher-income bracket) pay for private medical care where the treatment covers the spectrum of health issues including reasonably priced but high-quality surgery. An increasing number of health professionals are choosing to work in the private sector, which is not helping the already beleaguered public sector.

There is no state-funded healthcare provision for foreigners, and all medical and dental care must be paid for in full, even in the public clinics and hospitals. In general, costs are reasonable. The majority of treatments have to be paid for at the time of administration, and most hospitals and clinics will accept credit card payments. Individuals, families, or companies usually subscribe to medical and dental care insurance plans. Further information can be obtained from the Central Council for Medical Schemes (Private Bag X88, Pretoria 0001).

Practitioners are listed in the telephone directory (under "Medical Practitioners" and, for Afrikaans speakers, *Mediese Praktisyns*). It is advisable to ask friends and colleagues for recommendations. The city hospitals are generally equipped with the most advanced facilities, certainly of all the African nations and comparable with most Western cities.

Public hospitals tend to be crowded, and the medical and nursing staff are invariably overworked, although the standard of patient care remains remarkably high. Private hospitals generally offer a lot more comfort and individual attention, but are, of course, more expensive.

For more information on healthcare in South Africa see Health Systems Trust, www.hst.org.za, and South Africa Department of Health: www.doh.gov.za/index.html.

ENVIRONMENT ISSUES

The water in Johannesburg is safe to drink. Air pollution is not a major concern.

ECONOMIC OVERVIEW, 2008

GDP growth	3.8%
Inflation	11.8%
Unemployment	21.7%

INFRASTRUCTURE

Utilities and transport: Public transport in Johannesburg is extensive but usually quite crowded, and the high crime rate means that people avoid public transport if they can afford to.

Air travel: Johannesburg International Airport is South Africa's major international and domestic airport, serving both Johannesburg and Pretoria;it is the busiest airport on the continent of Africa.

The airport is situated 24 km from the city center. It offers a good choice of flights to Western European and African destinations and a fair range of departures to most other parts of the world.

All car rental kiosks can be found in the Domestic Arrivals area. Taxis can be found outside the arrivals area of Terminal A. A trip to the center of Johannesburg costs around ZAR 150 and takes around 25 to 35 minutes. Taxi kiosks are located in the baggage reclaim areas in Terminals A and B.

Impala Bus Company runs regular services into the city center. The service runs between 6:15 A.M. and 8:30 P.M., with buses leaving every 45 minutes. Many of the major hotels provide their own shuttle services that meet international flights. This usually has to be arranged in advance of arrival. Generally, the cost of this service is about ZAR 150.

Public transport: Metropolitan Bus Services (Tel: +27 11-403-4300) run buses within the Greater Johannesburg Metropolitan area. The service is available between 6 A.M. and 7 P.M., and there are 108 routes covering the city. Bus fares work on a zonal system (between Zones 1 and 6). The center of the zonal system is Gandhi Square bus terminus on Main Street. A single ticket for Zone 1 costs ZAR 2 and a single ticket to enter Zone 6 costs ZAR 7. Tickets can be purchased on the bus from the driver. A strip of ten-trip clipcards can be purchased from kiosks at the Gandhi Square bus terminus.

Taxis must always be telephoned for in advance. In the center you will find taxi ranks outside the Carlton, the Sandton Sun and the Sandton Towers hotels, and the railway station. All taxis operate meters, which, unfortunately, vary considerably in their fares. Taxis are relatively expensive, and if your journey is anything more than a "hop" across town it is advisable to ask the driver for an estimate of the fare. It is also advisable to check that he knows how to get you to your destination. The initial meter charge is usually ZAR 5, and the rate per kilometer is around ZAR 4–6.

Minibus taxis are available within the city. These cruise around the city and can be hailed in the street. Main routes are generally served between 5 A.M. and 9 P.M. These are fast (sometimes too fast) and tend to be overcrowded. You should use these taxis with extreme caution.

Car: The best way to get around Johannesburg is by car. Road signs tend to be poor and local drivers pushy, but the city's grid pattern makes it easy to find your way around. Familiarity with a few key roads and careful map reading makes getting around relatively straightforward. The Witwatersrand Street Guide is the best and can be found at CAN newsstands.

City rush hours are between 7 and 9 A.M. and 4 and 6 P.M. on weekdays. Traffic is often dense and slow moving, partly because there are so many one-way streets.

SHOPPING AND AVAILABILITY OF CONSUMER GOODS

Johannesburg offers a great shopping experience with huge varieties of products and shops to choose from. Mall shopping hours are generally Monday through Saturday, 9 A.M. to 5 P.M. and Sunday 9 A.M. to 2 P.M., although the bigger department stores and supermarkets may remain open until 6 P.M. For an excellent overview of shopping in Johannesburg, see www.sa-venues.com/attractionsga/johannesburg-shopping.htm; for details on shopping malls by location (city center, north, south, east, and west), see www.joburg.org.za/content/view/182/9."

South Africa produces some of the best meat, fruit, vegetables, and seafood in the world. Most consumer items for daily use can be found in the larger supermarkets. A wide selection of alcoholic beverages is available, and it is possible to purchase almost any model of car.

RECREATION AND ENTERTAINMENT

Restaurants: There is a very good choice of restaurants in Johannesburg. There is no such thing as "South African" cuisine in the sense of a single, coherent philosophy of food. The region is ethnically diverse, and cuisine is drawn from many parts of the world. However, the traditions of some colonial and immigrant groups have been especially influential. It is worth sampling some of the traditional Cape cuisine, which is an interesting mixture of Malay and Dutch. Natal has a significant Indian population and is a good place to try Indian cuisine.

Cinemas: There are plenty of cinemas in Johannesburg that show a variety of films. Ster-Kinekor and Nu Metro manage the main movie complexes, some of which boast 10 or more screens. Ster-Kinekor also runs the "Cinema Nouveau" in Rosebank Mall, which features art cinema. Tickets are available at the cinemas, from Computicket outlets at shopping centers, or online (some booking systems let you choose your seats as well as the venue and time).

Culture and entertainment: A wide choice of cultural events is available in Johannesburg. The Civic Theatre in Braamfontein is Johannesburg's premier scene for theater and opera productions, but there are other interesting locations, along with innovative companies such as the Johannesburg Youth Theatre.

The National Symphony Orchestra plays regularly at Linder Auditorium in Parktown, and dance companies such as the Moving into Dance Academy and the Dance Factory in the Newtown Cultural Precinct have given new life to the artistic side of Johannesburg.

Sports: South Africa offers a wide range of sporting opportunities, and Johannesburg can provide many sporting and leisure activities with excellent amenities. See the city's official site, www.joburg.org.za/content/view/317/9, for listings of golf courses, soccer venues, jogging courses, extreme sports, swimming pools, and recreation centers.

Nightlife: There are many bars located in the Hillbrow, Berea, and Troyeville areas. In the northern suburbs, bars are usually found in the shopping centers. There are many nightclubs located in Johannesburg.

Several publications encompass Johannesburg's events and nightlife. The *Mail & Guardian* publishes a weekly guide, and the Johannesburg Publicity Association publishes *Johannesburg Alive*. However, FM radio stations are the best guides for upcoming events. Tickets for most events can be booked through Computicket (www.computicket.co.za; Tel: +27 11-445-8445 for information or Tel: +27 11-445-8000 for credit card purchases).

SOCIOCULTURAL ENVIRONMENT

There are no formal limitations on freedom of speech and movement in South Africa. The free practice of religion is guaranteed by law.

There are two national television channels in South Africa, and satellite television is also available. Some international newspapers are on sale in Johannesburg. Government censorship has been lifted, but there is some informal pressure on the media.

DEMOGRAPHIC/WORKFORCE OVERVIEW

Population	44,187,637 (2006 estimate)
Population density	36.2 inhabitants per km^2
Age structure	0–14 years, 30%
	15–64 years, 65%
	65 years and over, 5%
Life expectancy at birth	
Total population:	42.73 years
Male	43.25 years
Female	42.19 years

WORKPLACE CULTURE

In general, South African business people are relatively conservative and reserved and prefer formal and low-key business contact. It is necessary to make appointments for business meetings, and punctuality is expected. However, protracted and tough bargaining is not part of South African business culture.

Business hours vary between companies; however, in general, working hours are Monday through Friday, 8 A.M. to 5 P.M. with an hour for lunch between 1 and 2 P.M.

Standard European business attire is the norm in South Africa. For meetings, men wear suits and ties, and women wear suits or conservative dresses.

NATURAL ENVIRONMENT

Johannesburg has a sunny and pleasant climate. Winters are usually mild, and temperatures rarely drop below 0°C. No natural disasters occur.

HOUSING

Johannesburg has a variety of suburbs, most of them within 30 to 40 minutes (commuting time) of the city center. The majority of them have poor public transport services, and it is usually necessary to travel into the city by car.

There are few difficulties finding rented accommodations in Johannesburg's suburbs. Both apartments and houses are available for rent, although houses tend to be more popular. The houses available in Johannesburg preferred by expatriates are limited. Individual housing is very common, and foreigners are allowed to own property in South Africa.

Districts that are favored by expatriates include Norwood, Parkmore, Bryanston, Sandton, Northern Suburbs, and Rosebank. Some residents prefer to live in housing complexes designed for security and protected by guards.

Household appliances and furniture are easily obtainable, and for household maintenance and repair, quality service is available at all times.

Property is usually found and rented through agents and newspaper advertisements, such as *The Star,* which can also be consulted online at www.iol.co.za. Agents usually charge between a 5 percent and 10 percent commission fee. House-hunting services are also available, and the usual charge is upwards of ZAR 200 for these services.

FINANCIAL ISSUES INCLUDING BANKING SERVICES AND TAXES

The banking system in South Africa is similar to and as sophisticated as those in most Western industrialized countries.

Currency may be exchanged at banks, hotels, and by authorized money changers. Some exchange controls are still in place but are gradually being lifted.

South Africa's currency is the Rand (ZAR). 1 rand = 100 cents. Notes come in denominations of ZAR 10, 20, 50, 100, and 200. Coins can be in denominations of ZAR 1, 2, and 5, and 1, 2, 5, 10, 20, and 50 cents.

Be careful that you do not mistake a ZAR 200 note for a ZAR 20 note, as they look very similar and you run the risk of an unscrupulous shop assistant taking advantage and short changing you. As the rand is a currency that fluctuates significantly, it is quite possible that you will get more rand for your unit currency when you arrive than when you leave. The exchange rate should always be checked before changing money as it can vary greatly in a short space of time.

Banks: Money can be changed at banks, which are located almost everywhere except in small towns. Banking hours are generally Monday through Friday, 9 A.M. to 3:30 P.M. and Saturday from 9 A.M. to 11 A.M., with banks in smaller towns usually closing for lunch. Banks are always closed on public holidays. In major cities, some banks operate currency exchange offices that stay open until 7 P.M. Outside banking hours, some hotels will change money, although they will charge a higher commission. Automated foreign currency exchange machines are available in some locations. ATMs are widely available; however, you should check with your bank to ensure that your card is compatible with the South African system. One of the many traps that tourists fall into is to accept assistance when at an ATM. Any such unsolicited offers of assistance are usually ploys to learn your PIN code and to steal any money you may have withdrawn.

Long-term visitors and residents find it convenient to have a Rand checking account at a local bank.

As Johannesburg is the main financial center in South Africa and home to the South African stock exchange, most international banks have established their branches in Johannesburg rather than in Cape Town.

In order to open an account, banks require a valid work permit and a letter from the employer confirming employment and sufficient funds. In addition to these documents, a valid passport and previous bank references are required. The post office offers savings accounts. It is not normally necessary to make a prior appointment in order to open an account with a bank in South Africa.

Credit cards: Visa and MasterCard (Access) are the most widely accepted cards in major cities, while American Express and Diners Club are accepted less frequently. Credit cards will not be accepted in small towns and rural areas where cash is needed for most transactions.

Traveler's checks can be exchanged at all commercial banks and larger international hotels. Some restaurants and shops will also accept traveler's checks, but may make a chargeable commission that can vary greatly. To avoid additional exchange rate charges at banks, it is advisable to take traveler's checks in GBP or USD; however, most major international currencies are accepted for exchange. There are foreign exchange bureaus in most major cities in South Africa.

Taxes: The tax year for individuals begins on March 1 and ends at the end of February the following year. Income tax is withheld by employers from salaries and wages on a pay-as you-earn (PAYE) basis. Taxpayers must file an annual return, and then the tax authorities issue an assessment notice for any tax that is due. However, all taxpayers earning less than ZAR 60,000 pay standard income tax through their employers and are exempt from filing a tax return.

Residents are taxed on their worldwide income, with certain exemptions and relief. An individual is considered a resident if

- he or she is "ordinarily resident" in South Africa or
- he or she is physically present in South Africa for more than 91 days in the current tax year and each of the three preceding tax years and for a period or periods of more than 549 days during the three preceding tax years.

Note that the 91 and 549 days are aggregates, and continuous daily presence is not required. However, a day includes a part of a day, so days of arrival in and departure from South Africa are included.

There are no tax concessions provided under the law for expatriates. However, expatriates usually qualify for a tax-exempt relocation allowance up to a maximum of one month's salary. Also, the Tax Act provides that where an employee is away from his usual places of residences, the employer can provide accommodations to the employee as a tax-free benefit. This needs to be structured correctly in order to qualify for the exemption.

INTERNATIONAL SCHOOLS AND EDUCATION

There is a good choice of schools for the international community in Johannesburg, with English, French, German, and Japanese schools offering kindergarten, primary, and secondary education.

Standards in local state schools have declined somewhat in recent years, but excellent local private school facilities are available.

- The American International School of Johannesburg (www.aisj-jhb.com): The curriculum is based on the American national curriculum but has an international flavor. Exams offered are the American graduation diploma and the International Baccalaureate. The school takes children between the ages of 4 and 18 years. A school bus service is provided. There is no uniform or dress code policy applied. There is a canteen available for children who wish to eat at school. School hours are Monday through Thursday, 7:40 A.M. to 2:55 P.M. and Friday 7:40 A.M. to 3:30 P.M.

- St. John's College (British school) (www.stjcollege.com): The curriculum is based on the English national curriculum. Exams offered include IEB examinations and the Cambridge Board A-levels. The school takes boys aged between 5 and 18 years. Girls are admitted into sixth form (the last two years of secondary school, for students age 16 to 18) only. A school bus service is provided at an additional cost. The school applies a uniform policy, and a canteen is available for children who wish to eat at school (cost ZAR 2,380). Hours are Monday through Friday, 7:40 A.M. to 2:55 P.M.

- Ecole Française Jules Verne (French school) (www.lyceefrancais.co.za): The French national curriculum is followed. Exams offered include the French Baccalaureate. The school takes children between the ages of 2 and 18 years. A school bus service is provided at an additional cost. There is no canteen available. School hours are Monday through Thursday, 8 A.M. to 3:30 P.M., Friday 8 A.M. to 2:35 P.M. (Lycée and Collège); Monday through Thursday, 8:10 A.M. to 2:10 P.M.,, Friday 8:10 A.M. to midday (Primaire); Monday through Thursday, 7:50 A.M. to 2 P.M., Friday 7:50 A.M. to midday (Maternelle).

- Deutsche Schule (German school) (dsj@dsjmail.co.za): The German national curriculum is followed. Exams offered are the Matric and Abitur. The school accepts children between the ages of 5 and 18 years. A school bus service is provided at an additional cost. The school does not apply a uniform policy. School hours are Monday through Friday, 7:55 A.M. to 1:10 P.M.

- The Japanese School of Johannesburg (jsj@icon.co.za, www.icon.co.za): The school follows the Japanese curriculum. A school bus service is provided at an additional cost. The school does not apply a uniform policy. There is no canteen available at the school. School hours are Monday through Friday, 8 A.M. to 3:50 P.M.

South Korea: Seoul

PERSONAL SAFETY AND SECURITY ISSUES

The internal political situation is somewhat unstable due to efforts to liberalize the economy and increase democracy in the country. Demonstrations and strikes are commonplace, but do not normally affect everyday life. They can, however, become confrontational and violent. Seoul is a relatively safe city, but with the increase of tourists and foreigners, the number of crimes such as bag snatching and sexual assaults has risen. One should avoid going out alone at night.

MEDICAL ISSUES

The healthcare system in South Korea is based on the following principles:

- Combination of Western and traditional Korean (*hanyak*) medicine, the latter is based on Chinese herbal remedies and acupuncture.
- Most healthcare resources are privately owned.
- Patients must first visit a primary care doctor, who will refer them, if necessary, to a general or university hospital.

Medical treatment is good in both public and private hospitals, and most medicines are readily available. Due to hot weather, the number of cases of dysentery has increased. It is thus advisable to filter and/or boil tap water. It is recommended to have inoculations against cholera, typhoid, and polio prior to entry, although these are not requirements for entry into the country. Waste removal and sewage services are usually functional throughout the city. Mosquito-borne encephalitis is a danger between June and October; therefore, protection against bites is highly advisable. Air quality is deteriorating and respiratory problems are increasing.

Medical treatment in Korea may be quite different from what you may be used to back home. Foreigners often complain that physicians seem abrupt and uncaring. Korean doctors are used to seeing a lot of patients in a limited time in a clinic setting. Also, Koreans do not have the same sense of privacy as most Westerners do, and this may create problems. Several of the larger hospitals in Seoul have foreigners' clinics staffed by physicians who speak English, or by an English speaking nurse who will coordinate appointments for you with specialists who speak at least a little English.

The foreign Community Service (FOCUS, Tel:+82 2-798-7529) provides referrals to hospitals, doctors, lawyers, schools, and other services in South Korea. The office is open Monday through Friday between 9 A.M. and 5 P.M., with voice mail service after hours. Membership is required; volunteers are available.

ENVIRONMENT ISSUES

Sanitation is very good in Seoul, although elsewhere old sewerage systems can cause problems from time to time. Improvements are being made outside main cities; however, it is advisable not to drink tap water. Despite this, there is little chance of contracting serious intestinal infections.

ECONOMIC OVERVIEW, 2008

GDP growth	4.2%
Inflation	5.0%
Unemployment	3.3%

INFRASTRUCTURE

Utilities and transport: Telephone, mail, water, and electricity services operate to a high standard. Seoul has a good public transport network, including an underground and an urban railway system. Road traffic is often congested even beyond the rush hour. The airport, Incheon International Airport, is situated 65 km from the city center and it takes almost 90 minutes to reach. It offers flights to most Asian destinations, plus some to Western Europe and North America.

With 16,500 inhabitants per km^2, Seoul is one of the world's most densely populated cities in recent years; the Seoul Metropolitan Government has taken various steps to deal with the city's transport-related problems. On July 1, 2004, bus routes, fares and schedules were integrated with the metro system, thus providing a far-superior overall public transport system. Metro lines have been expanded and measures have been taken to curb the harmful impacts of excessive car use and to encourage public transport use, walking, and cycling.

Air: The airport, Incheon International Airport, is situated 65 km from the city center and it takes a journey of almost 90 minutes to reach There are two terminals in the airport and both have a variety of facilities, including shops, restaurants, bureaus de change, banks, a pharmacy, and a post office.

It offers flights to most Asian destinations, plus some to Western Europe and North America. Buses from the airport to Seoul operate at 10–15-minute intervals. The most convenient and cheapest way to get to Seoul is the Limousine bus. Several kinds of taxis are available at the airport. Deluxe taxis are black and regular taxis are grey. There are also jumbo taxis that are able to carry up to nine passengers.

Metro (www.seoulmetro.co.kr): Although Seoul's underground can be very crowded during rush hours, it is a very convenient and efficient way to travel. The metro system in Seoul consists of ten lines. The lines are color coded and announcements are multilingual. Ticket counters, station names, and transfer signs are both in English and Korean. Since July 1, 2004, tickets can be used for both metro and bus services. There is a multipurpose, stored-value smart card (called T-money) that can be used for the entire network.

Bus: In 2004, the bus route network was entirely redesigned to enhance the structure and integrate over 400 different bus routes. All bus services are now grouped into four types, with buses color coded to help passengers distinguish between them. Blue buses are long-distance express buses that connect outlying suburbs with each other and with the city center. Red buses are long-distance buses that connect the satellite cities with the city center. Green buses provide local services throughout the metropolitan area to feed metro stations and express bus stops. Yellow buses provide local services within the city center.

Taxis are very popular in Seoul. Regular taxis calculate the fare from both the distance traveled and the time taken. For regular taxis, fares increase between midnight and 4 A.M. Taxis can be hailed from the street or caught at one of the taxi stands. Deluxe taxis are black with a yellow sign. For deluxe taxis, there are no surcharges for night hours. These taxis can be found at stands at hotels, major city streets, and at bus and underground stations. Most of the taxi drivers have mobile telephones, and foreigners can use an "interpreter service" system free of charge to state their destination.

You can also call for a taxi (Tel: +82 2-414-0150-5). All taxis in both Seoul and Busan have meters, and a receipt can be issued on request. The fare is paid according to the fare shown on the meter.

SHOPPING AND AVAILABILITY OF CONSUMER GOODS

Most daily consumables are in good supply, although some specific international products are not commonly available due to import restrictions. This also applies to alcoholic beverages and some models of cars.

Insa-dong district, widely known as Mary's Alley among the expatriate community, has the biggest concentration of shops dealing in arts, crafts, antiques and reproductions. Visit several shops to compare prices before purchasing any item. It is essential to get an official export certificate for any genuine antique (more than 50 years old).

Namdaemun Market, located in the very center of Seoul, is the biggest traditional market in Korea selling clothing for children, men, and women, daily miscellaneous goods, kitchenware, and local and imported products. Most shops have their own factories and make the products themselves, offering both wholesale and retail at very low prices. Every conceivable item can be found there.

Ever since its opening in 1905, Dongdaemun Market has been one of the major markets in Korea. Over the years, Dongdaemun Market has grown tremendously and now houses 30,000 stores within its 30 shopping centers. It is the largest wholesale and retail clothing market area in the nation, with 50,000 wholesalers.

A shopping district in the heart of Seoul is Myeongdong with upmarket shops, large shopping malls, and department stores. The headquarters of banks and securities brokers and many Western and traditional restaurants are also located here.

RECREATION AND ENTERTAINMENT

Restaurants: There is good choice of restaurants serving quality food. If you are entertaining Korean clients or business colleagues, it is advisable to take them to a Western restaurant rather than a Korean restaurant, however prestigious it may be and however familiar you may be with Korean table etiquette. Inexpensive meals can often be found in the basement restaurants of large department stores, in large underground railway stations, and underground shopping malls.

Culture and entertainment: Korea's entertaining scene blends traditional culture with the increasing influences of foreign countries. There are many choices, from discos to classical concerts to casinos. Seoul has a varied entertainment scene. There is a good selection of cultural events such as operas, theaters, concerts, and cinemas. Sports and leisure activities are available at private clubs.

Sports: Baseball and soccer are the most popular sports. Both are played at the Tongdaemun Stadiumin Seoul. Since Seoul hosted the 2002 Soccer World Cup, several new stadiums have been built. Tae kwon do is Korea's national sport. There are courses and demonstrations run at the Kukki-won Gym in Seoul.

Nightlife: Although the military-imposed midnight curfew has long since vanished, most restaurants and bars are still required to close their doors at midnight. But you can find some places open late and some places running all night long. Some indoor sports facilities, including bowling alleys and billiard rooms, also open after midnight.

Korean clubs expect you to buy a minimum amount of drinks and overpriced food when you sit at a table. If you want to dance, it is much better to frequent clubs near U.S. military installations where you are only charged for what you drink. All the major hotels have discotheques with the latest sound and lighting effects.

SOCIOCULTURAL ENVIRONMENT

Freedom of speech and religion is permitted. Local media may be under political pressure, especially when covering delicate subjects that touch on North Korea. International newspapers can be found at major hotels. Satellite television is available.

DEMOGRAPHIC/WORKFORCE OVERVIEW

Population	49,044,800 (2007 estimate)
Population density	491.7 inhabitants per km^2
Age structure	0–14 years, 18%
	15–64 years, 72%
	65 years and over, 10%
Life expectancy at birth	
Total population:	77.2 years
Male	73.8 years
Female	80.9 years

WORKPLACE CULTURE

Generally, business is conducted formally, with great value placed on punctuality and efficiency. Koreans are generally highly disciplined and hard working, but they can also be distrustful of outsiders and extremely nationalistic. Korean behavior is largely determined by Confucianism, which teaches respect for superiors, duty to family, and loyalty to friends. Workers generally respect the companies they work for and are driven to help their business succeed. Among co-workers, people of higher status and age are respected by those of a lower rank.

Business office hours are 9 A.M. to midday and 1 P.M. to 6 P.M., Monday through Friday, and 9 A.M. to 1 P.M. on Saturday. However, it is common to work later. Junior staff stays until their bosses leave the office. The prevailing six-day work week was shortened to a five-day work week in July 2004.

Men usually wear three-piece suits for business. Businesswomen are expected to dress conservatively, both in and out of the office. Business meetings are very formal and prior appointments are important. Koreans are more at ease as a group than as individuals and become uncomfortable when people speak as individuals instead of as a group, or when they make statements that are not in harmony with the group's view.

NATURAL ENVIRONMENT

The climate is moderate and has four seasons. The hottest part of the year is during the rainy season in July and August, while the coolest is during December and January.

Seoul has been subject to numerous typhoons causing landslides, damage to property, and disruption to traffic and communication.

HOUSING

Furnished and unfurnished accommodations are available, although it is not always possible to find accommodations of a good standard at a reasonable cost. Many expatriates live in residential areas with walled compounds and 24-hour security guards.

Western-style houses and apartments are also available for rent, but accommodations in Seoul are among the priciest in the world. At the same time, housing is often much smaller than that which some Westerners are accustomed. Often the size of accommodations are measured in *pyong*, where one pyong equals 3.3 square meters or 35 square feet. House-hunting services and accommodation agencies operate in the major cities.

Apartments are in giant complexes of similar buildings of more than five stories. Freestanding houses are usually quite common. A villa (or town home) is another option. These are constructed on large lots and are more spacious than apartment complexes. They usually have three or four stories. A watchman and a manager take care of security and maintenance.

A refundable deposit of KRW 5,000,000 to KRW 10,000,000 is required. Sometimes two or even three years' advance rent payment is requested. In this case, a discount is generally given.

Areas popular with expatriates include Sungbuk Dong, Nonhyung Dong, Itaewon Dong, Yong San, and Hannam Dong. The availability and quality of household appliances and repair services have improved considerably.

FINANCIAL ISSUES INCLUDING BANKING SERVICES AND TAXES

Most banking services are available, but they may not fully meet international standards. Delays are common for international transactions.

Currency: The currency in South Korea is the Won (KRW). The Bank of Korea issues the currency and mints coins. Currency units are in won notes of 1,000, 5,000, and 10,000, and won coins of 1, 5, 10, 50, 100, and 500 (although the 1- and 5-won coins are not used in general circulation).

There are numerous currency exchange counters at airports, banks, hotels, and major department stores (for example, Hyundai and Lotte). The exchange rates vary little from one to another. Hotel exchange desks have longer opening hours and are open on Sundays.

There are no restrictions on the amount of foreign currency that can be exchanged, but for amounts over USD 10,000 or equivalent, a customs declaration is necessary. The U.S. dollar and the Japanese yen are the most acceptable currency for exchange, but most other foreign currencies are easily exchanged at banks. It is advisable to keep all exchange certificates because they may be requested if you convert Korean currency back to foreign currency at the airport exchange desks. Bank drafts for large amounts (normally drafts of KRW 100,000) are available. Bank checks in denominations of KRW 100,000, 500,000, and 1,000,000 can be used, but merchants often add a surcharge for handling them, especially if they were issued by a bank in a different city.

Credit cards: In general, South Korea is a cash-oriented economy. Major international credit cards are, however, widely accepted.

Traveler's checks are accepted but may be difficult to exchange in smaller towns. When applying for a credit card in Korea, most companies require a Korean guarantor. The card credit limit available is determined by the nature of the employment of the Korean guarantor and the applicant, as well as the monthly salary of the applicant.

Banks: The Bank of Korea (BoK) (www.bok.or.kr) under the Ministry of Finance is the Central Bank with overall responsibility for banking supervision and control of money supply and credit. Over 50 foreign banks have branches or representatives in South Korea; however, only Citibank and the Hong Kong and Shanghai Banking Corporation (HSBC) offer retail services through their local branches. All remaining international banks engage only in corporate banking services such as loans in the local or U.S. dollar currency and foreign exchange or spot/forward transactions and guarantees.

It is advisable to check with your personal bank regarding services and facilities they offer expatriates. Banking hours are 9:30 A.M. to 4:30 P.M. on weekdays only.

You will have to visit a branch office in person, bringing identification (passport, Certificate of Alien Registration) with you. Then you will have to complete an application form—the staff may help you do this. After opening an account, you will receive a bankbook and the associated bank cards.

Taxes: All individuals in Korea are classified as listed below for income tax purposes.

- Citizen: Korean national.
- Resident: Non-Koreans having a domicile or residence within Korea for one year or more, individuals having an occupation that would generally require them to reside in and who retain substantial assets in Korea. Generally, residency is determined on a facts and circumstances' test, evaluated on an individual basis.
- Nonresident: An individual who is not deemed to be a resident.

Korean citizens and individuals considered residents for tax purposes are subject to Korean income tax on worldwide income. An expatriate who is deemed to be a nonresident is taxed only on Korean-source income. A nonresident is not allowed all the personal deductions granted to residents, except a basic deduction of KRW 1,000,000.

INTERNATIONAL SCHOOLS AND EDUCATION

There is a good choice of international schools in Seoul. There are international, American, British, French, German, and Japanese schools, which offer both primary and secondary levels of education. Schools to consider include the following:

- Deutsche Schule Seoul (www.dsseoul.org): The school follows German curriculum. There is a wide range of after-school activities provided such as sports, theater, and cooking.
- International Christian School (www.icseoul.org): The school follows an American program, including an AP program for some areas. There is a bus service available. A canteen is available for children who wish to eat at school. Two different playgrounds are available. Certain documents have to be provided as admission requirements. School hours are 8 A.M. to 5 P.M.
- Japanese School in Seoul (www.sjshp.or.kr): The school follows Japanese curriculum. It provides bus services. There is no canteen. The school offers after-school activities on Mondays, Tuesdays, and Thursdays. A playground is available for students during break time. Student registration certificate and application forms are needed for admission. School hours are Monday through Saturday, 8:25 A.M. to 5:30 P.M.
- Lycée Français de Seoul (www.lfseoul.org): The school follows the French curriculum and offers a bus service.
- Seoul Foreign School (www.sfs.or.kr): The school follows three different styles of education programs: British, American, and international. It provides children with a bus service. The school applies a uniform only for the British section. A canteen is available, and a lunch service is provided. A wide range of after-school activities is offered including sports, drama, and computing. Certain documents have to be provided as admission requirements. School hours are 8:20 A.M. to 3 P.M.

Taiwan: Taipei

PERSONAL SAFETY AND SECURITY ISSUES

Strikes are rare. Demonstrations occur occasionally but these hardly disturb everyday life. Taipei is quite a safe city and violent crimes are uncommon.

Taiwan suffers greatly from petty crime and theft; however, foreigners are seldom victims of serious crime. Crime is contained to local natives and their property. Pickpocketing is common in markets, especially in the night markets. The police rarely enforce the law. Corruption in politics and authority is rife. Statute law in Taiwan in practice is replaced with a system of reprisals. Again, foreigners are detached from this culture, although it is recommended that you keep personal details and those of your family discreet, as cases have been known to occur. More than two-thirds of Taiwanese taxi drivers are convicted criminals. It is prudent to not enter a taxi alone if you are a female, not to accept anything to eat or drink offered by the driver, and avoid being dropped off directly in front of your house.

Credit card fraud has now become so prevalent that some card issuers advise against using your credit card in Taiwan if possible. Criminals commonly use card readers in ATMs other than at banks and post offices, which are now replaced by card swipe readers.

MEDICAL ISSUES

The standard of health in Taiwan is relatively good, especially when compared to other countries in Asia. Universal healthcare is provided, and labor insurance is cheap and available to every worker. Health facilities in Taiwan provide routine and emergency medical treatment and are of a high quality. Physicians are highly qualified and many have studied in the United States, consequently speaking good English. Medical equipment is among the best in the world and is available at many clinics and hospitals. Ambulances are also available, although there are no trained emergency medical system technicians accompanying the ambulance, unless you live within two kilometers of the National Taiwan University Hospital or Veterans General Hospital (both located in Taipei). Ambulances are generally used purely as transport to the hospital. Drivers rarely speak English and have little medical training. Normally they will transport you to the nearest hospital, not necessarily the one of your choice.

The structure of health service in Taiwan differs from Western systems in several ways. There are few general practitioners; if you have a heart problem, you should go directly to the heart specialist and wait in a queue to visit them, rather than await a referral. It helps if you can make an appointment in advance; however, you can simply turn up at a hospital, seek out the relevant specialist, and wait your turn in line; the doctor will not leave until all the patients have been attended to.

Should you fall ill in Taiwan, you are eligible to visit any doctor or hospital for treatment. Problems can arise if your health insurance is not valid or does not cover you on that occasion. It is strongly recommended that you obtain the best possible travel insurance for your stay in Taiwan. Medical care is generally very inexpensive in Taiwan as many of the government clinics and hospitals are state subsidized, although emergency cases can cost you enormously.

There is an abundance of Chinese medicine practitioners throughout Taiwan. Their treatments/remedies are considered unorthodox and are very rarely used by foreign nationals, who prefer conventional medical care.

Doctors and hospitals in Taiwan expect immediate cash payment for health services. Many travel agents and private companies offer insurance plans that will cover healthcare expenses incurred in Taiwan, including emergency services such as medical evacuations. If you have a valid work permit and an alien resident's card, you will most likely qualify (after four months for Taiwan's National Health Insurance Program that covers routine checkups. The standard of healthcare is fairly good, although expatriates normally undertake major treatments outside the country. Most medicines are readily available.

Severe acute respiratory syndrome (SARS) and avian influenza (bird flu) have been contained, and there has been no evidence of further outbreaks. The government has made an effort to monitor and control the situation.

Ensure that your inoculations are all up to date, in particular, including hepatitis A and typhoid. A recent outbreak of dengue fever has led to travelers to the south of the island to use insect repellents and to take measures to avoid being bitten by mosquitoes.

The SARS virus is no longer considered to be a risk in Taiwan and was taken off the watch list in June 2003.

ENVIRONMENT ISSUES

Drinking tap water may cause minor intestinal upsets; therefore, most people prefer bottled water. Waste removal and sewage systems are functional.

Air pollution is a major concern in Taipei. It was acute a decade ago, but vast improvements have been made in air quality in the last few years. The air may probably never be really clear due to the fact that Taipei City is located in a natural depression surrounded by mountains, but it is not threatening to an asthmatic visitor. Heat stroke in the steamy summer months, also caused by the basin configuration of Taipei, is much more likely.

Common sense precautions concerning food are necessary. Raw fruits and vegetables must be carefully washed and meats must be cooked thoroughly as some are bought from open-air markets.

The health department rarely monitors any food sources or food preparations; however, in restaurants, as their reputations are at stake, few higher-class establishments take risks. The health department does checks when the restaurant opens and sporadically thereafter, but self-regulation is practiced and effective. Although illnesses from food or drinks sold by street vendors are rare, it is still not advisable for someone just off the plane to eat from hawkers. The food is prepared in the open air, at times without proper refrigeration, and the utensils are often less than clean. Water must be boiled prior to usage, or alternatively you can buy bottled water.

ECONOMIC OVERVIEW, 2008

GDP growth	1.9%
Inflation	1.9%
Unemployment	4.4%

INFRASTRUCTURE

Utilities and transport: Taipei's public transport system is efficient and cheap. Taipei is divided into north, south, east, and west. Chunghsiao Road dissects the city north to south. Chungshan Road bisects the city into the east and west sections of the grid. Addresses are identified by the position of the road on a compass grid and by the section of the road. A section is generally about three blocks long. The side roads are lanes and these do not have names but numbers. The number of the lane usually relates to the number of the building at the intersection with the main road.

The public transport system is improving. It includes the Taipei Metro, which consists of seven lines, with a few more under construction. Traffic in Taipei is almost constantly congested, and driving can be hazardous.

Metro: The Mass Rapid Transport (MRT) system runs throughout the city and development is underway to extend the service, which consists of the metro style underground trains and electric urban trains. A single journey ticket costs from TWD 20 to 65 depending on the distance traveled. A one-day unlimited pass is TWD 150. Trains run from 6 A.M. until midnight. You can take your bicycle on the MRT in Taipei; the government is making every effort to encourage residents to use their bicycles and the public transport system instead of cars.

Buses are frequent although signs are in Chinese only, making it difficult for foreigners to navigate the area. Bus prices for a single journey in the city cost between TWD 20 and 25. Caves Books and Lucky bookshops in Taiwan sell a bus guide written in English.

Taxis are also abundant, although again, the language could prove to be a barrier, as drivers rarely speak English. Rates are TWD 70 for the initial meter charge and just under TWD 17 for each kilometer. Taxis within the cities are metered, although it's common for the driver to switch off the meter outside the city and you will have to negotiate a price. It is wise to find out in advance what the journey should be, as you are likely to be charged much higher than the usual rate otherwise. If you are overcharged there is nothing you can do about it; it is advisable to try and use a taxi from the same company and request the same driver if you use taxis frequently.

Air: Chiang Kai-shek International Airport is located in Tayuan Township, Taoyuan County, about 40 kilometers from Taipei City. It provides good connections to other Asian cities, plus a fairly good selection of flights to Western Europe and North America.

It can take an hour to travel by road between the airport and the center of Taipei. In the rush hour traffic, it can be even longer. Hotel shuttle buses offer the best service compared to the slow airport bus service and expensive taxis. Taxis are located outside the arrivals hall around the clock. A 50 percent surcharge is added, exclusive of motorway tolls. Hotel shuttle buses should be requested in advance but can be arranged through the tourist information desk at the airport. Most hotels offer a limousine service. Taxi and bus drivers rarely speak any English, so it is important to get someone to write down your destination in Chinese before you make your journey.

The airport limousine buses run every 15 to 20 minutes from 6:30 A.M. to 10 P.M. There are two routes. The No. 2 bus runs along the Chungshan North Road and stops at the main railway station, the Hilton and Lai Lai Sheraton hotels; the other bus goes to Sungshan Domestic Airport and the northeast side of the city. Airport facilities include a tourist information office, post office, hotel reservation desk, and currency exchange office. Unused Taiwan currency may be exchanged at the Bank of Taiwan office in the departure lounge.

SHOPPING AND AVAILABILITY OF CONSUMER GOODS

Shopping is huge in Taiwan and is growing all the time. Taiwan has some of the largest and most modern stores in Southeast Asia. For an excellent discussion of shopping opportunities in the north (Taipei), central (Taiching), and south (Kaohsiung) regions of the island, as well as a listing of all major department stores and shopping centers, see http://eng.taiwan.net.tw/lan/Cht/multichoice/multichoice_detail.asp?id=2.

A wide variety of consumer goods is available, catering to both Asian and European tastes. Imported items are available but can be expensive.

RECREATION AND ENTERTAINMENT

The choice of restaurants in the city is fairly wide and the food served is of good quality. Cultural events are frequent, even by international standards. Sports and leisure facilities are available through both public and private clubs.

Restaurants: Eating out in Taipei and Kaohsiung is extremely popular, as there is an excellent choice at very reasonable prices. This often works out cheaper than shopping in supermarkets and cooking for oneself, as supermarket products are expensive. Taipei is principally concerned with Chinese cuisine and is renowned for having some of the best Chinese restaurants in the world. Much of the food from street hawkers is of excellent value and as food is kept boiling at high temperatures there is little risk of illness. Produce is fresh and tasty. The Taiwanese are averse to "hot" foods, and if you like your food spicy you will probably have to find a specialty restaurant. Much of the food is rice based and vegetarians will have no difficulty in finding a wide variety of choice; in fact, a relatively high percentage of Taiwanese are vegetarians themselves, as a result of Taiwan's long history of Buddhism. Although the food may be inexpensive in Taiwan, the cost of alcohol is not and may add substantially to the bill.

The restaurants here are too numerous to list; dining out is a Taiwanese way of life. A good current list of Taipei restaurants can be found at www.lonely planet.com/taiwan/taipei/restaurants. Many of the Western snack bars are springing up in Taipei, such as McDonald's, Subway, KFC, and Pizza Hut. There are some pizza restaurants available in the city and many burger and sandwich bars, especially in the shopping malls and around entertainment venues. The international hotels are usually home to the more upmarket restaurants. French cuisine is available at the Ritz and the Hilton hotels; Chinese (including Taiwanese, Cantonese, and Sichuan cuisine) is available at the Lai Lai Sheraton, the Hilton, the Ritz, and the Howard Plaza hotels. Sushi restaurants are abundant, popular, and very inexpensive. Swiss, Mexican, Thai, Korean, European, Japanese, and Indian food are also available.

Culture and entertainment: The Chinese Culture and Movie Centre and the world-renowned National Palace Museum are both located within the Shi Lin district and cover both the banks of the Keelung River and spill into the surrounding mountains. Shi Lin is best known for hosting Taipei's largest night market, the Shihlin Night Market.

The Taiwan Provincial Museum, Botanical Gardens, Chang Foundation Museum, andthe huge Chang Kai-Shek Memorial Hall that also houses the National Theater and National Concert Hall are located in Taipei's Zhong Zheng district.

Nightlife: The best place for information on nightclubs in Taiwan is found at the Taipei Night Life Web site www.taiwannights.com/886nights. Well-known international DJs are found in clubs such as the Ministry of Sound in Taipei, and there are other popular nightspots such as Plush, an upmarket hip hop and R&B club located on the 12th floor in Living Mall of Bade Road.

The Tavern (www.tavern.com.tw) near the Grand Hyatt hotel is another pub-style bar popular with the foreign community. It is open from 11:30 to 1 A.M. The Pig and Whistle is a very popular pub frequented by expatriates who enjoy the wide selection of imported beers available. Located in Tienmu, the bar is open from midday until 2 A.M. (until 3 A.M. on weekends). Sports are shown on a large screen.

SOCIOCULTURAL ENVIRONMENT

In 1987, the martial law under which Taiwan was governed for four decades was replaced by a new national security law, embodying some broadening of political freedom. There is tolerance regarding religious practices and the government is gradually relaxing political controls. International newspapers are available, as is satellite television.

DEMOGRAPHIC/WORKFORCE OVERVIEW

Population	22,858,872 (2007 estimate)
Population growth rate	0.3% (2007 estimate)
Age structure	0–14 years, 18%
	15–64 years, 72%
	65 years and over, 10%
Life expectancy at birth	
Total population:	77.56 years
Male	74.65 years
Female	80.74 years

WORKPLACE CULTURE

Business hours are typically from 8:30 A.M. to midday and 1 to 5:30 P.M. Monday through Friday. Government office business hours are 8:30 A.M. to 12:30 P.M. and 1:30 to 5:30 P.M. Monday through Friday. Saturday hours are the same as other businesses, 8:30 A.M. to midday. Some Taiwanese workers will nap for half an hour after lunch. It is advisable to refrain from scheduling appointments until at least 2 P.M. for this reason. In addition Taiwanese business culture frequently involves late nights at bars or restaurants; therefore, scheduling morning appointments is best avoided. Business breakfasts are also not practiced.

The work ethics in Taiwan is particularly strong and it is not uncommon to work 12 to 15 hours a day. Deadlines in Taiwan frequently pass their agreed dates; it is quite usual for the deadline to carry over for at least a week. This can be part of the negotiation ploy to destabilize the other party and you should never complain about deadlines being passed. Professional, conservative, and modest working attire is recommended for both men and women.

It is quite common for you to be directly questioned about your salary or the cost of any material items you own. You should always answer such questions by either giving a few details or by responding indirectly.

Modesty is a revered quality in Taiwanese culture. When complimented you should not accept the statement with a "thank you," rather you should reply that you are not worthy of such a comment. The notion of saving face runs strongly throughout Taiwanese business and social culture. It is important that you never say anything that could embarrass or belittle any business counterparts. Strong business relationships are forged on respecting each other's dignity.

NATURAL ENVIRONMENT

The climate in Taipei is hot and humid in the summer and cold and wet in the winter. Taiwan is located near a fault line and severe earthquakes have affected the island. Taipei is occasionally subject to typhoons and floods that can be very serious.

HOUSING

A wide variety of good-quality apartments and houses are available for rent in Taipei. Peitou, Jasper, Eastern Downtown, Tien Mou, and Yang Ming Shan are some of the districts popular with expatriates. Household appliances, furniture, and repairs of good quality are available.

Most expatriates find accommodations through real estate agencies. English-speaking agents advertise in the *China Post, China News,* and the *Taipei Times.* Agents generally charge a commission fee. If you are looking for an apartment other than through an agent, it is always advantageous if you can take along someone who speaks Chinese, as many private landlords do not speak English. In Taipei, it is usual for car parking or garages to be included in the rental price; however, if this is not the case, the average prices are between TWD 5,000 and 10,000, again determined by the area.

In Taipei, you would normally pay two months' rent in advance as a deposit; for a house you should expect to pay three months' rent in advance.

In Taipei, rental costs for houses have decreased slightly; prices for apartments have remained stable. Accommodation prices in Kaohsiung have remained stable as well. Accommodation costs vary greatly depending on the area and size of the property. For a furnished two-bedroom apartment in Taipei, prices range from TWD 65,000 to 115,000 and TWD 50,000 to 100,000 for an unfurnished apartment. A three-bedroom furnished house is between TWD 100,000 and 190,000 per month; unfurnished properties of the same size are from TWD 90,000 to 180,000.

FINANCIAL ISSUES INCLUDING BANKING SERVICES AND TAXES

Currency: The unit of currency is the New Taiwan dollar (TWD), also referred to as kuai, which totals 100 cents. The coins come in denominations of TWD 1, 5, 10, and 50. Notes come in units of TWD 100, 500, 1,000, and 2,000.

Currency may be exchanged at banks and hotels. Most banking services are available, although they do not always reach international standards. Delays may occur when making foreign currency transactions. Taiwan's currency has fluctuated greatly in the last few years.

There are no bureaux de change in Taiwan. Currency must be exchanged either at a government-designated bank or at a hotel. The official exchange rate is used at the exchange office at the airport, the Bank of Taiwan, and the International Commercial Bank of China (ICBC). The bank at CKS Airport (Taipei) is open when flights are departing and arriving. In Taipei, ICBC or the Bank of Taiwan are the best places to change money, although hotel rates are sometimes slightly lower. When exchanging currency, it is important to keep the receipt issued, as you will have to present this when leaving the country; it is illegal for New Taiwan dollars to be taken out of the country, so all local currency must be exchanged.

Traveler's checks may be cashed at branches of the Bank of Taiwan or in some larger international hotels if you are a guest. It is worth shopping around when changing traveler's checks, as commission costs can vary greatly.

Credit cards: Major international credit cards are widely accepted in any outlets catering to foreigners, particularly in Taipei, but they may not be accepted for small transactions under the value of TWD 1,000.

Banks are open 8:30 A.M. to 3:30 P.M., Monday through Friday and 8:30 A.M. until midday on Saturday. The Central Bank of China (CBC) is both the government's bank and an agency under the Executive Yuan. The CBC issues the local currency; controls the money supply, credit, and public debt via its control over interest rates and local banks' reserve/asset ratios; plus acts as the government's fiscal agent and oversees all foreign exchange operations.

There are around 23 commercial banks (in 13 of these, the government has a majority stockholding). The Bank of Taiwan is the leading domestic bank here.

As a general rule, foreigners wishing to open up an account in Taiwan must produce a valid work permit and resident card. Some banks will only request a passport, although this is unusual. Application forms for an account are usually in Chinese; either bring a Chinese-speaking friend to the bank with you for assistance or you may be lucky and find staff who speak English and will fill out the form in Chinese for you.

It is important to be aware that ATMs in Taiwan only accept four-digit PIN codes; therefore, if you have a six-digit PIN you will not be able to withdraw money.

Banking with a branch of your own bank from your native country will not mean that you can access the overseas account from Taiwan. Regulations stipulate that they must remain separate. International banks offer a wide range of foreign currency accounts, direct debit, and online facilities as well as savings accounts and loan opportunities. Personal checks are rarely issued in Taiwan's cash-based society. To pay utility bills, it is recommended that you set up a direct debit which is usually the most convenient, or pay in cash at any post office or bank.

Taxes: Any Taiwanese citizen or foreign national (residing in Taiwan for over 90 days per year) is eligible for taxes. Taiwanese taxes range from 6 percent to 40 percent and are among the highest in Asia. Most employers will deduct tax at the source from their employee's salary. The withheld tax is credited against the annual sum of tax owed. Tax returns must be filed by March 31 the following year and should be accompanied by any outstanding tax owed.

Taxable Income (TWD)	Tax on Lower Amount (TWD)	Tax Rate
0–369,999	0	6%
370,000–989,000	22,200	13%
990,000–1,989,999	102,800	21%
1,990,000–3,719,999	310,700	30%
3,720,000+	832,700	40%

INTERNATIONAL SCHOOLS AND EDUCATION

There are international, American, English, French, German, and Japanese schools in Taipei. Like many other countries, Taiwan's educational system begins with one to two years of preschool education and nine years of compulsory education, including six years of elementary education and three years of junior high school education. After finishing compulsory education, students take national exams in order to receive senior secondary education, which includes three years of senior high school, three years of vocational high school, or five years of junior college. Schools to consider include the following:

- British School Taipei (www.taipeieuropeanschool.com): The curriculum is based on the British national curriculum with an international content. The Nursery and Infant School serves children aged 3–6 years, Junior School 7–10 years, and Secondary School (key stage 3) 11–14 years. Bus services are available. There is a school uniform policy. French and Chinese language and culture forms a part of the core curriculum from age 12. All pupils from the French, German, and British sections, on reaching the age of 14, attend the TES High School, where they spend two years studying for the International Certificate of Secondary Education, followed by the International Baccalaureate (or the TES High School diploma for students who have not attained the level of the IB).
- Deutsche Schule Taipei (www.taipeieuropeanschool.com): The curriculum is based on the German national curriculum; language acquisition is given priority. Mandarin is also taught. There is a school bus service available. Hours are kindergarten, 8 A.M. to 12:30 P.M. (until 2:30 P.M. once a week); other classes are 8 A.M. to 2:50 P.M. Students have an hour for lunch from 12:30 until 1:30 P.M.

- Ecole Française de Taipei (www.taipeieuropeanschool.com): The curriculum is based on the French national curriculum. The school serves children aged from kindergarten (preschool) to 14 years. A school bus service is available. There is no uniform policy. A canteen is available for children to eat at school. School hours are kindergarten, 8 A.M. to 2:15 P.M. and primary and secondary, 8 A.M. to 3:20 P.M.

- Taipei American School (www.tas.edu.tw): The curriculum is international and based on the U.S. core curriculum and students can work towards exams for the Advanced Placement Program or the International Baccalaureate Diploma. The school serves children aged between kindergarten and grade 12. There is a school bus service available. There is no uniform policy. A canteen is available for children who wish to eat at school. The school provides a wide range of extracurricular activities. School hours are Lower School, 7:45 A.M. to 2:30 P.M. and middle and upper schools, 7:45 A.M. to 3:15 P.M.

- Taipei Japanese School (www.taipeijs.org): The school provides bus services. There is no canteen available. School hours are Monday through Friday, first and third Saturday, 8:10 A.M. to 3:40 P.M.

Thailand: Bangkok

PERSONAL SAFETY AND SECURITY ISSUES

The relationship between Thailand and most other countries is generally stable, but there are periodic border clashes with Burma/Myanmar. Historically, the country has been internally unstable. Martial law was declared, but has now been partially revoked. A new constitution has been approved, which will lead to the return of democratic elections. Violent crimes occur, but are not a major concern, providing normal precautions are taken. Corruption and bribery are widespread, and laws are sometimes contradictory or not applied.

While it is very easy to enter or leave Thailand as a tourist, visas and work permits for residents are expensive and difficult to obtain. A work permit is required if working one day or more in Thailand, and takes at least six weeks to process. As in any other large city, pickpocketing, purse snatching, and other petty crimes are common on Bangkok public buses and in areas where tourists/foreigners gather. Extra precautions should be taken with regard to the safety of personal belongings. When using taxis at the airport or downtown, travelers should avoid unlicensed taxis. A growing number of travelers have reported being robbed after consuming drugged food. There are a number of scams reported by visitors to Bangkok involving the purchase of jewelry to export. Credit card fraud is on the rise.

MEDICAL ISSUES

The standard of sanitation and healthcare varies dramatically depending on the location in Thailand. Private hospitals in Bangkok offer excellent services, although medical expertise may not reach the highest standards. The quality of dental services is very good. Medical supplies are freely available, with or without prescription. Bangkok has a very high incidence of AIDS, and it is also necessary to take precautions against malaria, hepatitis, yellow fever, and gastrointestinal diseases. The severe acute respiratory syndrome (SARS) has been kept within limits, and another outbreak seems unlikely. The government has made an effort to monitor and control the situation. The avian influenza (bird flu) situation is likewise being monitored by the authorities.

Healthcare in Bangkok matches the standards of healthcare in Western cities. There are many excellent medical and dental practitioners in Bangkok. Details can be found in the local telephone directory. Private hospitals include Bangkok Adventist Mission Hospital, Bangkok Christian Hospital, Bangkok General Hospital, BNH Hospital, Bumrungrad Hospital, Central General Hospital, Chao Phya Hospital, and Phyathai Hospital. Government-run hospitals include Chulalongkorn University Hospital, Police Hospital, and Rajavithi General Hospital. Dental treatment in Bangkok is available at the Dental Hospital.

Pharmacies can be identified by an illuminated green cross sign and can usually be found in shopping centers. Opening hours are generally daily from 8:30 A.M. to 9 P.M. Unlike in the West, many medications can be bought over the counter without prescriptions for symptoms not acute enough to warrant seeing a doctor.

ENVIRONMENT ISSUES

Drinking tap water is not advisable, but bottled water is plentiful and cheap. Waste removal services are not completely functional, which makes some city areas unpleasant. Sewage systems are not totally reliable and most of the city's canals are polluted as a consequence.

Air pollution is a major problem in Thailand.

ECONOMIC OVERVIEW, 2008

GDP growth	4.7%
Inflation	6.3%
Unemployment	1.4%

INFRASTRUCTURE

Utilities and traffic: The quality of telecommunications is very good, and services are reliable and efficient. Mobile phones and pagers are widely available. Mail services are generally of average quality, but express services are available. Public transport is very cheap, currently provided by taxis, tuk-tuks, minibuses, regular bus services, ferries, and riverboats. A modern elevated metro system (Skytrain) operates within major business areas of the city. Traffic is a very severe problem in Bangkok, where entire areas, including highways, can often be completely blocked for hours. It is essential to allow plenty of time for all journeys.

Air travel: The main airport (Suvarnabhumi Airport), which opened in 2006, is located 25 km east of downtown Bangkok, and is one of the busiest airports in Asia. Bangkok has excellent air services to the rest of Asia, and a good range of direct flights to North America, Western Europe, and the Middle East. However, travelers to and from destinations in Africa and Latin America may need to catch a connecting flight.

Bangkok Transit System (BST) (www.bts.co.th) or Skytrain has two lines. The Sukhumvit Line starts in eastern Bangkok at Sukhumvit Soi 81 (on Nut Station) and ends at the old Mor Chit bus terminal in the north of the city (Mo Chit Station). It passes along Sukhumvit Road, Ploenchit Road, Rama I Road, Phyathai Road, Victory Monument, and Phahonyothin Road. The Silom Line starts at the foot of King Taksin Bridge (Sathorn Bridge) on the Bangkok side of the river and ends east of Banthat Thong Road near the National Stadium. From Sathon Road, it proceeds north to Naradhiwas Rajanagarindra (the junction with Klong Chongnonsee) where it turns east to join Silom Road before running along Ratchadamri Road and Rama I Road.

Two types of tickets are available: single-journey tickets and stored-value tickets. Both tickets are purchased from ticket offices, which are located in every station. Fares vary between THB 10 and THB 40, depending on the distance traveled (Zones 1–7).

Trains operate daily from 6 A.M. to midnight, with departures every three minutes during rush hours and every five minutes during off-peak hours.

Mass Rapid Transit Authority of Thailand (MRTA) (www.mrta.co.th) has regular operations here. Two types of tickets are available: single-journey tickets and stored-value tickets. Both tickets are purchased from ticket offices, which are located in every station. Fares range from THB 14 to THB 36, depending on the number of stations traveled.

Bus services are operated by the Bangkok Mass Transit Authority (BMTA) (www.bmta.co.th). Bus route maps are available in hotels and bookshops.

Buses are classified as follows:

- Non-air-conditioned regular bus (red-cream color): This is the cheapest bus service. Fares are THB 5 for any journey. Services usually operate between 5 A.M. and 11 P.M. Some red and cream buses travel on the expressway, in which case the fare is THB 6.50. These buses usually have a yellow sign in the front. All night buses run between 11 P.M. and 5 A.M.. Other types of regular service buses in white-blue color and privately owned mini-buses in green run on some routes. The fare is THB 6 for any distance for the white-blue bus and THB 4.50 for the green mini-buses. The green mini-buses are notorious for the nerve-wracking maneuvers of their drivers.

- Air-conditioned buses (cream-blue color): The bus fare depends on the distance traveled and ranges from THB 9 to THB 17. Services usually operate between 5 A.M. and 11 P.M. Air-conditioned buses (white-pink color) are only available on some routes.

The fare is THB 10. Services usually operate between 4:30 A.M. and 11 P.M.

- Euro II bus (yellow-orange color): These buses are air conditioned and relatively new. Services operate between 5 A.M. and 11 P.M. The fare ranges from THB 11 to THB 21, depending on the distance traveled.
- Micro-bus (purple or red color) is an alternative privately owned bus service. The 20-seat passenger buses are air conditioned. The fare is a flat THB 20 regardless of the distance. Micro-buses stop taking passengers once the seats are filled.

Train: There are only a few train services offering stops in Bangkok and the suburbs. There are two routes: Bangkok-Chachoengsao-Prachinburi and Bangkok-Ayutthaya-Lopburi-Kaengkhoi. Fares range between THB 10 and THB 30, depending on the distance and class. Advance tickets are available daily at all principal stations from 5 A.M. to 11 P.M. or at the Bangkok Advance Booking Office at Hua Lampong Station from 8:30 A.M. to 4 P.M.

Taxi: Metered taxis are available in Bangkok. They can be hailed in the street or taken from taxi stands. Always ensure that the meter is turned on. The initial meter charge is THB 35, and then THB 5 for every kilometer traveled. Passengers have to pay the charges for the toll roads. Make sure you have small change for the fare, as drivers often have no change. Tipping of taxi drivers is not really a Thai practice, though rounding the fare up to the nearest THB 5 or THB 10 is fairly common. All licensed taxis have yellow and black number plates. Unmetered taxis are also available, but the price should be negotiated prior to the commencement of the journey. The price will vary depending on the distance, traffic, and weather. Average fares around Bangkok are THB 50 to THB 200. If you are not near any taxis, you can phone 1661 and order one to pick you up. This costs the meter fee plus THB 20.

Tuk-tuks: Tuk-tuks are three-wheeled, open-air vehicles powered by a two-piston engine. They take two passengers (three or four at a squeeze). Tuk-tuks offer an "interesting" ride and are better taken for shorter trips during off-peak hours. For passengers who are over 1 m 80 tall (6 ft), they can be quite uncomfortable as head height is limited. Be aware also that you may be subject to much dirt and pollution while riding in a tuk-tuk. Fares must be negotiated before getting in, and generally range from THB 40 to THB 150, depending on the distance you wish to travel. Tuk-tuks can be found mainly in the Bangkok area and are popular among tourists.

Boat: On the Chao Phraya River, boats run between Ratchasingkhorn Temple and Pak Kred in Nonthaburi province. There are regular stops along the way. The total traveling time is approximately 1 hour, 45 minutes. Check your destination before getting into the boat as they do not stop at every port, and some boats do not go beyond Nonthaburi town. The fare is THB 10 throughout the route. Boat taxis are classified by a flag system. Daily standard express boats (without flags) depart every 20 minutes between 6 A.M. and 6:40 P.M. During weekday rush hours, special express boats stop at certain docks on the Nonthaburi to Ratburana

Route (yellow flags), Nonthaburi to Sathorn Route (red/orange flags), and the Pak Kred to Ratchasingkorn Temple Route (green flags).

On Saen Saeb Canal, boats depart daily every 15 minutes between 5:30 A.M. and 7:30 P.M. The fare is THB 5–15, depending on the distance. Boats start from Sriboonruang Temple and then dock at around 20 stops until they terminate at Panfah Leelard Bridge. The total traveling time is about 1 hour. Boats return along the same route.

On Lard Prao Canal, boats depart daily between 5:30 A.M. and 7:30 P.M. Fares cost between THB 7 and THB 15, depending on the distance. They start the journey from Saphan Mai near Ying Charoen Market and terminate at Prakanong, stopping at around 12 docks on the way. Boats return along the same route. The total travel time is about 1 hour, 30 minutes.

Car: Driving in Bangkok requires a great deal of patience. This is not the most advisable way to travel around Bangkok, as good knowledge of the city is required to be able to find your way. The density of the traffic and the number of lanes mean that drivers always need to know which lane to be in. There are a number of expressways crossing the city, with clearly signposted exits, but during the rush hours (7 to 9 A.M. and 4 to 6 P.M.), the traffic is often grid-locked. However, car rentals are available in the city; companies include Avis, Budget, and Hertz.

SHOPPING AND AVAILABILITY OF CONSUMER GOODS

Food is plentiful in Bangkok and of very good quality. A few items such as imported meat (veal, lamb, etc.) may be hard to find. Fruit and vegetables are available in good supply and there are no problems with quality. Other daily consumption items, both local and imported, are widely available, although replenishment of stocks in retail shops is irregular. There is a good choice of alcoholic beverages. There is a good selection of brands and models of cars, and the waiting times for imported cars have been significantly reduced. Bangkok is one of the most popular shopping locations in Asia because prices are relatively inexpensive, quality is generally high, and the range and variety are innumerable. The Silom Road area is one of the main shopping centers. The Sukhumvit Road area has a street market that is open daily, morning until evening.

Shops are generally open seven days a week, from 10 A.M. to 10 P.M. Siam Paragon (www.siamparagon.co.th) is a luxury shopping mall on the site of the former Intercontinental Hotel in Siam Square, which houses shops, car showrooms, aquaria, food courts, fountains, cinemas, restaurants, and serviced apartments. The Emporium consists of shops, a department store, food court, and cinema complex. Central World Plaza has shops, restaurants, cinemas, and an ice skating rink. Designer shops are available at Gaysorn Plaza, and Sogo department store and fast-food outlets are found in Amarin Plaza. Erawan, Peninsular Plaza, All Seasons Place, Siam Discovery Centre, MBK Centre, Central Plaza, and Central City are other shopping centers.

Popular department stores, with many branches throughout the city, include Central and Robinson. Big C is a hypermarket with several stores located throughout the city. Carrefour and Tesco Lotus are others. Many street markets are located in Bangkok: Chatuchak Weekend Market is an open-air market that sells everything. It is located on Phayathai Road and is open on Saturdays and Sundays. Patpong Night Bazaar begins at 7 P.M. in the Patpong area and Silom Road.

RECREATION AND ENTERTAINMENT

Bangkok has an excellent choice of both Thai and foreign restaurants of all types and price ranges. Concerts starring world-famous names are becoming more common, but the choice of theater, opera, etc. is more restricted. Cinemas have a fairly wide variety of local and foreign movies; however, English-language films that are shown are not the most recent. There is a good choice of sports and leisure facilities of all types, including over 100 golf courses, although some of these may be a long way outside the city.

International associations and clubs in Bangkok area include The British Council (www.britishcouncil.or.th), Alliance Française (www.alliance-francaise. or.th), Goethe Institut (www.goethe.de/so/ban/enindex.htm), American Women's Club of Thailand (www.awcthailand.org), British Club Bangkok (www .britishclubbangkok.org), and The Japanese Association (www.jat.or.th).

Restaurants: There are plenty of restaurants in Bangkok. The following are only a few recommendations. Excellent Thai, other Asian, and continental cuisines are widely available. French restaurants are usually considered the premier places to entertain business guests and to enjoy good food and a pleasant atmosphere. Thai Cuisine, Le Café Siam, Supatra River House, Salathip, Baan Khanitha, Ban Klang Nam, Lemon Grass, Suda, and Ad.Makers are others. International cuisine can be obtained at Biscotti (Italian cuisine) and Angelini's (Italian cuisine), New York Steakhouse, Shenanigans, Charley Brown's (Mexican cuisine), and William Tell (Swiss cuisine).

Culture and entertainment: Current events, performances, cinema screenings, and festivals are advertised in the English language newspapers *The Bangkok Post* (www.bangkokpost.net) and *The Nation* (www.nationmultimedia.com). TAT (Tourism Authority) also publishes a weekly events magazine, *Where,* which has a comprehensive listings of events.

The Bangkok National Theatre stages Thai drama, concerts by the Bangkok Symphony Orchestra, and occasional performances by visiting artists. Thailand Cultural Centre hosts Thai classical dance and cultural evenings. Chalerm Krung Royal Theatre hosts Thai drama and plays. Patravadi Theatre is an outdoor theater hosting modern adaptations of classical Asian literature; show times are on Friday, Saturday, and Sunday. Bangkok Playhouse hosts modern dramas.

Museums include the National Museum, National Gallery (has traditional and contemporary Thai art); Prasart Museum (has Thai antiquities); Princess

Maha Chakri Sirindhorn Anthropology Centre (http://av.sac.or.th/SAC_E/index.html) (showcases different sociocultural developments in Thailand, ethno-archaeology, Thai ceramic collections, as well as the Princess Maha Chakri Sirindhorn's biography); Bangkok Folk Museum (this is a traditional house converted into a private museum); Science Museum and Planetarium; Jim Thompson's House and Museum (www.jimthompsonhouse.com, a former home of the man who saved the Thai silk industry from collapse); Supatra River House (a two-storey traditional Thai house showcasing cooking demonstrations; it also has a restaurant); and the Royal Barges Museum.

Full listings of films, cinemas, and show times can be found online at the Movieseer, Thailand (www.movieseer.com/Index.asp?Channel=2). Many of the cinemas that show English-language films are located around Siam Square.

Entertainment for children: Future Park Rangsit is an amusement park and fun world for children. Others are the Lumpini Park, Sanam Luang (flat field for strolling, picnicking, and soccer); Ancient City (www.ancientcity.com), Bangkae Amusement Park (computer games and fun rides), The Ngamwongwan Water Park and Playland (play land for children under 135 cm); Samut Prakarn Crocodile Farm and Zoo; and Yoyo Land (entertainment zone with activities for children aged 3–10 years).

Nightlife: There is more to nightlife in Bangkok than adult entertainment, even though the city has developed a worldwide reputation for it. Bangkok offers a wide range of nightlife, including nightclubs, pubs, cocktail lounges, restaurants, cinemas, pool halls, and cabarets. For up-to-date information on the best nightlife venues, see Bangkok.com (www.bangkok.com/nightlife/index.html), which has listings of what is going on in the city and where to find it.

Bars include Woodstock (www.woodstockbkk.com), The Londoner Brew Pub (English-style micro-brewery), Old German Beerhouse, Gulliver's Travellers Tavern, The Dubliner Irish Pub, Huntsman Pub, Riverside Lounge, and The Barbican (London-style bar).

Nightclubs include the Mystique Night Club (hip hop, R&B, house music), Q Bar Bangkok (house music, hip hop), Lucifer (pop/dance to hard-core techno and trance music), Narcissus, La Nina Latin Heat Café (regular Latin dance and singing contest, fashion shows, and exotic theme nights), and Concept CM2.

Sports: Popular and traditional spectator sports include Thai boxing (*muay Thai*), Takro (a game passing a small rattan ball), motorcycle racing, soccer, kite-fighting, horse racing, and boat racing. There are national competitions for each of these sports. In Bangkok, horse racing takes place every Saturday at the Royal Bangkok Sports Club, Henri Dunant Road, or every Sunday at the Royal Turf Club, Phitsanulok Road. Thai boxing matches are held at the two main stadiums in Bangkok: Lumpini, Rama IV Road (Tuesday, Friday, and Saturday) and Ratchadamnoen, Ratchadamnoen Nok Road near TAT (Monday, Wednesday, Thursday, and Sunday). Tickets can be purchased at the gate. Thailand offers great opportunities for a whole range of water sports, including diving, snorkeling, windsurfing, canoeing, sailing, and rafting. Rental of equipment and instruction are widely available at Thailand's many beach resorts. Sports facilities in Bangkok include a range of fantastic golf clubs and fitness centers.

Sports for children: Imperial World Ice Skating (www.bangkok.com/sport-ice-skating/index.html) has the only Olympic-size rink in Bangkok complete with skating facilities like first aid, a training room, changing room, and pro shop. Skating lessons are available. Cycling (www.bangkok.com/cycling-tours/index.html) allows a fun way to see Bangkok by bike. Most biking tours also accommodate children (aged 12 upwards). Dance (www.bangkok.com/sport-bangkok-dance-fever/dance-schools.html) schools offer various kinds of classes, some specializing in a certain type of dance. Most parks (www.bangkok.com/sport-parks-&-activities/index.html) have sports facilities such as a tennis court, swimming pool, soccer pitch, and other amenities, which can be hired for a very small fee. Tae kwon do classes are available at all ages and levels, starting with the Little Dragons program for children aged 4–6 years.

The Tourism Authority of Thailand (TAT) (www.tourismthailand.org) operates tourist information services at various locations in Bangkok.

SOCIOCULTURAL ENVIRONMENT

Personal freedom is guaranteed by the constitution, but in reality it is restricted by corruption. There are restrictions on the freedom of action of trade unions. The freedom of students (for example, to conduct a protest) has been relaxed. Making disrespectful remarks about the Thai royal family must be avoided, as this can be considered a capital offense punishable by death. There is free practice of religions, and Thais are traditionally very tolerant in this respect. All types of media, including satellite television, free TV, and cable TV with more than 36 channels are available, but movies and publications are subject to censorship. Newspapers are unrestricted in their publication of political opinions, although objectivity could be hampered by corruption.

DEMOGRAPHIC/WORKFORCE OVERVIEW

Population	65,068,149 (2007 estimate)
Population density	126 inhabitants per km^2
Age structure	0–14 years, 21.6%
	15–64 years, 70.1%
	65 years and over, 8.2%
Life expectancy at birth	
Total population:	72.5 years
Male	70.2 years
Female	75.0 years

WORKPLACE CULTURE

Thai people have a strong sense of identity and history. Disparaging remarks about any member of the royal family are ill advised and illegal.

Thai respect for rank and authority demands that all documents, requests, and proposals must travel up the entire chain of command before they reach the actual decision maker; therefore, decision-making is a slow process. Thais will go to great lengths to avoid giving an outright "no" and believe it is not possible to be too polite. Decisions are made at the top, and subordinates shield high-level executives so they do not have to deal with situations for which they are not prepared.

Punctuality is becoming a norm, and arriving on time for a meeting will earn you respect. However, do not be surprised if your Thai associate is late as the business pace is relaxed. Your first meeting could be a business lunch, at which business might not be discussed at all. Thais like to take time to get to know their potential business partners. When talking business, do not ask questions that require a direct response or a judgement. Bluntness, and its potential for confrontation, will make a Thai uncomfortable and could be considered impolite. If Thais laugh for seemingly no reason, they are embarrassed and it is best to change the subject.

Thai women have long been active and highly visible at all levels of business and are treated the same as men. Foreign women can expect to be treated with respect and taken seriously, but they will find they are more easily accepted if they speak softly.

It is important to make prior appointments, and business cards are widely used. Business cards should be printed in both Thai and your national language or English. Thais generally prefer business to be conducted face to face rather than on the telephone. The maintenance of "harmony" in all relationships is important to Thais, and consequently any conflict, confrontation, or criticism will usually cause offense and embarrassment. Differences of opinion are settled through negotiation, informal discussion, or subordinates' deference to superiors.

Entertaining is an important aspect of developing business relationships and negotiating contracts. Invitations to lunch or dinner are the rule and whoever issues the invitation normally pays the bill. After dinner, your Thai host may suggest you move on to a bar for drinks. It would be impolite to refuse such an invitation. It is customary to exchange small gifts with business associates in Thailand. Appropriate gifts include liquors, something from your home country, or books. Gifts should be modest. Thais love bright colors, so gifts should be wrapped in brightly colored gift wrap and ribbons. Remember, however, that ripping open the wrapping paper is offensive.

Government offices are open Monday through Friday, 8:30 A.M. to 4:30 P.M., with a lunch break between midday and 1 P.M. Businesses are generally open from 8 A.M. to 5 P.M.

Business attire is very often used to project and assess status, and it is advisable for men to dress formally in dark-colored business suits, ties, and polished shoes.

Businesswomen should wear tasteful, conservative dresses or suits with long sleeves (never sleeveless), high collars, and below-the-knee-length skirts.

Thais do not normally shake hands except in more Westernized groups. The traditional and most common Thai greeting is the *wai*. This is made by placing both hands together in a prayer position at the chest and bowing slightly. Do not be surprised if you are addressed by your first name instead of your surname, though you should use surnames until invited to use first names by your counterparts.

NATURAL ENVIRONMENT

Thailand has three seasons. Between October and January it is cool and dry, while between February and May it is hot and dry. The monsoon season is between June and September, when torrential rains fall throughout the country. Extreme temperatures are rare in Bangkok. The monsoon rains often cause local flooding in Bangkok, which is badly drained, and light earthquakes are sometimes registered. Floods resulting in extensive material damage and loss of life have occurred within the last two decades. In Bangkok, the average high temperature is 35°C in April, which is usually the hottest month. The temperature falls to 21°C in December.

HOUSING

Apartments, houses, condominiums, and townhouses are all available here. The more prestigious districts include Sathorn, Sukhumvit, and the Dusit area. Household appliances and furniture are available, but with wide fluctuations in quality and variety. Maintenance and repair services tend to be either very expensive or of low quality.

The Bangkok Post (www.bangkokpost.net) and *The Nation* (www.nationmultimedia.com) have real estate and rental listings. "For Rent" signs are often posted outside available accommodations, although often the sign is only in Thai.

A few real estate agencies are CB Richard Ellis (www.cbre.co.th/en/index.asp), Andrew Park Co. Ltd. (www.andrewpark.com), and Thailand Top Properties Sales and Rentals (www.thaitopproperties.com).

Lease periods are usually for two years and are renewable. One-year leases are possible, but owners will have the option to increase the rent after the first year if you decide to stay on longer. Some owners, however, will prefer leases on a year-by-year basis. Most landlords require one month's rent to be paid in advance and the equivalent of two month's rent as a security deposit. This deposit is usually refundable. Houses and apartments—good areas: Pholyothin; very good areas: Sukhumvit; best areas: Sathorn.

Sukhumvit is situated within 30 minutes of the city center. Many expatriates live in this area due to its convenient location and facilities such as shopping malls, public gardens, and playgrounds. An apartment or resident with a 24-hour security guard is recommended.

There is a fair choice of furnished apartments available in Bangkok with a full range of services and facilities provided. Unfurnished accommodations are also available. The cost of accommodations can vary considerably depending on the area and type of housing. The average cost of a two-bedroom, unfurnished apartment in a very good area in Bangkok is THB 90,000 per month. For apartments, parking places are generally included in the rent. However, with houses a monthly charge is usual for parking facilities. Water supply is usually included in the monthly rent; other utilities are sometimes included in the rent, but this is not standard procedure and should be specifically set out in the lease. Garbage collection services pass about twice a week in Bangkok, and the cost is generally around THB 30 per month. Full-time, part-time, and live-in domestic help is available. For part-time cleaning staff, the pay rate is around THB 80 to THB 100 per hour. For childcare services, the cost is around THB 70 to THB 90 per hour.

FINANCIAL ISSUES INCLUDING BANKING SERVICES AND TAXES

The Thai Baht is convertible, although it is difficult to exchange outside Asia. The import and export of foreign currency is unlimited. Many international banks now operate in Thailand due to a recent drive aimed at opening up the country to financial services. However, few of these offer consumer banking services. Although some local banks have worldwide networks, the quality of their services remains average. The ongoing banking and finance sectors' restructuring is expected to improve the quality. E-banking has been introduced, and many banks can provide this service.

Currency: The unit of currency in Thailand is the Baht (THB); 1 baht = 100 satang. Notes are in denominations of THB 1,000, 500, 100, 50, 20, and 10. Coins are in denominations of THB 10, 5, and 1, and 50 and 25 satang.

Banks and checks: Foreign currency can be exchanged at banks, hotels, and bureaux de change offices. Banks generally offer the best rates. Hotels tend to charge high commission fees. It is recommended to carry smaller denominations of notes and also carry coins. Traveler's check can be exchanged in banks, large hotels, and some shops. Major international credit cards are accepted in most establishments. MasterCard and Visa are the most commonly accepted. American Express and Diners Club are not as widely accepted. Some merchants will apply a surcharge of 5 percent for the use of a credit card. Also, make sure you receive the carbon copies, as theft and forgery can be a problem. ATMs are widely available. Siam Net and Bank Net Cards may be used at banks other than the issuing bank, provided the ATMs work on the same network. There is usually a handling fee of 1.5 percent on every withdrawal transaction from another bank.

Foreign visitors may open a savings account without any problem, but they must be residents to open a checking account. Checks can be deposited into saving accounts, and funds are generally made available within a day. Checks written on foreign accounts may take up to three months to clear. Foreign currency accounts with any commercial bank in Thailand are also available to foreigners. As long as the funds originate from abroad, there are no restrictions imposed by the government on the maintenance of and withdrawal from the account. However, banks may apply their own rules. When opening an account, you will require an official piece of identification (passport).

Taxes: Thailand taxes its residents and nonresidents on their assessable income derived from employment or business carried out in Thailand, regardless of whether such income is paid in or outside of Thailand. Residents, defined as persons residing in Thailand at one or more times for an aggregate period of 180 days or more in any tax year (calendar year), who derive income from abroad are taxable on that income if remitted into Thailand in the year in which it is received. Short-term residence is not defined under Thai tax regulations. Expatriate tax concessions are typically not provided. Possible concessions may be available where an individual is working in Thailand under an economic or technical cooperation agreement between Thailand and his or her home country.

INTERNATIONAL SCHOOLS AND EDUCATION

There are many educational possibilities in Bangkok, including international, English, French, Swiss/German, Swedish, and Japanese schools. In total, there are almost 52 international schools in Bangkok, located in various parts of the city. A number in the outskirts are difficult to reach, and some are expensive. Most local schools teach in Thai, but there are some church-managed high schools and vocational schools that teach in English. Standards at these schools are generally below average. Some universities also use English as a medium of instruction, but the general level of education is low.

- The International School of Bangkok (www.isb.ac.th): The curriculum is based on the U.S. standard. Programs offered are AP (Advanced Placement) and IB (International Baccalaureate). Exams offered are ACT, AP, IB, MAT, PSAT, SAT, and TOEFL. The school takes children from kindergarten to grade 12. There is a school bus service provided, and a canteen is available for children who wish to eat at school. The school applies a uniform/dress code policy.
- The American School of Bangkok (www.asb.th.edu): The curriculum is based on the U.S. curriculum. The school takes children from pre-kindergarten to grade 12. School bus services are available. The school applies a uniform/dress code policy, and a canteen is available for children who wish to eat at school (grades 1–5, meals are included in the school fees). School hours are 7:30 A.M. to 2:45 P.M.
- The Bangkok Patana School (British school) (www.patana.ac.th) is based on the British curriculum. Exams offered are PSAT, SAT, GCSE, International General Certificate of

Secondary Education (IGCSE), and International Baccalaureate Diploma. The school takes children from pre-kindergarten to grade 12. School bus services are provided. The school applies a uniform/dress code policy. Two cafeterias are available, offering light snacks or full lunches. School hours are 7:40 A.M. to 1:50 P.M. (kindergarten) and 7:40 A.M. to 2:30 P.M. (primary and secondary).

- The Lycée Français International de Bangkok (French school) (www.lfib.ac.th) is based on the French curriculum. Exams offered are Brevet des Collèges and Baccalaureate. School bus services are run by a private company. A canteen is available for children who wish to eat at school. School hours are 7:30 A.M. to 12:40 P.M.

- The Deutschsprachige Schule Bangkok (German school) (www.dssb.org) follows the Swiss and German curricula. The school takes children from kindergarten to grade 12. School bus services are provided. The school applies a uniform/dress code policy. A canteen is available for children who wish to eat at school.

- The Japanese Association School (www.tjas.ac.th) is based on the Japanese curriculum. School bus services are provided. There is no canteen. School hours are Monday through Friday, 8 A.M. to 3:20 P.M., and twice monthly on Saturdays from 10:10 A.M. to 11:50 A.M.

Turkey: Istanbul

PERSONAL SAFETY AND SECURITY ISSUES

The relationship between Turkey and neighboring countries is complex. The Cyprus dispute continues to cloud relations with Greece. Occasional terrorist attacks are carried out by Kurdish separatists; however, the number of these incidents has slightly decreased recently. Violent crimes occur and crime, in general, is on the increase. Common sense precautions should be taken.

MEDICAL ISSUES

The standard of public health and sanitation in the larger cities of Turkey are generally good. Nevertheless, they are still below the standard of other European cities or those in the United States. The medical and health facilities in Istanbul are generally adequate. Hospitals are well equipped and the standard of care is usually good. Turkey has many private hospitals emerging over the last few years in response to the lengthy queues and impersonal service found in state hospitals. Even though state hospitals are better, private facilities are often favored by the upper and middle classes as well as the expatriate population. State hospitals lack hygiene and staff; some of the best surgeons are found in state hospitals, in particular, university hospitals. Staff will usually speak English (especially in the private sector); however, in Istanbul, some of the hospitals funded by foreign communities include a higher proportion of their own native speakers, such as

French, German, and Italian. Some of Turkey's best medical care is at the Red Crescent hospitals (Turkey's equivalent of the Red Cross).

ENVIRONMENT ISSUES

Although tap water is usually chlorinated in the larger cities, it is not necessarily treated; therefore, it is advised to avoid drinking tap water where possible. Bottled mineral water is widely available. If you find a water source marked *içilir, içme suyu,* or *içilebilir,* then the water is safe for drinking; if it is marked *içilmez* then it is unfit for consumption.

All fresh fruits and vegetables should be washed thoroughly with drinking water, and meat and fish should be well cooked. Changes in diet can often cause upsets to the digestive system; therefore, you should eat only a small amount of food on arrival until you get used to the different food stuffs in Turkey. Air pollution is still a concern in Istanbul, although it has improved in recent years.

ECONOMIC OVERVIEW, 2008

GDP growth	3.5%
Inflation	11.0%
Unemployment	11.0%

INFRASTRUCTURE

Utilities and transport: The electricity supply is usually reliable, but there are occasional interruptions. Voltage changes are rare. Water services are generally reliable, but some disruptions occur. Telephone services in Istanbul are excellent, and the mobile telephone network is extensive. Postal services have a reputation for being unreliable and consequently fax services are becoming more widely used for written communication.

Public transport is fairly extensive but can be inefficient. Traffic is congested for much of the day, especially during the rush hours.

There is a huge variety of public transport available in Istanbul, especially with its coastal location opening up possibilities of water transport. Public transport is fairly extensive but can be inefficient. Traffic is congested for much of the day, especially during the rush hours. All forms of transport takes either tickets or tokens. A good way to save money if you are using public transport on a frequent basis is by purchasing a smart ticket called an *Akbil.* These can be purchased at all main bus stations and can be used in almost all forms of transport, offering you a discount between 10 percent and 25 percent. The "key" is plastic and has a rechargeable battery.

Taxi (*Taksi*): As with Ankara, taxis in Istanbul are plentiful and are yellow in color, making them easy to identify. The meter should be on day rate (*gündüz*) from 6 A.M. until midnight and night rate (*gece*) from midnight until 6 A.M. The initial meter charge is slightly higher than in Ankara, although the price per kilometer is less. If your journey takes you over the Bosphorus bridges, you are also required to pay the tolls.

Dolmus (*Dolmuş*): Istanbul also has a very popular dolmus taxi/bus hybrid, which follows certain routes, but you can descend wherever you please and not just on scheduled stops. A sign in the bottom right side of the windscreen will tell you the direction and destination of the dolmus. It is a cheaper alternative to taxis, but more comfortable and less crowded than buses. Depending on demand, taxis can turn into dolmus and occasionally can levy a special (higher) rate for unusual journeys or when bad weather increases demand.

Bus (*Otobüs*): Istanbul has two principal bus operators. Belediye Otobüsü is the municipal run bus line which accepts payment by the Akbil smart key as well as normal tickets and various discount ticket cards. The privately owned Halk Otobüsü accepts only cash or payment using the Akbil key. These bus fares are of the same price as those on the municipal owned buses. The Halk Otobüsü company has a number of double-decker buses that are popular especially when others suffer from overcrowding. If you pass over the Bosphorus Bridge, you will have to use three tickets—all other journeys require two. Again, as the buses are privately owned, it is not possible to use the tickets here; however, cash and Akbil payments are equally acceptable forms of payment.

Metro (*Hafif Metro*): Istanbul's metro system is only partially underground and consists of three lines, one stretching from Eminönü to Zeytinburnu via Aksaray; Aksaray to Yenibosna, passing through Otogar and also serving Atatürk International Airport; and Levent via Sisli to Taksim. The Akbil key is valid for the metro or you can purchase a discount card for the metro from any of the station's ticket booths.

Tunnel (*Tünel*): The tunnel is a welcome alternative to climbing the steep street from Karaköy to Beyoğlu. The coach is now run by electricity and is a very short funicular open from 7 A.M. to 9:30 P.M. daily (Sundays 7:30 A.M. to 9 P.M.); tokens for a single journey cost TRY 0.75.

Tramway (*Tramvay*): The short journey between Taksim and Tünel is closed to all traffic—aside from walking the old tram is the only alternative form of transport along Istiklal Street. Tram tickets can be bought preferably in advance or from the driver once on board.

Ship (*Vapur*): The ships in Istanbul go from one side of the Bosphorus to the other and sometimes to distant points that are on the same side. The two companies are Princes' Islands ships or Bosphorus cruises; prices for tokens will vary depending on the operator.

Motorboat (*Motor*): These are small boats that take you the short distances between various "water bus stops" around the Istanbul coast. They are found next to ship ports and operate the following lines: Kad köy-Eminönü-Kad köy;

Beşiktaş-Üsküdar-Beşiktaş; and Karaköy-Üsküdar-Karaköy. You should buy your ticket from the staff once on board.

Ferry Car (*Araba Vapuru*): Car ferries operate daily between Sirkeci and Harem. Tickets are bought prior to boarding.

Sea Bus (*Deniz Otobüsü*): These buses operate to Australia, Bangladesh, China, Hong Kong, India, Indonesia, Japan, Malaysia, New Zealand, Pakistan, Philippines, Singapore, South Korea, Sri Lanka, Taiwan, Thailand, and Vietnam.

Suburban Train (*Banliyö Treni*): Suburban trains operate from Sirkeci on the European side of Istanbul and from Haydarpaşa on the Anatolian side. They provide a good alternative during peak traffic hours but they can be dirty and not at all comfortable. Akbil payment is accepted on the suburban trains as well as tickets or discount cards purchased at the station.

Air: The airport, Ataturk International Airport, is situated 24 km from the city center and can be reached after a bus journey of 50 minutes. The airport offers a good choice of flights to Western Europe, the Middle East, and some destinations in the United States. Most other journeys require a connecting flight.

The Havas airport bus connects to Taksim Square and the bus terminal. Probably the easiest way to reach the center of Istanbul from the airport is by metro. Buses run daily from 6 A.M. until 11:30 P.M. approximately every half hour from the airport to Taksim Square and on demand from the airport to the bus terminal. Taxis are available directly outside the arrivals terminal. The journey to the city by taxi takes approximately 30 minutes. There is a 50 percent surcharge for journeys late at nigh and an additional charge for luggage.

Airport facilities include banks, ATMs, and bureaux de change as well as tourist information and hotel reservation desks, bars, restaurants, duty-free shopping, a conference center, a post office, 24-hour left luggage, and a first aid post.

Both Turkish Airlines and British Airways have their own lounges. There is a millennium lounge for first- and business-class passengers of scheduled flights.

SHOPPING AND AVAILABILITY OF CONSUMER GOODS

Istanbul offers a full variety of excellent quality food, consumer goods, and alcoholic beverages. There is a good selection of automobile brands available for purchase.

Istanbul has a wide variety of shopping, whether it be in supermarkets, department stores, weekly bazaars, or the many antique emporiums and craft shops. The bazaars (known as *bedestans*) are very popular but you must be sure to bargain hard for everything. It is usual to offer 50 percent of the initial price and then be prepared to go up about 25 percent to 30 percent of the initial price asked. Beware that you don't start bargaining for something that you don't want to buy, as this is considered rude. Even in shops where the prices are fixed, you may be able to bargain a reduced price if you are purchasing more than one item.

The large shopping malls are open daily from 10 A.M. to 10 P.M., but these can get very crowded on weekends. Wikipedia (http://en.wikipedia.org/wiki/List_of _shopping_malls_in_Istanbul) gives a good list of the historic malls (including the Grand Bazaar, going back to 1461), almost 50 modern ones, and more than a dozen projected ones.

RECREATION AND ENTERTAINMENT

Restaurants: Turkish cuisine has an excellent reputation. Throughout the country, whether you eat at a street-side café or luxury restaurant, it is likely that you will experience delicious food. Eating establishments are available in abundance, particularly in the cities. As Turkey is a predominantly Muslim country, you will rarely find pork dishes. Lamb is the basic meat of Turkish cuisine.

Different dishes from each region contribute to the complexity of Turkish cuisine. For example, due to heavy rains, the Eastern Black Sea region specializes in dishes which rely mostly on corn and corn flour, as wheat is difficult to grow. The Southeast Anatolian region is famous for Kebaps (roasted meat dishes, which Americans might refer to as "kebabs"), as livestock in the area is plentiful. The Aegean region, known for its olive production, is famous for its delicious vegetables marinated in olive oil and herbs, while the Thrace offers tasty and varied pastries.

Alcohol is available in Turkey. The national alcoholic drink, *raki,* is made from grapes and aniseed (this is usually mixed with water or ice and served as an aperitif or sipped throughout the meal). Good wines include Doluca and Kavaklidere, available in red (*kirmizi*) or white (*beyaz*). The most popular local beer is Efes Pilsen.

There is an excellent choice of restaurants offering traditional Turkish food as well as those providing international cuisine such as French, Italian, and Chinese food.

Many restaurants do not accept credit cards, unless they are more upmarket or part of a hotel. Visa, MasterCard, American Express, and occasionally Diners are most commonly accepted.

Culture and entertainment: There is a wide range of entertainment in Istanbul, from the traditional folk dance and theatrical groups to the internationally acclaimed Istanbul International Festival held from late June to mid-July. During the festival performances of modern and classical music, ballet, opera, and theater are found throughout the city. Tickets and further information are available from the tourist information offices and the Istanbul Foundation for Culture and Arts.

The Istanbul State symphony, ballet, and dance companies perform at the Atatürk Kültür Me kezi. There are chamber music performances at the Beyaz Kösk and Hidiv Kasri organized by the Touring and Automobile Club. There is no central ticket agency; therefore, tickets can be purchased from the venue or by applying in advance to the organizers. Full details of entertainment venues and shows can be found at www.mymerhaba.com.

The AKM houses the Istanbul State Symphony Orchestra and Chorus, Istanbul State Modern Folk Music Ensemble, and Istanbul State Classical Turkish Music Chorus. The State Symphony Orchestra gives concerts every Friday at 7 P.M. and Saturday at 11 A.M. You can attend to these concerts either by subscribing beforehand or buying a ticket the same day. Sports and leisure facilities of a high standard are available.

Nightlife: There are a number of night clubs (see Fodor's lists of clubs by type and region at www.fodors.com/world/europe/turkey/istanbul/nightlife.html) and restaurants (see Fodor's reviews of almost 50 restaurants at www .fodors.com/world/europe/turkey/istanbul/restaurants.html) throughout Istanbul, which offer a variety of entertainment programs throughout night.

SOCIOCULTURAL ENVIRONMENT

In Turkey, there are a few minor regulations limiting personal freedom, although some journalists and writers speaking on behalf of the Kurdish people or about other sensitive political issues have faced government reprisals. Free practice of religion is guaranteed.

Most local television and radio is now in private ownership. International cable television is available. Nearly all international newspapers are available in Istanbul.

DEMOGRAPHIC/WORKFORCE OVERVIEW

Population	71,158,600 (2007 estimate)
Population growth rate	1.0% (2007 estimate)
Age structure	0–14 years, 25%
	15–64 years, 68%
	65 years and over, 7%
Life expectancy at birth	
Total population:	72.9 years
Male	70.4 years
Female	75.5 years

WORKPLACE CULTURE

Businesses are normally open Monday through Friday, 8:30 A.M. to 12 noon and 1 P.M. to 5 or 6 P.M. and closed on Saturdays and Sundays. Turkish males may attend the Friday Congregational Prayer called the *Cuma Namazi* at 1 or 1:30 P.M. on Friday afternoons. It is advisable to avoid traveling to Turkey on business between the months of June and August, as many Turks take extended vacations to spend time with their families.

Business dress in Turkey is conservative. Men are expected to wear a suit and tie. Women should wear smart professional attire.

NATURAL ENVIRONMENT

Istanbul has a warm Mediterranean climate. Summers are very hot, and winters are mild. The rainy season is from November to March.

Several major fault lines cross Turkey. Although fairly low, there is a possibility of severe earthquakes occurring. Heavy rains have caused flooding in Istanbul in recent years.

HOUSING

There is an acceptable range of apartments and villas available to rent, although the price paid is often high considering the quality of the property. The most prestigious residential areas of the city include Bosphorus, Bebek, Ulus, Yenikoy, Etiler, Levent, Emirgan, and Arnavutkoy.

As with Ankara, fully furnished houses in Istanbul can be difficult to find; there are usually few problems encountered when looking for unfurnished properties. There is an acceptable range of apartments and villas available to rent, although the price paid is often high considering the quality of the property. In Istanbul, prices for a furnished three-bedroom house start at around USD 3,500 for a good area, rising to USD 8,000 per month in the best areas. For a furnished two-bedroom apartment, prices range from USD 1,700 to USD 3,000 a month depending on the area. Unfurnished properties of comparable size are from USD 1,300 to USD 2,600. Rental prices have been consistent for the last 12 months in Istanbul.

Parking or garage space is normally included in the rental price. It is usual to pay two months' rent as a refundable deposit or to pay the rental charges in advance.

There is a very good choice of household appliances and furniture. Maintenance services are available and are of good quality, though there is generally a wait for such services. The *Turkish Daily News* is an English language paper where most of the larger real estate agencies (*Emlakç*) advertise. Landlords usually advertise accommodations in local newspapers and you can deal with them directly.

FINANCIAL ISSUES INCLUDING BANKING SERVICES AND TAXES

In Istanbul, many foreign financial institutions are represented by branches or subsidiaries. Banking services are usually reliable.

Currency: The official currency of Turkey is the New Turkish Lira (TRY). It was introduced on January 1, 2005, whereby six zeros were dropped from the previous currency, the Turkish Lira (TRL), and the sub-unit New Kuruş was created. Other than this change of six zeros, there was no revalue or devalues in the Turkish currency. Both currencies were used side by side until December 31, 2005. Old Turkish lira bank notes, which are no longer in circulation, may be redeemed until December 31, 2015 in Turkish banks.

Yeni Kuruş (New Kuruş) is the sub-unit of the New Turkish Lira. 100 New Kuruş make 1 new Turkish Lira. Coins are in denominations of 1, 5, 10, 25, and 50 New Kurus, plus there is a 1 TRY coin. Notes are in denominations of 5, 10, 20, 50, and 100 TRY.

It is essential that all exchange certificates and purchase receipts be retained in order to prove that legally exchanged currency was used for purchases in Turkey.

Traveler's checks: The easiest way to get cash liras is to use a home bank card or credit card in a Turkish ATM. Cash can be exchanged at a currency exchange office (*Döviz Bürosu*). Many people will not accept large bills/notes for small payments, so it may be necessary to ensure a range of value notes.

Traveler's checks can be cashed immediately on presenting proof of identity at some banks and all PTT (post office) branches. In order to avoid additional exchange rate charges it is recommended that traveler's checks are taken in GB pounds or U.S. dollars. *Döviz* are currency exchange offices. They will exchange traveler's checks at the best rates but will also levy a service fee.

Credit cards are widely accepted throughout Turkey to pay for most goods and services. Visa, MasterCard, and Eurocard are the most popular, although many of the larger hotels and upmarket restaurants accept American Express. Some merchants still practice the custom of adding the credit card fee on top of the price of the goods purchased, which can range from 2 percent to 4 percent. Despite this being labeled illegal in 2003, foreigners in particular may face this. The service fee is called a *komisyon.*

ATMs are available at most Turkish banks and you can withdraw cash either on your credit card or by using your Cirrus or Plus card. Credit card fraud is rife in Turkey. It is important that you do not let the card out of your sight when handing the card to shop assistants and waiting staff. Request that you swipe the card yourself if possible to avoid it being scanned illegally and your card information being passed onto criminals.

Banks: Istanbul is Turkey's financial center; hence most foreign banks that operate in Turkey have branches in Istanbul rather than the capital, Ankara. Banking hours are 8:30 A.M. to 12:30 P.M. and 1:30 P.M. to 5 P.M. Monday through Friday.

Expatriates usually open an account in one of the major international banks represented in Turkey. It is possible to open a lira account in any Turkish bank, however, checks can take a long time to clear and there is a lot of paperwork to complete each time. In order to open a bank account, you require a valid passport, a letter confirming your credit, and a valid Turkish work permit.

Some foreign banks may request your personal tax number. Joint accounts are available for married couples only. Some accounts require an initial deposit of around EUR 1,000 and others require simply that a certain minimum balance is maintained in order to keep the account alive.

Taxes: The tax year in Turkey is the calendar year. Tax returns are normally filed before the end of March. Individuals who have resided in Turkey for at least six months of the year are considered to be tax payers in Turkey and are taxed on their global income. Those who are resident in Turkey for less than this period are considered to be limited tax payers. Turkish income tax rates vary from 15 percent to 40 percent depending on the level of income.

Expatriates who are employed by a nonresident employer for a limited duration in Turkey are exempt from Social Security payment provided they are insured abroad. Salaries paid in foreign currency by employers who are not involved in any trade, industrial or service activity in Turkey and whose business centers are not in Turkey are exempt from Turkish Tax.

INTERNATIONAL SCHOOLS AND EDUCATION

There is a good choice of schools catering to the international community of Istanbul. There are international, English, American, German, French, Italian, and Japanese schools offering both primary and secondary levels of education.

- British International School (www.bis.k12.tr): The school follows the British national curriculum, with a heavy emphasis on foreign languages, followed by the International Baccalaureate. Students sit GCSE examinations in year 11 and are offered the International Baccalaureate in year 12. There is a uniform policy. A school bus service operates and a canteen is provided. School hours are 9 A.M. to 4 P.M. The school takes children between the ages of 5 and 18 years. The admission process may require an examination and an interview.

- Istanbul International Community School (www.iics.k12.tr): The curriculum is international although it is also recognized by the Turkish Education Authorities. The language of instruction is English. Students are accepted from the ages of 3 to 19 years. The school has two campuses: the Hisar campus (Rumeli Hisar) for children aged 3 to 9 and the Marmara Campus near Alkent 2000 for children aged 3 to 18. The school is accredited by the European Council of International Schools and is authorized by the International Baccalaureate Organization. Extracurricular activities include soccer, cross-country running, needlework and crafts, gymnastics, cooking, and theater. School hours are 8:30 A.M. to 3:30 P.M. A school bus service as well as a canteen are available for students. There is no uniform policy.

- Lycée Français Pierre Loti (www.pierreloti.k12.tr) follows the French state national curriculum. The school is officially recognized by the Ministère de l'Education Nationale. There is no school bus, although the school has negotiated a special tariff for students with a local bus company. The school is divided into two campuses; Beyoglu is where the kindergarten and primary school is located and the Tarabaya site is for the collège and lycée. A canteen is available at the Tarabaya site. The medium of instruction is in

French. The school accepts children from the ages of 3 to 18 years. The French baccalaureate is awarded, as this school allows children direct access to the French Higher
Education system.

- Deutsche Schule Istanbul (www.ds-istanbul.de): The curriculum is based on the
  German national curriculum. The language of instruction is in German although
  Turkish children can undertake certain lessons in Turkish. There are school buses available. A uniform policy is in operation. A canteen provides lunch facilities for children
  who wish to eat at school. The school takes children from kindergarten age to the end
  of grade 12.
- Robert College (American school) (www.robcol.k12.tr): The curriculum is based on U.S.
  and international curricula. The students work towards the International Baccalaureate.
  The school takes children from 8 to 18 years of age:; elementary, 8 to 10 years; middle
  school, 11 to 14 years; and high school, 14 to 18 years. The language of instruction is
  English. The school provides a bus service, and there is a canteen available for children
  who wish to eat at school. School hours are 8:30 A.M. to 4 P.M. There is no uniform policy.
  A placement test is part of the admission process. Extracurricular activities include drama,
  radio, musical activities, and Braille club.

United Arab Emirates: Dubai

PERSONAL SAFETY AND SECURITY ISSUES

The relationship between the United Arab Emirates and neighboring countries is
generally good, although there are some disagreements such as the dispute with
Iran over Abu Musa Island and the Tunbs island group. The internal political situation is very stable due to strong government controls. Serious crimes are rare in
the Emirates and penalties are very harsh. Drink and drug offenses are regarded
very seriously. Most of the European and North American nationals do not
require any visas except a valid passport for entry into the Emirates. For other
nationals, in order to obtain a visa, one must have an invitation or a sponsor
and a certificate or other evidence of religion may be needed. A few categories
of foreign nationals may obtain a visa on arrival. Nevertheless, Dubai is the most
stable city in the Middle East.

MEDICAL ISSUES

The general standard of public health and sanitation is good. Facilities in the
new hospitals are among the most modern in the world. Many doctors have
been trained in the West and consequently speak good English. Pharmacies are
abundant and hold extensive stocks of drugs and healthcare products.
It is still advisable to take necessary precautions against malaria and to drink bottled water. Dysentery and minor intestinal ailments are the main health problems, although cholera is present in some areas of the country. Air pollution is

not a major concern in Dubai. You should peel fruit and cook vegetables, meat, and fish well. For further information on medical issues in the UAE, visit www.gulfmd.com.

For dentists, see www.dubaihealthcare.com. For doctors and tips on health, see www.theemiratesnetwork.com. Listed under "Web site directory—health and medicine" are many Web links to private and public hospitals and clinics, including alternative healthcare centers. Hospitals in Dubai have well-equipped medical facilities. The Dubai Health and Medical Service specializes in maternity and diabetes care.

The Dubai Hospital is one of the best medical centers in the Middle East, with a large range of specialized clinics. The American Dental Clinic provides a wide range of services (www.american-dental-clinic.com). There is also a large number of pharmacies in Dubai. Some pharmacies are open 24 hours; local newspapers are the best place to look for details of pharmacies that operate an out-of-hours roster system. Hospitals usually dispense pharmaceuticals when the prescriptions have been issued there. Drugs are strictly controlled in the UAE, so if you are bringing medication for personal use, ensure you check with the UAE Customs Service prior to bringing pharmaceuticals into the country. Many international brands are available in the Emirates, but it is a good idea to note the generic name as well as the brand name of any medication you use, should that particular manufacturer not be represented in the state.

Full listings of clinics, hospitals, and pharmacies can be found at www.dubaihealthcare.com (Dubai), www.ameinfo.com, www.dhcc.ae (Dubai), and www.dohms.gov.ae (Department of Health and Medical Services). Note that government medical clinics have separate sections for males and females. If you have a son, for example, after a certain age his mother will not be able to take him into the clinic, and he will have to be accompanied by his father or another adult male.

ENVIRONMENT ISSUES

The general standard of public health and sanitation in the UAE is good, and air quality issues through pollution are not a major concern in the region. Water in Abu Dhabi and Dubai is deemed quite safe to drink, although expatriates tend to drink only bottled water.

ECONOMIC OVERVIEW, 2008

GDP growth	6.4%
Inflation	12.0%
Unemployment	4.0%

INFRASTRUCTURE

Utilities and traffic: Electricity and water supplies are reliable and operate without interruptions. The telephone system in the United Arab Emirates is reliable and local; long-distance and most international calls can be dialed directly. Internet and electronic mail services are provided by the telephone department and have become popular recently. The postal service is adequate although there is no home delivery service. Express mail is available for overseas post. Public transport is extensive and efficient in Dubai, but road traffic is sometimes congested during rush hours.

Air travel: The airport is located within a 30-minute journey to the city center and offers an excellent choice of departures to Asia, Western Europe, North America, and within the Middle East. Dubai International Airport (www.dubai airport.com) is Dubai's award-winning airport and is regarded as one of the best in the world. Currently, three terminals serve the airport. Most international flights arrive and depart from Terminal 1. Approximately 100 airlines fly in and out of Dubai, connecting the city to over 140 destinations across the world.

Facilities available for departing passengers are impressive and include a health center which has a swimming pool, jacuzzi, and sauna; a business centers includes Internet access, fax, and telephone, and secretarial services are available 24 hours; 24-hour banking facilities; and 25 food and drink outlets serving a range of international cuisine, from fast food outlets to an à la carte restaurant are other features. A mother's lounge and children's play area, a post office operating full services on a 24-hour basis, and a fully equipped medical center (one of only few such centers in world airports) are also located here. Lounges include first class, business class, individual airline lounges, and a free of charge "quiet" lounge with special reclining chairs. The Dubai duty-free shopping complex is one of the largest and most comprehensive in the world. Special needs services and prayer rooms are also offered by the airport.

As with Abu Dhabi, Dubai International Airport has a VIP check-in area called *Val Majlis* and provides special baggage clearance facilities as well as immigration and check-in services. This facility is open to all passengers. A fee is payable and reservations must be made at least 24 hours in advance. The passengers enjoy both VIP and VVIP very very important person) services, including private office facilities, showers, and exclusive dining. There is an airport shuttle service between the two terminals, and the airport is easily accessible by public transport. Taxis operate around the clock. Bus numbers 401 and 402 connect the airport to the *Al Sabkha* or *Al Ghubaiba* bus stations in Dubai. A ticket will cost AED 3, and buses run every 30 minutes from 5:30 A.M. until 8:30 P.M.

The **public transport system** is run by Dubai Municipality. They have an extensive network reaching across the city including the airport and the free port zone of Jebel Ali. They also operate six express bus lines with limited stops. The Web site has a comprehensive map of the area. Monthly tickets are available from AED 95 per month (tickets may be restricted to certain zones). This includes an

AED 5 fee for a ticket card, which you then "load" with credit for AED 90 a month. Other options include being able to charge the card in multiples of AED 10 or AED 20, thereby giving the holder a 10 percent discount off the normal fare. These cards do not automatically mean you have a valid ticket. Smart cards must be inserted into the machine on the bus to obtain a ticket. Individual tickets require exact change for use in the machine; passes must be handed to the driver for inspection. Animals are not permitted on the buses, and the first three rows are reserved for females only. Customer services can be contacted on a toll free number: 800-4567.

The Dubai Municipality is also responsible for the water link between Deira and Bur Dubai. This crossing is by traditional rowing boat or motorized boat. Costs to cross the creek are AED 1 and Fils 50, respectively. The Big Bus Company (www.bigbus.co.uk) operates open-top sightseeing buses in Dubai seven days a week from 9 A.M. until 5 P.M. The bus tickets are valid for 24 hours and permit an "available on line hop-on hop-off" facility. Dubai taxis are generally reliable; day tariff, AED 3 plus AED 1.17 per kilometer and night tariff, AED 3.5 plus AED 1.7 per kilometer. Expatriates generally use Dubai Taxis (other taxi companies are very small). National Taxi is a subsidiary of Dubai Taxi.

SHOPPING AND AVAILABILITY OF CONSUMER GOODS

A wide choice of food, fresh fruits, and vegetables is offered, and a full choice of consumer goods is on sale. Alcoholic beverages can be bought in hotels and restaurants. For home consumption, non-Muslims can obtain a special permit to buy alcohol from liquor shops. There is a complete range of car models available, catering for all segments of the market.

Shopping is said to be an experience in Dubai. There is an abundance of goods, from souvenirs to electrical items, many designer labels, and goods imported from all over the world, all at very competitive prices. The majority of large shopping malls will remain open during the long early-afternoon break. Other shops will usually open between 9 A.M. and 9 P.M., closing between 1 P.M. and 4 P.M. Supermarkets are normally open straight through the day, every day except Friday.

Following is a selection of shopping malls, department stores, and supermarkets which represent the shopper's paradise that is the UAE. The *Souks* (markets) are an experience, too, for the traveler. There are many souks all over the Emirates; some are known for trading in particular goods, such as gold or textiles. Souks span both sides of the creek. In Bur Dubai, Al Fahidi Street and Cosmos Lane are particularly known for their electronic goods and textiles, whereas the Karama area is home to a lot of replica merchandise. Situated on the other side of the creek in Deira, the souks are well known for their spices and gold. One good place to visit in the old gold souk is Chetan Jewellers who can custom make jewelry in just 24 hours. Haggling is expected in souks and you can get some worthwhile bargains. Some retailers in the souks do not accept credit cards, and not all people here speak English. Many traders are now Indian, rather than Arab, but the markets still have the same bustling ambiance that they have always enjoyed. The supermarkets and department stores provide many imported goods for their large expatriate clientele. If you prefer to shop online, check www.expatshopping.com, where you can order British food online for delivery to the UAE.

Dubai's malls are social hubs in addition to offering a shopping experience. All malls in Dubai are air conditioned and are very modern. Most locals tend to do their shopping in the evenings. Details of many of the shopping malls listed below can be found at www.deira.com. Al Ghurair Shopping Center, Deira, one of the most popular shopping centers, has the choicest and best quality of products equivalent to that elsewhere in the Emirates. At the BurJuman Center, you can find just about anything you want under one roof. With shops covering three floors, you will also find many restaurants and cafés situated on the top floor. The Deira City Centre, on Beniyas Road, is an impressive new shopping and entertainment center, with over 300 shops, fast food outlets, restaurants, and leisure facilities, including The Planet, the largest entertainment complex in the Gulf. Other features include the Textile Market and an Arabian home living section. The Garoleus Mall is the first 360°-screen cinema and is located in Jebel Ali. Mercato Mall is one of the latest shopping malls. It has Heliau decorations and is extremely popular with a Spinneys Supermarket and is located in Jumeriah. The Al Mulla Plaza, Al Ghusais, is popular among bargain hunters. Famous for its huge discounts on end-of-line and discontinued items, this mall is generally frequented by locals. Wafi Shopping Mall, found on Al Wasl Road, is an immense shopping center, with stylish boutiques selling quality goods often from Europe. The impressive entertainment, seasonal decorations, and displays make this a popular center to visit. The Hamarain Centre promotes itself as an upmarket shopping center, being attached to the five-star JW flagship Marriot Hotel. Shopping is on three levels and the center has a huge food court. Some of Dubai's streets are particular centers for certain goods. For example, the Al Maktoum Street is known for its watch shops; the Satwa and Karama districts are famous for Indian shops; and the Al Fahidi Street and Al Nasr Square are known for their good selection of electronics shops.

Department stores and supermarkets: Al Futtaim is home to Toys R Us and the British Marks and Spencer Department store. The Oasis Centre is somewhere between a department store and a small shopping mall; with five anchor stores selling shoes, items for babies, and household goods, it is situated in the center of Dubai. Lu Lu Hypermarket is somewhere between the department store and supermarket category; situated in Al Ghusais, this huge hypermarket offers a wide range of food and household goods. This has been a popular store from the start, particularly as it is so well situated for the residents of Ghusais and Sharjah, who previously had to go to Deira. This is mostly frequented by the Asian community.

There are many supermarkets in Dubai—possibly the most well known is Spinneys (www.spinneys.com) which is found in Bur Dubai opposite the Al Khaleej shopping mall. Produce from all over the world is widely available in this and most other supermarkets that serve the needs of a large and diverse expatriate population. Carrefour is the most popular supermarket (and most affordable) with a wide range of French products. It is located in Dubai in the City Center and Shingara Street, Abu Dhabi, Al Ain, and in the Northern Emirates. Cooperative Society is a popular supermarket amongst locals, selling a wide variety of fresh vegetables that are well priced.

RECREATION AND ENTERTAINMENT

Dubai is a cosmopolitan city and has a very good range of restaurants locally, including branches of all the major international restaurant chains. There are few theatrical productions, but a good selection of films is shown at the city's cinemas. Latest movies are also available on videos and DVDs. A good number of sports clubs are also available. The UAE government gives special attention to sport and leisure activities and sponsors many shows and tournaments. Some useful phrases for foreigners learning Arabic can be found online at www .phrasebook.com.

Restaurants: Unless part of a hotel, no restaurant in Dubai can serve alcohol. All of the Emirates (with the exception of Sharjah) permit the consumption of alcohol by non-Muslims. You will usually find that where alcohol cannot be consumed, a yoghurt drink (*Ayran*) or a strong black cup of coffee is served. Hotels often have several high-quality restaurants, with varying themes, although bistros are just as easily found in shopping malls and anywhere frequented by tourists. *Time Out* magazines (www.timeoutdubai.com and www.timeoutabudhabi.com) have extremely good guides to eating out.

An excellent site to visit before you eat out is www.diningindubai.com, which lists over 350 restaurants in Dubai, from the finest restaurants in the city to fast-food establishments. An online table reservation facility is available for some establishments. Eating out in Dubai is an immensely popular pastime. There are literally hundreds of fast food establishments, bistros, cafés, and elegant award-winning restaurants right across the city; Dubai city alone has four Russian specialty restaurants and ten Irish restaurants.

The very upmarket restaurants are found only in hotels. Al Dawaar is a revolving restaurant which offers spectacular views over the city and the sea and boasts an impressive buffet menu with some upmarket dishes. Friday lunch buffets are a family affair for a quieter and more elegant experience. The Al Mahara, furnished and decorated as a submarine with fish swimming in portholes and staff dressed as submarine officers, is a unique dining experience and more subtle and romantic for dining than its theme would suggest. Cuisine is international and is principally seafood. The Automatic Restaurant and Grill is a popular chain of restaurants offering quality Arabic/Lebanese food, served simply; these are very popular in Dubai, and branches are found at Jumeria and Bur Dubai. Benihana is a luxurious fish restaurant where you can either sit near the chef while he prepares the food (excellent for parties) or in a regular seating area.

Entertainment: A good reference for entertainment in Dubai is the *Time Out* guide (www.timeoutdubai.com), available from main bookshops and newsstands. For theaters and concert halls, check www.timeoutdubai.com and www.dubailook.com. A Web site for Dubai nightlife is www.asiatraveltips.com/BarsinDubai.shtml. For an up-to-date roundup of all local and regional events and places, go to www.dwtc.com.

The Dubai World Trade Centre is a huge exhibition complex. Many exhibitions are free to enter (www.dubai.fm). Many restaurants offer theme nights; often with live music and dancing. Dubai has come to be a center for 1970s and 1980s retro music of late. Bands from the era such as Kim Wilde and Blondie have performed in Dubai.

The Dubai Museum is located within the Al-Fahidi Fort; this museum contains 4,000-year-old relics and artifacts from Emirati history, including items from ancient trading partners in Africa and Asia. Entrance fee is AED 3 for adults and AED 1 for children. Jumeirah Mosque is not exactly a museum but you can visit this stunning mosque every Thursday and Sunday morning at 10 A.M. with a guide from the Sheikh Mohammed Centre of Cultural Understanding. Sheikh Saeed Al Maktoum's House is the former home of the late ruler of Dubai; this palace that dates back to the end of the nineteenth century has been restored and now houses a museum of photographs and money. Entrance fee is AED 2 for adults and AED 1 for children, and hours are daily from 8:30 A.M. until 9:30 P.M. Cinemas include Century Cinemas (9 screens), Cinestar Cinemas (11 screens), and Galleria Cineplex (2 screens).

Entertainment for children: The Dubai Zoo, located on Jumeirah Beach Road, is always a popular attraction for children. Fantasy Kingdom is a fun place for children as well. Tennis lessons for young children and juniors are provided periodically throughout the year at Dubai's Aviation Club. If you want a break for a short while to have a coffee and pastry without the children, Liwa Café in Dubai has a well supervised, free childcare facility. Inline skating is popular at the Dubai Creek Side Park; at the Mamzar Park, Deira, children can ride on camels or miniature trains. Parks usually charge for entry between AED 2 and 5. The Wonderland Family Park is a huge adventure theme park with cart racing, a roller coaster, simulators, and water attractions covering an 18-hectare site.

Sports: Sport is a strong element running right through the cultural fabric of the UAE. Traditional sports such as camel riding, endurance (horse) racing, and sailing dhows (traditional Arab boats with one or more sails) are heavily promoted and subsidized, ensuring that sport remains alongside the more international sports such as soccer, show jumping, polo, golf, powerboat racing, yachting, motor racing, tennis, cricket, boxing, chess, snooker, ice hockey and ice skating, basketball, and rugby.

The UAE has the infrastructure required to maintain sporting facilities at a world-class level. Sports clubs are normally at the center of expatriate cultural life as well as a hub for sporting activities. Golf clubs are excellent here. The Aviation Club is a sports and entertainment center very popular with the expatriate population of Dubai. With world-class sports facilities, aerobics studios, a 13-hole golf course, a tennis stadium, and swimming pools, there are also a multitude of bars and restaurants, with the Irish Village and Century Village containing some of the most popular venues in the country. International music stars play regularly at the club. Some of the top sports personalities in the world compete at the club as well. The Al Nasr Club is chiefly a soccer club; however, there are many other activities offered by the center, including handball, volleyball, basketball, karate, tennis, judo, tae kwon do, athletics, swimming, cycling, and table tennis. The Dubai Country Club is a family leisure retreat offering many activities, with emphasis on water sports, windsurfing, water skiing, boating, and swimming. There is a pool plus a restaurant and bar. Dubai Creek Golf and Yacht Club boasts an 18-hole championship course and a golf academy run by PGA professionals. The course is floodlit, permitting play until late into the night. A health club and gymnasium offering everything from swimming instruction to nutritional advice is available as is a choice of six restaurants. Four Wheel clubs are very popular throughout the UAE. One of the larger organizations is the Dubai 4x4 Club, which organizes off-road excursions to the desert and a forum for off-road enthusiasts.

Sports for children: Manchester United Soccer School (www.muss.ae) offers a world-class coaching program, emphasizing teamwork, discipline, and fun. The David Lloyd Tennis Academy is an environment where everyone can learn, develop, and grow as well as participate in leagues and events for more competitive players. Jebel Ali Equestrian Club is an approved branch of the British Pony Club for both children and adults. Alreland Nasr Leisu houses one of Dubai's two ice-skating rinks as well as tennis, squash, bowling, boxing, fitness, and swimming facilities.

Tourism Information Offices (www.dubaitourism.ae) can give detailed information.

SOCIOCULTURAL ENVIRONMENT

The United Arab Emirates is governed by a council composed of the rulers of the Emirates. In practice, the presidency of the council is always held by Abu Dhabi and the Prime Minister is from Dubai. No elections or political parties are permitted. The UAE has a strict Islamic religious and social structure. The vast majority of the population is Muslim, and Islamic culture, law, and economics permeate every aspect of life.

Freedom of speech is guaranteed by national law, but in practice there are strict limitations due to government controls and censorship. For expatriates, particularly women, adapting to life in the United Arab Emirates may require major changes in lifestyle. Not all religions are tolerated and discrimination is widespread, particularly against Judaism.

A wide range of satellite television channels and international newspapers are available in the UAE.

DEMOGRAPHIC/WORKFORCE OVERVIEW

Population	5,000,000 (2006 estimate)
Population density	60 inhabitants per km^2
Age structure	0–14 years, 26.7%
	15–64 years, 70.4%
	65 years and over, 2.9%
Life expectancy at birth	
Total population:	74.7 years
Male	72.3 years
Female	77.3 years

WORKPLACE CULTURE

Two main factors differentiate the Middle East from Western cultures. In the United Arab Emirates, women generally play a totally different role from that of their Western counterparts; life and law in the UAE is dominated by religion. The main religion in the UAE is Muslim, and the religion plays a pivotal role in all aspects of life there. Some laws are deemed to be governed by religious law and carry sentences such as lashings for violations. These penalties only apply to practicing Muslims; others are given alternative punishments. Religion also dictates dress and the structure of the day as well as prohibiting alcohol and the consumption of some food—unfamiliar practices to those more used to a Western culture. It is crucial that the Muslims are allowed to practice their religion in their country without observing any disrespectful behavior from foreign visitors. The United Arab Emirates is very tolerant of other religions; more so than elsewhere in the Middle East.

The change in the role women play in the UAE came with the discovery of oil half a century ago. The sudden wealth within the country gave rise to many factors, opening the doors for women. The Emirati infrastructure was hungry for a labor force that the population could not produce. Women were finding themselves occupying roles, albeit unskilled and menial, but, nevertheless, outside the home and away from the profession of mother, wife, and housekeeper. This change is happening fast; today twice as many women as men attend University in the UAE; women occupy nearly half of all posts within the civil service; nearly two-thirds of teachers are women and a huge majority of health service workers are female. However, equality groups stress that there is a lot of work still to be done, as women in these sectors do not reach supervisory or managerial levels and hence women in top-level businesses are extremely rare. Although women are found today working in the banking and finance sectors, it is unlikely that they would be included in any of the social functions associated with the post. A point to remember is that although women in the UAE enjoy a much more liberal lifestyle than others in the Gulf, the society is still very much rooted in strong patriarchal tradition. Women may receive unwelcome comments from time to time; however, one advantage of being a woman in the UAE is that women are normally served first, and banks and post offices, police stations and other government offices frequently have separate queues for women. Women are also given seats set aside at the front of the bus, and some public areas are reserved for women only.

For some public offices in the UAE, the weekend is on Thursday afternoons and Fridays, although this is changing to align with Western practices. For private offices, the weekends are on Friday and Saturday. Working hours vary depending on the organization, but generally, businesses work from 8 A.M. until 6 P.M. with an hour's lunch break from 1 to 2 P.M. Some organizations will adjust their hours slightly according to the season, opening and closing an hour earlier in summer, although this is very rare. Arabs tend to make arrangements for business meetings at times of the day rather than at specific hours/minutes. In general, business in Dubai operates on European principles; more and more companies in Abu Dhabi are adopting the same regimes.

Remember that during the month of Ramadan, business hours are limited to six hours per day; government departments are closed in the afternoons during Ramadan. It is not uncommon for employees to spend between two and four hours commuting each day to work, due to the intense congestion on the roads in and around the cities.

Business dress: Men should wear smart trousers and a shirt during the day, with a collar and tie for night. Women have more freedom of dress in the UAE than elsewhere in the Middle East, but business dress should still be conservative and never revealing. It is strictly forbidden for foreigners to wear the Emirati local or traditional dress.

Most business is now conducted along the same lines as in the United States or in Western Europe. But you should observe carefully until you are confident of the etiquette that your company and associates use in conducting business. It is usual to use "*Sayed*" (Mr.) or "*Sayeda*" (Mrs.) followed by the first name. The name should always be prefixed with the person's title when conducting business. The UAE rates personal image very highly. Attractive employees have been known to beat other more experienced and capable employees to promotions and job positions, purely because they look good. Resumés must always include a photograph.

If you are not married, but you live with your partner, it is unwise to mention this. Cohabitation outside marriage is against Muslim religion. You should shake hands with everyone who is present, except the women.

The value of networking in the UAE is not to be underestimated. Personal contacts both within the expatriate community and in the Emirati culture are invaluable. It is widely acceptable for Arab businessmen to be late in the United Arab Emirates; however, it is considered rude for a Western businessman to attend a meeting late. You should arrive on time, but expect to be kept waiting. Never get emotional or animated. Business culture is always conducted calmly and it is important to not deviate from facts. Arabs do not discuss business on the first meeting. Expect to have several encounters before you are able to discuss business issues. Learning and practicing the art of negotiation is essential when working in an Arab culture. It is a custom that is popular among citizens of the UAE and foreigners are expected to participate.

Strikes and labor unions are illegal in the Emirates. The Arabs will respect someone who has a firm grasp on their argument, as long as they remain courteous. It is important to distinguish between this and the notion of quarrelling which is abhorred. Business entertaining is lavish in the UAE, but you must be careful to not assume that the more lavish the affair, the better your negotiations will proceed. Extravagant entertaining can be a way of letting people down gently. Giving business gifts in the UAE is difficult, as most items can be bought for less in the UAE and citizens are used to quality, usually handmade items. It is normal for the recipient to open their gift on presentation and look for a hallmark or stamp of distinction on the gift. The giving of counterfeit goods is seen as highly disrespectful to the recipient.

Discussions in business are similar to those in social occasions. Winning a debate for an Arab in not important, rather they work on enriching the knowledge of each of the participants. English is widely spoken in business circles, but translation services will usually be available. You should never ask about an Arab's wife; instead refer to "the family." Secretaries in the UAE do not take appointments for their bosses. Often it is better to turn up to see someone on the off-chance that they might be available rather than try to arrange an appointment. You should have business cards printed with English on one side and Arabic on the other. It is important not to schedule business meetings or appointments during prayer times; check the local newspapers for listings of prayer times. Web sites for good information on the United Arab Emirates are www .britishexpats.com, www.expatmum.com, and http://dwc.hct.ac.ae/expatinfo/ dubaiuaegeneralinfo.htm.

NATURAL ENVIRONMENT

From June to September the weather is very hot and humid, with temperatures rising as high as 48°C. During the winter, temperatures at night can drop considerably. Natural disasters do not occur.

HOUSING

In Dubai it is possible to find excellent but expensive housing within a short distance from the metropolitan area. Luxury apartments with leisure facilities have become popular. Districts favored among the international community include Sheikh Zayed Road, Bur Dubai and Um Suqueim, and Jumeirah, where a residential colony has been developed. A good choice of domestic appliances and furniture is available, and maintenance and repair services of quality exist.

There are many real estate agencies located throughout the country. A full list can be found in the *Yellow Pages Directory* or online at www.yellowpages.ae. Two major online agencies are www.amlaki.net and www.ikaar.com. Other real estate agencies are Better Homes, Asteco Real Estate, and Alpha Properties.

Lease and rental conditions may vary between landlords; however, in general, a refundable deposit equivalent to six months' rent is required. Most landlords will expect the full annual rent to be paid in advance, but this may be negotiated down to two, six-month payments. In many cases, parking spaces are included in the rental costs. New properties often have covered car parking. Most rented accommodations are unfurnished although you may find kitchens at least partially equipped. It is advisable to look for properties that have air conditioning; many new apartments and houses have a central air-conditioning system already installed. Some residential complexes will provide a daily maid service.

Houses in districts in Dubai—good areas: Garhoud, Barsha, Mirdif; very good areas: Garhoud, Jumeirah, Springs, Meadows; best areas: Jumeirah, Umm Suqueim. Apartments in good areas—Bur Dubai, The Greens, Garhoud; very good areas: Emaar Projects; best areas: Jumeirah, Umm Suqueim, Sheikh Zayed Road, Dubai Marina.

Rental costs vary considerably depending on the type of accommodations and location. The average monthly cost of a two-bedroom unfurnished apartment in a very good area is AED 12,500 (approximately USD 3,400) in Dubai.

FINANCIAL ISSUES INCLUDING BANKING SERVICES AND TAXES

Traveler's checks and foreign currency may be freely exchanged at exchange offices and hotels. The U.S. dollar, in the form of cash or traveler's checks, is by far the easiest currency to exchange, followed by British pound sterling. Most major foreign banks are represented in Dubai. Banking services are efficient and reliable and international services are available. Major international credit cards are widely accepted.

Currency: The currency of the United Arab Emirates is the Dirham (AED). Given the economic strength of the UAE, the currency is stable and is index-linked to the U.S. dollar. Dirham notes are available in the following denominations: 5, 10, 20, 50, 100, 200, 500, and 1000. 100 fils make a dirham. Fils are found in coins of 1, 5, 10, 25, and 50 (although the 5 and 10 coins are rarely used). The value on coins is written in Arabic only, but one can easily recognize them.

Cash, traveler's checks, and credit cards: Foreigners will have no difficulty paying for goods and services or withdrawing cash from ATMs with almost any international credit card. There are many banks in all the cities in the UAE that offer a comprehensive range of exchange services and are both efficient and reliable. Money can be easily exchanged in not just banks, but also at exchange offices, in markets, shopping centers, and in hotels. Almost any denomination can be changed at these places and exchange rates are usually good. Money changers can be located near to the Central Souk, off Liwa Street in Abu Dhabi; in Dubai head to the central Deira and Bur Dubai, where you will easily find places to change money.

Cash payments in both Dirhams and American dollars are accepted in the Emirates in hotels, larger restaurants, and in shopping malls, although if you pay in dollars you will usually receive your change in Dirhams. Otherwise, it is a good idea to keep some small denomination notes in Dirhams available to pay for taxis and in smaller shops, restaurants, and the markets. The UAE is essentially a cash-driven society; once away from the main tourist and business areas, payment is more than likely required in cash. The markets too will usually require cash payments for goods.

Banks and hotels can change traveler's checks; however, the best rate of exchange for traveler's checks is found at privately owned bureaux de change. Unlike banks, the exchange offices are also open in the afternoon, and sometimes on Friday. Additionally you can find some money changers in the souks that exchange traveler's checks. These can offer variable rates, but some good deals can be found; it is advisable to check the daily exchange rate listed in most local newspapers to make accurate comparisons. Taking traveler's checks in U.S. dollars is recommended, as these are the easiest to change. Pounds sterling traveler's checks are also widely accepted. Banks charge approximately AED 10 for changing traveler's checks. Hotels tend to offer less-favorable exchange rates.

Payment by credit card is the norm in most hotels, larger shopping centers, and restaurants; however, a considerably lesser number of smaller establishments accept card transactions. If they do, be prepared to pay a 5 percent supplement for the processing of the card. Almost all international credit cards are accepted in the UAE including MasterCard, Diners, American Express, and Visa. Many international ATM cash cards will also allow you to withdraw money from

UAE. Both the Emirates Bank International and the Abu Dhabi Commercial Bank are on the Global Access, Cirrus, and Plus networks. Some banks have Switch facilities.

Banks: The UAE's banking system is efficient and modern. Regulated by the UAE Central Bank, many of the world's top banks have branches in the UAE, including ABN Amro, HSBC, Deutsche Bank, and Citibank. The Emirates have their own banks such as the National Bank of Dubai and the Emirates International Bank, which provide a full range of services. Internet banking is advanced in the UAE and most accounts can be fully managed remotely from the bank. Banks are usually open from 8 A.M. until 1 P.M. Saturday through Wednesday and until 12 P.M. on Thursday. Banks are closed on Friday and on public holidays. Women should use their own counters in banks when provided. An advantage for women is that the queues are frequently shorter. Most of the banks in Abu Dhabi and Dubai are located in close proximity to each other; in Abu Dhabi you will find banks on the Sheikh Hamdan bin Mohammed Street and in Sheikh Khalifa bin Zayed Street, in the center of the city. Dubai's banks are generally along the Khalid bin Al Waleed Road, in the Bur Dubai district.

Opening an account: Salaries earned in the UAE must be paid into an account based within the state. To open a bank account you will need to take along a photocopy of your passport (plus the original to validate the copy). If you require a joint account, your spouse will need to attend and bring his or her original passport plus a photocopy. Personal checks are not widely used in the UAE. Normally residents use checks only to pay their utility bills. Once you have written a check, it cannot be stopped, plus there are legal implications if you write a check without proper funds. MasterCard and Visa cards are available through your UAE account, although you can still retain your credit card from your own country if you prefer, but you will have to inform them of your change of contact and address details. The primary bank in the UAE is the Emirates Bank International (www.ebi.ae). Located in cities throughout the Emirates, this bank offers an impressive array of services and products for their clients. As pioneers of Internet banking in the Middle East, the bank now offers account information accessible via SMS mobile phone. EBI has 30 branches within UAE alone. The Web site has full contact details of all offices.

Taxes: In the United Arab Emirates, there is no personal income tax. There are neither social charges nor income taxes to pay on employee's wages; the employer makes no payment either. There are no capital gains taxes in the UAE. The only taxable revenue within the country is payable by some oil companies and foreign banks.

INTERNATIONAL SCHOOLS AND EDUCATION

There is a good choice of international educational facilities in Dubai including American, English, German, and Japanese schools offering all levels of education. Several American, British, Australian, Indian, and Pakistani universities have opened campuses in Dubai and Sharjah, where they offer a wide range of graduate and postgraduate courses. Primary and secondary education is provided for all UAE citizens. The existing educational structure, which was established in the early 1970s, is a four-tier system covering 14 years of education. Kindergarten is for children aged 4 to 5 years old; primary is for children aged 6 to 12 years old and is compulsory for all UAE citizens; preparatory is for children aged 12 to 15 years old; and secondary is for children aged 15 to 18 years old and the Secondary School Leaving Certificate is awarded. Technical secondary school is for children aged 12 to 18 years old, and the Technical Secondary Diploma is awarded.

- American School of Dubai (www.asdubai.org) offers the U.S. curriculum. The school takes children from kindergarten to grade 12. The school does not provide bus services nor does it apply a uniform/dress code policy. A canteen is available for children who wish to eat at school. After-school activities are offered to all students.
- Deutsche Schule Sharjah (German school) (www.dssharjah.org) offers the German national curriculum. The school takes children from kindergarten to grade 8. School bus services are provided, and after-school activities are offered to all students.
- Dubai Japanese School (www.japanese.sch.ae) offers the Japanese curriculum. The school provides bus services at an additional fee of AED 3,600 per year. The school does not apply a uniform/dress code policy. A canteen is available for children who wish to eat at school, and after-school activities are offered to all students.
- Emirates International School (www.eischool.com) offers international curriculum, mainly UK and U.S. The school takes children from kindergarten to grade 12 (ages 4–18 years.) The school provides bus services at an additional fee of AED 2,650 per year. The school applies a uniform/dress code policy. A canteen is available for children who wish to eat at school, and after-school activities are offered to all students.
- Jumeirah College (English school) (www.jc-dxb.sch.ae) offers the English national curriculum. The school takes children from nursery to grade 12. The school does not provide bus services. The school applies a uniform/dress code policy. Children must bring their lunch from home. After-school activities are offered to all students.
- Lycée Georges Pompidou (French school) (www.lgp.ae) offers the French national curriculum. The school does not provide bus services, nor does it have a uniform/dress code policy. After-school activities are offered to all students.

Appendix 1
Securing Work Permits and Visas

Note: Generally, visas are needed only for extended stays of 90 days or more. There are many exemptions for tourists, usually depending on the traveler's country. Check with a travel agent or the host country's government site managing visas.

Visa type	Documentation Needed
Australia	
Visa	• Non-citizens need a valid visa or Electronic Travel Authority (ETA)—either of these is an authority to enter and spend time in Australia. • An ETA is equivalent to a visa, but there is no stamp on your passport. Applications can be submitted through travel agencies or airlines when you are arranging your travel. Most travel agencies and airlines issuing ETAs will charge a processing fee. Applications can also be done online at www.eta.immi.gov.au for a service fee of AUD 20. Otherwise, there is no Government charge for ETAs, though long-term business entrants must pay AUD 65. • Citizens of 32 countries qualify for ETAs (mostly in Western Europe, but also Brunei, Hong Kong, Japan, Malaysia, Singapore, South Korea, and the United States). • Other nationals must apply for a "label" visa, either tourist or short-stay business visa.

Visa type	Documentation Needed
China	
Visa	• Valid passport (with at least two blank pages). • Completed visa application form. • One recent passport-sized photograph. • Visa fee.
Work and residence permit	• Valid passport and visa. • A valid lease or deed for the residence rented or bought by the applicant. • Two recent passport-sized photographs. • A health certificate issued by the Health Quarantine Station. • Fee.
Czech Republic	
Visa	• Completed and signed application form. • Two recent passport-sized photographs. • Valid passport. • Application fee (usually payable in cash only). • Proof of sufficient funds to cover your stay. • Proof of transport (airplane or train return or onward tickets) with specified dates. Open tickets are not permitted. • Medical travel insurance. • For long stay visas: • Proof of assured accommodation in the Czech Republic. • Police clearance certificate (criminal history records) from your country of origin. • Application for police clearance certificate (criminal history records) from the Czech Republic (to be requested at the Czech embassy). • Documents regarding the purpose of your stay in the Czech Republic. The documents will vary depending on the purpose of your stay. All official documents presented as proof must be notarized if issued in the Czech Republic or have an *Apostille* if issued in a different country. *If you will be working in the Czech Republic you will need to show the original work permit*
Work permit	• Personal details of the foreigner. • Travel document number and name of the issuing authority.

Visa type	Documentation Needed
	• Identification information of the future employer (name, registered seat, identification number). • Job description. • Place of work and length of contract. • Any other information required for the performance of the job. • Photocopy of the first page of the employee's passport. • A declaration by the employer that it will employ the foreigner. • A notarized copy of a document of professional competence for the field in which the foreigner is to work in the Czech Republic (vocational certificate, certificate of matriculation, university diploma, etc.). • A health certificate (not more than one month old). • Other documents may be requested.
Egypt	
Visa	• Valid passport (valid for at least six months and with a blank page for the visa stamp; if your passport does not fulfill these criteria then you should apply for a new passport and secure your visa in that one). • One passport-sized photograph. • Completed application form and visa fees (cash, check or money order—payable to "Consulate of Egypt"). Note: the check must be certified—personal or business checks are not accepted. • A computer-generated flight itinerary from your travel company, so the Egyptian Embassy knows when you are due to arrive and depart. • If you are sending the above by mail and will not attend the consulate in person, then you need to enclose a self-addressed prepaid express/certified mail envelope in order for the consulate to return your passport. Applicants for a business visa (entry visa) need to enclose a letter from their company along with their standard visa form. The letter should state the following: • Duration of stay. • Purpose of the trip. • Who is responsible for travel expenses. • Who is responsible for accommodation costs.
Work permit	• Passport with valid residence in Egypt. • Seven passport-sized photographs.

Visa type	Documentation Needed
	• Two copies of the employment contract • Two copies of the Tax ID Card. • A copy of the company commercial register. • Two copies of the employee's certificates of academic degrees and experience, plus any professional licenses where applicable. • A memorandum justifying the recruitment of the foreigner for the job. • The letter should state the reasons for not recruiting an Egyptian as well as the tasks assigned to the foreigner. • Approval of the related Authority (e.g. Investment Authority, Egyptian General Petroleum Corporation, etc.). • Official company delegation of authority to the person within the company who is going to apply for the work permit on behalf of the foreigner. • A certificate from a public hospital or a recognized laboratory such as the vaccination laboratory of the Ministry of Health, confirming that the foreigner is free of HIV. • The approval of the concerned security authorities. This can be arranged through the department of work permits at the Manpower and Training Directorate at the Tahrir Complex.
Hong Kong	
Visa	• Passport (valid for another six months and with blank visa pages). • Completed application form. • Valid travel documents (onward or return tickets and accommodation bookings). • Proof of sufficient funds to cover the stay in Hong Kong. • One recent passport-sized photograph. • Application fee. • For business visas, a letter of invitation from a ministry, company, or an official Hong Kong organization is required.
Hungary	
Visa	• Passport valid for at least six months from the date of departure from Hungary. • Completed and signed application form.

Visa type	Documentation Needed
	• One passport-sized photograph. • Application fee. • Return ticket for the entire journey or ticket reservation confirmation. • Proof of lodgings: hotel reservation or an official invitation letter from a friend or relative endorsed by the Hungarian Immigration Authorities. • Proof of Financial means to cover your stay in Hungary (bank statement, traveler's checks, credit card, etc.). • Travel insurance. • If you are traveling on business or to a conference, an invitation letter from your Hungarian business partner or the conference organizer to this effect.
Work permit	• Application form filled out by the Hungarian employer. • Letter of assignment. • Certified copy of the employee's diploma. • Photocopy of the employee's passport (valid for at least 18 months). • Application fee. • Job description of the employee. • Health Certificate. • Certified copies of the corporate documentation of the Hungarian company (that is, Articles of Association, Registration at the court of Registration, Specimen of Signature Rights, Social Security, and Tax Registration form/numbers).
India	
Visa	• Passport valid for a minimum of six months beyond the date of intended departure. • Two passport-sized photos. • Foreigners holding other nationalities (other than the country where applying for the visa) should submit proof of legal or permanent residence in the country (where applying).
Work and residence permit	• Foreigners Regional Registration Office (FFRO) application. • Residential permit application. • Notarized letter by a guarantor accepting responsibility for living expenses if you intend to stay in India.

Visa type	Documentation Needed
	• Photocopies of your passport. • Five passport-sized photographs.
Indonesia	
Visa	• Two color passport-sized photographs. • Two completed visa application forms (available from your nearest Indonesian Embassy or Consulate). • Original passport. • Fee (your local consulate will inform you of the current fee). • Proof of identity. • Letter of recommendation from a sponsor (either in your home country or in Indonesia). • Return or onward travel tickets (for Single Visit and Transit Visa, and Visa on Arrival arrangements). • In the case of employees who will be working in the fields of scientific research or education, social studies, or religious missions: a letter of recommendation (plus a copy) is required from the institution you will be working for. • For employees who will be working for foreign aid organizations as technical professionals or on a domestic investment venture, you will have to provide letters of recommendation (plus copies of each) from the Technical Department of the Government relative to your discipline, the Department of Manpower, and the Investment co-coordinating board.
Business	**Employee:** • Copy of passport (all pages including all blank pages). • Color photographs (2x3cm—10 copies; 3x4cm—6 copies; 4x6cm—15 copies). • A copy of the employee's degree certificate. • A copy of the curriculum vitae/resume. • A copy of the marriage certificate and birth certificate for each family member if residing with the employee in Indonesia. • TA-01 Recommendation from the Ministry of Manpower to the Immigration Office. • VITAS statement from the Immigration Office. • KITAS Limited Stay Permit. **Employer:** • Copy of the company's business license. • Copy of the RPTKA for PMA companies and the Ministry of Manpower report for the company.

Visa type	Documentation Needed
	• Copy of employment contract covering the employee's work in Indonesia. • Copy of company's registration document. • Copy of company's tax registration document (NPWP). • Copy of employment agreement of Indonesian counterpart for manager level plus a copy of the KTP of the Indonesian counterpart for manager level (if the company is operating under Foreign Capital Investment Law—PMA companies).
Israel	
Visa	• Completed application form. • Three identical recent passport-sized photographs (write your name and passport number on each photo). • Return ticket. • Copy of tenancy or mortgage agreement. • Bank statement for last 3 months (to prove you have the financial means to support yourself while in Israel). • Self addressed envelope. • Letter of invitation from friends/contact/company in Israel.
Work permit	• Updated resume/CV. • Copies of all qualifications (diplomas or transcripts). • Current and proposed job description. • Full salary and benefits package (employment contract). • Declarations from the company's CPA and authorized salary manager. • Copies of the last three 102 forms (*Bituch Leumi*). • Copy of the registration certificate (from the company registrar). • Number of current Israeli employees and expatriates. • Company profile; product brochures; recent press clippings; etc. • Evidence of accommodation in Israel. • Evidence of health insurance in Israel. • Dates of prior visits to Israel. • Power of attorney.
Japan	
Visa	• Valid passport. • Two recent passport photos. • Two official visa application forms, available at the embassy or consulate. • Documents certifying the purpose of the visit.

Visa type	Documentation Needed
Work and residence permit	**Investor/business manager:** In cases where the person concerned intends to commence the operation of international trade or other business, or to invest in the business, the following documents are required: • A business plan, copies of the company registration, and a statement of profit and loss. • Material showing the number of full-time staff except the foreign national concerned, and in the case where the number of the full-time staff is two, copies of resident cards or certificates of alien registration and documents regarding wage payments of the staff concerned. • Material showing the outline of the business office. In cases where the person concerned intends to engage in management of international trade or other business on behalf of the foreign national who began or invested in the business concerned or is engaged in management of the business concerned which was begun or invested in Japan, the same three sorts of material are required, plus: • Documents certifying the career of the person concerned and his or her certificate of graduation with a major in management or administration. • Documents certifying the activity, its duration, the position, and the remuneration of the person concerned. **Intra-company transferee:** • Documents certifying the relationship between the business office in a foreign country and the business office in Japan. • Copies of the company registration and a statement of profit and loss of the business office in Japan, and material describing the business activities. • Documents certifying the details of the employee's responsibilities and employment duration at the business office in a foreign country. • Copies of the company registration of the business office in a foreign country, and material showing its outline. • Documents certifying the activity, its duration, the position, and the remuneration of the person concerned. • A diploma and documentation certifying the career of the person concerned. **Skilled labor:** • Copies of the company registration and a statement of profit and loss of the recipient organization.

Visa type	Documentation Needed
	• Materials describing the business undertaken by the recipient organization. • A personal history and documents issued by the official organization which is certifying the career and the qualification regarding the activity of the person concerned. • Documents certifying the activity, its duration, the position, and the remuneration of the person concerned. **Trainee:** • A training plan showing the substance of the training, its necessity, location, duration, and the conditions of stay. • Documents certifying that the person concerned intends to engage in a duty that requires the technique, skill, and knowledge learned during the stay in Japan after returning home. • A diploma and documentation certifying the professional career of the person concerned. • Documents certifying the professional career of the trainer regarding the training concerned. • Material showing the outline of the foreign organization which is sending the person concerned. • Copies of the company registration, a statement of profit and loss, a list of full-time staff of the organization inviting the person concerned, and a list of trainees. **Dependent:** • Documents certifying the personal relationship between the person concerned and the person who is to support him or her. • Copies of the certificate of alien registration or the passport of the person who is to support the person concerned. • Documents certifying the profession and the income of the person who is to support the person concerned.
Malaysia	
Visa	• Passport valid for at least six months from the date of entry into Malaysia or valid travel document. Two photocopies of passport. • Two recent passport-sized photographs. • Application fee (usually cash only). • Completed and signed visa application forms (Form IMM.47) with two photocopies.

Visa type	Documentation Needed
	• Proof of sufficient funds (original and photocopy of most recent bank statement or travelers checks) to show financial capability during stay in Malaysia. • Onward or return ticket or official travel itinerary with two photocopies. • If applicable, yellow fever vaccination certificate (for travelers coming from infected areas). • Letter of introduction (and photocopy) from the applicant's employer or university.
Employment pass	• Cover letter • Letter of Authorisation from the Company • DP11 Form • Approval Letter from the relevant government agency (such as the Expatriate Committee (JKPD)/Malaysian Industrial Development Authority (MIDA)/ Ministry of International Trade and Industry (MITI)/ Construction and Industrial Development Board (CIDB)/ Ministry of Domestic Trade and Consumer Affairs (KPDNandHEP)/ Ministry of Education (KPM) • Companies' registration Forms 9, 13, 24 and 49 • Employment contract (should include: position; contract period; monthly salary; employer's and expatriate's signature)—stamping fee RM10 • Personal resume, academic certificate and experience • Full copy of expatriate's passport containing expatriate details • Passport size photo
Work permit	• Cover letter. • List of foreign workers' names. • Details of employer's form. • Details of foreign workers and their dependents. • Bank guarantee. • Medical report. • Form IMM.12 (one copy). • Form IMM.38 (one copy), if applicable. • Company's registration, that is, Forms 9, 13, 49, and 24. • Photograph (black and white) measuring 3.5 cm x 5 cm. • Passport and travel document.
Professional visit pass	• Cover letter. • Form IMM.12 (two copies).

Visa type	Documentation Needed
	• Form IMM. 38 (two copies), if relevant. • Two photographs measuring 3.5 cm x 5.0 cm • Photocopy of passport/travel document. • Security bond (stamped). • Letter of request from Malaysian company to the foreign company requesting assistance. • Letter from the foreign company accepting the request and confirming in the letter the following details: The expatriate's name;the expatriate's position; the salary of the expatriate to be paid overseas; the duration of services by the expatriate in Malaysia. • Details of the project with which the expatriate will be involved in Malaysia (such as name and location of project, commencement and completion date of project, the nature of project, project schedule, and project contract). • Certified true copies of the expatriate's graduation certificates and resume (to be translated into English if the documents are in other languages). • A security deposit is required. The amount depends on the nationality of the applicant. • Photocopies of company brochure or annual report, Forms 9, 13, 24, and 49 issued by the Companies Commission of Malaysia.
New Zealand	
Visa	• Fee. • Passport (for each person on your application). • Recent passport-sized photograph (for each person on your application). • Evidence of financial support while in New Zealand (either NZD 1000 per person per month; or NZD 400 per person per month where accommodation is provided; or a "Sponsorship form for Visiting New Zealand," completed by a sponsor (friend or relative) already residing in New Zealand). • Evidence of onward travel from New Zealand. • Or the above sponsorship form, guaranteeing repatriation or evidence of sufficient funds in New Zealand that will enable you to fly to another country where you have right of entry.

Visa type	Documentation Needed
Philippines	
Visa	• Completed and signed application form. • Two recent passport-sized photographs. • Passport (valid for six months beyond the intended departure date from Philippines). • Proof that your visit is of a tourist or business nature. • Application fee. • Onward or return tickets. • If travel is for business purposes, a letter from the company.
Work permit	**From the sponsoring company:** • Affidavit of Support signed by company representative. • Employments contract. • Articles of Incorporation, Bylaws, and SEC registration of the company. • Latest income tax return of the company and audited financial statements. • Latest General Information Sheet of the Company filed with the Securities and Exchange Commission (SEC). • Certification as to the number of foreign nationals employed. **From the employee and family:** • Photocopy of passport of the employee and each accompanying family member. • Three original CV's detailing both employment history and educational qualifications. • Two passport-sized photos of the employee. • Two passport-sized photos of each accompanying family member. • Job description and job title. • Salary and compensation details. • Original, certified marriage certificate (officially translated if not already in English). • Original, certified birth certificates of all accompanying children, showing names of both parents (officially translated if not already in English).
Work visa	• Passport valid for at least six months. • Two completed application forms. • Four identical passport-sized photos.

Visa type	Documentation Needed
	• Medical and physical examination report by an authorized physician. It must include a chest x-ray film, laboratory reports and a certificate that the applicant does not have AIDS. The medical examination report is acceptable only if submitted to the quarantine officer at the port of entry in the Philippines, together with the visa. • Police clearance, issued by the police authorities of the place where the applicant resides. • Visa application fee.
Poland	
Visa	• Completed application form, signed by the applicant. An online visa application form in several languages can be downloaded at www.msz.gov.pl/Polski,wniosek, wizowy,1805.html • One recent passport-sized photograph. • Valid passport or travel document. Passport must be valid for at least three months after the planned departure date from Poland. It must have at least one blank page for the visa sticker. • Proof of sufficient funds to cover your stay in Poland (bank statement, credit card, etc.). • International health insurance valid for the period of your stay
Russia	
Tourist	• Completed visa application form (from the Consulate, travel agency, or online at www.visatorussia.com/russianvisa.nsf/consulate_form.html). • Valid original passport with at least one blank page. The passport must be valid for at least six months after the intended departure date from Russia. • One recent passport-sized photograph. • The original Tourist Voucher from an authorized travel agency stamped and signed by an authorized person. • A standard Tourist Confirmation (in Russian language) of acceptance from the authorized Russian travel agency or a hotel, registered with the Russian Ministry of Foreign Affairs. The confirmation must contain the agency's reference number and registration number.

Visa type	Documentation Needed
	• Application fee. • Medical insurance (depending on your country of origin).
Private visa	• Completed visa application form obtainable from the Consulate or from any travel agency. • Valid original passport with at least one blank page. The passport must be valid for at least six months after the intended departure date from Russia. • One recent passport-sized photograph. • The original invitation. • Application fee. • HIV certificate (for visas over more than three months). • Medical insurance (depending on your country of origin).
Business	• Completed visa application form (from the consulate, travel agency or online at www.rbcc.co.uk/travel/visaapp.htm). • Valid original passport with at least one blank page. The passport must be valid for at least six months after the intended departure date from Russia. • One recent passport-sized photograph. • An invitation issued by the local representative of the Passport and Visa Department of the Ministry of Interior (PVU). The invitation must contain an official stamp and legal address of the host institution, the document registration number, date of registration, signature and name of the official authorized to invite foreigners to Russia, travel itinerary, dates of stay, and the names of the persons invited. • An introductory letter from your company (or from yourself if you are self-employed) giving full details of the traveler, destinations, terms, and purpose of the visit. The letter must indicate who is financially responsible for your stay in Russia. Self-employed persons should produce copies of their bank statement for the last three months. • Application fee. • HIV certificate (for visas over three months).
Transit visa	• Completed visa application form (obtainable from the Consulate, travel agency, or online at www.rbcc.co.uk/travel/visaapp.htm). • Valid original passport with at least one blank page. • One recent passport-sized photograph.

Visa type	Documentation Needed
	• The original and a copy of your confirmed tickets via Russia. • A valid visa for the destination country (if applicable). • Application Fee.
South Africa	
Short-term visa	• Valid passport with at least two blank pages. • Two recent passport-sized photographs. • Completed application form. • Application fee. • A valid Yellow Fever Certificate (if traveling through or from yellow fever endemic area). • Proof of sufficient funds to cover visit. • Onward or return ticket. • Certificate from local police stating you do not have a criminal record.
Short-term business	• Completed application form. • Valid passport with at least two blank pages. • Two recent passport-sized photographs. • Business letter from the parent company, on company letterhead, stating financial responsibility for applicant while in South Africa and providing purpose, nature, and duration of the visit as well as full names and addresses of business contacts to be visited in South Africa. • Flight details from travel agent/airline or onward/return ticket. • Application fee (fees vary depending on the applicant's passport). • A valid yellow fever certificate (if traveling through or from a yellow fever endemic area).
Work permit	• Completed application forms BI-1738. • Passport valid for no less than 30 days after the intended stay in South Africa, with at least two blank pages. • Two recent passport-sized photographs. • A vaccination certificate where applicable. • A letter from the employer, with press clippings of advertisements relative to the specific position from a South African publication. Alternatively, the employer must state why no advertisement was placed. • Proof that despite a job advertisement complies with the requirements in terms of regulation 28(6), no qualified

Visa type	Documentation Needed
	South African citizen or permanent resident is available. The employer may have to submit proof that all short-listed candidates have been interviewed. • Contract of employment stating occupation, position, maximum duration of employment, and remuneration offered. • Certified copy of the applicant's highest educational degree and any additional qualifications, in addition to testimonials or certificates of employment from previous employers. • Medical certificate. • Proof of sufficient funds for personal expenses. • Cash deposit or bank guarantee in the case that the applicant fails to comply with conditions of the permit or if it becomes necessary for the applicant to be repatriated to his home country. The amount collected is normally equivalent to the cost of an air ticket to the applicant's home country and may be refunded on his/her departure from South Africa. • Application fee.
South Korea	
Visa	• Completed visa application form. • Original copy of the certificate for confirmation of visa issuance. • Passport with remaining validity of at least six months. • One recent passport-type color photograph
Work and residence permit	• A resume. • An affidavit of identification (notarized). • An employment agreement. • A certificate for establishing a company (where relevant). • Letter of invitation. • A diploma or qualified license (if any). The application must be made by your Korean employer to a Korean consulate.
Taiwan	
Visa	• Duly completed visa application form (available from the Bureau of Consular Affairs in Taiwan, or from Overseas Missions of the Republic of China). You should send your

Visa type	Documentation Needed
	application form either directly to the Bureau of Consular Affairs or to the ROC (Republic of China) Overseas Mission in your country. If you apply for a resident's visa prior to entering Taiwan, you will be issued the visa by the Overseas Mission in your home country. If you apply when you are already in Taiwan, you will be issued the visa by the Consulate officer; however, they may request an interview with you to support your application. • Passport with at least six months' validity. • An alien resident certificate (ARC) is required by all foreign nationals residing in Taiwan. Application for the ARC must be made within 15 days of arrival. This is applied for at the local police department once the Resident Visa is issued. See below for application procedures.
Work permit	• Application form (available from the Bureau of Consular Affairs, the Ministry of Financial Affairs, or any branch offices). • Copy of passport of the company's responsible person. • Company or business registration and business permit. • Copy of employment contract. • Copy of graduation certificate. • Original copy of receipt for the processing fee (TWD 500). • Any other documentation required by the relevant Central Government Authority.
Thailand	
Transit visa	• Passport or travel document with validity of not less than six months. • Completed visa application form. • One recent passport-sized photograph. • Evidence of means of transportation (confirmed air ticket paid in full). • Evidence of adequate financial means (THB 20,000 per person and THB 40,000 per family). • Visa for the next country in a passport or travel document. • Letter of invitation stating the application's participation in sports activities in Thailand (if applicable). • Consular officers reserve the right to request additional documents as deemed necessary. • Visa fee: THB 800 per entry.

Visa type	Documentation Needed
Tourist	• Passport or travel document with validity of not less than six months. • Completed visa application form. • One recent passport-sized photograph. • Air ticket (paid in full). • Financial means (THB 20,000 per person and THB 40,000 per family). • Consular officers reserve the right to request additional documents as deemed necessary. • Visa fee: THB 1,000 per entry.
Non-immigrant visa	• Completed visa application form. • Passport or travel document with validity of not less than six months and one photocopy. • Two passport-sized photographs taken within the past six months. • Evidence of adequate finance (THB 20,000 per person and THB 40,000 per family). • Letter of acceptance from the Ministry of Labour and Social Welfare.
Turkey	
Visa	• Application forms are available from any Turkish Consulate or the Consular Section of the Turkish Embassy. Applications should be made at your nearest Embassy or Consulate—usually in your home country. • Valid passport. • Recent passport-sized photograph. • Completed application form (form available from your local Consulate or Embassy or often by visiting their Web site and downloading the form). • Appropriate fee and registered stamped addressed envelope if applying by post.
Work and residence permit	• Four application forms (they must be completed in typeset, not handwritten). • Four passport photographs (one attached to each application form). • Passport which should contain a working visa issued by a Turkish Embassy abroad. • A letter from your employer in Turkey.

Visa type	Documentation Needed
	• Completed residence declaration form. • Permission granted to the company. • The appropriate fee.
United Arab Emirates	
Visa	• A copy of the intended visitor's passport (with at least six months' validity remaining). • Two passport-sized photographs. • Application form in duplicate. • Letter or fax from the sponsor in the UAE to the embassy concerned showing proof of sponsorship (if applying through your embassy). • A letter (and an extra copy) from the applicant's company/organization stipulating position held and purpose of visit. The sponsor's name, contact details, and occupation (or nature of business if a company) must be noted. The letter must also state that the employee is guaranteed both return transportation and financial support for the duration of the visit. • Fee.
Work permit	• You will need your original degree, diploma, or further education certificate to be authenticated. To do this you need to have the certificate authorized by the educational establishment or local education authority in your own country. Then the diploma certificate and the certificate of authorization are sent to the Department for Foreign Affairs (again in your own country) in order to further authenticate your qualifications. • You then need to send your attested certificates to your new employer along with the letter from the Department of Education verifying your certificates. Also include a copy of your passport, a signed employment contract, and a passport-sized photograph. • Your employer will submit the documents to the Ministry of Labor and Social Affairs in the UAE. It takes two to three weeks to issue an employment visa providing all the documents are in place.

Appendix 2
Salary/Price Differentials for Managers (Compared to New York City, United States), 2007 (converted to USD)

Net pay is simply gross pay after average taxes.

To compute the median gross or net pay for a country other than the United States, multiply the base amount times 100% plus or minus the percentage differential. For example, median gross pay in Japan is USD 88,500 x 117%, or USD 103,545, but net pay is USD 67,945 x 115%, or USD 78,136.

	Median Gross Pay	Median Net Pay
United States	88,500	67,945

Country	Gross Pay Differential	Net Pay Differential
Australia	18%	10%
China: Beijing	−52%	−50%
China: Shanghai	−48%	−45%
Czech Republic	−34%	−37%
Egypt	−53%	−50%

Country	Gross Pay Differential	Net Pay Differential
Hong Kong	−3%	14%
Hungary	−36%	−57%
India	−37%	−43%
Indonesia	−65%	−65%
Japan	17%	15%
Malaysia	−54%	−55%
New Zealand	−9%	−19%
Philippines	−66%	−69%
Poland	−11%	−33%
Romania	−57%	−60%
Russia	−38%	−30%
South Korea	−13%	−5%
Taiwan	−30%	−23%
Thailand	−51%	−46%
Turkey	16%	−2%
United Arab Emirates	28%	58%

Appendix 3
Safety Abroad: Corporate Concerns

Country	Safety Abroad
Australia	While Australia is considered to be a safe country, obviously it is still wise to avoid certain situations. Larger cities, especially Sydney, can get quite rough at night. Australians are heavy drinkers, so be cautious after drinking hours. Women can walk around freely, but it is advisable to travel in groups at night. The police are generally efficient and courteous. All common sense precautions should be taken to avoid being the victim of petty crime. Foreign business visitors are often the targets of thieves in any large city, and this is no different in Australia. Consequently, purses, laptops, and briefcases will require additional security. Do not leave valuables on show in cars or on tables in cafés. Information regarding risks that may be present in the area you are visiting or staying is usually available from the local visitor information bureau. • Avoid dark public spaces when alone. • Always let someone know where you are and where you are going. • Take care when using ATMs and secure your cash quickly. • Keep valuables out of sight and secure while traveling. • Don't carry unnecessary valuables around with you. • Don't leave any valuables in your car when leaving it parked.

Country	Safety Abroad
	• When driving ensure you have road maps. • Drink alcohol in moderation and never drink and drive.
China	Terrorism is rare in China. Overall, China is a relatively safe country with a low crime rate. But recently the crime rate has been on the increase, so it is advisable to take commonsense precautions with regard to personal safety and safeguarding personal property. Petty theft, mainly pick pocketing, is noticeable around tourist destinations and on the public transport systems. Violent crime against foreigners is very rare, however incidents do occur. Never carry large amounts of money around unnecessarily, and always have a supply of smaller notes to pay for taxi fares etc. Never exchange money illegally on the streets, always use a bank or official exchange bureau. Never walk alone in quiet or dimly lit areas. Always carry personal identification with you. It is advisable to make photocopies of passports, visas, permits etc. and keep them in a safe place.
Czech Republic	The Czech Republic is relatively safe and generally has a low crime rate, but common sense precautions should be taken with regard to personal safety and care of belongings. Street crimes such as pickpocketing and mugging are not uncommon, especially in major tourist areas in Prague and on public transport; nevertheless, the situation is no more dangerous than in any other European capital.
Egypt	Egypt is generally a fairly safe place for visitors. Egyptian law enforcement and security officials have increased their counterterrorism activities and security presence throughout the country.
Hong Kong	Hong Kong is generally considered a very safe city, both at night and during the day. The Hong Kong Police Force (HKPF) (www.info.gov.hk/police) has stations and reporting centers throughout the territory. Hong Kong police are polite, efficient, and honest. Any problems or crimes reported to them will be dealt with promptly. Unlike many Western cities of similar size, Hong Kong is relatively safe. There are organized gangs, known as Triads, that run drugs, gambling, prostitution, and money-lending services but have little impact on foreigners. The heavy police presence makes

Country	Safety Abroad
	it unlikely that you will encounter any problems. The biggest problems are pickpocketing and occasional purse snatching. Take basic common sense precautions. Avoid flashy displays of wealth; dress and behave conservatively. Avoid carrying too much cash around with you.
Hungary	Hungary has a low rate of violent crime but petty street crime does exist. The usual common sense approach to personal safety and caring for belongings is necessary. Pickpocketing has become more common, especially on the public transport system and in tourist areas. Purses, laptop computers, and briefcases are high target items for theft. It is inadvisable to carry large sums of cash with you. Always ensure that you do not leave any valuables in a parked car. Car theft is on the increase especially the more prestigious makes and models.
India	Some terrorist groups are active in India. Although they have not targeted foreign nationals specifically in the past, civilians have been killed or injured in blasts and explosions that have taken place in public places such as markets or on public transport. Demonstrations can occur spontaneously and can on occasions be violent. Foreigners are also requested to be extra vigilant around festival times when large crowds ensure petty theft and minor injuries are rife.
Indonesia	The September 9, 2004, terrorist bombing of the Australian Embassy in Jakarta, the previous bombing of the JW Marriott hotel in August 2003, and the 2005 Bali bombings have exacerbated concerns in the area over security initiated by the bombing of a Bali nightclub in October 2002. These targets were all identifiably Western. Expatriates and visitors are advised to be extra vigilant in areas where Westerners, particularly Americans, British, and Australians, have traditionally congregated, such as hotels, restaurants, schools, places of worship, and clubs. Travelers are requested to maintain a low profile, to vary routines, and to avoid any large crowds or demonstrations. Embassies strongly advise foreign nationals to register with their embassy or consulate on arrival in Indonesia, in order to facilitate any evacuation plans that may be required. Travelers are encouraged to read local newspapers and to keep up to date with regional

Country	Safety Abroad
	political affairs. Sectarian and ethnic attacks also put foreigners at risk in various parts of the island. Religious, political, and business targets have all been affected by domestic attacks. Jakarta International Airport and Indonesian government buildings have all suffered bombing attacks since 2003. Unrest in West Timor and Papua are causing grave concerns for security. Kidnapping is a threat in nearby Malaysia and the Philippines.
Israel	It is strongly advised that foreign nationals living in Israel take particular care over their personal security arrangements and remain vigilant against indiscriminate attacks. Most foreign embassies advise their expatriates to register with them on arrival in Israel. Consulates and embassies advise against travel along Israel's borders with Lebanon and to take particular care when crossing between Israel and Jordan. Visits to the occupied territories is strongly discouraged, especially at night, and visits to the Gaza Strip should be for essential purposes only as there is still a risk of kidnapping in the area. The Israeli government often imposes travel restrictions during periods of unrest, for example to the West Bank and Gaza areas where the safety of visitors would be at risk. In Jerusalem, travelers should exercise caution, especially on religious and holy days. You should adhere to all government or foreign embassy warnings with regard to safety and security issues. Despite Israel's reputation as a "high risk" country, it is a relatively safe place to live. Muggings and other forms of street crime are very uncommon; however, car thefts and burglaries do occur. All the usual common sense precautions should be exercised with regard to personal safety, for example don't carry excessive amounts of money around unnecessarily, and don't walk alone in unlit streets at night. If you are a victim of crime you should report the incident immediately to the local police and your embassy or consulate. Security is generally high around government buildings and public places. Your bags may be regularly searched when entering buildings, cinemas, restaurants, etc. This is common practice to ensure higher safety standards and should not be alarming or taken as an insult.

Country	Safety Abroad
Japan	In general, the Japanese are honest and law-abiding people. Japan has one of the lowest crime rates in the world, so personal safety is not too much of a concern; theft and drug-related crimes are relatively rare. Bicycle theft, however, is extremely common. To discourage petty crime, there is a police box (*koban*) in every neighborhood. You must carry a piece of identification at all times, for example, your passport or permit. The police have the right to arrest anyone who fails to do so. They rarely stop foreigners but car drivers are more frequently checked. If you are found without a valid ID, the police will accompany you to your home to collect it. Japan is an earthquake-prone country, so you should take all necessary precautions
Malaysia	The overall crime rate in Malaysia is low and violent crime involving tourists is relatively uncommon. Petty theft, particularly purse snatchings and pickpocketing, is the most common criminal activity. Thieves on motorcycles commit "snatch thefts" in crowded shopping areas, when the passenger on the back snatches a purse, handbag, or cellular telephone. These thefts occur at all hours and sometimes in front of large groups of witnesses. Automobile burglaries also occur and the usual common sense precautions should be taken when parking or leaving your car. Credit card fraud is a growing problem in Malaysia. Credit cards should only be used at established businesses, preferably outlets of internationally recognized firms, and credit card numbers should be closely safeguarded at all times. If you do need to report a crime in Malaysia, are lost, or are in need of help, many larger cities have tourist police stations which can provide assistance. Tourist police officers can be recognized by their uniforms (checkered hatbands, dark blue shirts, and trousers). They wear a red and blue badge with the letter "I" (for information) on their breast pocket. Regular police stations can also help and the regular police officers are dressed in blue trousers and shirts and are armed with small handguns. Traffic officers are dressed in black trousers and white short-sleeved shirts and are armed with small handguns.
New Zealand	Crime in New Zealand is relatively low, although there has been an increase in property crime over the past few years.

Country	Safety Abroad
	Most of this involves vehicle theft. Personal attacks are estimated to be around the same per capita as the United States and the United Kingdom. Any crime should be reported immediately to the New Zealand Police Service; www.police.govt.nz. Despite the relative safety of New Zealand, normal common sense precautions should be taken with regard to personal safety. It is recommended that items of value should be kept in a safety deposit box. Do not leave valuable items on view inside a car, but lock them in the trunk instead. Pickpocketing and purse snatching do occur, especially around bus and rail stations, public parks, and tourist areas. Do not display large amounts of cash and jewelry in public.
Philippines	You should always remain vigilant with regard to personal safety and caring for personal possessions. Pickpocketing and credit card fraud are common. Like in many major cities, drug related crimes, robbery, and assault are also prevalent in Manila and large amounts of jewelry should not be worn. It is inadvisable to carry large amounts of money around. Common sense precautions should be taken at all times. Don't walk alone in dark or unpopulated areas. When driving, the car doors should be kept locked. Children should never be left unsupervised. House alarms are highly recommended and some expatriate families hire security guards. There are many rural areas where it is not safe to travel as there are risks of kidnapping or general harm; therefore, before visiting any areas unknown to you, it would be wise to check safety with the tourist information services or the Philippine embassy.
Poland	Crime rates in Poland vary in different areas. Warsaw and Krakow, along with other major cities, have higher rates of crime against residents and foreign visitors. Organized groups of thieves and pickpockets often operate in major tourist destinations, railway and bus stations, and on public transport. It is advisable to be extra vigilant with personal possessions and valuables when traveling. One of the major crimes in Poland is car theft. It is advisable to park your car in a car park that has security and it is also important not to leave any personal possessions or valuables inside an

Country	Safety Abroad
	unattended car. It is relatively safe to walk around at night but crime rates are on the increase and common sense precautions should be taken with regard to personal safety. In Warsaw, it is advisable to avoid the central railway station at night.
Romania	Street crime, for example theft, is on the increase and it is advisable to take common sense precautions, particularly after dark or in crowded public places. While most crimes in Romania are nonviolent and nonconfrontational, there has been an increase in the number of crimes in which the victim suffers personal harm. Crimes against tourists (robbery, mugging, pickpocketing, and fraud) are a growing problem. Organized groups of thieves and pickpockets operate in train stations and on public transport systems in major cities. Panhandlers—often groups of children—can be very persistent and have resorted to grabbing or tearing clothing in their efforts to steal. Credit card fraud is on the increase. The level of assistance that can be expected from the Romanian Police varies. Authorities are often ineffective at deterring crime and their response to emergency calls can be too slow to disrupt incidents in progress. If a victim desires a thorough response by the local authorities, they must be prepared to devote time and effort to wade through local bureaucracy.
Russia	It is advisable to check with the consulate/embassy that any regions you may wish to travel to are safe for tourists or foreigners. There are certain areas that are not considered safe for travel. The usual common sense precautions should be taken with regard to personal safety. As with any large city, Moscow and St. Petersburg have their fare share of crime. Theft and pickpocketing incidence is high, especially on the public transport systems and around tourist areas. It is essential to remain vigilant at all times and keep personal belongings close. Do not carry unnecessary large amounts of money and keep your credit cards in a safe place. Visitors are required to carry identification at all times; those who do not have a national identity card should carry the hotel card (*propusk*) and preferably a photocopy of the first pages of their passport. Law and order is maintained by the "*militsia*" (militia or police), recognizable by their blue-grey uniforms.

Country	Safety Abroad
	Traffic police usually wear white belts. In general, the *militsia* are very helpful; however, if you run into serious trouble it is advisable to contact your embassy for assistance.
South Africa	Insecurity due to crime is probably one of the most serious difficulties facing the country. However, crime follows a demographic pattern and the greatest proportion of violent crime takes place in the poorer areas such as in the townships. On a more positive note political violence has decreased significantly since the end of apartheid; nevertheless it is still prudent to avoid large gatherings especially on national holidays such as Human Rights Day, Freedom Day, and Workers Day. Police officers are not widely present outside city centers and major tourist venues. Police officers will keep a low profile since they are barely respected, underpaid, shot at, under-equipped, and demoralized. If you are feeling unsafe and see a police officer, feel free to ask for an escort. In case of a robbery, do not expect much action (nor getting back your property), but the police report will be needed for insurance purposes. Many middle-class people subscribe to the services of armed private security firms to protect their property; a theme that has become a national obsession. This is obvious by the large number of alarms, bars, high walls, and electronically controlled gates, not only in the suburbs but also in less deprived areas of some townships. The Central Business District (CBD), Braamfontein and Newtown, are the most dangerous districts; Joubert Park, Hillbrow, and Berea are somewhat safer, and Yeoville and Observatory even more, but attention is still needed in these neighborhoods. If you are mugged, take very seriously the usual advice not to resist; running can work, but some muggers have guns and might use them. If you have money or valuables, leave some of them easily available, so that the mugger will not look further. Criminal activity such as assault and armed robbery is particularly high in public transportation areas or where there are hotels. Another risk is car jacking. To be safe, always keep all car doors locked and windows up, and never wait in an unlocked car. The most dangerous times are when leaving or returning to a car, so be attentive, park in secure and preferably guarded parking, and do not stay in parking lots more than the

Country	Safety Abroad
	needed time. At traffic lights, keep a good distance between you and the car in front, verify that all windows are closed and doors locked, check your mirrors and keep your foot near the accelerator. Late at night, many motorists do not stop for red lights. Visitors to game parks and reserves are strongly advised to remain in the vehicle at all times, even if you are accompanied by a guide. Unfortunately there have been several incidents of attacks by wild animals resulting in serious injuries and even death.
South Korea	The internal political situation is somewhat unstable due to efforts to liberalize the economy and increase democracy in the country. Demonstrations and strikes are commonplace but do not normally affect everyday life. They can, however, become confrontational and violent. This is relatively a safe place, but with the increase of tourists and foreigners, the number of crimes such as bag snatching and sexual assaults has risen. One should avoid going out alone at night.
Taiwan	Taiwan suffers greatly from petty crime and theft; however, foreigners are seldom victims of serious crime which is contained to local natives and their property. Pickpocketing is common in markets, especially in the night markets. The police rarely enforce the law in Taiwan, and corruption in politics and authority is rife. Statute law in Taiwan is in practice replaced with a system of reprisals. Again, foreigners are detached from this culture although it is recommended that you keep personal details and those of your family discreet as cases have been known to occur. More than two thirds of Taiwanese taxi drivers are convicted criminals. It is prudent to not enter a taxi alone if you are a female; not to accept anything to eat or drink by the driver; and avoid being dropped off directly in front of your house. Credit card fraud has now become so prevalent that some card issuers advise against using your credit card in Taiwan if possible. Card readers used by criminals are common in ATMs other than at banks and post offices and have recently been used to replace the card swipe reader on entering ATMs within banks out of hours.
Thailand	Thailand is generally considered a safe country; however, the usual common sense safety precautions should be followed.

Country	Safety Abroad
	There are certain areas/regions in Thailand where tourists should exercise extreme caution if visited (for example, the Thai-Myanmar border area). Most embassies or consulates publish travel alerts and advice and it is recommended that you seek such advice prior to planning a trip. As in any other large city, pickpocketing, purse snatching, and other petty crimes are common on the Bangkok public buses and in areas where tourists/foreigners gather. Extra precautions should be taken with regard to the safety of personal belongings. Avoid carrying large sums of money around, unless really necessary, and don't wear flashy jewelry. When using taxis at the airport or downtown, travelers should avoid unlicensed taxis and only enter taxis from the airport's official taxi stand or licensed taxis. Alternatively, use the airport limousine service where you can hire a car and a driver. A growing number of travelers have reported being robbed after consuming drugged food or drink offered to them by a friendly stranger, sometimes posing as a fellow traveler. Never accept any food or drink from strangers while traveling. There are a number of scams reported by visitors to Bangkok involving the purchase of jewelry to export. These scams are well orchestrated, and a friendly passerby will let you into a "great secret," followed by a tour of the city in a tuk-tuk whereby the route takes you to an export jewelry dealer; most victims have paid over the market value for goods and sometimes the jewelry has turned out to be fake. Go by the simple rule: if it seems too good to be true it probably is. Credit card fraud has also been increasing. Travelers may wish to take extra precautions with credit cards and use them only in known or established businesses.
Turkey	Many foreign nationals find themselves injured each year through accidents on the road, whether as a pedestrian or in a vehicle. Turkey has one of the highest accident rates in the world and particular mention is given to the high risk incurred when on Turkish roads. Turkey has received media attention of late due to a spate of terrorist attacks. The main city centers are believed to be targets; however, the current areas to avoid are the border areas between Turkey and Syria, Iran and Iraq. Bomb attacks in the last few years in Istanbul, Ankara, Izmir, and Adana have resulted in injuries and

Country	Safety Abroad
	deaths; the bombings of two tourist hotels in Istanbul in August 2004 and the November 2003 attacks against the British Consulate-General, HSBC Bank, and synagogues in Istanbul highlight the current threat. It is advisable to avoid any large crowds partaking in demonstrations or protests as in the past these have quickly degenerated into violence. Women should bear in mind the local customs and religions and dress conservatively mostly when traveling outside of major cities.
United Arab Emirates	The United Arab Emirates are currently under significant threat from terrorism against Western interests. Elsewhere in the region, attacks have been indiscriminate and civilian organizations have been targeted. In June 2004 an Al Qaeda Web site carried threats to attack Western residential areas, military bases, oil facilities, and transportation (including aviation) interests in the Gulf States. A senior Al Qaeda operative was arrested in Dubai two months later. Personal security arrangements should be assessed and all people within the UAE are requested to remain vigilant. Nevertheless, Dubai is the most stable city in the Middle East, and daily life has been unaffected by the death of the Palestinian Authority Chairman Yasser Arafat. Women should respect Muslim laws and dress conservatively, particularly in public places, and try to avoid traveling alone at night. A reputable taxi company should always be used. Incidents of street crime are rare, although it is advisable to keep a close watch on your personal possessions and to refrain from walking in unlit areas at night. Westerners are advised to stay in the main public areas.

Appendix 4
Healthcare Abroad

Country	Healthcare Abroad
Australia	There are no specific health risks in Australia. Standards of hygiene and sanitation are very high. Water is potable, milk is pasteurized, and meat and vegetables are safe to eat. Travelers to north Queensland and the Northern Territory should use insect repellents and sleeping nets to guard against the risk of contracting mosquito-borne diseases such as dengue fever and Ross River fever. There have also been reports of cases of Murray Valley Encephalitis (MVE), a potentially fatal mosquito-borne disease, in the Northern Territory. Australia has one of the highest skin cancer rates in the world, so special care should be taken with regard to sun exposure. Protect both yourself and your children against possible heat and sunstroke, as in summer temperatures can reach 40°C. You must wear high factor sun protection cream at all times while in the sun.
China	It is extremely important to visit your doctor or travel health clinic at least 6–8 weeks prior to leaving for China. You can then receive all the most up-to-date advice and vaccination recommendations for your journey. Typhoid, polio, hepatitis A, and hepatitis B vaccinations are advised by many national health authorities but are not a requirement for entry. A cholera vaccination may be required if you are

Country	Healthcare Abroad
	traveling from a tropical or infected area. A certificate of vaccination against yellow fever is required by those traveling from infected areas, including Central America, South America, and Africa. For persons intending to stay in China for longer than one year, an AIDS test is required. Malaria is a risk in certain areas throughout China, but not in urban areas or densely populated plain areas. In general, malaria prophylaxis is not necessary unless one is traveling to a remote rural area within the following regions: Hainan, Yunnan, Fujian, Guangdong, Guangxi, Guizhou, Sichuan, and along the Zangbo River. In large cities and towns, food and water are for the most part safe to eat and drink. The Chinese themselves, however, will rarely drink straight from the tap and usually boil and store drinking water in a thermos flask. It is advisable to boil all water that is to be used for drinking or brushing teeth. Bottled water is available. Most Chinese food is well cooked, although some care should be taken with shellfish or fish and under-cooked meat. All fruits and vegetables should be thoroughly washed prior to consumption. Respiratory infections are very common during the winter months. Travelers often refer to it as the "China syndrome" and it can sometimes be far more serious than a simple flu. Symptoms include fever, chills, weakness, and sore throat. The condition is aggravated by cold weather, changes in diet, and air pollution. Traveler's diarrhea is often a problem for newcomers to China and is caused principally by the change in diet and different strains of bacteria.
Czech Republic	Traveling to the Czech Republic poses no great health risks; however, it is advisable to see your doctor or visit the travel clinic at least six weeks before departure from your home country to seek advice and information. It is recommended that you keep current with all standard immunizations. Tap water is considered relatively safe to drink but it is usually chlorinated and may cause mild abdominal upsets. Bottled water is widely available and advised. Milk is generally pasteurized and dairy products are safe for consumption. Local meat, poultry, fish, and produce are generally of good quality and safe to eat. Special care should be taken if there is to be an abrupt change in climate from your home

Country	Healthcare Abroad
	country. The weather in the Czech Republic can be unpredictable and it is always a good idea to dress with this in mind. Even in the summer a sweater or light jacket can be necessary in the evenings. The Czech Republic's winters tend to be long and dark and can aggravate colds, influenza, and throat infections. Depression and seasonal disorders are also common ailments due to the lack of sunlight in the winter months. Vitamin supplements, a balanced diet, and an active lifestyle are usually effective in counteracting the effects of darkness.
Egypt	Cholera, typhoid, and polio vaccinations are advisable. It is important to take prompt care of cuts and skin irritations since flies can quickly spread infection. Bilharzia infects the Nile waters and it is strongly advised not to bath or walk bare-foot in the river. There is a very limited risk of Malaria in Egypt; the only location being highlighted at present is in the El Faiyum governorate (50 miles southwest of Cairo); although there have been no cases reported since 1998. Pro-phylaxis is not recommended. Air pollution is a major con-cern in Cairo.
Hong Kong	It is important to consult your doctor or local travel health clinic before moving to Hong Kong. They will advise you on all health matters and recommend vaccinations for the area. Care is necessary only in some rural and island areas where water is still drawn from wells. It is recommended to boil tap water before drinking. Bottled water is widely available in hotels, restaurants, and convenience stores. Food purchased from street vendors is also generally safe; however, during summer, beware of heat-related problems. Milk and dairy products are pasteurized and safe for consumption. Local meat, poultry, seafood, fruit, and vegetables are usually of a high standard. Avian flu and severe acute respiratory syn-drome (SARS): As of now, there are no travel restrictions to Hong Kong. But you should avoid contact with living or dead poultry and avoid any chicken farms or markets.
Hungary	There are no special requirements for travel to Hungary. The normal common sense precautions should be followed with regard to food and drink. The water in Hungary is generally safe to drink; however, bottled water is widely available, and

Country	Healthcare Abroad
	many people prefer to drink this. Milk is pasteurized and safe for consumption. Local produce is usually of a good standard and safe to eat. It is advisable to visit your doctor and keep up to date with all the standard vaccinations that are administered in your home country.
India	Contaminated drinking water is a serious problem. To be safe, stay away from ice, uncooked food, unpasteurized milk and milk products, and drink only water that has been boiled for at least 20 minutes or bottled. Also turn down offers of "filtered" water; water is often filtered to take out particles, but this doesn't mean it has been purified to kill off parasites. Check the caps of water bottles to make sure they have not been tampered with, as bottles are sometimes refilled with tap water. You should avoid raw vegetables and fruit that have been peeled before they are brought to you. Peel your own fruit and choose varieties with thick skins. Pork products should be avoided; make certain that other meats are thoroughly cooked. Stomach upsets often are due to both the richness of Indian food as well as a lack of hygiene. Many hotel restaurants tend to cook Indian dishes especially with a large amount of oil, which can trigger "Delhi belly." Ask the chef to use less oil. Fried foods from street vendors often look delicious, but check the oil; if it looks as old as the pot, it could be rancid and lead to trouble. Remember to wash your hands before you eat anything, even snacks. A useful tip is to carry premoistened towelettes to use when soap and water are not available. The sun can be intense in India. Beware of overexposure even on overcast days. To avoid sunburn, use a sunscreen with a sun protection factor of at least 30. To be safe, also wear a wide-brimmed hat and be sure to drink plenty of water. All cities in India are heavily polluted. Pollution-control regulations and devices were introduced in 1995, but the majority of India's vehicles continue to use diesel (although most public service vehicles now use more environmentally friendly means of power). People with breathing problems, especially asthma, should carry appropriate respiratory remedies. Take toilet paper with you and carry it around. You will usually find it at nicer hotels and restaurants, but it is not generally provided. Traditional Indian toilets are covered holes in the

Country	Healthcare Abroad
	ground. In many Indian bathrooms you will notice a faucet and/or bucket with a beaker or other small vessel, which Indians rinse with after using the toilet. You should never place toilet paper or anything else in a toilet in India, as the septic systems cannot handle it. In many bathrooms you will find sanitary bags for disposal purposes. If you travel into forested areas during or just after the monsoon, protect yourself against leeches by covering your legs and by not wearing sandals. When a leech clings to your clothing or skin, dab it with a pinch of salt and the leech will fall off. If itching persists, apply an antiseptic; infection rarely occurs. For bedbugs, buy a bar of *Dettol* soap (available throughout India) to be used when bathing to relieve itching and discomfort.
Indonesia	A yellow fever vaccination certificate is required for visitors traveling to Indonesia from infected areas. Indonesia considers the countries and areas included in the endemic zones as infected. Malaria is a risk throughout Indonesia with the exception of the city of Jakarta, major cities, and in the tourist areas of Bali and Java. It is recommended that travelers consult their doctor on whether an anti-malaria treatment is necessary. Doctors recommend that travelers take precautions to cover exposed skin from being bitten by mosquitoes. Nets around the bed are recommended and the use of an insect repellent is advised. Visitors are advised to have booster vaccinations against typhoid and polio, diphtheria, tetanus, and measles, mumps, and rubella. Although malaria, hepatitis A and B, and Japanese B encephalitis are present in rural areas, it is recommended that all travelers to Indonesia obtain precautions against contracting these illnesses, even if travel outside the cities is not envisaged. It is advised to avoid drinking tap water and to boil any water for brushing teeth. Expatriates sometimes have water coolers installed in the home. To avoid incidences of gastroenteric illnesses, it is recommended to drink only bottled water.
Israel	There are no particular health precautions to be taken in Israel. All persons traveling to Israel should ensure they have current routine immunizations, such as tetanus-diphtheria, measles, and varicella (chickenpox). An outbreak of West Nile Virus infection in 2000 led to 452 cases and 29 deaths, mainly in the central and northern parts of the country.

Country	Healthcare Abroad
	Subsequent years have seen up to 72 deaths caused by this mosquito-borne disease. Travelers in these areas of the country are advised to take precautions against mosquito bites between August and November. Water is generally safe to drink; however, it is normally chlorinated and may cause some mild abdominal upsets. Hence it is advisable to initially purchase bottled water, which is widely available. In rural areas it is essential to sterilize all tap water. Local meat, produce, and dairy products are usually of good standards and are safe for consumption. Israel is a hot, sunny country and you should ensure that sun protection is used at all times to avoid damage to the skin.
Japan	For the most part food and drink are safe. It is advisable to take the usual personal care if traveling from a different climate to Japan's seasonal weather conditions. Tap water is safe to drink throughout Japan, but you should avoid drinking directly from streams or rivers. It is also not a good idea to walk barefoot through flooded paddy fields, due to the danger of waterborne parasites. With regard to food, you should have no fears about eating raw seafood or fish, including the notorious *fugu* (globefish). However, raw meat and river fish are best avoided. Japan has high standards of health and hygiene, and there are no significant diseases to worry about. Japan is an earthquake-prone country, so you should take necessary precautions.
Malaysia	The general standard of sanitation and environmental health services is good, particularly in the towns and cities. The usual care should be taken if there is to be an abrupt change in diet and climatic conditions from your country of origin. It is advisable to ask friends and colleagues to recommend good general practitioners and dentists. Although it is considered safe to drink water straight from the tap, it is recommended that tap water be boiled, filtered, or treated before drinking. Bottled mineral water is readily available. Milk is sometimes unpasteurized and should be boiled before drinking. Nevertheless, pasteurized milk is also available. Fruit and vegetables should be thoroughly washed and peeled before consumption. All meat and fish should be cooked well. You should consult your doctor or traveler's

Country	Healthcare Abroad
	health clinic at least six weeks before your departure for Malaysia. There are certain vaccines that are recommended (although not compulsory) for travel to the region. Basic immunizations should also be kept current. You may also need anti-Malaria medication depending on which area you are traveling to. Avian flu and severe acute respiratory syndrome (SARS): As of now, there are no travel restrictions to Malaysia. It is recommended, however, to avoid contact with living or dead poultry and not to visit any chicken farms or markets.
New Zealand	Food and water are safe to eat and drink. Air pollution is not a major concern in Auckland. Sand flies, ants, and cockroaches are common in New Zealand but are considered a nuisance rather than a health hazard.
Philippines	It is advisable to visit your doctor or travel clinic at least six weeks before leaving for the Philippines. There are vaccinations that are recommended for travelers to the region and your doctor can advise you of all health precautions necessary. Water used for drinking, brushing teeth, or making ice should always be boiled or sterilized first. Bottled water is available and recommended for drinking. Unpasteurized milk should also be boiled; however, it is advisable to use powdered or tinned milk that is reconstituted with pure water. You should try and avoid any dairy products that are likely to have been made from unsterilized or unboiled milk. Meat and fish should be thoroughly cooked and served hot. Vegetables should be washed and well cooked and fruit should always be washed and peeled. If you are living in, or visiting, a malaria risk area it is important to ensure that you take the proper precautions and medications to protect yourself. Malaria risk exists throughout the year in areas below 600 meters, except in the provinces of Aklan, Bilaran, Bohol, Camiguin, Capiz, Catanduanes, Cebu, Guimaras, Iloilo, Leyte, Masbate, northern Samar, Sequijor, and metropolitan Manila. No risk is considered to exist in urban areas or in the plains. The recommended prophylaxis in risk areas is mefloquine (World Health Organization recommendation).
Poland	There are no special health requirements for traveling to Poland. The normal common sense precautions should be

Country	Healthcare Abroad
	followed with regard to food and drink. The water in Poland tends to be chlorinated and may cause slight stomach upsets. It is advisable to boil all drinking water or to buy bottled water, which is widely available. Milk and dairy products are generally pasteurized and safe for consumption. Local produce is usually of a good standard. Winters in Poland are long and with very little sun. Common colds, flu, seasonal disorders, and depression can be frequent. Balanced nutrition and exercise can help ease the effects of the lack of sunlight by keeping your immune system strong. Some people find that light therapy also helps ease the symptoms of "the winter blues." Be prepared for unpredictable weather that can shift in very little time. Carry an umbrella and an extra sweater and dress warmly.
Romania	It is advisable to visit your doctor or travel clinic at least six weeks before departure to receive medical advice. There are no required vaccinations necessary for entry into Romania; however, it is recommended that you keep up to date with all standard immunizations. In Romania, tap water is usually chlorinated and while it is safe for drinking it may cause stomach upset. Bottled mineral water is widely available and recommended. The water supply in mountain or rural areas usually comes from the local mountain springs and is safe for drinking. Milk and dairy products are generally pasteurized and safe for consumption. Local meat, poultry, seafood, fruits, and vegetables are usually of good quality and safe. Stray dogs are a problem in Bucharest. Although no cases of rabies have been reported, they have been known to attack joggers and passersby; therefore, it is advisable to keep at a safe distance. It is worth noting that Bucharest and many other cities in Romania are located in active seismic zones. The last major earthquake in Bucharest took place in 1977. Since that time, numerous smaller tremors have taken place, including in 2005. These smaller tremors are usually harmless but can be very frightening and you should try to avoid panicking. Civil authorities have plans in place for major disasters, but they could become overwhelmed in a major event. Romania experiences severe winters, and it is important to note that roads are not maintained to the same

Country	Healthcare Abroad
	standard as in other Western countries. It is essential to take extra care while driving in winter.
Russia	It is advisable to visit your doctor or travel clinic before your departure. There are no vaccinations compulsory for entry into Russia, but you should have your standard immunizations current. You should also have a standard health check. All persons staying in Russia for a period of over three months must produce an HIV test certificate. Drink only bottled water. If there isn't any available, make sure you boil the water you will drink. Water filtration systems are also available for purchase. The tap water in St. Petersburg is definitely not drinkable. There are many poplar trees in Russian cities. People with allergies should be aware that in the summer they shed very large quantities of cotton-like fur which fills the air and triggers allergy symptoms. During the winter there is very little daylight, especially in St. Petersburg. Colds, flu, seasonal disorders, and depression are common. Balanced nutrition, exercise, and vitamin sup-plements can help ease the effects of the lack of sunlight by keeping your immune system strong. Be prepared for unpre-dictable weather that can shift in very little time. Carry an umbrella and an extra sweater and dress warmly. Russia has the highest HIV/AIDS epidemic in Europe, mainly due to a very high rate of injected drug abuse. Unprotected casual sex should be avoided.
South Africa	Vaccinations against typhoid, hepatitis A, and polio are recommended. Routine immunizations (e.g. tetanus) should also be kept current. It is highly recommended that you visit your doctor or local traveler's health clinic for advice before leaving for South Africa. Although there have been no cases of polio reported in South Africa since 1989, you should still be immunized before arrival in the country. Depending on which areas you are visiting, you may wish to seek precautions against cholera. An outbreak was reported in the Nkomazi area in Mpumalanga Province on the Mozambique border in early 2004. Hepatitis B inoculations are recommended for children up to the age of 12 who have not completed the series of injections as infants. Booster doses for tetanus and measles are also advised. Tap water is generally safe to drink throughout South Africa; however, in

Country	Healthcare Abroad
	rural areas it is advisable to boil all water before usage. In some areas the water can be very mineral rich and may cause a little gastro upset, but this will pass in a couple of days when you are used to it. In the Cape area, some water contains humic acid, which gives the water a brown hue; however, the water is quite safe to drink. You can drink from pure mountain streams but not from other streams and rivers where you are at risk from waterborne diseases. Swimming is safe along the entire coastline, but rivers and lakes in the eastern and northern regions might carry the bilharzia parasite. Usually, warning signs are posted. Sun can be intense, so remember to use high-factor sun protection at all times. Malaria is endemic in tropical Africa. Many Africans have it in their bloodstream and get occasional bouts of fever. Most of South Africa is free of the disease, but before visiting the game reserves and parks of the Northern, Mpumalanga, and KwaZulu-Natal provinces, anti-malaria precautions should be taken. Anti-malaria tablets are available without prescription at South African drugstores. AIDS and other venereal diseases are widespread in southern Africa in both men and women. About one in five South African adults is HIV positive (5.3 million), and more than 800 South Africans die every day of the disease. Tickbite fever can be an issue but is easily treated. Hepatitis inoculations are recommended. It is advisable to wear a hat from 10 A.M. to 4 P.M. and to wear sunglasses to protect against the strong South African sun. Sunscreen must be worn at all times; even on a cloudy day or if you are dark skinned but from a cooler climate you are still at risk from being burned. The Government's Department of Health Web site is www.doh.gov.za.
South Korea	Sanitation in Seoul is very good, although elsewhere, old sewerage systems can cause problems from time to time. Improvements are being made outside main cities; however, it is advisable not to drink water straight from the tap. Despite this there is little chance of contracting serious intestinal infections. Police stations are identified by a yellow illuminated sign. The Korean National Tourist Organization (KNTO) operates an advice/complaint service in most major cities (Seoul: +82 2-735-0101). Seoul City Tourist Information Center (+82 2-735-8688) will also assist,

Country	Healthcare Abroad
	including calling an ambulance on your behalf or relaying your call to the appropriate authorities. However, these services are available only during office hours (9 A.M. to 6 P.M. daily). Outside office hours, contact International SOS, Tel: +82 2-3140-1924, www.internationalsos.co.kr, which provides a 24-hour emergency service for foreigners, acting as a link between the patient and the Korean hospitals for a fee.
Taiwan	The standard of health in Taiwan is relatively good, especially when compared to other countries in Asia. Universal health care is provided, and labor insurance is cheap and available to every worker. Every major city has several large hospitals staffed by thousands of overseas-trained doctors, and every small town has a clinic, although the quality of care might be lower. Pollution in Taipei City was acute a decade ago, but vast improvements have been made in air quality in the last few years. The air may probably never be really clear due to the fact that Taipei City is located in a natural depression surrounded by mountains, but it is not threatening to an asthmatic visitor. Heat stroke in the steamy summer months, also caused by the basin configuration of Taipei, is much more likely. Common sense precautions concerning food are necessary. Raw fruits and vegetables must be carefully washed and meats must be cooked thoroughly as some are bought from open-air markets. The health department rarely monitors any food sources or food preparations; however, in restaurants, as their reputations are at stake, few higher-class establishments take risks. The health department does checks when the restaurant opens and sporadically thereafter, but self-regulation is practiced and effective. Although illnesses from food or drinks sold by street vendors are rare, it is still not advisable for someone just off the plane to eat from hawkers. The food is prepared in the open air, at times without proper refrigeration, and the utensils are often less than clean. Water should never be drunk straight from the tap, as the plumbing in some places of Taipei is old and inadequate. Water must be boiled before usage, or you can buy bottled water. Vaccination certificates for yellow fever and cholera are required for those arriving from infected countries. It is advisable to ensure your inoculations are all current, including

Country	Healthcare Abroad
	hepatitis A and typhoid. A recent outbreak of dengue fever has led to travelers to the south of the island to use insect repellent and to take measures to avoid being bitten by mosquitoes. The SARS virus is no longer considered to be a risk in Taiwan and was taken off the watch list in June 2003.
Thailand	The general standard of sanitation and healthcare varies dramatically depending upon your location in Thailand. Healthcare in Bangkok matches the standards of healthcare in Western cities, whereas the standards in rural areas are only adequate. Both private and public healthcare facilities are available. Private institutions generally have higher standards. Medical supplies are freely available, with or without prescription. It is necessary to take precautions against malaria, hepatitis, yellow fever, and gastrointestinal diseases. Since 2004, the severe acute respiratory syndrome (SARS) has been kept within limits, and there seems no evidence of another break out. The government has made efforts to monitor and control the situation. The avian influenza (bird flu) is also being monitored by the authorities. You need to visit your doctor or travel health clinic at least six weeks before your departure for Thailand. There are recommended vaccinations that you should consider having (for example, typhoid, hepatitis A, tetanus), and your doctor will be able to advise you on the appropriate treatment. Precautions against mosquito and ant bites are necessary. Insect screens, mosquito nets, and insect repellent treatments are definitely required. Dehydration is a common problem for visitors to Thailand, due to the heat and the humidity. You must drink plenty of water and be careful on the consumption of alcohol. Food and waterborne diseases are common. Tap water is not fit for consumption unless it is boiled before use. Bottled water is widely available and is recommended for drinking, making ice, and brushing teeth. Only use pasteurized milk and other dairy products. Meat and fish should be well cooked and hot and never reheated. Avoid raw vegetables and unpeeled fruits. Many people experience stomach upsets after arrival in Thailand. This is often due to the vast changes in climate and dietary intake.

Country	Healthcare Abroad
Turkey	The standard of public health and sanitation in the larger cities of Turkey are generally good. Nevertheless, they are still below the standard of other European cities or those in the United States. The standard of medical care and dental care varies although there is a good choice of private hospitals covering most specialties. Ankara and Istanbul like most cities have their share of pickpockets and thieves; it is recommended that valuables are stored or carried safely and obvious displays of wealth are discouraged. Turkey can be a politically sensitive country at times and it is prudent to refrain from voicing any anti-state views or opinion. Cholera is active in Turkey although it is very unlikely that any visitors will come into contact with the disease which is generally confined to some of the rural areas with substandard sanitation. Hepatitis A vaccinations are recommended for all non-immune travelers and hepatitis B vaccinations are recommended for all visitors wishing to stay in Turkey for three months or over. Cases of malaria are reported countrywide, but the majority are reported from southern and eastern Turkey, particularly along the Mediterranean coast, including Diyarbakir and Siirt Provinces, and the provinces bordering Syria, Iraq, and Iran. Vivax malaria accounts for 100% of cases; Chloroquine prophylaxis is recommended in risk areas. There is no malaria in Istanbul, Ankara, or Izmir. Polio and typhoid vaccinations are recommended as a precautionary measure. Although tap water is usually chlorinated in the larger cities, it is not necessarily treated; therefore, it is advisable to avoid drinking tap water where possible. Bottled mineral water is widely available. If you find a water source marked *içilir*, *içme suyu* or *içilebilir*t hen the water is safe for drinking, if it is marked *içilmez* then it is unfit for consumption. All fresh fruit and vegetables should be washed thoroughly with drinking water and meat and fish should be well cooked. Changes in diet can often cause upsets to the digestive system; therefore, it is advisable to eat only a small amount of food on arrival until you are used to the different food stuffs in Turkey. Turkey is a hot country, and heat stroke is a common ailment, especially among visitors. It is advised that you drink at least a glass of water each hour and avoid excessive physical exertion during the day. Sunblock,

Country	Healthcare Abroad
	sunglasses, and a sun hat are all recommended especially in the hottest part of the day.
United Arab Emirates	The general standard of public health and sanitation in the UAE is good and air quality issues through pollution are not a major concern in the region.

Appendix 5
Celsius to Fahrenheit Conversion Chart

°C	°F	°C	°F	°C	°F	°C	°F
50	122.0	27	80.6	4	39.2	−19	−2.2
49	120.2	26	78.8	3	37.4	−20	−4.0
48	118.4	25	77.0	2	35.6	−21	−5.8
47	116.6	24	75.2	1	33.8	−22	−7.6
46	114.8	23	73.4	0	32.0	−23	−9.4
45	113.0	22	71.6	−1	30.2	−24	−11.2
44	111.2	21	69.8	−2	28.4	−25	−13.0
43	109.4	20	68.0	−3	26.6	−26	−14.8
42	107.6	19	66.2	−4	24.8	−27	−16.6
41	105.8	18	64.4	−5	23.0	−28	−18.4
40	104.0	17	62.6	−6	21.2	−29	−20.2
39	102.2	16	60.8	−7	19.4	−30	−22.0
38	100.4	15	59.0	−8	17.6	−31	−23.8
37	98.6	14	57.2	−9	15.8	−32	−25.6
36	96.8	13	55.4	−10	14.0	−33	−27.4
35	95.0	12	53.6	−11	12.2	−34	−29.2
34	93.2	11	51.8	−12	10.4	−35	−31.0
33	91.4	10	50.0	−13	8.6	−36	−32.8

32	89.6	9	48.2	−14	6.8	−37	−34.6
31	87.8	8	46.4	−15	5.0	−38	−36.4
30	86.0	7	44.6	−16	3.2	−39	−38.2
29	84.2	6	42.8	−17	1.4	−40	−40.0
28	82.4	5	41.0	−18	−0.4	−	−

Source: National Climatic Data Center, U.S. Department of Commerce

Index

Auckland, New Zealand, 149–58
   demographic/workforce overview, 154
   economic overview, 150
   environment issues, 150
   financial issues including banking
      services and taxes, 156–57; banks,
      157; currency, 156; taxes, 157
   housing, 155–56
   infrastructure, 150–51; air travel, 150–
      51; bus, 151; metro, 151; taxi,
      151; utilities and traffic, 150
   international schools and education,
      158
   medical issues, 150
   natural environment, 155
   personal safety and security issues,
      149–50
   recreation and entertainment, 152–54;
      bars, 154; casinos, 154; culture and
      entertainment, 153; entertainment
      for children, 153; museums and
      galleries, 153; restaurants, 153;
      sports facilities, 154
   shopping and availability of consumer
      goods, 151–52
   sociocultural environment, 154
   workplace culture, 155
Australia, general, 19–24
   demographic/workforce overview, 21
   economic overview, 20
   environment issues, 20
   financial issues including banking
      services and taxes, 22–24; banks, 22;
      cash, traveler's checks, and credit
      cards, 22; currency, 22; taxes,
      23–24
   medical issues, 20
   personal safety and security issues, 19
   sociocultural environment, 20
   workplace culture, 21–22

Bangkok, Thailand, 218–30
   demographic/workforce overview, 225
   economic overview, 219
   environment issues, 219
   financial issues including banking
      services and taxes, 228–29; banks
      and checks, 228–29; currency, 228;
      taxes, 229
   housing, 227–28
   infrastructure, 219–22; air travel, 220;
      Bangkok Transit System (BST), 220;
      Boat, 221–22; bus, 220–21; car,
      222; Mass rapid Transit Authority of
      Thailand (MRTA), 220; metro, 211;
      taxis, 211–12; train, 221; *Tuk-tuks*

(jitneys), 221; utilities and traffic, 219–20
international schools and education, 229–30
medical issues, 218–19
natural environment, 227
personal safety and security issues, 218
recreation and entertainment, 223–25; bars, 224; culture and entertainment, 223; entertainment for children, 224; international associations and clubs, 223; museums, 223–24; nightclubs, 224; nightlife, 224; restaurants, 223; sports, 224–25; sports for children, 225
shopping and availability of consumer goods, 222–23
sociocultural environment, 225
workplace culture, 226–27
Beijing, 49–54,
environment issues, 49
housing, 53–54
infrastructure, 50–51; air travel, 50; bus, 50–51; car, 51; metro, 50; taxis, 50; transport, 50
international schools and education, 54;
medical issues, 49;
natural environment, 53;
recreation and entertainment, 51–53; cinemas, 52; clubs and bars, 52–53; entertainment for children, 52; restaurants, 52; social clubs, 51–52; sports facilities, 53; theaters, 52
shopping and availability of consumer goods, 51. *See also* China, general
Brisbane, 24–29,
housing, 28–29
infrastructure, 24–26; air travel, 24; bus, 25; ferry, 25–26; rail, 25; taxis, 26; utilities and traffic, 24
international schools and education, 29
medical issues, 24
natural environment, 28
recreation and entertainment, 26–28; casinos, 28; cinemas, 27; culture and entertainment, 26–27; entertainment for children, 27; museums, 27; nightlife, 27–28;

restaurants, 26; sports for children, 28
shopping and availability of consumer goods, 26. *See also* Australia, general
Bucharest, Romania, 175–85
demographic/workforce overview, 181
economic overview, 176
environment issues, 176
financial issues including banking services and taxes, 183–84; banks, 183; currency, 183; expatriate tax concession, 184; taxes, 183–84
housing, 182
infrastructure, 176–78; air travel, 176–77; buses and trams, 177; metro, 177; taxi, 177–78; utilities and transport, 176
international schools and education, 184
medical issues, 175–76
natural environment, 182
personal safety and security issues, 175
recreation and entertainment, 178–80; cinemas, 179; culture and entertainment, 179; entertainment for children, 179–80; nightlife, 180; restaurants, 178–79; sports, 180
shopping and availability of consumer goods, 178
sociocultural environment, 180–81
workplace culture, 181–82
Budapest, Hungary, 88–100
demographic/workforce overview, 95
economic overview, 89
environment issues, 89
financial issues including banking services and taxes, 98–99; banks, 98–99; currency, traveler's checks, and credit cards, 98; taxes, 99
housing, 96–98
infrastructure, 89–92; air travel, 90; bus, 91; car, 92; inter-city bus travel, 90; metro, 91; public transport, 91; rail, 91; taxi, 91–92; train, 91; utilities and transport, 89
international schools and education, 99–100
medical issues, 89

natural environment, 96
personal safety and security issues,
88–89
recreation and entertainment, 93–95;
casinos, 94–95; cinemas, 94;
entertainment, 93; entertainment for
children, 94; international
associations and clubs, 93; museums,
94; nightlife, 94; restaurants, 93;
sports facilities, 95; theaters and
concert halls, 93–94
shopping and availability of consumer
goods, 92–93
sociocultural environment, 95
workplace culture, 95–96

Cairo, Egypt, 66–78
demographic/workforce overview, 73
economic overview, 67
environment issues, 67
financial issues including banking
services and taxes, 76–77; banks, 76;
cash, traveler's checks, and credit
cards, 76; currency, 76; opening an
account, 76; taxes, 77
housing, 74–76
infrastructure, 67–69; air travel, 67–68;
bus, 68; metro, 68; taxis, 68–69;
utilities and traffic, 67
international schools and education,
77–78
medical issues, 66–67
natural environment, 74
personal safety and security issues,
66
recreation and entertainment, 70–72;
casinos, 72; cinemas, 71;
entertainment for children, 71;
international associations and clubs,
70; museums, 71; nightclubs, 72;
nightlife, 71; restaurants, 70; sports
facilities, 72; theaters and concert
halls, 71
shopping and availability of consumer
goods, 69–70
sociocultural environment, 72
workplace culture, 73–74
Canberra, 29–34,
housing, 33–34

infrastructure, 30–31; air travel, 30;
bicycles, 31; bus, 31; taxis, 31;
transport, 30; utilities and traffic, 30
international schools and education, 34
medical issues, 29
natural environment, 33
recreation and entertainment, 31–33;
casinos, 33; entertainment, 32;
entertainment for children, 32;
museums, 32; nightclubs, 33;
nightlife, 32–33; restaurants, 32;
sports facilities, 33
shopping and availability of consumer
goods, 31. *See also* Australia, general
China, general, 44–49
demographic/workforce overview, 46
economic overview, 45
environment issues, 45
financial issues including banking
services and taxes, 47–49; banks,
47–48; credit cards, 48; currency,
48; taxes, 48–49
infrastructure, 46
medical issues, 44–45
personal safety and security issues, 44
sociocultural environment, 46
workplace culture, 46–47

Dubai, United Arab Emirates, 239–53
demographic/workforce overview, 247
economic overview, 240
environment issues, 240
financial issues including banking
services and taxes, 250–52; banks,
252; cash, traveler's checks, and
credit cards, 251–52; currency, 251;
opening an account, 252; taxes, 252
housing, 250
infrastructure, 240–42; air travel, 241;
public transport system, 241–42;
utilities and traffic, 241
international schools and education,
252–53
medical issues, 239–40
natural environment, 250
personal safety and security issues, 239
recreation and entertainment, 244–46;
entertainment, 245; entertainment
for children, 245; restaurants,

244–45; sports, 245–46; sports for
children, 246
shopping and availability of consumer
goods, 242–44
sociocultural environment, 246–47
workplace culture, 247–49

Hong Kong, 78–88
demographic/workforce overview, 84
economic overview, 79
environment issues, 79
financial issues including banking
services and taxes, 85–87; banks, 86;
cash, traveler's checks, and credit
cards, 85–86; currency, 85; taxes,
86–87
housing, 84–85
infrastructure, 79–80; air travel, 79–80;
bus, 80; metro, 80; taxis, 80
international schools and education,
87–88
medical issues, 79
natural environment, 84
personal safety and security issues,
78–79
recreation and entertainment, 81–83;
culture and entertainment, 81–83;
nightlife, 83; restaurants, 81; sports,
83
shopping and availability of consumer
goods, 81
sociocultural environment, 83–84
workplace culture, 84

India, general, 100–105
demographic/workforce overview, 102
economic overview, 101
environment issues, 101
financial issues including banking
services and taxes, 103–5; banks,
104; cash, traveler's checks, and
credit cards, 103–4; currency, 103;
taxes, 104–5
medical issues, 100–101
personal safety and security issues, 100
shopping and availability of consumer
good, 101
sociocultural environment, 102
workplace culture, 102–3

Istanbul, Turkey, 230–39
demographic/workforce overview,
235–36
economic overview, 231
environment issues, 231
financial issues including banking
services and taxes, 236–38; banks,
237–38; credit cards, 237; currency,
236–37; taxes, 238; traveler's
checks, 237
housing, 236
infrastructure, 231–33; air, 233; bus,
232; *dolmus* (taxi/bus), 232; ferry
car, 233; metro, 232; motorboat,
232–33; ship, 232; suburban train,
233; taxi, 231–32; tramway, 232;
tunnel, 232; utilities and transport,
231
international schools and education,
238–39
medical issues, 230–31
natural environment, 236
personal safety and security issues,
230
recreation and entertainment, 234–35;
culture and entertainment, 234;
nightlife, 234; restaurants, 234
shopping and availability of consumer
goods, 233–34
sociocultural environment, 235
workplace culture, 235–36

Jakarta, Indonesia, 114–23
demographic/workforce overview,
119
economic overview, 116
environment issues, 116
financial issues including banking
services and taxes, 120–22; banks,
121; cash, traveler's checks, and
credit cards, 121; currency, 120;
taxes, 122
housing, 120
infrastructure, 116–17; air travel, 116;
bus, 117; taxi, 117; utilities and
traffic, 116
international schools and education,
122–23
medical issues, 115–16

natural environment, 120
personal safety and security issues,
    114–15
recreation and entertainment, 118–19;
    cinemas, 118; culture and
    entertainment, 118–19; nightlife,
    119; restaurants, 118; sports, 119
shopping and availability of consumer
    goods, 117
sociocultural environment, 119
workplace culture, 119–20
Johannesburg, South Africa, 194–201
    demographic/workforce overview, 198
    economic overview, 195
    environment issues, 195
    financial issues including banking
        services and taxes, 199–200; banks,
        199–200; credit cards, 200;
        currency, 199; taxes, 200; traveler's
        checks, 200
    housing, 198–99
    infrastructure, 195–96; air travel, 195;
        car, 196; public transport, 195–96;
        taxis, 196; utilities and transport,
        195
    international schools and education,
        200–201
    medical issues, 194–95
    natural environment, 198
    personal safety and security issues, 194
    recreation and entertainment, 196–97;
        cinemas, 197; culture and
        entertainment, 197; nightlife, 197;
        restaurants, 196–97; sports, 197
    shopping and availability of consumer
        goods, 196
    sociocultural environment, 197
    workplace culture, 198

Kuala Lumpur, Malaysia, 141–49
    demographic/workforce overview, 146
    economic overview, 142
    environment issues, 142
    financial issues including banking
        services and taxes, 147–49; banks,
        148; cash, traveler's checks, and
        credit cards, 148; currency, 147–48;
        taxes, 148–49
    housing, 147

infrastructure, 142–44; air travel,
    142–43; cars, 144; buses, 143–44;
    Light Railway Transit (LRT), 143;
    monorail, 143; taxis, 144; train
    services, 143; utilities and transport,
    142
international schools and education,
    149
medical issues, 141–42
natural environment, 147
personal safety and security issues, 141
recreation and entertainment, 144–46;
    cinema, 145; culture and
    entertainment, 145; nightlife, 145–
    46; restaurants, 144–45; sports, 145
shopping and availability of consumer
    goods, 144
sociocultural environment, 146
workplace culture, 146–47

Manila, Philippines, 158–66
    demographic/workforce overview, 163
    economic overview, 159
    environment issues, 159
    financial issues including banking
        services and taxes, 164–65; banks,
        164–65; cash, traveler's checks, and
        credit cards, 164; expatriate tax
        concession, 165; taxes, 165
    housing, 164
    infrastructure, 159–61; air travel, 160;
        bus, 160; "Jeepneys," 161; metro,
        160–61; rail, 160; sea and river
        travel, 160; taxis, 161; utilities and
        traffic, 159
    international schools and education,
        165–66
    medical issues, 158–59
    natural environment, 163
    personal safety and security issues, 158
    recreation and entertainment, 161–62;
        cinemas, 162; culture and
        entertainment, 162; nightlife, 162;
        restaurants, 161–62; sports, 162
    shopping and availability of consumer
        goods, 161
    sociocultural environment, 163
    workplace culture, 163
Melbourne, 34–39,

housing, 38
infrastructure, 34–36; air travel, 35;
    buses, 35; car rental, 35; taxis, 35;
    trains, 35; tram, 35; utilities and
    transport, 34–35
international schools and education,
    38–39
medical issues, 34
natural environment, 37
recreation and entertainment, 36–37;
    cinemas, 37; culture and
    entertainment, 36–37; events, 36;
    entertainment for children, 37;
    museums, 37; restaurants, 36; sports
    for children, 37
shopping and availability of consumer
    goods, 36. *See also* Australia, general
Moscow, Russia, 185–93
demographic/workforce overview, 190
economic overview, 186
environment issues, 186
financial issues including banking
    services and taxes, 191–93; banks,
    192–93; credit cards, 192; currency,
    191; taxes, 193; traveler's checks,
    192
housing, 190–91
infrastructure, 186–88; air travel, 186–
    87; bus and tram, 187; *Marshrutki*
    (route-taxis), 188; metro, 187; taxi,
    187; utilities and transport, 186
international schools and education,
    193
medical issues, 185
natural environment, 190
personal safety and security issues, 185
recreation and entertainment, 188–89;
    cinemas, 188–89; culture and
    entertainment, 189; nightlife, 189;
    restaurants, 188; sports, 189
shopping and availability of consumer
    goods, 188
sociocultural environment, 190
workplace culture, 190
Mumbai, 105–9,
housing, 108
environmental issues, 105
infrastructure, 105–7; air travel, 105–6;
    bicycle and scooter hire, 106; bus,

106; rail, 106; sea and river travel,
    106; taxis, 106–7; utilities and
    transport, 105
international schools and education,
    108–9
natural environment, 107
recreation and entertainment, 107;
    cinema, 107; culture and
    entertainment, 107; nightlife, 107;
    restaurants, 107; sports, 107. *See also*
    India, general

New Delhi, 109–14,
housing, 112–13
environment issues, 109
infrastructure, 109–11; air travel, 110;
    bicycle, 110; bus, 110; car travel,
    110; metro, 111; rail travel, 110;
    rickshaws, 111; taxi scooter, 111;
    taxis, 111
international schools and education,
    113–14
natural environment, 112
recreation and entertainment, 111–12;
    cinema, 111; culture and
    entertainment, 111; nightlife, 121;
    restaurants, 111; sports, 111–12. *See
    also* India, general

Prague, Czech Republic, 59–65
demographic/workforce overview, 62
economic overview, 59
environment issues, 59
financial issues including banking
    services and taxes, 64–65; banks,
    64; cash, traveler's checks, and credit
    cards, 64; currency, 64; taxes, 65
housing, 63–64
infrastructure, 59–60; air travel, 60;
    funicular, 60; metro, 60; public
    transport, 60; tram and bus, 60
international schools and education,
    65
medical issues, 59
natural environment, 63
personal safety and security issues,
    59
recreation and entertainment, 61–62;
    cinema, 61; culture and

entertainment, 61–62; nightlife, 62; restaurants, 61; sports, 62
shopping and availability of consumer goods, 60–61
sociocultural environment, 62
workplace culture, 63

Seoul, South Korea, 201–8
demographic/workforce overview, 205
economic overview, 202
environment issues, 202
financial issues including banking services and taxes, 207–8; banks, 207; credit cards, 207; currency, 207; taxes, 208; traveler's checks, 207
housing, 206
infrastructure, 203–4; air, 203; bus, 203; metro, 203; taxis, 203; utilities and transport, 203
international schools and education, 208
medical issues, 202
natural environment, 206
personal safety and security issues, 201
recreation and entertainment, 204–5; culture and entertainment, 204–5; nightlife, 205; restaurants, 204; sports, 205
shopping and availability of consumer goods, 204
sociocultural environment, 205
workplace culture, 205–6
Shanghai, 55–58,
environment issues, 55
housing, 57–58
infrastructure, 55–56; air travel, 55; bus, 55–56; metro, 56; rail, 56; sea and river, 56; taxis, 56; utilities and transport, 55
international schools and education, 58
natural environment, 57
recreation and entertainment, 57; entertainment, 57; nightlife, 57; restaurants, 57; sports facilities, 57
shopping and availability of consumer goods, 56–57. *See also* China, general
Sydney, 39–44,

environment issues, 39
housing, 42–43
infrastructure, 39–41; air travel, 40–41; bus, 39; ferry, 40; metro, 39–40; rail, 39; taxis, 40; utilities and transport, 39
international schools and education, 43–44
medical issues, 34
natural environment, 42
recreation and entertainment, 41–42; cinemas, 41; entertainment for children, 42; museums, 41–42; sports facilities, 42; theaters and concert halls, 41
shopping and availability of consumer goods, 41. *See also* Australia, general

Taipei, Taiwan, 209–18
demographic/workforce overview, 214
economic overview, 211
environment issues, 210–11
financial issues including banking services and taxes, 215–17; banks, 216; credit cards, 216; currency, 215–16; taxes, 217; traveler's checks, 216
housing, 215
infrastructure, 211–12; air, 212; buses, 211; metro, 211; taxis, 211–12; utilities and transport, 211
international schools and education, 217–18
medical issues, 209–10
natural environment, 215
personal safety and security issues, 209
recreation and entertainment, 212–13; culture and entertainment, 213; nightlife, 213; restaurants, 212–13
shopping and availability of consumer goods, 212
sociocultural environment, 214
workplace culture, 214–15
Tel Aviv, Israel, 123–32
demographic/workforce overview, 128
economic overview, 125
environment issues, 124–25
financial issues including banking services and taxes, 130–32; banks,

131; cash, traveler's checks, and
credit cards, 131; currency, 130–31;
taxes, 131–32
housing, 129–30
infrastructure, 125–26; air travel, 125;
buses, 125–26; taxis, 126; utilities
and transport, 125
international schools and education,
132
medical issues, 124
natural environment, 129
personal safety and security issues,
123–24
recreation and entertainment, 126–28;
cinemas, 127; culture and
entertainment, 127; nightlife, 128;
restaurants, 126–27; sports, 128
shopping and availability of consumer
goods, 126
sociocultural environment, 128
workplace culture, 129
Tokyo, Japan, 132–41
demographic/workforce overview, 138
economic overview, 134
environment issues, 133
financial issues including banking
services and taxes, 139–40; banks,
140; cash, traveler's checks, and
credit cards, 139; taxes, 140
housing, 138–39
infrastructure, 134–35; air travel, 134;
car, 135; bus, 135; rail, 134–35;
taxis, 135; utilities and traffic, 134
international schools and education,
141
medical issues, 133
natural environment, 138

personal safety and security issues,
132–33
recreation and entertainment, 136–37;
cinema, 136; culture and
entertainment, 136–37; nightlife,
137; restaurants, 136; sports, 137
shopping and availability of consumer
goods, 136
sociocultural environment, 137
workplace culture, 138

Warsaw, Poland, 166–74
demographic/workforce overview, 171
economic overview, 167
environment issues, 167
financial issues including banking
services and taxes, 172–73; banks,
173; credit cards, 172–73; currency,
172; taxes, 173
housing, 172
infrastructure, 167–69; air travel, 167;
bus/tram/metro, 168; car rental,
168–69; taxis, 168; utilities and
transport, 167
international schools and education,
174
medical issues, 166–67
natural environment, 171
personal safety and security issues, 166
recreation and entertainment, 169–70;
cinemas, 169; culture and
entertainment, 170; nightlife, 170;
restaurants, 169; sports, 169–70
shopping and availability of consumer
goods, 169
sociocultural environment, 170
workplace culture, 171

About the Author

MERCER is a leading global provider of consulting, outsourcing, and investment services, with more than 25,000 clients worldwide, including most of the
Fortune 500. Mercer's global network of more than 18,000 employees, based
in over 40 countries, provides integrated, worldwide solutions in financial and
retirement security, healthcare, productivity, and employment relationships.